CHANGED FOREVER
Volume II

SUNY series, Native Traces

Jace Weaver and Scott Richard Lyons, editors

Changed Forever

Volume II

AMERICAN INDIAN BOARDING-SCHOOL LITERATURE

Arnold Krupat

On the cover: Chauncey Yellow Robe (Timber), Henry Standing Bear, and Richard Yellow Robe (Wounded) at the time they entered Carlisle Indian School in 1883 and three years later, in 1886, both photographs taken by John N. Choate. Courtesy of Dickinson College Carlisle Indian School Project.

Published by State University of New York Press, Albany

© 2020 State University of New York

For information, contact State University of New York Press, Albany, NY
www.sunypress.edu

LIBRARY OF CONGRESS CATALOGING-IN-PUBLICATION DATA
Names: Krupat, Arnold, author.
Title: Changed forever: American Indian boarding-school literature. Volume II / Arnold Krupat. Other titles: American Indian boarding school literature
Description: Albany, NY : State University of New York Press, [2020] | Series: SUNY series, Native traces | Includes bibliographical references and index.
Identifiers: LCCN 2017022009 (print) | LCCN 2018005523 (ebook) | ISBN 9781438480084 (e-book) | ISBN 9781438480077 (hardcover : alk. paper) | ISBN 9781438480060 (pbk)
Subjects: LCSH: Off-reservation boarding schools—United States—Biography. | Boarding school students—United States—Biography. | Indian students—United States—Biography. | Hopi Indians—Biography. | Navajo Indians—Biography. | Apache Indians—Biography. | Autobiographies—Indian authors.
Classification: LCC E97.5 (ebook) | LCC E97.5.K78 2018 (print) | DDC 371.829/97—dc23
LC record available at https://lccn.loc.gov/2017022009

10   9   8   7   6   5   4   3   2   1

For Gerald Vizenor

What has become of the thousands of Indian voices who spoke the breath of boarding-school life?

—K. Tsianina Lomawaima

We still know relatively little about how Indian school children themselves saw things.

—Michael Coleman

Boarding-school narratives have a significant place in the American Indian literary tradition.

—Amelia Katanski

CONTENTS

Part III. A Range of Boarding-School Autobiographies

ILLUSTRATIONS

INTRODUCTION

FROM THE MOMENT THEY SET FOOT UPON THESE SHORES, THE EUROPEAN invader-settlers of America confronted an "Indian problem."[1] This consisted of the simple fact that Indians occupied lands the newcomers wanted for themselves. To be sure, this was not the case for the earliest Spanish invaders of the Southeast and Southwest in the mid-sixteenth century, whose intent was to find treasure and to convert and missionize the tribal peoples they encountered. But in the Northeast, the English, from the early seventeenth century, and then the Americans, as they made their way across the continent, came to understand that broadly speaking, America's Indian problem permitted only two solutions: extermination or education. Extermination was costly and dangerous, and in time it came to be thought *wrong*.

It then began to appear wiser, as the title of Robert Trennert's introduction to a study of the Phoenix Indian School put the matter, for policymakers to proceed according to the assumption that "The Sword Will Give Way to the Spelling Book" (1988 3), thus offering—again to cite Trennert—an "alternative to extinction" (1975). Educating Native peoples—teaching them to speak, read, and write English; to convert to one or another version of Christianity; and to accept an individualism destructive of communal tribalism, ethnocide rather than genocide, was a strategy that might more efficiently and with fewer pangs to the national conscience free up Native landholdings and transform the American Indian into an Indian-American, uneasily inhabiting if not quite melted into the broad pot of the American mainstream.

In a fine 1969 study, Brewton Berry remarked that so far as the choice between "coercion" and "persuasion" was concerned (23), "Formal education has been regarded as the most effective means of bringing about assimilation" (22). In these respects, Trennert writes, when the Phoenix Indian School was founded in 1891, it was "for the specific purpose of preparing Native American children for assimilation ... to remove Indian youngsters from their traditional environment, obliterate their cultural heritage, and replace that ... with the values of white middle-class America." Complicating the

matter, he adds, was the fact that "the definition of assimilation was repeatedly revised between 1890 and 1930" (1988 xi).[2] Further complicating it well
in to the 1960s and beyond was the fact that "white middle-class America"
was not generally willing to accommodate persons of color regardless of
whether they shared its values or not.

In the *Annual Report of the Commissioner of Indian Affairs* for 1890, the
"Rules for Indian Schools" stated clearly that the government, in "organizing
this system of schools," intended them to "be preparatory and temporary;
that eventually they will become unnecessary, and a full and free entrance
be obtained for Indians into the public school system of the country. It is
to this end," the "Rules" continued, that "all officers and employees of the
Indian school service should work" (in Bremner 1971, 2: 1354). Although
Native Americans could obtain a "full and free entrance" to all public schools
in the United States—as African Americans could not—on those occasions
when they availed themselves of that right, they were not always welcomed or
well served. Indeed, as Wilbert Ahern has written, "The local public schools
to which 53% of Indian children went in 1925, were even less responsive
to Indian communities than the BIA schools" (1996 88). And some of the
Indian Office's Catholic schools, from about the 1880s through the 1960s,
as we will see, provided their own particular forms of disservice to their
Native students.

In her study of the St. Joseph's Indian boarding school in Kashena,
Wisconsin, Sarah Shillinger affirms that "Assimilation was an important, if not a more important goal than education to the supporters of the
boarding-school movement" (2008 95). Her conclusion, however, is that
the boarding schools' "results were closer to an *integration* of both cultural
systems [Indian and white] than ... to assimilation into Euro-American
society" (115, my emphasis). This seems to me accurate, and I will quote
other writers on the subject who state roughly similar conclusions in different ways. But the degree to which any single individual could successfully
integrate "both cultural systems," and what it meant to her to do so, varied
a good deal. As we will see, some boarding school students had little trouble
"living in two worlds," as the metaphor is often given—a metaphor that is
usually unexamined.[3] Others found the two "cultural systems," Native and
settler, to be substantially in conflict, so that "bridging the gap"—another
largely unquestioned metaphor—was painful and difficult. Further complicating the matter is the fact that one of the "cultural systems" was backed
by the overwhelming power of the colonial state.

By the turn of the twentieth century, as David Adams has written, "Those responsible for the formulation of Indian policy were sure of one thing: the Indian could not continue to exist as an Indian." Indian people, therefore, "had to choose ... between civilization or extinction" (1995 28), and in order to become civilized, Indians needed to be educated. "By the early 1890s," according to Ahern, "Thomas Jefferson Morgan, commissioner of Indian affairs, had designed the means to extinguish American Indian cultures by going after the children, pulling them from their homes, and indoctrinating them with 'American civilization'" (1996 88). To cite Adams once more, "The boarding school, whether on or off the reservation, was the institutional manifestation of the government's determination to completely restructure the Indians' minds and personalities" (1995 97). As Superintendent Cora Dunn of the Rainy Mountain School said in 1899, "Our purpose is to change them forever" (in Ellis 1996b xiii). I have adapted her words for the title of this book.

ಙ

It was in 1879 that the bright light and pre-eminent model of the boarding-school movement, the off-reservation Carlisle Indian Industrial School in Pennsylvania, was founded by Captain Richard Henry Pratt. First established in 1751 as a munitions depot prior to the American Revolution, Carlisle had later become a stop on the Underground Railroad for slaves fleeing the South, and then a Civil War battleground as part of the 1863 Gettysburg Campaign. Jacqueline Fear-Segal notes that in 1871 it "became the U.S. Army Cavalry School, where young recruits were trained to fight Indian tribes out west" (2004 129); then, when the Cavalry School was moved farther west, the Carlisle Barracks became available for Pratt's purposes.[4]

Pratt was a complicated man and much has been written about him. The early, nearly hagiographic biography by Elaine Goodale Eastman called him "the Red Man's Moses," a term first applied to him, she observed, in a 1900 commencement address given by Indian Commissioner Merrill Gates (Eastman 1935 219). More recently, Ward Churchill's revisionist account of Pratt presents him as founder of a genocidal policy (2004), a charge to which I will return. Pratt also wrote his own story.[5] Dr. Martin Luther King is said to have remarked that the white South loves individual black people but hates the race, while it is the reverse in the North. Pratt would seem to

1 Superintendent Richard Pratt (center) with members of the Carlisle staff, a group of students, and—probably—a few staff children, about 1900. Courtesy of the Yale Collection of Western Americana, Beinecke Rare Book and Manuscript Collection, Yale University, New Haven, Connecticut.

have had the South's view of Indians. He got along well with a great many individual Indians, at first some of the Kiowa, Cheyenne, and Apache prisoners of war at Fort Marion, in Saint Augustine, Florida, where he was in charge in the 1870s; and over the years he showed affection for many of his Indian students, a number of whom clearly reciprocated that affection. Yet as Jacqueline Fear-Segal (2007 18–19) and Jacqueline Emery (2017) have observed, Pratt had established Carlisle on a carceral model, whether consciously or not—he was neither highly educated nor an intellectual. In Emery's words, "The containment and seclusion of the fort [Fort Marion] provided what Pratt believed were ideal conditions for civilizing Native Americans," and "he would later recreate this model at the Carlisle Indian Industrial School" (2017 15).

But Pratt genuinely liked Indian people, while—so far as he knew them—he detested Indian cultures. His often-quoted motto was, "Kill the Indian and save the man!"[6] and the regimen at Carlisle sought—sometimes aggressively and sometimes only half-heartedly—to do just that. For all the violent determination of the slogan, in hindsight it was a vain and naive oxymoron, lacking all imagination, and was even programmatically unnecessary: all of Pratt's students learned English and engaged with American dress and religion while remaining proudly Indian. But, again, what it meant for each of them in his or her time to be Indian is a complicated matter. In some cases it might accurately be said, as Genevieve Bell has written, that Carlisle was "a site at which to promulgate a certain kind of new *Indian* identity" (1998 vi, my emphasis). But then, if that new Indian identity was that of an "American (Indian) *citizen*" (38, my emphasis), as Bell also wrote, in what exactly would a parenthetical "Indianness" consist? In many ways, as Timothy Braatz has written, "Carlisle was itself a contradiction: a place to acculturate Native children, but in a segregated setting that affirmed their Indianness" (2010 vii).

Although a great many Native people who attended Carlisle, worked at Carlisle, or otherwise engaged with Pratt had much good to say about him, his reputation today is roughly that of Custer. There are, however, a number of Pratt's Indian students on record with a far more positive assessment of the man. At Arlington National Cemetery where Pratt is buried, his private memorial reads:

VETERAN OF THE CIVIL WAR

FRIEND AND COUNSELOR OF THE INDIANS

FOUNDER AND SUPERINTENDENT OF

THE CARLISLE INDIAN SCHOOL (1879–1904)

ERECTED IN LIVING MEMORY BY HIS STUDENTS AND OTHER INDIANS

At Carlisle students took half a day of very basic instruction, mostly in literacy and simple arithmetic, along with half a day of manual instruction for the young men and some form of "domestic science" for the women.[7] There were offerings in art and music, along with a range of sports and athletic activities. The Carlisle football team and its star Jim Thorpe were nationally celebrated, and Carlisle competed against—and sometimes beat—some of the best American college teams. That team was for the most part made up of college age men (or older), but Carlisle was in no way a college, offering no more than a ninth grade education. (Many of the boarding schools did not go past the sixth grade.) Students who wished to stay on and go further would enroll at nearby Dickinson College.

Pratt had been a soldier and he ran the school like a military academy; students marched, saluted, drilled, wore uniforms, and were punished for disciplinary infractions.[8] Corporal punishment, typical of the late nineteenth century, was employed, and Carlisle also had a jail—one in which, as we will see, the eminent Lakota chief Spotted Tail (Sinte Gleska) was enraged to find a young family member. Genevieve Bell reports that Carlisle had "three different lock-ups in its history" (287), but that these were used only for serious infractions, and used only once with any given malefactor. A student who had been incarcerated, Bell notes, would be expelled for any further infraction of the rules (288). Carlisle's program of regimentation and discipline served as a model for most if not all of the off-reservation boarding schools and played a major part in the effort to change Native people forever. It was not until the mid-1920s that reforms were introduced, and not until the 1930s that Commissioner of Indian Affairs John Collier "ended the military system for all Indian boarding schools" (Gram xiv), at least officially.

The young men also learned gardening, farming, and the proper handling of livestock. Carlisle's industrial programs taught them carpentry, blacksmithing, harness-making, and tinsmithing.[9] The "domestic science" young Indian women studied at Carlisle, as also at the other boarding schools, consisted in such things as how to set a table and how to use stoves, irons, and washing machines—most of which, at least in the early decades of the school, would be absent, rare, or largely disapproved of once they returned home.

Important to Pratt's program at Carlisle was what he called the "placing-out," or simply the "outing" system, something he had begun to develop at his prior posting at Hampton Institute under General Samuel Armstrong, its superintendent.[10] Pratt's outing program at Carlisle sent a number of young Indian men and women to live for a time with local white families, to whom they provided labor or domestic service in return for their board and some very modest pay. This was not compulsory; students had to request or agree to an outing assignment, although it is not clear that all of them understood they had a choice in the matter. Most of the families to whom Native students were "outed" were farm families living not far from the school. The theory was to expand these young people's experience of white ways beyond the school grounds and to make them appreciate the jingle of a couple of quarters in their trouser or apron pockets. In practice, however, the outing system for the most part provided cheap labor for the host families with lessons primarily in subservience for the guest Indians. Although it soon became clear that the outing system was "a way for white families to obtain cheap servants" (Reyhner and Elder 2004 139), and that it "did more than any other [boarding school practice] to reinforce the concept of the suitability of Indians for menial labor" (Child 1998 81–82), it was nonetheless practiced by those off-reservation boarding schools whose location made it feasible. It should also be said that many students found their situation congenial and asked to stay on, working and attending the local school, when they might have returned to Carlisle. Pratt usually granted permission.

Carlisle students—and students at the other boarding schools—were supposed to leave school and return home as substantially Americanized individuals who would become workers and farmers, wives and mothers, in approximately the same way as their working-class, non-Native contemporaries. There is no accurate tabulation of how many did this or of the degree to which they did this. The school did, however, make a consistent effort to check up on the condition of its returned students, regularly mailing them to ask what and how they were doing and receiving a good number of replies. There were many who did not reply, and it is impossible to say why they did not. Some of them had surely "returned to the blanket," in the disparaging phrase of boarding-school proponents, referring to the fact that they had gone back to speaking their Native languages rather than English, abandoned the Christianity upon which the schools insisted, and did not live in the "civilized" manner that had been imposed upon them. In this regard, it is interesting to note that some Carlisle students participated in the Ghost Dance revitalization movement of the 1890s.

For example, among those who made the trip south in the last decade of the nineteenth century to meet Wovoka, the Paiute "Messiah" and instigator of the Ghost Dance, were three former Carlisle students. In the spring of 1891—(interest in Wovoka and the Ghost Dance did not cease after the 1890 massacre of Lakota people at Wounded Knee)—a delegation of Cheyennes and Arapahos traveled "to visit the messiah in Nevada and bring back the latest news from heaven," and "Arnold Woolworth, a Carlisle student, acted as interpreter" (Mooney 1973 900). Woolworth, an Arapaho whose Indian name was Big Tall Man, had been at Carlisle from 1881 to 1886. Later, in August 1891, another Arapaho delegation traveled to see Wovoka. Among them were Grant Left Hand and Casper Edson. Edson had attended Carlisle—not continuously—for no fewer than ten years, entering at the age of twenty in 1880 and leaving in 1890, by which time he had reached the sixth grade. Grant Left Hand was the son of Left Hand (Niwot or Nawot), the principal chief of the southern Arapahos, and he too had been to Carlisle. He bizarrely appears in the school records as U.S. Grant, having entered in 1879 and left because of poor health in 1881. James Mooney, the great chronicler of the Ghost Dance, wrote of him that "notwithstanding several years of English education, ... [he] is a firm believer in the doctrine and the dance, and the principal organizer and leader of the auxiliary 'crow dance' in his own tribe" (Mooney 1973 1038).

Achieving a certain notoriety in the aftermath of the Ghost Dance and Wounded Knee was another returned Carlisle student. This was Plenty Horses (Carlisle records also list him as Plenty Living Bear), a Lakota, who had entered first grade at the school at the age of fourteen in 1883, leaving in 1889, by which time he had completed the fourth grade. Returned home to the Rosebud reservation, he "donned blanket and moccasins ... wore his hair in long braids" (Utley 1974 17), and participated in his People's Ghost Dance ceremonies. He was not present at Wounded Knee Creek on the Pine Ridge reservation at the end of December 1890, when the Seventh Cavalry massacred Big Foot's band of Minneconjou Sioux, but he was near enough to hear the guns and then to engage in skirmishes with U.S. troops. On January 8, 1891, he was in the vicinity of a council between army officers and several Lakota chiefs convened to discuss arrangements for peace. The participants included, on one side, Red Cloud, Bear Lying Down, and He Dog and, on the other, Lieutenant Edward Casey and several emissaries of General Nelson Miles. At some point Plenty Horses, from horseback, fired a single rifle shot and killed the mounted Casey. He was arrested for murder just over a month later. At trial his lawyers offered in his defense the fact that a state of war had existed between the Sioux and the U.S. at the time Casey was killed, and therefore Plenty Horses, regardless of the circumstances of his act, could not be prosecuted for killing an enemy combatant.

This meant that to obtain a guilty verdict against Plenty Horses for murder, the government would have to claim that no state of war had existed between the Indians and the United States at the time of the shooting. But if no state of war had then existed, the soldiers who had earlier participated in the killings at Wounded Knee would also have to be tried for murder. The trial ended in a deadlocked jury. A second trial was held, at which testimony by General Miles was entered into the record. Miles stated emphatically

2   Plenty Horses with his father and others around the time of his trial in 1891.
Top row, standing, left to right: Rock Road, White Moon, Bear Lying Down, and
Broken Arm. Seated, left to right: He Dog, Jack Red Cloud, Plenty Horses, and
his father, Plenty Living Bear. Plenty Horses is the only one wearing a blanket
and moccasins (his father may also be in moccasins).

that at the time his troops had engaged at Wounded Knee, a state of war
between the parties had existed, nor had it ceased to exist at the time Casey
was killed. On the basis of Miles's testimony, the judge halted the trial and
instructed the jurors to find for the defendant. Plenty Horses was acquitted.

Why had Plenty Horses shot the army lieutenant? Valentine McGillycuddy, former Indian agent at Pine Ridge, was the foreman of the jury that
acquitted Plenty Horses. In a biography of her husband, *McGillycuddy, Agent:
A Biography of Dr. Valentine T. McGillycuddy* (1941), his widow Julia reported
her husband quoting Plenty Horses as follows: "Five years I attended Carlisle
and was educated in the ways of the white man. When I returned to my
people, I was an outcast among them. I was no longer an Indian. I was not
a white man. I was lonely. I shot the lieutenant so I might make a place for
myself among my people. I am now one of them. I shall be hung, and the

Indians will bury me as a warrior" (272). Plenty Horses was not hanged. He responded to a 1910 questionnaire sent out by Carlisle, writing that he was then a farmer at Pine Ridge. He died in 1933.

ಐಐ

Pratt was dismissed from Carlisle in 1904 and the school closed for good in 1918, near the end of the First World War. Ten years later, the 1928 government survey *The Problem of Indian Administration,* generally known as the Meriam Report, appeared and was intensely critical of the boarding schools. The report contained this noteworthy passage: "The position taken…is that the work with and for the Indians must give consideration to the desires of the individual Indians. He who wishes to merge into the social and economic life of the prevailing civilization of this country should be given all the practicable aid and advice in making the necessary adjustments. He who wants to remain an Indian and live according to his old culture should be aided in doing so"[11] (86).

In 1929, a year after the Meriam Report's publication, Indian Commissioner Burke "issued circular #2526 … forbidding corporal punishment altogether at Indian schools" (Trennert 1989, 603). Shortly afterward, under John Collier's tenure as commissioner of Indian Affairs (1933–45), some of the boarding schools were closed, others were substantially altered, and some became public high schools. Collier ended the military system and made religious observances for students voluntary; also, the curriculum now might include elements of Native culture and history, and materials were developed to teach some Native languages. Despite the shift in official policy, however, the changes were not always implemented. For example, corporal punishment, although forbidden, continued at a great many schools throughout Collier's tenure as commissioner. Carole Barrett and Marcia Britton observe that although schools differed in their practices, the English-only language policy was not actually "eliminated from many schools until the late 1960s" (1997 22).

That was partly because Collier's liberal commitments began to be reversed after his resignation as commissioner in 1945, the year the Second World War ended, and the year President Franklin Roosevelt died. After Collier's departure, "In the late 1940s, conservative critics across the country launched attacks against progressive education" generally (Watras 2004

99), and specifically against Collier's commitment to pluralism at the Indian schools. Having become president upon Roosevelt's death, Harry Truman appointed William Brophy to succeed Collier and to reverse his policies. Hampered by ill health, Brophy and his like-minded successors, Acting Commissioner William Zimmerman, and Commissioner John Nichols, served only briefly. But in 1950 Dillon Myer became commissioner of Indian Affairs. Myer had administered the Japanese internment camps during the war—two of them on Indian reservations—and strongly opposed allowing cultural differences among any minority populations in the United States. He ordered broad, regressive changes in the Indian schools, leading overall to an "Erosion of Indian Rights," as a critique by Felix Cohen in the *Yale Law School Journal* termed it.[12] These were the years, as we will see, when Lydia Whirlwind Soldier, Walter Littlemoon, and Mary Crow Dog suffered terribly in their South Dakota boarding schools.

In her interviews with former boarding school students at Saint Joseph's Indian Industrial School, Sarah Shillinger found that "a theme that runs through the students' remembrances is physical abuse" (2008 14). As I have said, this occurred widely in the schools even when federal policy forbade it, and it is a subject that comes up frequently in the narratives I examine. But it was only in the 1990s that some of the darkest aspects of the boarding schools began to be brought to light. That the schools often provided inadequate nutrition, hygiene, and health care had been clear for some time and was abundantly evidenced in the Meriam Report. But even that extremely critical 1928 account did not look into the matter of sexual abuse at the schools. For example, Basil Johnston, a Canadian Ojibwa, in his 1989 autobiography of more than 250 pages, *Indian School Days*, mentioned no molestation or sexual abuse at St. Peter Clavier's Indian Residential School in Canada, which he attended. But in 2007, in a moving foreword to Sam McKegney's *Magic Weapons*, Johnston told of having suffered these things regularly. Tomson Highway's autobiographical novel, *Kiss of the Fur Queen* (1998), graphically detailed the sexual abuse of young boys by teaching Brothers at the Catholic Residential School in Canada that Highway and his brother attended.[13]

Here in the U.S., the Navajo poet Berenice Levchuk's recollections of her boarding school experiences at the Fort Defiance School include the memory of "a nine-year-old girl [who] was raped in her dormitory bed during the night," and "a certain male teacher who stalked and molested girls" (1997

184). The accounts of Lydia Whirlwind Soldier and Mary Crow Dog also include their observation and experience of sexual abuse at Saint Francis Mission School, as does Tim Giago's account of his time at the Holy Rosary Mission School (1978). Several of the Catholic boarding schools as well as the Catholic dioceses have repeatedly been sued, and the legal briefs including allegations of abuse suffered by the Indian students of those schools are both abundant and horrifying. It was also the case, as Johnston noted, that older boys sexually abused younger boys, something to which Giago attests as well, and something that is strongly hinted at in Jim Northrup's brief account of his time at the Pipestone Indian School.

Historians of the boarding schools have recorded these things, and they have been careful to note as well that that the history is not exclusively one of victimization and suffering. Diana Meyers Bahr found that among graduates of the Sherman Institute in Riverside, California, "Even alumni whose memories are depressing or ambivalently fond and regretful retain an undeniable attachment to the school" (2014 3). Generally, as Myriam Vuckovic writes, Haskell's "indigenous students' reactions ranged from complete rejection to enthusiasm, and most felt ambivalent about their boarding school years" (2008 2). Irene Stewart (see volume 1) and Esther Burnett Horne (this volume), both of whom attended Haskell in the mid-1920s, were among those who viewed their time there very positively.

Lawney Reyes, who attended the Chemawa School in Oregon for two years in the early 1940s—Chemawa had been the second federal boarding school to be opened—wrote, "Chemawa may have succeeded in 'civilizing' me, but it did not separate me from the Indian culture. It did the opposite. Chemawa introduced me to my culture ... by enabling me to meet and get to know several Indian boys my age.... This," he continued, enabled him "to learn, appreciate, and differentiate between several Indian cultures. It would have been impossible to do this back home" (134). As Michael Coleman concluded, "No Hopi or Navajo or Sioux response to the schools emerged" (1993 94); individual young Indian people experienced their boarding-school education in very different ways.

Thus when K. Tsianina Lomawaima interviewed former Chilocco Indian School students about a Miss McCormick, a particularly harsh head matron, she found that "the range and disparity within student responses to this one individual indicate the difficulty of making generalizations about key facets of boarding-school life" (1994 48). Lomawaima wrote that in terms of morale, the Chilocco Indian School "falls somewhere between the depiction of boarding schools as irredeemably destructive institutions" and the opinion of one of the former students she interviewed that Chilocco "'really was a marvelous school'" (1994 164). Kim Brumley's recent compilation (2010) of the recollections of twenty-nine Chilocco students, from the class of 1933 to the class of 1980, is in accord with this finding. Sally McBeth's study of "the boarding school experience of west-central Oklahoma Indians," found the schools to be "a concrete and definite topic of conversation" among them, and one "perceived by the Native community as an important topic" (1983 4). The boarding schools were remembered, on the one hand, as emblematic of oppressive "*government control* of Indian people" but, on the other, as representative of "*government obligations* to Indian people" (1983 117, italics in original). The former students McBeth consulted were mostly women, and among them, "The Indian boarding schools seemed to foster a sense of belonging and eventually became acceptable symbols of an Indian ethnic identity" (1983 114). For them, she writes, "the memory of the boarding school experience operates as a symbol of group solidarity and identity. Even the few people who consider the boarding school experience as essentially harmful still may respond to it as responsible for stimulating group consciousness and contributing to group survival" (1983 142).

In *Boarding School Seasons* (1998), and in subsequent publications, Brenda Child has also been scrupulously careful in presenting the many different responses of former students to the schools. Nonetheless, what is currently taken to be "true" about the boarding schools is that they were an unmitigated disaster. There has developed, as Child has written in an important essay, "a tension between history and memory," between the historical record and the "way in which American Indian people remember [boarding-school] experience."[14] So great is this tension that, as she has observed, "Learning of happy students and satisfied parents—Indians who liked boarding school—can be mystifying, even troubling to Indian people today" (2014 275). For many Native communities the boarding schools, to cite the subtitle of an essay by Michael Kenny, have operated as "The Interface between Individual and Collective History" (1999).

Indeed, as Child writes, the boarding school has come to serve as "a useful and extraordinarily powerful metaphor for colonialism"; it has become "symbolic of American colonialism at its most genocidal" (Child 2014 268). The schools now serve as "an adaptable metaphor Indian people ... use to describe and encapsulate many different forms of colonialism and historical oppression" (279). Further, "Boarding school is now the ancestor in a genealogical line of terrible offspring—alcohol abuse, family and sexual violence, and other dysfunction" (268). Serving as "the primary explanation for social dysfunction and adverse conditions on the reservation" (271), the boarding schools are often cited as a major source "of historical trauma and unresolved grief" (271).

Michael Kenny has observed that the Holocaust suffered by European Jews as a result of the Nazis' attempted genocide has sometimes "become a model for construing the histories of other disadvantaged and 'traumatized' groups" (Kenny 1999 420–21). Among American Indian people, "Holocaust memories have become a paradigm," Kenny writes, "as has the rhetoric of genocide" (426). Thus we find Ward Churchill's study of Pratt and the boarding schools called *Kill the Indian, Save the Man: The Genocidal Impact of American Indian Residential Schools*. For Churchill the boarding schools were akin to what Kenny, with reference to indigenous Australian commentary, has called an "aboriginal Auschwitz" (Kenny 1999 436). In similar fashion, the Ziibiwing Center of Anishinaabe Culture and Lifeways, established in 2004 by the Saginaw Chippewa Indian Tribe of Michigan, published "A Supplementary Curriculum Guide" titled *American Indian Boarding Schools: An Exploration of Global Ethnic and Cultural Cleansing*.[15] Berenice Levchuk also wrote of Carlisle and the boarding schools generally as a "phase of our Native American holocaust" (1997 185), while Tom Gannon, who suffered beatings at the Holy Rosary Mission School, titled "a talk on [his own] Indian Boarding School experience 'A Holocaust of the Mind'" (2014 114–15). Child has cited Canadian authors referencing "an aboriginal holocaust" (2014 270).

Earlier, noting that Indian boarding-school experiences were being compared to experiences of "the Holocaust, Hiroshima, slavery, and imprisonment," Robert Warrior argued that "the boarding-school experience ... is in and of itself irreducible to any other experience" (2005 118). This is a useful warning against careless comparisons as I develop the matter further. But to compare the boarding-school experience to the other human tragedies Warrior references is not to reduce it to or equate it with any one of them.[16] Significant individual and communal events are both historically unique—different in their specifics and particularities—and in some measure comparable. For example, in that the definition of "holocaust"—lower case "h"—is destruction or slaughter on a mass scale, intentional and systematic or not, one can indeed speak of the colonial history of the United States as having produced a "Native American holocaust." Nonetheless, it is mistaken to speak of the boarding schools as an "aboriginal Auschwitz." This is to say that while it would have been deplorable if Auschwitz had been established to turn Jews into good Germans, that was not its purpose. Its purpose was to exterminate the Jews. The boarding schools, however, *contra* Ward Churchill, simply were not committed to genocide; and to insist on that fact is to make no excuse for the ethnocide to which they were committed. Nonetheless, memory of the schools has given rise to what Kenny has called "survivor syndrome" (1999 422). With reference here to Canada, he writes that rather than "reconstruct history as it actually was … what emerges instead is the history of Native Canadians as metaphorical Jews." He continues, "Native people who endured the schools have a story to tell, but only lately has a space been opened up for the story to be not only told, but heard, and not only heard but perpetuated in the collective memory" (431).

These stories, sometimes passed on by persons with no experience or little knowledge of the schools themselves, now constitute a body of survivor discourse that I suggest has become a genre of the oral tradition. The stories that constitute it have been passed down, not since ancient times, to be sure, but for a long time, from the late nineteenth century to the present: so the elders have said—at least so far as communal memory is concerned. To these stories has accrued the authority of the oral tradition. Used as a metaphor for all the worst abuses of colonialism in exactly the manner described by Child, and marshalling the authority of what has become oral tradition, boarding-school survivor discourse may be deployed in the service of what Kenny has called the contemporary "ethnopolitics of the disadvantaged" (1999 421)—or, more plainly, of the oppressed and colonized.

Nonetheless, despite the fact that the now traditional narrative, embodying the communally agreed-upon memory of the past, has come to have a certain historical truth, it should be said again that not all of it is historically factual. Carlisle was not Auschwitz, nor was a single one of the other off-reservation boarding schools, destructive though they were, engaged in the systematic murder of Indian people. A considerable number of former boarding school students, as we have seen and will see further, have stories to tell that are quite unlike any that could be told by those who survived the death camps. As the historians have found and the present study shows, the

narratives written by former boarding-school students themselves present
a range of responses.

ಬಃ

The earliest studies of the boarding schools worked largely from the perspective of the government—although many involved in teaching at or
administering the schools were themselves extremely critical of that perspective, none more so than some of the young women who entered the
Indian Service to teach at the schools.[17] In the last twenty years or so, that
perspective has been supplemented by attention to what the Indian students,
communities, and families themselves felt and said about the schools. Thus,
in the third edition (1999) of her 1974 book *Education and the American
Indian,* Margaret Connell Szasz writes that "between the late 1970s and the
late 1990s [she has] been moving away from an earlier focus on policy to
a more recent focus on the Indian community itself" (xi). The recent work
of Brenda Child, Amanda Cobb, Clyde Ellis, Tsianina Lomawaima, Sally
McBeth, Clifford Trafzer, Myriam Vuckovic, and others has indeed turned
to the "Indian community itself," examining letters from and engaging in
interviews with a great many former boarding school students.

A quarter century ago Michael Coleman observed: "We still know relatively little about how Indian school children themselves saw things" (1993
194); we know a bit more today, but there remains much to learn. One way
to do this is to look closely at what "Indian school children themselves"
had to say in a range of autobiographical texts. (Coleman's study, it should
be noted, was based on autobiographical texts.) It is in these texts that we
may hear "the thousands of Indian voices who spoke the breath of boarding
school life" (Lomawaima 1994 xii). As Jeffrey Ostler has observed, "Only
the most resilient children later wrote their experiences, whereas those who
suffered deeper damage did not" (2004 154), and of course the children
who rest in the boarding-school cemeteries did not live to tell their stories. Ruth Spack has claimed that "the dearth of accounts reveals that the
overwhelming majority of students remained silent" (2002 109). But "the
dearth of accounts" she speaks of is only a relative dearth; the written record
left by the boarding-school students, only a minority of them, to be sure, is
very rich—far richer, as this study shows, than has so far been recognized.

These "Indian voices" speak of a range of experiences, and they reference a number of what I call *scenes of initiation* or *initiatory loci,* and also

a number of *topoi* as they are encountered by boarding-school autobiographers. Thus, for example, the dining room is an initiatory locus—new and strange things happen in this place—while food—its kind and quality or lack thereof—is a topos. In view of the large quantity of oatmeal of widely varying quality and preparation that they were served, some of the students gave the generic name "mush" to the strange and often unpleasant foods they encountered. Discipline, predominantly in the form of corporal punishment, is a topos, but one that has no particular locus in that it might be administered in the classroom, in a teacher's office, in the dining room, or almost any other place—perhaps a jail—at a given school. The topos clock time, or what Myriam Vuckovic has termed "Living by the Bell" (2008 59), is also encountered everywhere: the dormitory, the dining room, the classroom, with movement to each and in each regulated by the bell or whistle or bugle—sometimes a triangle that was loudly struck. In each of these loci students woke, ate, studied, marched, or played according to the clock.

Naming—that is, the de-individuating bestowal of Tom, Dick, Harry, and Sally to replace the highly distinctive names each student brought—is a topos,[18] along with what I call the cleanup: the scrubbing and, in particular, the hair cutting that took place almost immediately upon each student's arrival. The dormitory is the locus for the students' nightly rest and also on occasion for the *topos* sex. But sexual relations among the students (or with others at the schools, when they occurred) certainly do not only take place in the dormitory. The *topos* outing labor might have a family farm as locus—that was its rationale, based upon the substantial farming community around Carlisle—but Native student workers might have a variety of tasks assigned to them—like, for example, Luther Standing Bear's unique summer outing in the John Wanamaker department store in Philadelphia. Identity is an important and complex topos but what one can say about it for any particular student depends on shifting loci of home, family, school, and other matters, all of these varying over time. It is important to emphasize that not a single one of the many boarding school students considered in this book ever entirely abandoned a sense of being Lakota, Ojibwe, Kiowa, or Arapaho, although they understood their tribal identity in a variety of ways. For some, an active reclamation of national and cultural identity, as we will see, was a major step in healing the damage done by the schools' assault on being Indian.

ന

Along with an introduction, this second volume of *Changed Forever* consists of three parts and two appendices. Part I examines seven Dakota autobiographies that deal with the boarding-school experiences of their authors—three of them well-known. Within each part, the studies are arranged chronologically by date of birth of authors (with two exceptions that I will note). Part II offers readings of six Anishinaabe—Ojibwe or Chippewa—boarding-school autobiographies, one of them a book-length account of its author's "Life in an Indian Boarding School," and another a record of its author's time not in an Indian boarding school but in a residential institution for dependent children, somewhat like the boarding schools. Part III, "A Range of Boarding-School Autobiographies," considers the experiences of Native people from different tribal nations in boarding schools around the U.S., along with a single brief Canadian example. This volume and the one that preceded it are intended to call attention to a great many texts, the majority of them not well known, although I make no claim to have "covered" or fully "surveyed" what turns out to be a wide field. Especially for the texts that are not well known, my discussions here, as I noted as well in volume 1, in some measure offer annotated critical editions that I hope will be useful to both teachers and students.

I had intended to close this book with a fourth section to be called "The Legacy of the Boarding Schools in Native American Literature." This was projected as a study of drama, fiction, and poetry by Native American authors, from just past the turn of the twentieth century to the present, that referenced the boarding schools or dramatized events taking place in those schools. It might have begun with Francis LaFlesche's *The Middle Five* (1900), continuing to Louise Erdrich's representation of her characters' experiences of Catholic boarding schools. As for drama, in addition to some other plays, we have two by N. Scott Momaday set at boarding schools. A study of boarding-school poems—nineteenth-century to 1920s—might begin with the "Boarding School Poems" Robert Dale Parker included in his anthology *Changing Is Not Vanishing*, and then go on to a consideration of verse by Louise Erdrich, Luci Tapahonso, Laura Tohe, and others. But this is the second volume of this study, it is already long, and even were I to extend it further, it would be impossible to do justice to the legacy of the boarding schools in Native American literature in this book.

My subtitle "American Indian Boarding-School Literature," was chosen on the assumption that this book would indeed include readings of Native American poetry, fiction, and drama—obviously literary genres—in which the boarding school played a part, and I have taken Amelia Katanski's observation that "Boarding school narratives have a significant place in the American Indian literary tradition" as one of the epigraphs for this book. Believing that nonetheless to be true even when the narratives considered are all autobiographies, I've retained the subtitle—rather than altering it to, say, "American Indian Boarding-School Autobiography." I mean to insist upon the fact that these autobiographies are indeed literature and that they are treated here as literature. To do this, and to present some of "the thousands of Indian voices who spoke the breath of boarding school life," in order to understand better just "how Indian schoolchildren themselves saw things," is the aim of this study.

Consistent with this aim are the two appendices. The first reprints a letter from a returned boarding-school student that has been out of print for more than 130 years. The second lists the names, tribal affiliations, and schools attended for all the Indian students mentioned in volume 1 and 2 of *Changed Forever*: of the many who have been forgotten, may these names live in memory.

PART I

DAKOTA BOARDING-SCHOOL AUTOBIOGRAPHIES

1

Charles Eastman's *From the Deep Woods to Civilization*

CHARLES ALEXANDER EASTMAN WAS BORN IN 1858 TO MANY LIGHTNINGS, a Santee Sioux, and Wakantewin, or Mary Nancy Eastman, daughter of the artist and army officer Seth Eastman and his Native wife. As their fifth and last child, he was given the birth-order name Hakadah, and because his mother died soon after he was born, that name has frequently been translated as "the pitiful last."[1] At about the age of four he received an honor name, Ohiyesa, "winner" (*Indian Boyhood* 32), for success at lacrosse (37). After many years of schooling he received his medical degree from Boston University Medical School in 1890, at the age of thirty-two, becoming one of the first Native American doctors.[2]

Eastman's first medical posting was to the Pine Ridge Agency, where he arrived in November 1890. In the last days of December that year he found himself ministering to his fellow Dakotas shot by federal troops at Wounded Knee Creek.[3] For the most part, however, Eastman's professional career did not involve medical work. Upon leaving Pine Ridge he served as physician at the Crow Creek Agency and for a time attempted to establish a private practice in Saint Paul, Minnesota. For most of his life, however, he worked in administrative and bureaucratic capacities. He spoke at the Chicago Columbian Exposition in 1893, and was "outing agent"—not school doctor—for Richard Pratt at the Carlisle School for a year in 1899. In formal attire, Eastman attended Mark Twain's seventieth birthday party in New York City in 1905. Between 1903 and 1909 he served the Bureau of Indian Affairs in a project to provide new names for the Sioux, and he was a founding member of both the American Indian Association (1892) and the Society of American Indians (1911), having played a part in the establishment of the Boy Scouts of America in 1910. He addressed the First Universal Races Conference in London in 1911 and, in 1923, was a member of Secretary of the Interior Hubert Work's Advisory Council on Indian Affairs, known as the Committee of One Hundred. Eastman was the first recipient of the award for distinguished achievement given by the Indian Council Fire at the Chicago World's Fair in 1933. He frequently appeared as a paid lecturer and also published nine books and a considerable number of essays.[4] Eastman died in 1939.

For a time critics examining Eastman's life and work disparaged him as an accommodator of federal assimilationist policies, one who had largely abandoned his identity as an American Indian in order to become a successful, if hyphenated, Indian-American. Thus in an early study Marion Copeland concluded that Eastman "fell into the role of functionary to one faction after another whose primary concern was to control and convert the Indian" (1978 8). Later Robert Warrior cited Eastman's response to John Oskison in 1911 at the first meeting of the Society of American Indians—Eastman said to those who thought "a great deal of injustice" had been "done to our tribes," that "really no prejudice has existed so far as the American Indian is concerned" (in Warrior 1999 6)—as indicative of his "blinding progressivistic optimism" (7). A recent reevaluation of Eastman, however, is represented by Kiara Vigil's estimate that Eastman's "work as a political activist required negotiating civilizationist thinking and rhetoric while recognizing indigenous sovereignty" (2015 48). I would qualify this only by observing that a full recognition of what is understood today by the term "indigenous sovereignty" was hardly possible historically until perhaps the last ten years or so of Eastman's life, if then.

But Vigil's recognition of Eastman's engagement in complex *negotiations* of rhetoric and praxis in this difficult period of sustained assault on Native American cultures, languages, and sovereignty is important. It builds upon Hertha Wong's earlier assertion of the "uneasy alliance" (142) between "assimilationist and traditional Sioux values" in Eastman's work (148). Philip Deloria offered a useful summary of these "uneasy alliances" or "negotiations" on Eastman's part, writing that "Eastman's Indian mimicry [he often performed in headdress and regalia] invariably transformed his construction of his own identity—both as a Dakota and as an American. He lived out a hybrid life, distinct in its Indianness but also cross-cultural and assimilatory" (1998 123). Like other prominent "progressives," he "worked actively to preserve elements of Native cultures and societies from destruction" (Deloria 2013 26).

At the elite private institutions Eastman attended, he was either the sole Indian student or one of only a few. He would certainly have known— to take a phrase from W. E. B. Du Bois to which I will return—how it feels to be a problem. Before turning to Eastman's writing about his education, I want to engage briefly a matter that has occupied Eastman's critics: whether and to what degree ideas and values expressed in his books derive from the participation of his wife, Elaine Goodale Eastman, in their composition.

Goodale (1863–1953), a graduate of Smith College, was first employed as a teacher to the Indians at the Hampton Institute, during which time she met Richard Pratt. Although she strongly favored reservation day schools over the off-reservation boarding schools championed by Pratt, she was nonetheless sufficiently impressed by his efforts to write the first (and thus far the only) biography of him, tellingly entitled, *Pratt: The Red Man's Moses* (1935). Goodale served as supervisor of Indian schools in the Dakotas, based at the Pine Ridge Agency, and it was there that she met Charles Eastman upon his arrival from the east in November 1890. The two became engaged on Christmas day of that year, and less than a week later Goodale assisted as her fiancé tended to the Lakota survivors of the Wounded Knee massacre. The two were married in New York in June 1891 and would work together and raise a large family before separating in 1921.[5]

In an autobiographical text, Goodale wrote that "in an hour of comparative leisure," she had "urged" her husband "to write down his recollections of the wild life, which [she] carefully edited" (E. Eastman 2004 173). He did so, and his first texts appeared in several of the periodicals of the day, some of which her husband included in his first autobiography, *Indian Boyhood* (1902). In the last chapter of his 1916 autobiography, *From the Deep Woods to Civilization: Chapters in the Autobiography of an Indian*, Eastman noted that the book was "the eighth that [he had] done, always with the devoted cooperation of [his] wife" (185), adding that although "but one book, 'Wigwam Evenings', bears both our names, we have worked together" (185–86). It is the nature of that work that remains in dispute.

David Reed Miller believed that "Elaine was indispensable to her husband's writing," noting—as others have—that "after his separation from her in 1921, he published nothing new" (66).[6] Margaret Jacobs, on the basis of a careful reading of some of Goodale's letters and a late autobiographical sketch, concluded that Goodale herself believed she had "cowritten every book attributed to Charles alone" (39). A contrary view was expressed by H. David Brumble (1988). To dwell on this matter no longer,[7] I share Theodore Sargent's assessment that Goodale was, on occasion, "critically important in putting Charles's words into acceptable [!] English" (2005 87), but that she altered few of his meanings. Eastman never shared his royalties with Goodale, and among other possible reasons, this may be because of his strong sense that whatever her aid, the books were indeed his work alone. It is also worth noting that he may have been particularly sensitive to the issue of what constituted an author's original composition as the consequence of an incident in his schooling when he was accused of plagiarism (considered later). In what follows I take Eastman's meanings and almost all of his words to be his own, noting the rare occasion when I suspect a trace of Goodale's hand.

ཚ

Dr. Charles Alexander Eastman had more years of formal education than any Native writer before him, and this fact is worth more attention than it has received. As Bernd Peyer long ago compiled the details, Eastman "attended Santee Normal Training School (1874–76), Beloit College (1876–79), Kimball Union Academy (1882–83), Dartmouth College (1883–87), and Boston University" (232). Even this substantial listing does not include his first year of schooling at the day school in Flandreau, South Dakota (1873–74), his two years at Knox College in Galesburg, Illinois (1879–81), and the three summers (1887–90) he attended Northfield Mount Hermon School while studying at the Boston University medical school. Not one of these was a government boarding school; as Eastman would write in *Deep Woods*, during his first years in school "the Government policy of education for the Indian had not then been developed" (49). Only Flandreau and Santee were Indian schools, and all the others were elite mainstream institutions, but I have thought it worthwhile in the context of this study to look at Eastman's educational experiences nonetheless.

It is near the conclusion of his first autobiography, *Indian Boyhood*, that Eastman details the event that changed his life, ushering in his many years of schooling.[8] He writes that when he was fifteen, he had felt an "unusual excitement" one day upon returning to camp and seeing "a man wearing the Big Knives' clothing … coming toward [him] with [his] uncle" (246).[9]

His uncle—he had adopted the boy when the family believed his father had been hanged for his part in the 1862 Sioux uprising in Minnesota—informs him that the man is his father, that he has "adopted the white man's way," and come "for [him] to learn this new way, too" (246). His father, Many Lightnings, now calls himself Jacob Eastman, and, Eastman notes, he "had brought [his son] some civilized clothing," the adjective offering a description, not an evaluation of the attire provided. "At first," Eastman recalls, he "disliked very much to wear garments made by the people [he] had hated so bitterly," but "the thought that ... they had not killed [his] father and brothers, reconciled [him], and [he] put on the clothes" (246). Under these circumstances, he does not, of course undergo a cleanup and certainly no hair cutting before donning the "civilized clothing."

It is on the way to Flandreau, after Ohiyesa has heard and seen for himself "the fire-boat-walks-on-mountains" (247)—a train—that he first encounters Christian practice engaged in by an Indian. The young man is about to go out to hunt when his father "stopped [him] ... and bade him wait." His father "was accustomed every morning to read from his Bible, and sing a stanza of a hymn." To this, Eastman writes, he "listened with much astonishment. The hymn contained the word *Jesus*. [He] did not comprehend what this meant." His father explains "that Jesus was the Son of God who came on earth to save sinners, and that it was because of [Jesus] that he had sought [Ohiyesa]." Looking back, Eastman notes that "This conversation made a deep impression on [his] mind" (246), although he could not at the time have understood concepts like the son of God or the salvation of sinners. The final paragraph of *Indian Boyhood* describes Ohiyesa's arrival at his father's home in 1873 and his coming school days: "Late in the fall we reached the citizen settlement at Flandreau, South Dakota, where my father and some others dwelt among the whites. Here my wild life came to an end, and my school days began" (247).

Jacob Eastman had settled at Flandreau in 1869, after being released from four years' imprisonment in Davenport, Iowa, where along with his older son, John, he had been converted to Christianity by Stephen Return Riggs and Thomas Williamson. Riggs not only spoke Dakota but had served as interpreter for the Dakotas on trial by the government, and he had also translated the Bible into the language. He and Williamson would both have worked hard to make such concepts as "the Son of God," "sinners," and "salvation" comprehensible to their potential converts. But none of this is treated in *Indian Boyhood*, which was written for what we would now call a young adult audience.[10]

From the Deep Woods to Civilization,[11] Eastman's second autobiographical volume, opens by revisiting the conclusion of *Indian Boyhood*.[12] The last chapter of that book was titled, "First Impressions of Civilization"; the first chapter of this one is called "The Way Opens," and in it Eastman provides details he had not given in *Indian Boyhood* while omitting others included in the earlier book.[13] In just three paragraphs Eastman summarizes his Indian boyhood from the perspective of a man who has attained a number of mature and critical "impressions of civilization." He notes having been trained as a boy "to be a warrior and a hunter," and "not to care for money or possessions;" that is, to become, "in the broadest sense a public servant" (1), a responsible member of his tribal nation. Indian warfare he describes as akin to college athletics (2), very different, he observes, from "civilized war" because in it, there "was no thought of destroying a nation, taking away their country or reducing the people to servitude." At least there was not, Eastman writes, until his people "had adopted the usages of the white man's warfare for spoliation and conquest" (2). Ironies of this sort are frequent.

An exception to tribal warfare as intercollegiate competition, he writes, involved conflict with the Americans. He "was taught," Eastman explains, "never to spare a citizen of the United States" (3). Although his people "were on friendly terms with the Canadian white men," this was not the case with the Americans. This was because they had "pretended to buy [Dakota] land at ten cents an acre, but never paid the price," and "the debt stands unpaid to this day."[14] The Sioux protested, and when they received no redress, there "finally came the outbreak of 1862 in Minnesota, when many settlers were killed, and forthwith our people, such as were left alive, were driven by the troops into exile" (3). His father was among those who fled and was later captured. Eastman says "we were informed that all were hanged."[15] "This was why," he explains, his uncle "had taught [him] never to spare a white man from the United States" (3).

Eastman describes his traditional upbringing "in the upper Missouri region, and along the Yellowstone River" (4), until, in "the winter and summer of 1872," his people "drifted toward the southern part of what is now Manitoba" (5). It is there that his father comes to find him a year later, and Eastman retells the story of the day on which his father arrived. In this telling Eastman has his father immediately proceed to an "eloquent exposition of the so-called civilized life, or the way of the white man"

(7). Although he "could not doubt" his father, he nonetheless acknowledges "a voice within saying to [him], 'A false life! a treacherous life!'" Both his father's voice and that inner voice would speak to him throughout his life.

Jacob Eastman, his son writes, "had been converted by Christian missionaries" who gave him "a totally new vision of the white man, as a religious man and a kindly" (7). Although the father continues to believe that the traditional life of the Dakota "is the best in a world of our own, such as we have enjoyed for ages" (8), he knows there is no resisting the power of the whites. "Above all," he says, "they have their Great Teacher … Jesus" (8). Thus, Jacob Eastman has concluded that "the sooner we accept their mode of life and follow their teaching, the better it will be for all of us" (8). Whatever doubts the boy may yet have, he nonetheless agrees to return to the United States with his father.

Eastman describes the eventful trip, which now does reference his father's Bible reading and hymn singing—all in Dakota—and mentions an encounter with the loud "monster with one fiery eye" (13), a Northern Pacific train. They arrive at "Flandreau, in Dakota Territory," on a "peaceful Indian summer day," as it happens, one when "the whole community gathered together to congratulate and welcome us home" (13). Soon Jacob Eastman says, "'It is time for you to go to school my son,' … with his usual air of decision" (16). Ohiyesa asks what he is to do at school, and his father's response specifies learning "the language of the white man … how to count your money and tell the prices of your horses and furs." These will involve learning "A, B, C, and so forth"; his father has learned only a few of these letters himself (17). Ohiyesa is soon off "to the little mission school, two miles distant over the prairie" (17).

Once at the school, Eastman is met by "thirty or forty Indian children" (21) observing the newcomer as curiously as he observes them. He finds the children dressed in "some apology for white man's clothing," the "pantaloons" and coats they wear all oddly sized. "Some of their hats were brimless, and others without crowns, while most were fantastically painted" (21). He does not describe his own attire. The schoolboys have short hair, and Eastman notes something that had not been described for Indian students elsewhere: that their hair "stood erect like porcupine quills" (21). Eastman observes that the "boys played ball and various other games," until "the teacher came out and rang a bell, and all the children went in." After a while, he "slid inside and took the seat nearest the door" (21).

When the teacher speaks to him in English, he has "not the slightest idea" what is meant. When the teacher then "asked in broken Sioux: 'What is your name?'" Eastman informs the reader that the teacher had probably "not been among the Indians long, or he would not have asked that question" (22). This is because, he says, "It takes a tactician and a diplomat to get an Indian to tell his name!"[16] (22). When the teacher addresses the class in English, the children show their comprehension by opening their books and themselves speaking "the talk of a strange people" (23). Ohiyesa observes the students whispering among themselves about him, and when "one of the big boys" calls him "Baby"—doubtless in his own language—he mounts his pony and rides off, as the children call after him, "there goes the long-haired boy!"[17] (23) It is his intention to tell his father that he "must go back to [his] uncle in Canada" (24).

Returning to the Flandreau settlement, he first encounters his grandmother, who, when his father returns, repeats her skeptical view of "these new manners" (24). But Jacob Eastman holds firm to his conviction that "there is no going back," and finally his son admits that "father's logic was too strong for me." The consequence of that admission is that "the next morning," as Eastman writes, he "had his hair cut"—by his father, probably—"and started in to school in earnest." From that point forward, he "obeyed … father's wishes, and went regularly to the little day-school" (25). Because his doubts—still supported by his grandmother—persist, he goes, he says, "where all [his] people go when they want light—into the thick woods" (26). After a time, he emerges with his heart "strong," desiring "to follow the new trail to the end." He once more uses the simile of the brook, although I think this time (with the possible exception of "resistless") it is more likely Eastman's than his wife's. The new trail, he writes, "like the little brook … must lead to larger and larger ones until it became a resistless river" (26).

Although Ohiyesa is now attending school on a daily basis, Eastman says absolutely nothing about what transpired there. Rather, we continue to hear of his grandmother's ongoing doubts, and much more about his father's unyielding convictions. Jacob Eastman steadfastly praises the white man's religion and speaks of the value of writing (28), so that soon Ohiyesa "began to be really interested in this curious scheme of living that [his] father was gradually unfolding." At last even his "grandmother had to yield … and it was settled that [he] was to go to school at Santee Agency, Nebraska, where Dr. Alfred L. Riggs [the son of Stephen Return Riggs] was then fairly started in the work of his great mission school" (29–30). Like any proud alumnus, Eastman adds that Riggs's school "has turned out some of the best educated Sioux Indians" (30), and somewhat oddly calls the school "the Mecca of the Sioux country" (30).[18]

One "of the best educated Sioux Indians" himself, Eastman situates his story by observing that "Sitting Bull and Crazy Horse were still at large [!]," and that "General Custer had just been placed in military command of the Dakota Territory" (30). He begins his next chapter, "On the White Man's Trail," by giving an exact date, writing: "It was in the fall of 1874 that [he] started from Flandreau ... with a good neighbor of ours on his way to Santee" (31).

Ohiyesa is dressed in his "hunting suit, which was a compromise between Indian attire and a frontiersman's outfit." He also has taken along "a blanket, and an extra shirt" (31). Ohiyesa's "blanket" is a reminder that whatever he had or had not learned at Flandreau, he is very far from "civilized." Eastman reports his father's parting words: "it is the same as if I sent you on your first war-path. I shall expect you to conquer" (31–32). Similar words would be addressed to Luther Standing Bear by his father.

Ohiyesa and his Indian neighbor Peter both hunt successfully on their first night out, and "it seemed ... more like one of our regular fall hunts than like going away to school" (32). Peter, like Eastman's father, also makes use of "his Bible and hymn-book printed in the Indian tongue" (32), and finding the place where they have camped plentiful with game, he decides to remain and trap. Ohiyesa is greatly tempted to do the same, but "the thought of [his] father's wish kept [him] on [his] true course." He asks Peter to tell his father that he will "not return until [he] finish[es his] war-path," recalling "how he had said that if [he] did not return, he would shed proud tears" (34). Taking his "blanket on his back," the boy "started for the Missouri on foot" (34). The distance to Santee is about 150 miles.

Eastman describes coming "upon a solitary farm-house of sod" late one afternoon and encountering its owner, "a white man—a man with much hair on his face" (35). The young traveler is hungry and fortunately has some money given him by his father to offer for sustenance, although he "hardly knew the different denominations." When the man sees it he becomes more "cordial," and Ohiyesa is invited to eat with the farm family, who say grace before the meal. After eating, he again offers the farmer money, which the man declines. Invited to remain with the family indoors, the young man

chooses instead "the bank of a stream near by, where [he] sat down to medi-
tate." As he does, he hears "a peculiar weird music, and the words of a strange
song." He did not know then, but does know now that it "was music from a
melodeon ... and the tune was 'Nearer, my God, to Thee.'" Eastman writes
that "strange as it sounded to [him] ... there was something soothing and
gentle about the music and the voices" (37).

Later he sees the farmer shaping "an old breaking-plow ... on his rude
forge," and the man's physique and manner make him look "not unlike a
successful warrior just returned from the field of battle." So impressed is the
young man with the sight that he resolves to "learn that profession," should
he "ever reach the school and learn the white man's way" (38). Although the
man signs to him to join the family and sleep indoors, Ohiyesa declines, and,
as he later recalls, "every star that night seemed to be bent upon telling the
story of the white man." After breakfast he again offers money, and when it is
once more refused, Eastman writes, "Then and there I loved civilization and
renounced my wild life." The following sentence, however, makes clear that
this renunciation is not yet—nor will it ever be—absolute. Eastman writes,
"I took up my *blanket* and continued on my journey" (39, my emphasis).

"Thirty miles from the school" Ohiyesa encounters Alfred Riggs, from
whom he "received some encouraging words ...., for he spoke the Sioux
language very well" (40). In that he and Riggs recognize each other, they
must have met before. Arriving at the school, the young man is greeted by
his "older brother John, who was then assistant teacher." John, whom he
had not mentioned before, "introduced [him] to [his] new life" (40).[19] This
begins with a bell marking clock time, the "bell of the old chapel at Santee
[summoning] the pupils to class" (40). To class—or more likely to chapel, for
Eastman describes "our principal," Alfred Riggs, reading "aloud from a large
book," after which he offered prayer and "conducted devotional exercises in
the Sioux language" (40). Although he can understand the language—as students attending services at the English-only government boarding schools
usually could not—Eastman nonetheless writes that the "subject matter was
... strange, and the names he used were unintelligible to [him]. 'Jesus' and
'Jehovah' fell upon [his] ears as mere meaningless sounds" (40). This can't
entirely be true, for the concluding page of Eastman's *Indian Boyhood*, as
I'd noted, had his father singing a "hymn [that] contained the word *Jesus*,"
a word which, at that time, to be sure, he "did not comprehend" (247). But
his father, he had written, had then "told [him] that Jesus was the Son of

God who came on earth to save sinners" (247), and in the year Eastman had spent with his father at Flandreau, he would have heard of Jesus and Jehovah many times.

While others "were ordered to various rooms under different instructors," Eastman finds himself "left in the chapel with another long-haired young man"—after cutting his son's hair for school at Flandreau, Jacob Eastman had allowed him to let it grow long again, as we will later learn (44). The long-haired man was "a Mandan from Fort Berthold ... one of our ancient enemies" (41). Enemy or not, Eastman is impressed with Alfred Mandan, as he will be called, who "became a very good friend of [his]" (42). This matter is dropped as Eastman writes of learning "the rules of the school and what was expected of us" from Riggs himself, who permits him to avoid "study that first day," so that he can "fill up the big bag he brought ... with straw from the straw pile back of his barn" (42) to serve as a mattress. The straw-filled bag will go on "a bunk or framework for [his] bed" (42–43). Then Ohiyesa "filled a smaller bag for a pillow, and having received the sheets and blankets, [he] made [his] first white man's bed under [Riggs's] supervision." "When it was done," Eastman observes, "it looked clean and dignified enough for anyone" (43). But sleeping arrangements similar to this would almost surely have existed in his father's house at Flandreau.

Riggs explains that the bed must be made up "every morning like that before going to school" (43), and he gives instructions for a daily cleanup using "a tin basin or two on a bench just outside the door, by the water barrels" (43). Riggs then gave him "a little English primer to study, also one or two books in the Dakota language, which [he] had learned to read in the day-school," something he had not previously revealed. In addition, there "was a translation of the Psalms, and of the Pilgrim's Progress" (44), translations that had been done by Alfred Riggs's father. In spite of his growing enthusiasm for Christian civilization, Eastman finds these "the dullest hunting [he] had ever known!" (44).

That evening, Eastman writes, "a company of three young men arrived from up the river—to all appearance full-fledged warriors" (44). He admires "the handsome white, blue, and red blankets worn by these stately Sioux youths," and states that he "had not worn one since [his] return from Canada" (44). In that he had traveled the 150 miles from Flandreau to Santee with his own blanket, one may wonder at this statement. He will definitely not wear a blanket any longer, because his "brother," Eastman writes, "got [him] a suit of clothes, and had some one cut [his] hair which was already over [his] ears, as it had not been touched since the year before." He writes that he "felt like a wild goose with its wings clipped" (44), although, unlike many Native students, he does not take the hair cutting as a violation of his Indian identity.

"How well I remember the first time we were called upon to recite," Eastman writes (45). With him in the "primer class" were the three young Indian men whose arrival he had noted. All four of these "youthful warriors were held up and harassed with words of three letters ... those little words, rat, cat, and so forth," that "tore, bled, and sweated" them "until not a semblance of [their] native dignity and self-respect were left" (46). Tellingly, Eastman points out that they "were of just the age when the Indian youth is most on his dignity." In battle, he says, they could easily outdo "Custer or Harney"[20] because they "had been bred and trained to those things." But when they "found [them]selves within four walls and set to pick out words of three letters [they] were like novices upon snow-shoes—often flat on the ground." The young man admits that he hardly "ever was tired in [his] life until those first days of boarding-school" (46), and despite having several times voiced strong support for "civilization," he acknowledges an ongoing ambivalence: "At times I felt something of the fascination of the new life, and again there would arise in me a dogged resistance" (46–47). The necessity to manage this tension is often present in Eastman's texts, as it was in his life.

"Aside from repeating and spelling words," he writes, "we had to count and add imaginary accounts" (47). "It seemed now that everything must be measured in time or money or distance" (47). This, he notes, ran counter to all he had known. "And when the teacher placed before us a painted globe, and said that our world was like that," he feels his "foothold deserting [him]. All [his] savage philosophy was in the air, if these things were true." But "when Dr. Riggs explained ... the industries of the white man, his thrift and forethought," Eastman claims that he and his fellows "could see the reasonableness of it all" (47). Indeed, Eastman compares Alfred Riggs to his father, stating: "Next to my own father, this man did more than perhaps any other to make it possible for me to grasp the principles of true civilization" (48). The "Rev. Dr. John P. Williamson," he notes, was also someone who powerfully influenced him (48). Both men would have taught that civilization could only be founded upon Christian faith.

Meanwhile, Eastman's father "wrote to [him] in the Dakota language" (48), offering encouragement and inspiring him to the point that he "studied harder than most of the boys." He writes that the "white man in general had no use for the Indian" at that point in time when "Sitting Bull and the Northern Cheyennes were still fighting in Wyoming and Montana, so that the outlook was not bright for [him] to pursue [his] studies among the whites, yet now it was [his] secret dream and ambition" (49). The reason "the outlook was not bright," of course, was the widespread hostility "among the whites" to Plains Natives and to Indians in general. But Eastman continues to harbor his "secret dream and ambition." Like many boarding-school students, he notes that he has now come to possess "a little money of [his] own" (49), earned by sawing wood, "besides other work for which [he] was paid" (49). By the end of his second year he acknowledges that he still "could not understand or speak much English," although he "could translate every word of [his] English studies into the native tongue, besides having read all that was then published in the Sioux" (49). These are impressive achievements.

Despite his initial skepticism as to the uses of arithmetic, Eastman notes that he "had caught up with boys who had two or three years the start of me, and was now studying elementary algebra and geometry" (49–50). At this point two important events coincide: "Dr. Riggs came ... and said that he had a way by which he could send [him] to Beloit, Wisconsin, to enter the preparatory department of Beloit College" (50).[21] Then "on the eve of departure, [he] received word from Flandreau that [his] father was dead, after only two days' illness" (50). Eastman is now even more determined that his father's desire that he learn the white man's ways "should be obeyed to the end." Thus, he does not return home but, "in September, 1876, ... started from Santee to Beloit to begin [his] serious studies" (50).

Setting off for college, the eighteen-year-old Ohiyesa for the first time rides the "fiery monster," the train that had so frightened him at the end of *Indian Boyhood* and the beginning of *Deep Woods*. He reaches Beloit on "the second day of [his] pilgrimage," observing that it was "beautifully located on the high, wooded banks of Black Hawk's picturesque Rock River,"[22] and that the "college grounds covered the site of an ancient village of mound-builders" (52).[23] The new student "was taken to President Chapin's house, and after a kindly greeting, shown to [his] room in South College" (52).[24] There he overhears some banter between two young men, one of whom refers to him as "Sitting Bull's nephew," joking to the other to beware lest Eastman "have [his] scalplock before morning" (53). The exchange would seem to have been good-natured; Eastman writes that both of them "became good friends of [his] afterward" (53).[25]

Eastman makes clear "that this was September, 1876, less than three months after Custer's gallant command was annihilated by the hostile Sioux" on June 25 (53). We might remark Eastman's use of "gallant" in reference to Custer's Seventh Cavalry and of "hostile" in reference to his own western relatives. In part II of "The School Days of an Indian," the earlier version he had published, Eastman wrote: "I went to Beloit in September 1876, two months after Custer's command had been annihilated by the Sioux" (898). Neither "gallant" for Custer's command nor "hostile" for the Sioux appeared there.

The passage in *Deep Woods* continues with Eastman writing that he "was especially troubled when [he] learned that [his] two uncles ... left in Canada had taken part in this famous fight" (53). (He had not provided this information in 1907.) Eastman's father's brothers, it is clear, had taken a different view of white "civilization" than had Many Lightnings, going west to join Sitting Bull's Lakotas and the Cheyennes. As for the "Sitting Bull's nephew" reference, Eastman writes that "people were bitter against the Sioux in those days," and he thinks "it was a local newspaper that printed the story that [he] was the nephew of Sitting Bull." An unfortunate result of this misidentification was that when he "went into the town, [he] was followed by gangs of little white *savages*, giving imitation war whoops" (53, my emphasis), ignorant of his commitment to Christian civilization.

His "first recitation at Beloit," Eastman writes, "was an event in [his] life" (53). He is brought before "a remarkable looking man whose name was Professor Pettibone.[26] He had a long, grave face, with long whiskers and scarcely any hair on his head" (53–54), and Eastman thinks the man "the very embodiment of wisdom" (54). He doesn't dramatize this "event," representing, for example, what the formidable professor and the reticent young Indian student had said to one another, or how the class responded to their interaction. As I have noted, Eastman rarely dramatizes, preferring to narrate such things as his meeting with President Chapin, or his interaction with the fellows who pretended to believe he was Sitting Bull's nephew. But his descriptive narration at this point, I should note, is rich in metaphor (e.g., 54–55).

He writes that he was "diffident" about reciting, and it is only by great effort that he managed to speak English "quite fluently, although not correctly" (54). That the "expression of faces ... toward him" is "in general friendly" is "somewhat reassuring," and he poignantly observes of himself that he "absorbed knowledge through every pore. The more [he] got, the larger [his] capacity grew, and [his] appetite increased in proportion" (54). He alludes to the difficulties he had with the concept of grammar—"the idea of each word having an office and a specific name, and standing in relation to other words like the bricks in a wall" (55)—and to the differences between "history and geography" which to him had been "legends and traditions" rather than chronology and maps. Having more than once testified to the force of his father's "logic" and that of Alfred Riggs, he now reports that he "soon learned to appreciate the pure logic of mathematics" (55).[27] In particular he notes his participation in a "full share" of athletics; he states that he "spent no less than three hours daily in physical exercise ... throughout [his] college days" (55). Eastman would later become an outstanding athlete at Dartmouth.

The Pratt system of "outing" students to family farms had not yet been established, but Eastman decides on his own "to hire out to a farmer" (56) during his first summer vacation, not so much to immerse himself in civilization as to earn some money. He writes that he "set out in a southerly direction" (56), recalling "the troubles of that great chief of the Sac and Fox tribe, Black Hawk, who had some dispute with President Lincoln about that very region" (56). He had earlier mentioned "Black Hawk's picturesque Rock River" (52), although, as I noted, Black Hawk did not encounter that river anywhere near Beloit. Having died in 1838, Black Hawk could not have had any "dispute with *President* Lincoln" (56, my emphasis).[28]

Although the young Indian student is "armed with a letter of introduction from President Chapin," he nonetheless approaches the front door of "the first farm [he] came to ... with some misgivings" (56). When the farmer asks Eastman his business, the young man introduces himself as "a student of Beloit College" (56) seeking summer work. But this farmer's response is very different from what Ohiyesa had encountered at the South Dakota sod house. The man says with some heat, "'Oho! You can not work the New Ulm game on me. I don't think you can reproduce the Fort Dearborn Massacre on this farm'" (57). These historical references would probably not have been recognized by many of Eastman's readers in 1916, and they are far less familiar to readers today.

But the farmer himself has things confused. The "New Ulm game," as he calls it, had in fact been "worked" on the Indians some fifteen years earlier, not on the whites. After the failed rebellion of 1848 in the German states, many Germans emigrated to the Minnesota Territory—Minnesota

did not become a state until 1858—settling upon Sioux lands, the boundaries of which had not yet been clearly drawn. The town of New Ulm was
established in 1854, in an area the indigenous Nakotas had left for the winter,
as they did each year. On their return they found the settlers on their lands,
and upon confronting them, had the army called out against them. The town
of New Ulm became a liquor trading center, and its German residents were
among the first casualties of the 1862 uprising, with four hundred of them
killed. The farmer's other reference is to an incident that had occurred more
than fifty years earlier, during the War of 1812, in the vicinity of Chicago.
The Fort Dearborn Massacre, as I'll note further, was indeed an occasion on
which white settlers suffered at the hands of Indians.

The farmer concludes his angry outburst by asking Eastman, "'By the
way, what tribe do you belong to?'" When he responds that he is Sioux, the
man shouts, "'That settles it. Get off from my farm just as quick as you can!
I had a cousin killed by your people only last summer'" (57). Eastman offers
him no further word, writing that he "kept on [his] way until [he] found
another farmer to whom [he] made haste to present [his] letter. For him,"
Eastman says, he "worked all summer," adding with some irony, "and as treaties were kept on both sides, there was not occasion for any trouble" (57).
Although he offers no specifics, his experience on the farm seems to have
had just the effect intended by Pratt's outing program, leading him to an
expansive encomium upon "the greatness of Christian civilization, the ideal
civilization" (57). As for his People, he has come to understand: "There must
be no more warfare within our borders; we must quit the forest trail for the
breaking plow" (57–58). "For the first time," he writes, "I permitted myself
to think and act as a white man," (58) an extraordinary "permission" for the
young student who has thus far wavered—as he will again.

"At the end of three years," he continues, "other Sioux Indians had been
sent to Beloit, and I felt that I might progress faster where I was not surrounded by my tribesmen" (58). This is curious in that there never were very
many Native students at Beloit, nor should their presence have held him
back in any way. Nonetheless, Eastman apprises Alfred Riggs of his feelings
and "Dr. Riggs arranged to transfer [him] to the *preparatory* department of
Knox College of Galesburg, Illinois" (58, my emphasis), not to the college
proper.[29] There, Eastman writes, "I was thrown into close contact with the
rugged, ambitious sons of western farmers," and, in something of the manner
of Booker T. Washington, he provides a list of Knox "men who have become
well known and whose friendship is still retained" (58).[30]

Because Knox was "a co-educational institution," Eastman also "mingled for the first time with the pale-face maidens,"—perhaps the daughters "of western farmers"—"and as soon as [he] could shake off [his] Indian shyness, [he] found them very winning and companionable" (59). It is "through social intercourse with the American college girl that [he] gained [his] first conception of the home life and domestic ideals of the white man" (59), he writes, apparently discounting whatever he might have "gained" during his summer of work with the treaty-keeping farmer. It is at this time that he begins to wonder "what should be [his] special work in life," for he knows that "in civilization one must have a definite occupation—a profession" (59). This is very different from what most of the government boarding-school students had learned, the young men among them having been encouraged to aspire to a respectable *trade*, not a "profession." Eastman wishes to work on behalf of his "people," and to be "of service to [his] race," and he is well aware that for such service, "the ministry … was the first to be adopted by the educated Sioux" (60). He finds himself, however, more inclined toward either law or medicine, finally deciding to pursue the latter as his profession (60).

Back home for the summer, Eastman is told of Dartmouth College by Dr. Riggs, "and how it was originally founded as a school for Indian youth" (61). This is not quite accurate. He is intrigued by the prospect of attending, "and yet … hesitated," spending the fall term at home and teaching at "the little day-school where [his] first lessons had been learned" (61). In that this fifth chapter is titled "College Life in the East," there can be little suspense as to whether he will overcome his hesitation. Thus in January 1882 he set out for the East, "at a period when the Government was still at considerable trouble to subdue and settle some of my race upon reservations" (61). I note again both Eastman's concern to include Dakota history in his narrative along with a tendency, here, to distance himself from it, remarking on the government's "considerable trouble"—I do not think he is being ironic here—but not on the considerable trouble that the government's efforts to constrain them caused the Indians. Anticipating the long journey, he writes that he was "somewhat prepared," although "not yet conscious of the seriousness and terrific power of modern civilization" (62). He would become fully "conscious" of both these things when he found himself in one of modern civilization's great cities.

As his train pulls into Chicago, "the Fort Dearborn Massacre" mentioned earlier by the hostile farmer comes to mind, causing him to realize "vividly at that moment that the day of the Indian had passed forever" (62).

This powerful realization suggests that his consciousness of the "*terrific* power of modern civilization" may allude to "civilization's" power to *terrify* or *terrorize* Native people. As noted, the "Fort Dearborn Massacre"—the farmer had called it a "massacre"—occurred during the War of 1812, when the Potowatomis attacked American troops evacuating Fort Dearborn, Illinois Territory, in what is now the city of Chicago, killing many and burning the Fort. That particular "incident" could hardly demonstrate civilization's power in that the Potowatomis had been successful in their resistance. By 1816, however, the Fort had been rebuilt and the Indians removed, these latter events indeed testifying to the "terrific power of modern civilization," and perhaps contributing to Eastman's sense "that the day of the Indian had passed forever" (62).

This thought weighs heavily upon him as he walks the streets of Chicago. There he finds "a perfect stream of humanity rushing madly along" and notices that "the faces of the people were not happy at all. They wore an intensely serious look that to me was appalling" (62). The unhappy intensity of the citizens of Chicago must be particularly "appalling" to the young man if, as he has just stated, "the day of the Indian had passed forever" (62). He would, then, have no choice but to join the "perfect stream"—here, the adjective does assert a bitter irony—of humanity as it rushed "madly along." It does not help that Eastman recalls having been warned to "look out for pickpockets" in the city. As he writes, "Evidently there were some disadvantages connected with this mighty civilization, for we Indians seldom found it necessary to guard our possessions" (62). These parallel insights—that "the day of the Indian had passed," that the urban masses were "unhappy," and that there were indeed "some disadvantages connected with … civilization"—articulated here on his way to Dartmouth College, would in some degree remain with Eastman all his life.

Soon the young man is back on an eastbound train that takes him through Albany, New York, then to Boston (64), and "on to Dartmouth College" (65). As he approaches the college Eastman reflects in an elegiac manner upon "the time when red men lived here in plenty and freedom," believing himself "destined to come view their graves and bones." He has already learned the Western trope, "they shall not have died in vain," and he uses it to remind himself to "continue that which in their last struggle they proposed to take up, in order to save themselves from extinction." He will do what they did not; he will gain an education and establish a place for himself in American society. Developing this matter, Eastman states: "Had our New England tribes but followed the example of that great Indian, Samson Occom, and kept up with the development of Dartmouth College, they would have brought forth leaders and men of culture" (65). But this progressive reading of history is not accurate.

Shortly before the middle of the eighteenth century, Samson Occom, a Mohegan, had studied with the Reverend Eleazar Wheelock at the Moors Charity School in Lebanon, Connecticut. Later, in 1765, Occom went to England to preach and raise money for what Wheelock had proposed as a more substantial institution for the education of the Indians. Using monies Occom brought back, Wheelock did indeed found Dartmouth College in Hanover, New Hampshire, in 1769, and served as its first president. But the school catered to whites, not Indians, something Occom himself understood and lamented.[31] "In its first two hundred years," as Colin Calloway has written, "Dartmouth admitted only a trickle of Indian students and graduated only a handful" (xviii); in fact, "only nineteen Native Americans" attended Dartmouth prior to 1970 when a serious attempt to rectify this began (Vigil 42).[32] Thus Occom could not have "kept up with the development of Dartmouth College," nor could members of the "New England tribes" have done so until some two centuries later.

Eastman surely did not know this when he went to Dartmouth. But he does not seem to have learned much more by the time he wrote. To be fair, Occom's 1768 autobiography, the first by a Native American, was not published until 1982, and an edition of his collected writings did not appear until 2006. Nor is it surprising that Eastman was unaware of the fact that the New England tribes he mourned were not and are not "extinct." Believing them dead and gone, Eastman's elegy does not aim somehow to revive them, in the manner of most Native elegiac expression,[33] although it does inspire him to preserve his own Dakota people through education. "This was my ambition," Eastman writes, "that the Sioux should accept civilization before it was too late! I wished that our young men might at once take up the white man's way, and prepare themselves to hold office and wield influence in their native states" (65). He means by this surely the Dakotas, Minnesota, and perhaps New Hampshire. He does not seem to have imagined, in 1916, that they might "wield influence" in their sovereign tribal nations.

Eastman had come east to enroll at Dartmouth College, but "when he arrived at Dartmouth, he was judged not ready to enter the freshman class, and in January 1882 he began a year of preparation at Kimball Union Academy" (Calloway 116).[34] Calloway notes that during that year at Kimball Union, Eastman was found guilty of plagiarism. Having submitted an exercise as his own, he was confronted with the source from which he had copied two pages. His response was to claim "that he had been accustomed to that method of composition for years and did not realize he was doing anything wrong" (Calloway 116). Although academic conventions as to what constitutes plagiarism have varied over time, wouldn't he have known that offering two pages written by someone else as one's own work was unacceptable in the U.S. in the 1880s?

Nonetheless, Eastman's claim "that he had been accustomed to that method of composition" is interesting because "that method" is exactly the method by which the oral tradition is passed on. This is to say that no storyteller would ever claim that the story he or she told was "original" in the sense of newly created, or individually and independently authored. Very much to the contrary, oral narrative frequently includes phrases like, "so it is said," and "as we have heard." And while the extent to which any narrator introduces "new" material varies, the innovations are always subordinate to what is reproduced. Early in his education, Eastman, familiar with traditional oral narrative, might well have engaged in "that method of composition," although it is difficult to imagine that by the time he came to Kimball Union he would not have learned that it was unacceptable academically. In any case, Eastman subsequently submitted an exercise entirely of his own composition and continued his studies.

By "December [of 1882, he] was still 'not so ready as many' in his academic preparation" (Calloway 116), although upon his graduation from Kimball, he did go on "to old Dartmouth in the fall of 1883 to enter the Freshman class" (*Deep Woods* 67). Kiara Vigil has written that "much of Eastman's early life as an undergraduate at Dartmouth shaped his philosophy" (42), and I think that is correct. But given the fact that he entered Dartmouth at the age of twenty-five, "his philosophy" would already have been "shaped" a good deal by his experience and education up to that point. Vigil also observes that Eastman was the only Native American student in his freshman class (42), and surely that fact would have tested his ability to negotiate between his shifting sense of Indianness and his still-developing Americanness.

As for his studies at Dartmouth, Calloway writes that Eastman enrolled "in the Latin scientific curriculum, which required taking courses in English,

Latin, French, Greek, German, and linguistics," as well as "classes in zoology, botany, chemistry, physics, natural history, political science, philosophy, and geometry" (117), quite a rigorous course of study. It was at Dartmouth, Eastman writes, "that I had most of my savage gentleness and native refinement knocked out of me," an observation to which he immediately adds, "I do not complain, for I know that I gained more than their equivalent" (67). Nonetheless, one may well wonder whether whatever he "gained" did, in fact, amount to "more" than the apparently oxymoronic qualities of "savage gentleness," and "native refinement" that were lost. These are matters to which Eastman would return.

He would soon have a good deal more "knocked out of [him]" because, he writes, "On the evening of [the] first class meeting, lo! [he] was appointed football captain for [his] class" (67). He follows this observation by reporting the fairly predictable remarks of his fellow students about his "qualifications as a frontier warrior" (67), remarks he again takes as amiable banter, for all that they mark him as something other than just another American undergraduate.[35] Indeed, he writes that he "was a sort of prodigal son of old Dartmouth, and nothing could have exceeded the heartiness of [his] welcome," foreshadowing, as it were, the sentiment he expressed much later about Indians not having met any prejudice as Indians. He finds himself "a sort of prodigal son" who has returned because, as he once more writes, "The New England Indians, for whom [Dartmouth] was founded, had departed well-nigh a century earlier" (68). They had not all "departed," as I have said, although their presence would not have been apparent to Eastman—nor, to repeat, had Dartmouth actually been founded primarily for them.

Yet apart from the heartiness of his welcome and his captaincy of the freshman football team, there is not a word from Eastman about his four years of education at Dartmouth. He says nothing about his course work, his relations with classmates and faculty, nor about his substantial success at several sports.[36] Indeed, he writes of his departure from Dartmouth only a few pages after announcing his arrival, informing the reader that "after [his] graduation with the class of 1887, it was made possible for [him] to study medicine at Boston University" (71).[37] He does, however, speak retrospectively of his church attendance during his time at college (71), and, once more in a manner similar to Booker T. Washington, proudly states that at Dartmouth he "had met … Matthew Arnold, [who] … was kind enough to talk with [him] for a few minutes," and that he had on various occasions also spoken with "with Emerson,[38] Longfellow, Francis Parkman, and many other men of note" (72). It was during his attendance at Dartmouth, too, that Eastman delivered his first lecture ever "before the Wellesley girls" (72)—this was the first lecture for which he was paid (Wilson 32)—and "met society people of an entirely different sort to those [he] had hitherto taken as American types" (72–73), people of a higher class, apparently, than the "American types" he had encountered at Knox.

Eastman also reports attendance at a school not usually listed as part of his education, writing that during "the three years that [he] studied in Boston, [he] went every summer to Mr. Moody's famous summer school at Northfield" (73–74). Not only did he go to Mr. Moody's school, but he knew the man himself, "and was much interested in his strong personality" (74). Dwight Lyman Moody (1837–99) was a born-again evangelist who had made missionizing trips around the world before founding the Northfield Seminary for young ladies in 1879 and then the Mount Hermon School for Boys two years later, the two schools together known as Northfield Mount Hermon. Moody made it a point to seek out students of all backgrounds with few means, and, while it is not hard to understand why Eastman and Moody would have been interested in each other, it is not easy to understand why the Dartmouth graduate—and Eastman had taken a rigorous curriculum at Dartmouth—would be attending a college preparatory school during the summers he is at medical school. (It is also worth noting that he clearly did not need gainful employment during his summer vacations.) Eastman says little more of Moody and Mount Hermon, and describes nothing whatever of his experience at medical school, noting only "the date of [his] graduation [from Boston University medical college] in 1890," and the fact that he had applied for and "received [his] appointment to the position of the Government physician at Pine Ridge Agency in South Dakota" (74).

Before heading west, however, Eastman writes of visiting "the Lake Mohonk Indian conference" in New York, where he met several prominent people whose names he does not fail to provide. Reporting that he had listened "with great interest to their discussions," Eastman concludes this chapter by stating that what he had heard convinced him "that the Indians had some real friends" (75). I discern no irony here, Eastman's good opinion of the Friends of the Indian seeming to have held firm for more than twenty-five years. Charles Alexander Eastman's many years of formal education were at an end; his next chapter is titled, "A Doctor among the Indians."

ᐧᐧ

That chapter having been much discussed, and for the purposes of this study, I skip to the last chapter of *Deep Woods*. Called "The Soul of the White Man," it echoes the title of Eastman's 1911 volume, *The Soul of the Indian*. Both uses of "soul" recall an important earlier title, W. E. B. Du Bois's *The Souls of Black Folks* (1903).[39] Like other Native people who wrote about their experience of the American schools, Eastman speculates on his identity, and in many ways Du Bois is an important precursor on this matter. On the very first page of *Souls*, for example, Du Bois had posed a question Eastman himself must surely have raised on any number of occasions, "How does it feel to be a problem?" If one is a black American, Du Bois wrote, "One ever feels his twoness—an American, a Negro; two souls, two thoughts, two unreconciled strivings in one dark body, whose dogged strength alone keeps it from being torn asunder" (3). I don't know if Eastman had read Du Bois's book; I suspect he had. In any case, Dr. Eastman and Dr. Du Bois—Harvard PhD; ten years Eastman's junior—had been on the same panel at the First Universal Races Conference in London in July 1911, several months after Eastman's own "soul" book, *The Soul of the Indian*, had appeared.[40] Eastman's address was titled "The North American Indian" (in Spiller 367–76), and Du Bois's "The Negro Race in the United States of America" (in Spiller 348–63).

How to be both "an American," and "a Negro," was the problem specified by Du Bois; how to be both "an Indian" and "an American," was the problem Eastman had often confronted. His *Soul of the Indian* had looked deeply into the "soul of the white man," and his last chapter of *Deep Woods* is very much in dialogue with that earlier book. For example, in closing the first section of *Soul*, Eastman had written, "It is my personal belief, after thirty-five years' experience of it, that there is no such thing as 'Christian civilization.' I believe that Christianity and modern civilization are opposed and irreconcilable, and that the spirit of Christianity and of our ancient religion [that of the Indians] is essentially the same" (1911 24). He develops this belief in the last chapter of *Deep Woods*, "The Soul of the White Man," writing, "From the time I first accepted the Christ ideal it has grown on me steadily, but I also see more and more plainly our modern divergence from that ideal"

(1916 193). "Why," he continues, "do we find so much evil and wickedness practiced by the nations composed of professedly 'Christian' individuals? … Behind the material and intellectual splendor of our civilization, primitive savagery and cruelty and lust hold sway" (1916 194).[41]

The ascription by an Indian of "primitive savagery and cruelty" to the Americans is obviously telling; Dartmouth had not quite knocked the "savage gentleness" and "native refinement" (67) out of Charles Eastman. He continues by poignantly stating that when he "let go of [his] simple, instinctive nature religion, [he] hoped to gain something far loftier," and in accepting the "Christ ideal," he continues to believe that he did. But that "higher and spiritual life, though first in theory, is clearly secondary, if not entirely neglected, in actual practice" (194), Eastman writes. He continues, "When I reduce civilization to its lowest terms"—I suspect the ironic use of "lowest" here rather than "most basic" is intentional, and I suspect it was not a word chosen by Elaine Goodale—"it becomes a system of life based upon trade. The dollar is the measure of value, and *might* still spells *right*" (194, emphasis in original). Eastman remains "an Indian" because he has "never lost [his] Indian sense

3 Charles Alexander Eastman in 1897. National Anthropological Archives, Smithsonian Institution. BAE GN 034622A 06583800.

of right and justice," and he has come to understand that "the spirit of Christianity" and his people's "ancient religion is essentially the same" (*Soul* 24).

But of course he can no longer only be an Indian, at least not the sort of Indian he had been before his father sent him off to school. Thus he closes *Deep Woods* with the words, "Nevertheless, so long as I live, I am an American" (195). Just as Du Bois's "Negro" could not undo the "problem" of his "twoness" by rejecting the fact that he or she was an American, neither can Eastman, an Indian, reject the fact that he, too, is an American. Although American Christianity in practice is not at all what Eastman's father had learned from Stephen Riggs, nor what he himself had learned from his father and from Alfred Riggs, it was nonetheless from the Americans that "the Christ ideal" (1916 193) had come to him. So, too, had he gained the literacy and the professional competencies he possessed from the American schools. Whatever "uneasy alliances," whatever complex "negotiations" and mediations might be involved in sustaining his own particular "twoness," the highly educated Dr. Charles Alexander Eastman was, until the end of his life, both an Indian and an American.

4   Dr. Charles Alexander Eastman in Indian dress with tomahawk in 1913. National Anthropological Archives, Smithsonian Institution. BAE GN 3463.

2

Luther Standing Bear's
My People, the Sioux

BORN IN THE 1860S, LUTHER STANDING BEAR LIVED THROUGH SEVERAL important periods of Lakota and American history.[1] He was about eight at the time of the Custer fight (1876) and learned of it from persons who had taken part, as he would also hear firsthand of the death of Crazy Horse at Fort Robinson a year later. In 1879 he became, in his telling, "the first Indian boy to step inside the Carlisle Indian School grounds" (*My People the Sioux* 133),[2] although as we will see, he also provides information contradicting that claim. He left school in the summer of 1885 and knew of the Lakota Ghost Dances and the massacre at Wounded Knee (1890). A few years later he was hired as an interpreter and performer for Buffalo Bill Cody's Wild West, which he accompanied to England, where he "had the honor of being introduced to ... Edward the Seventh, the monarch of Great Britain" (*My People* 256).

In 1905, after the death of his beloved father, who he says had been chief, he in turn "became chief of the Oglala Sioux, the greatest Indian tribe in the United States" (*My People* 274).[3] Feeling stifled by life on the reservation under the Indian agent, Major John Brennan, Standing Bear traveled to Washington, where, after meetings with President Theodore Roosevelt's Secretary of the Interior Ethan Hitchcock, and Francis Leupp, the commissioner of Indian Affairs, he obtained the "fee patent for [his] whole section of land,"[4] making him "a citizen of the United States" (280), free to go and do as he pleased.[5] He worked for a time in Oklahoma, and having "heard a great deal about the wonderful climate of Southern California" (283), he wrote to the movie director of western films, Thomas Ince, who sent him funds for "transportation for Los Angeles" (283). Standing Bear began work in the movies in 1912, about that time also becoming somewhat active in Indian affairs. He notes that he was elected "president of the [shortlived] American Indian Progressive Association" (286) for two years during the First World War.[6]

He began work on *My People the Sioux* in 1925, with E. A. Brininstool serving as editor, and the book was published in 1928. Luther Standing Bear would go on to write three more books. *My Indian Boyhood*, an account of his traditional upbringing for young readers, was published in 1931. It was followed in 1933 by an ethnographic and autobiographical text, *Land of the Spotted Eagle*. Finally, there was *Stories of the Sioux*, giving Standing Bear's versions of a number of traditional Lakota tales and legends, published in 1934. He died in 1939,[7] on the set of *Union Pacific*, an ambitious film by Cecil B. DeMille. (Although he acted in the film, he is not listed in its cast.[8]) Standing Bear was buried in the Hollywood Forever Cemetery in Los Angeles along with his sacred pipe.

His boarding-school experiences at Carlisle in its first days of operation are represented in *My People, the Sioux* and also recalled at several points in *Land of the Spotted Eagle*.

ᖇᖇ

"I was the first Indian boy to step inside the Carlisle Indian School ground," Standing Bear wrote in *My People, the Sioux* (133). The date was October 6, 1879, the fall of the year Carlisle opened.[9] Standing Bear refers to "some of the Indian prisoners from Virginia"—that is, from the Hampton Institute—who had come to Carlisle with Pratt before he "could go to Dakota and return with his first consignment of scholars" (135),[10] and he would later mention a mixed-blood Creek boy who arrived earlier, so that Standing Bear was not literally "the first Indian boy" to come to Carlisle. He writes that his father, like Ohiyesa's father, had "realized that fighting would not get the Indian anywhere, and that the only recourse was to learn the white man's ways of doing things, get the same education, and thus be in condition to stand up for his rights" (98). But when he himself made the decision to go to Carlisle, "It did not occur to [him] at that time that [he] was going away to learn the ways of the white man" (128). Rather, his "idea was that [he] was leaving the reservation and going to stay away long enough to do some brave deed, and then come home again alive. If [he] could just do that, then [he] knew [his] father would be so proud of [him]" (128).

This was because two years earlier, when his father had taken him on his first raiding expedition, Standing Bear understood that his father "wanted [him] to do something of great bravery or get killed on the bat-tle-field." Indeed, he recalls the elder Standing Bear telling him that if he should fall in battle, "keep your courage. That is the way I want you to die" (76). Thinking back to this time, Standing Bear writes, "I was willing to do my father's bidding, as I wanted so much to please him" (76). Thus when Richard Pratt came to recruit Sioux children to go to the far-off Carlisle boarding school in September 1879, the "sweet talk … did not create much impression on [him]."[11] Rather, his "mind was working in an entirely differ-ent channel. [He] was thinking of [his] father, and how he had many times said … 'Son, be brave! Die on the battle-field if necessary away from home" (124). His thought was "that this chance to go East would prove that [he] was brave if [he] were to accept it" (124). Thus when his father asks, "'Do you want to go, son?'" (125) he replies that he does, and so his name will be entered "in a big book … as 'Ota Kte, or Plenty Kill, son of Standing Bear'" (125).[12] In both *My People* and *Land of the Spotted Eagle*,[13] we are several times reminded that once at school, he strongly keeps in mind his father's wish that he die a brave death, while hardly remembering his father's wish that he "learn the white man's ways of doing things" (98).

Once he has agreed to go off to school, he writes that his father "invited all the people who lived nearby to come to his place," and engaged in a tradi-tional giveaway: "He got all the goods down off the shelves in his store and carried them outside. Then he brought in about seven head of ponies. When all the people were gathered there, he gave away all these things because I was going away East. I was going with the white people, and perhaps might never return; so he was sacrificing all his worldly possessions" (125).

Standing Bear senior, a warrior who practices the old custom of the giveaway, has two wives and is the only Brulé to run a store. Although he has never been to school and knows no English, he wears white man's clothes (for the most part), and sometimes uses the name George.[14] His is the kind of complex Indian identity, a fluid mix of the traditional and the modern, that appears frequently during this time.

Standing Bear next describes his trip from the Rosebud Agency to Carlisle, Pennsylvania. It begins with his father and his sister—she "gave herself up to go with [him], doing this as an honor" (125)—taking him by wagon "to the place where the steamboat was to carry [them] part of the way," to "Black Pole" (126), or Rosebud Landing on the Missouri River. When the family camped for the night, they "met many other Indian boys and girls who were also going east with the white people" (126). Once they get to Black Pole, they pitch their tipis "to wait [sic] the arrival of the boat." When the boat arrives, Standing Bear's "sister suddenly experienced a change of heart. She concluded that she did not want any white man's education" (126–27). This suits him well enough in that he "figured that she would have been a lot of extra trouble for [him]," because "she was younger than [he]—and a girl, at that!" (127).[15]

The "Indian boys and girls who were going away were lined up, and as their names were called they went on board the boat," Standing Bear writes. At this last moment, however, "some of the children refused to go aboard, and nobody could compel them to. So [his] sister was not the only one who had 'cold feet,' as the white people say" (127). But young Ota Kte is ever stalwart: "When my name was called," he announces, "I went right on the boat without any hesitation" (127). As the boat pulls away, "the parents of the children stood lined up on the shore and began crying. Then all the children on the boat also started to cry. It was a very sad scene" (127). Because he does not see either his father or other members of his family crying, Standing Bear recalls, he "did not shed any tears," but stood silently "and watched the others all crying as if their hearts would break" (127).

A day later the boat docks, and Standing Bear describes the next stage of the journey not from his present perspective—that of a worldly man about sixty years old—but from the perspective of the boy he was then: "We walked quite a distance until we came to a long row of little houses standing on long pieces of iron which stretched away as far as we could see. The little houses were all in line, and the interpreter told us to get inside. So we climbed up a little stairway into one of the houses, and found ourselves in a beautiful room, long but narrow, in which were many cushioned seats" (128).

He takes a seat, and then switches to another, changing his "seat four or five times before [he] quieted down." The young people "admired the beautiful room and the soft seats very much," when "suddenly the whole house started to move away with us." He notes that the "boys were in one house and the girls in another" (128–29), and he is glad his "sister was not there" because "we expected every minute that the house would tip over, and that something terrible would happen. We held our blankets between our teeth, because our hands were both busy hanging to the seats, so frightened were we" (129). He explains what the reader will have gathered: "we were in [our] first railway train, but we did not know it. We thought it was a house" (129).

They "rode ... for some distance" before the interpreter "came into the room and told us to get ready to leave it, as we were going to have something to eat" (129). Standing Bear's description of the station stop, brief as it is, has considerable ethnographic and historical interest. Before getting off the train, some "of the older boys began fixing feathers in their hair and putting *more* paint on their faces" (129, my emphasis), having, it would seem, earlier painted their faces as if for battle. The train has stopped at Sioux City, and as Standing Bear notes, it is "but three years after the killing of Custer by the Sioux, so the white people were anxious to see some Sioux Indians" (129), and they turned out in great numbers.

Standing Bear, looking back, supposes that "many of these people expected to see us coming with scalping-knives between our teeth, bows and arrows in one hand and tomahawk in the other, and to hear a great war-cry as we came off that Iron Horse" (129). Of course none of the boys carries a weapon, but the crowd does get to see young Sioux Indians with painted faces and feathers in their hair. Headed for a restaurant, the young people find themselves surrounded by whites giving war whoops, and Standing Bear makes clear that they "did not like this sort of treatment" (130). Once inside the restaurant, the group finds whites now crowding against the windows, "waiting to see how we ate."

Then the train travels on to "Sotu Otun Wake ... 'smoky city' or [the] great city of Chicago" (130), where the children are astonished at the "big houses" and the enormous numbers of—not "'white people'" but "'Wasicun' [pl. of Wasichu] or 'Mila Hanska.' This latter," he translates, "means 'long knife'" (131), a term derived from the swords carried by army officers or the bayonets affixed to the rifles of some troops.[16] In the time between trains, the prospective students eat again. Then, in what was "possibly ... the waiting-room of the [train] station," they are "brought a big bass drum" (131), leading them to organize a dance, and allowing a "few white people ... to come inside and watch the dance, while there was a great crowd outside" (131).

They board the train once more and travel "all night, the next day and then another night." Having sat "all the way from Dakota in those straight seats," Standing Bear recalls that they "were getting very tired" (131). Then, moved by fatigue, boredom, or a dawning fear, the "big boys began to tell [the] little fellows that the white people were taking [them] to where the sun rises, where they would dump [them] over the edge of the earth." This seemed credible because all of them "had been taught that the earth was flat, with four corners, and when [they] came to the edge, [they] would fall over." In expectation of this, the "big boys were singing brave songs, expecting to be killed any minute" (131).

"First Days at Carlisle" is chapter 14 of *My People*, and it is a richly detailed account of those first days, which, as noted, were also the school's first days of operation. The young people's train arrived about midnight, on October 5, 1879. From the station the young Sioux "walked about two miles to the Carlisle Barracks" (133), where they encounter "a big gate in a great high wall." It is locked, and the party has "quite a long wait [before] it was unlocked and [they] marched through it" (133). Standing Bear, almost fifty years later, again notes, "At that time I thought nothing of it, but now I realize that I was the first Indian boy to step inside the Carlisle Indian School grounds" (133). The girls are "all called to one side," and "the girls' interpreter ... took them into one of the big buildings, which was very brilliantly lighted." Standing Bear recalls that the brightly lighted building "looked good to us from the outside" (133). Then the boys' interpreter "told us to go to a certain building." They run toward it, "expecting to find nice little beds like those the white people had" (133).

But "the first room we entered was empty" (133). There is only a cold cast-iron stove with an oil lamp on it. The boys explore the building's other rooms, but they are the same, "no fire, no beds" (133). The sorry conditions at the former Carlisle Barracks were not Pratt's fault. Rather, the bedding and furnishings he had requested from the Office of Indian Affairs had not arrived in time for the Lakotas' first night at Carlisle. Thus, tired as they were, the boys "went to sleep on the hard floor, and it was so cold!" (133). And their first breakfast—they are "called downstairs for breakfast" (134), no bells, or whistles, or bugles as yet—is only "bread and water" (134). Fortunately noon brings some "meat, bread, and coffee, so [they] felt a little better." Standing Bear assures readers that the fare is nothing like at "their far-away Dakota homes where there was plenty to eat," and that even when "the food began to get better ... it was far from being what [they] had been used to receiving back home" (134). But much of what his people, confined then to the reservation, were "receiving back home," were government-issued rations, which for the most part were neither especially palatable nor abundant.

During those first days at Carlisle, they "had nothing to do. There were no school regulations, no rules of order or anything of that sort. [They] just ran all over the school grounds and did about as [they] pleased" (135). Although for some time they "continued sleeping on the hard floor … one evening the interpreter called [them] all together, and gave each a big bag" (135). The boys are to go out behind the stable, where there "is a large hay-stack," and fill the bags with hay, which they then lug "across the yard and upstairs" (136), pretty much what Charles Eastman had done at Beloit. Despite having "no sheets and no extra blankets," that "night [they] had the first good sleep in a long time" (136).

At some point "the interpreter came … and told [them they] must go to school," despite the fact that, as Standing Bear describes it, they "were yet wearing [their] Indian clothes" (136). No cleanup or hair cutting has taken place, although the latter will be soon be described.[17] "[M]arched into a schoolroom," they are "each given a pencil and a slate." They are "seated at single desks, where they soon discover that these pencils are the sort that can make "marks on the slates" (136). The boys cover their "heads with [their] blankets, holding the slate inside so the other fellow would not know what [his neighbor was] doing" (136). Upon finishing, they "marched up to the teacher to show what [they] had drawn." The teacher "bowed her head as she examined the slates and smiled, indicating that [they] were doing pretty well—at least [they] interpreted it that way" (136). Although she is not named here, Standing Bear would later identify his "first school teacher at Carlisle" (287) as Mariana Burgess, about whom we will hear more.

Another day the boys come to class and find that "there was a lot of writing on one of the blackboards" (136). Standing Bear now provides an account of the boarding school *topos* I have called the naming; its *locus*, here, as often, is the classroom. First, the interpreter tells the class that each of the "marks on the blackboard" represents "a white man's name. They are going to give each one of you one of these names" (137). "None of the names were read or explained to us," Standing Bear writes, "so of course we did not know the sound or meaning of any of them" (137). The teacher now holds "a long pointed stick in her hand." The interpreter tells "the boy in the front seat to come up. The teacher handed the stick to him, and the interpreter then told him to pick out any name he wanted" (137).

Standing Bear notes that the "boy had gone up with his blanket on," because, unlike in the account in *Land*, the children have not yet been given new clothes to wear. When the pointer is given to this first boy, "he turned to us," Standing Bear writes, "as much to say … Is it right for me to take a white man's name?" The boy continues to hesitate thoughtfully, then finally "he pointed out one of the names written on the blackboard" (137). Neither the teacher nor the interpreter pronounces the name, nor, if he remembers it, does Standing Bear inform us what "white man's name" the first boy in his class at Carlisle chose.

He writes that "the teacher took a piece of white tape and wrote the name on it. Then she cut off a length of the tape and sewed it on the back of the boy's *shirt*" (137, my emphasis). But in order for her to attach the nametag to the boy's shirt, the Indian *blanket* he had been wearing must first have been removed. This illustrates how the naming is not only de-individualizing but de-Indianizing. The Indian boy in his blanket has now been replaced by a young man in a shirt with a white man's name sewn on it. Standing Bear will have much to say about the Indian and his blanket in *Land of the Spotted Eagle*.

Once the name-tape has been sewn on, Standing Bear recalls, "that name was erased from the board. There was no duplication of names in the first class at Carlisle School!" (137) Insofar as some eighty Sioux boys and girls as well as a number of children from other tribes entered Carlisle in the fall of 1879, it seems unlikely that first names were unique to each. When Standing Bear's "turn came, [he] took the pointer and acted as if [he] were about to touch an enemy," counting coup on the blackboard. He had long anticipated engaging in such a brave act, although he can hardly have imagined it taking the form it does here. "Soon," he continues, "we all had the names of white men sewed on our backs." But in the following days, when "the teacher called the roll, no one answered his name," requiring the teacher to "walk around and look at the back of the boys' shirts." Then, "When she had the right name located, she made the boy stand up and say 'Present.' She kept this up for about a week before we knew what the sound of our new names was" (137).

Standing Bear was "one of the 'bright fellows' to learn [his] name quickly" (137–38), and "proud … to answer, when the teacher called the roll!" He "would put his blanket down"—the boys appear sometimes to be wearing their blankets over the shirts to which their names had been attached—"and half raise [himself] from his seat, all ready to answer to [his] new name. [He] had selected the name 'Luther'" (138). "Next," he says, "we had to learn to write our new names." He makes the point that "our good teacher had a lot of patience with us," adding, "She is now living in Los Angeles, California, and I still like to go and ask her any question which may come up in my mind" (138).[18] The teacher first writes his name on the slate, "and then, by motions, indicated that [he] was to write it just like that. She held the pencil in her hand just so, then made first one stroke, then another, and by signs [he] was given to understand that [he] was to follow in exactly the same way" (138).

He follows the teacher's instructions with great determination. "The first few times I wrote my new name," he says, "it was scratched so deeply into the slate that I was never able to erase it. But I copied my name all over both sides of the slate until there was no more room to write. Then I took my slate up to show it to the teacher, and she indicated, by the expression of [sic] her face, that it was very good" (138). Having learned to write his name on the slate, he "took a piece of chalk downstairs and wrote 'Luther' all over everything [he] could copy it on" (138).

Although this seems to have come to him easily, when "the teacher wrote out the alphabet on [his] slate and indicated to [him] that [he] was to take the slate to [his] room and study," he is less successful (138). He looks "at those queer letters, trying hard to figure out what they meant," but, not having been given any information about them, he finds himself, for "the first time in [his] life really disgusted." Concluding for the moment that the alphabet "was something [he] could not decipher," he assuages his disgust with the recollection that "all this study business was not what [he] had come East for anyhow," adding with the wisdom of hindsight—"so I thought" (138).

At this time, he writes, "How lonesome I felt for my father and mother!" (139). And the recalcitrant slate is explicitly made the token of homesickness: "So it did me no good to take my slate with me that day," Standing Bear writes, "It only made me lonesome." The immediate result is that the "next time the teacher told me by signs to take my slate to my room, I shook my head, meaning 'no'" (139), a first act of resistance. Although she admonishes him, she is still kind and patient, offering no threats of discipline. Because she speaks to him in English, he "did not know what she was saying" (139). Fortunately, only a "few days later," the teacher "wrote the alphabet on the blackboard, then brought the interpreter into the room" (139).

The interpreter conveys to the students in their own language the teacher's desire that they repeat the letters after her. They do this, and Standing Bear writes, "This was our real beginning," the beginning, it would seem, of a literacy that he has not yet consciously decided to embrace. That first day, he sums up, "we learned the first three letters of the alphabet, both the pronunciation and the reading of them.... All [he] could think of was [his] free life at home" (139). The difference between the free life at home and the unfree life at Carlisle is now conveyed through the subject of mealtimes. "At home," Standing Bear states, "we could eat any time we wished, but here we had to watch the sun all the time." This sun-watching soon gives way to the more usual means of establishing clock time at the boarding schools. The "school people fixed up an old building which was to be used as our dining-room" (139), and then it is the ringing of a bell that announces to the students it is mealtime. Standing Bear, a bright fellow in this as in many things, "quickly learned to be right there ... and get in first" (139), as soon as he heard the bell.

Getting in first, he would "run along the table until [he] came to a plate which ... contained the most meat," and eat "without waiting for any one" (139). Obviously there is no saying grace at Carlisle at this time, nor does there seem to be an attendant or disciplinarian to correct the young man's haste at table. Standing Bear tells several anecdotes about bells and meals before stating what comes as something of a surprise, that after a fair amount of time at the school, "We were still wearing our Indian clothes" (139). This will change rapidly—but only after the inevitable hair cutting, which he describes next.

"One day," Standing Bear writes, "we had a strange experience," as the interpreter tells them that they are "to have [their] hair cut off." The students take this announcement in the culturally appropriate way; that is, as a proposal to which they must respond. This was something, Standing Bear writes, that "would require some thought" (140). Therefore, "that evening the big boys held a council" (140), the proper action to take before rendering a decision. At eleven years old or more, Standing Bear joins "the big boys" in "council." There, "Nakpa Kesela, or Robert American Horse, made a serious speech" (140),[19] in which he wittily offers the opinion: "'If I am to learn the ways of the white people, I can do it just as well with my hair on'" (140).[20] The big boys in council agree with him. But if the sense of this council was conveyed to anyone in authority, it was not, as one might guess, taken into account.

Thus a few days later, "we saw some white men come inside the school grounds carrying big chairs. The interpreter told us these were the men who had come to cut our hair" (140).[21] The boys go to class and notice that "one of the big boys named Ya Slo, or Whistler, was missing. In a short time he came in with his hair cut off. Then they called another boy out, and when he returned, he also wore short hair" (141). Standing Bear's reaction to this is complex. At first, he says, "When I saw most of them with short hair, I began to feel anxious to be 'in style' and wanted mine cut, too," something other young boarding-school students had felt as well. But when his hair is cut, the young man's reaction is very different.

Standing Bear writes, "When my hair was cut short, it hurt my feelings to such an extent that the tears came to my eyes. I do not recall whether the barber noticed my agitation or not, nor did I care. All I was thinking about was that hair he had taken away from me" (141). He reflects that "this hair-cutting affected [him] in various ways," most particularly as it was intended to affect him, to make him feel that he "was no more Indian, but would be an imitation white man" (141). But he arrives at the articulation of this feeling only after a line of reflection one might not have expected.

That is, Standing Bear reminds readers that he "always wanted to please [his] father in every way possible," and that he had understood his father's "instructions to [him to be] along this line: 'Son, be brave and get killed.' This expression," he writes, "had been moulded into [his] brain to such an extent that [he] knew nothing else" (141). But now the shock of having his hair cut—"It had been cut with a machine and was cropped very close" (141)—leads him to believe that his "father had made a mistake. He should have told me, upon leaving home," he writes, "to go and learn the white man's ways, and be like them. That would have given a new idea from a different slant; but Father did not advise me along that line. I had come away from home with the intention of never returning alive unless I had done something very brave" (141).

Of course, his father had most certainly told him of the necessity to "learn the white man's ways." But he had not registered that advice nor taken it to heart until the moment when the cutting of his long hair makes him feel "no more Indian." Could he actually "learn the white man's ways?" And, if he did become in some measure "like them," what would that mean? Would he continue still to be Indian—or only "an imitation white man?" It would take the young man much time to figure these things out.

Standing Bear observes that although the boys "still had [their] Indian clothes, they were all 'bald-headed.' None of [them] slept well that night; [they] felt so queer." But "in a short time," he writes, "I became anxious to learn all I could" (141). He makes this decision just before the students are told that at long last they are "to have white men's clothes." At this news, Standing Bear writes, "We were all very excited and anxious" (142). The clothes arrive in "wagons ... loaded with big boxes" (142). Once the boxes are unloaded and unpacked, the boys are "'sized up' and a whole suit" is handed to each of them: "The clothes were some sort of dark heavy gray goods, consisting of coat, pants, and vest. We were also given a dark woolen shirt, a cap, a pair of suspenders, socks, and heavy farmer's boots" (142).

Although, as we will soon see, military routine prevails, the clothes they are first given are not military uniforms; those will come later. For now, however, Standing Bear and his fellow Lakota students enjoy themselves greatly modeling their new attire. "As soon as we had received our outfits, we ran to our rooms to dress up." The "Indian prisoners," he notes, "were kept busy helping us to put the clothes on." The "suits were too big for many of us," and the "boots were far too large ... but as long as they were 'screechy' or squeaky, I didn't worry about the size. I liked the noise they made when I walked, and the other boys were likewise pleased.[22] How proud we were with clothes that had pockets and with boots that squeaked" (142).

The boys, Standing Bear writes, "walked the floor nearly all that night," and again no dormitory attendant or disciplinarian interrupts them. Some "even went to bed with their clothes all on" (142). Fondness for their new attire has nothing whatever to do with becoming less Indian; rather, it is an instance of "playing white man," to alter a phrase from Philip Deloria.[23] In "the morning, the boys who had taken off their pants had a most terrible time," unable to recall "whether they were to button up in front or behind." The matter is settled when those who "had kept all their clothes on ...showed the others that the pants buttoned up in front and not at the back. So here," Standing Bear writes, perhaps without irony, "we learned something again" (142).

So pleased was he with the clothing he had received that Standing Bear and a cousin of his named Waniyetula or Winter wish to have more. He writes that they "took all [their] money to the interpreter and asked him if he would buy [them] some nice clothes" (143). They have no idea how much money they had brought from home, although Standing Bear later discovers that they had spent about eleven dollars. Because the interpreter "had bought the cheapest things he could get" (143), in 1879 the sum was sufficient for each to receive a "a black suit of clothes, a pair of shoes and socks, [a] stiff bosom shirt, two paper collars, a necktie, a pair of cuffs, derby hat, cuff buttons, and some colored glass studs for [the] stiff shirt fronts" (143). He and his cousin, Standing Bear affirms, "were greatly pleased with [their] purchases"—and indeed young Luther had seen his father dressed in clothes like these.

Apparently there was a disciplinarian after all, a Mr. Campbell, and the next day the boys observe him carefully to see if they can figure out "how he put on his collar" (143). That evening they dress up, aided by the Indian "prisoner." When the "bell rang for supper," the boys descend to the meal decked out in their new suits. However they managed with their collars, they are quite a sensation. The Indians, Standing Bear writes, give a "war-whoop" and call them "white men"—approvingly—while the "white people were greatly pleased at [their] new appearance" (144). One can guess that the cousins played at dressing up many times, for Standing Bear notes: "We had only two paper collars apiece, and when they became soiled we had to go without collars" (144). The boys attempt to wear their neckties "without the collars," but Standing Bear observes in retrospect, "I guess we must have looked funny" (144).

It was now winter "and very cold." To ward off the cold, they "were supplied with red flannel underwear." The garments, he writes, "looked pretty to us, but we did not like the warmth [?] and the 'itching' they produced" (145).[24] Fortunately, his father has by this time sent him some more money and, along with "another boy named Knaska or Frog," he buys "some white underwear" made of soft cotton. The problem, however, is that "the rules were that we had to wear the red flannels." Because it is only during Sunday morning inspection that "Captain Pratt and others always looked us over ... very carefully"—carefully enough, it would seem, to determine whether they were indeed wearing the red flannel underwear—that was when the boys "would put the red flannels on," later slipping into their white underclothes "to attend Sunday School in town." This is the first mention of religious instruction or observance at Carlisle. Standing Bear writes that the students "were at liberty to go where they pleased to Sunday School. Most of us selected the Episcopal Church," and, indeed, he "was baptized in that church under the name of Luther" (145).[25]

Standing Bear's first Christmas at Carlisle is s approaching. "One night in December," he writes, "we were all marched down to the chapel" (146). This is the first mention of a chapel on the premises. There the students see "a big tree in the room, all trimmed and decorated.... Then a minister stood up in front and talked to us, but I did not mind a thing he said." And, in fact, as was the case with a great many clerical addresses to Indian boarding-school students, as Standing Bear tells us, "I could not understand him anyway" (146). Along with the others, he receives "several presents which had been put on [sic] the tree for [him]," and he also receives gifts from his "Sunday-School teacher, Miss Eggee" (146–47), and "from [his] teacher, Miss M. Burgess" (146). This is the first time Standing Bear's classroom teacher is named.

Mariana Burgess was an influential person at Carlisle. She not only taught but, as "Superintendent of Printing," produced its publications. She had come to Carlisle as "a practical printer" in its earliest days, when she was twenty-six (Fear-Segal 2004 123, 126), and she had also had four years' experience teaching the Pawnees. She came to the school with Anne S.

5 Frontispiece of Marianna Burgess' 1891 novel, *Stiya, a Carlisle girl at home.* The young woman pictured is not, however, the actual Carlisle student, Stiya Koykuri, from Laguna Pueblo, but another Carlisle student, Lucy Tsisnah, a San Carlos Apache woman.

Ely, twenty years her senior, who had also taught the Pawnees, and the two lived together openly at Carlisle (Fear-Segal 2004 134), where Ely would become supervisor of the school's "outing" program. Burgess has attracted attention for her novel *Stiya, a Carlisle Indian Girl at Home* (Embe 1891), which originally appeared in installments in the school's publication, *The Indian Helper.*[26] Burgess, the kind and patient teacher, is the only one of his teachers at Carlisle whom Standing Bear names. (Miss Eggee was a Sunday School teacher.)

After his first Christmas at school, Standing Bear again "began to realize that [he] would have to learn the ways of the white man," and that this would "please [his] father as well" as getting himself killed. He might, for example "become an interpreter for [his] father, as he could not speak English," or he "might be able to keep books for him if he again started a store." These thoughts move him to work "very hard" (147). About this time, the boys are assigned to learn trades, an important part of a Carlisle education. Standing Bear is "to be a tinsmith"— Pratt himself had been a tinsmith before joining the army—and although he "did not care for this," he applies himself and fashions "hundreds of tin cups, coffee pots, and buckets." These, he writes, "were sent away and issued to the Indians on various reservations." Ironically, after he "had left school and returned home, this trade did not benefit [him] any, as the Indians had plenty of tinware that [he] had made at school" (147).

"Mornings," he recalls, "I went to the tin shop, and in the afternoon attended school." He asks Pratt to allow him to drop the tinsmithing so he can "go to school the entire day" (147), but Pratt refuses. "Half school and half work took away a great deal of study time," Standing Bear writes (147). He calculated his study time at Carlisle as "about a year and a half," his year and a half of tinsmithing amounting to "wasted" time. In all, he remained at the school longer than the three years the Lakota parents had originally agreed upon, not leaving until the summer of 1885.

In addition to study and shop, young Luther Standing Bear, like many other Indian boarding-school students, takes up music. He and some others are called into a schoolroom where they find "a little white woman," and "a long table ... on which many packages were tied in paper" (147). Inside the paper are a number of band instruments, which the woman offers to them. Standing Bear received "a B-flat cornet" (148). The woman herself opens a black case and takes out "a beautiful horn and when she blew on it it sounded beautiful." She urges the boys to blow into their instruments, and shows them "how to wet the end of the mouthpiece." Misunderstanding her, Standing Bear writes, they "thought she wanted [them] to spit into the horns." This discourages her to the point "that she started crying" (148). Eventually some of the boys do manage to produce a sound from the horns, and, as one would expect, "It was terrible. But [they] thought they were doing fine" (148).

Standing Bear's days at school are now long: there is an hour's band practice in the morning, after which he changes clothes "to work in the tin shop," and then changes again for dinner (148). It seems that his academic study came in the afternoon and that his morning's work clothes were acceptable in the classroom. After he "had learned to play a little, [he] was chosen to give all the bugle calls" (149). This requires that he rise before the

6 Luther Standing Bear with his father on his visit to Carlisle. Photo by John Choate. Courtesy Cumberland County Historical Society.

others to blow the bugle for wake-up; at night he is to blow it again "at ten minutes before nine o'clock" to announce bed time, and then at "nine o'clock [when] the second call was given, ... all lights were turned out and [they] were supposed to be in bed." He notes that he later "learned the mess call, and eventually ... all the calls of the regular army" (149).

One Sunday morning in "the early part of 1880," when they "were all busy getting ready to go to Sunday school in town," there was a "great excitement among some of the boys on the floor below" (149). This, he learns, is occasioned by the arrival of his father. When he descends, he sees a great many boys crowded around the elder Standing Bear and, his son writes, "He was so glad to see me, and I was so delighted to see him." There is a problem, however, in that the students are not supposed to speak their own language and Standing Bear senior "could not talk English" (149). With what seems an extraordinary concern for the rules—and testimony to his having achieved at least a basic literacy—Standing Bear *writes* to Captain Pratt to ask if he might address his father "in Indian." Pratt agrees to the written request and invites the young man to bring his father to Pratt's house, where Standing Bear says they have a very pleasant visit (150). "Father was so well-dressed," Standing Bear writes proudly, "He wore a grey suit, nice shoes, and a derby hat. But he wore his hair long. He looked very nice in white men's clothes. He even sported a gold watch and chain" (150).

Standing Bear's father has brought him gifts, "some silver dollars and a gold watch and chain." The young man is "proud ... to receive the watch," and in the presence of others, he writes, he "always took out that watch and looked at it, imagining that [he] could tell the time," although in fact he "did not know how to tell the time by looking at a watch or clock" (151). Father and son receive permission from Pratt "to go downtown," where father "bought some fruits and candy" (151), which they take back to the school. Standing Bear observes that not only was "Captain Pratt ... very kind to his father during his stay," but that he also "took him to Boston, New York, Baltimore, Philadelphia, and Washington," accompanied by "a mixed-blood" interpreter named Stephen Moran (151).

This is a fair amount of travel for 1880, and Pratt surely must have been in communication with the elder Standing Bear prior to his appearance at Carlisle concerning the itinerary and other arrangements—as he would also have had to find a way to finance the trips. (I would guess neither man paid all the costs himself.) In the cities they visited, Pratt surely would have taken

his traveling companion to meet with supporters and prospective supporters of the school, as well as, in Washington, to meet with some government
officials. But Luther Standing Bear says no more of this trip than that his
"father was greatly pleased that he was given an opportunity to visit these
great cities" (151). In Pratt's own lengthy autobiography, there is no reference either to the elder Standing Bear's visit to Carlisle or to this trip to
Washington. "After he returned from the trip," Standing Bear writes, his
father told him "we will have to learn [the] ways [of the whites], in order
that we may be able to live with them. You will have to learn all you can,
and I will see that your brothers and sisters follow in the path that you are
making for them" (151–52). "This was the first time," Standing Bear says, "my
father had ever spoken to me regarding acquiring a white man's education,"
adding "it meant so much to me." But of course his father had spoken to
him several times before about learning the ways of the whites, for all that
the young man still persists in his intention to please his father by "getting
killed on the battlefield" (152). Perhaps "learning the ways of the whites," a
necessity he himself had realized after his hair was cut, will be easier now
that he understands it has his father's blessing.

"Toward the summer of 1881," Standing Bear recalls, the school "started
to make uniforms for the pupils." These make the young man "proud," and
he is especially pleased when the band put them on and "marched to the
bandstand in [the] new uniforms and made a splendid showing with [their]
music" (152). Standing Bear then provides an account of his first outing
experience. He, Robert American Horse, Julian Whistler, and Clarence
Three Stars[27] are sent to a farm where he remembers they "were presented
with straw hats such as the farmers in that section wore" (154). He recounts
several anecdotes concerning what and how much the young men ate, but he
describes no work of any kind, nor what the boys were paid. Perhaps that is
why he says of the return to school that it came "after the *vacation* trip was
over" (155, my emphasis). He again studies hard and is much impressed, as
Charles Eastman had been, to learn that the earth is round; he also gets to
observe an eclipse of the moon exactly at the time it had been predicted (155).

It is only at this point in his narrative that Standing Bear states: "We
slept in large dormitories" (156), the usual locus for sleeping, although one
that had not previously been mentioned. Then, as the Office of Indian Affairs
catches up on provisioning the school: "One day we were told that we were to
have night shirts to sleep in" (156). "Shortly thereafter," Standing Bear writes,

"Chief Spotted Tail came to visit the school" (157). This was in June 1880. Spotted Tail, or Sinte Gleska, the major Brulé chief at Rosebud Agency—it had earlier been called the Spotted Tail Agency—did not come alone, and the visit was of considerable importance to the Lakota people and also to Richard Pratt, although Standing Bear devotes only two paragraphs to it.

Standing Bear first assures readers that "When he arrived [Spotted Tail] did not get such a reception as had been accorded [his] father" (157). If this was true, it was not, as Standing Bear implies, because his father was a man of greater importance to the whites and to the Lakotas than Spotted Tail. Spotted Tail, as Standing Bear explains, "had three sons, one daughter, and a granddaughter" at the school.[28] He had come to Carlisle to see if what Pratt had told the Lakotas on his recruiting visit—that their children would be well cared for and well educated at Carlisle—was true.

There were several factions among the Brulés at Rosebud, and here, as elsewhere, denominating them "conservatives" or "progressives" can be misleading. Members of Spotted Tail's faction at Rosebud, as Jeffrey Ostler writes, had "petitioned the government in January 1880 for permission to visit Carlisle to 'see for ourselves how [the children] live, and are taken care of'" (154–55). But another faction, to which the elder Standing Bear belonged, sent a letter to the commissioner of Indian Affairs in May of that year expressing concern for what Spotted Tail might do when he got to Carlisle. They wrote to the commissioner, "although he is our chief [we] hope you will not listen to what he says'" (in Ostler 197). In June 1880, Ostler writes, Spotted Tail and the other leading men from Rosebud and Pine Ridge "spent a week at Carlisle before traveling on to Washington. On their return trip, the delegates stopped again at Carlisle" (155).

Standing Bear does not refer to two stays at Carlisle for Spotted Tail and the other chiefs, but the single visit he represents is surely the second, on the return from Washington. He writes that Spotted Tail "was shown all around, but he did not like the school, and told Captain Pratt that he was going to take all his children back to the reservation with him" (157). Pratt responds that he can take his children but he must leave his granddaughter.[29] According to Standing Bear, Spotted Tail nonetheless took his granddaughter along with his children, and that is the end of the matter so far as it is recorded in *My People, the Sioux*. There was, however, much more to it.

In *Battlefield and Classroom* Pratt states that on first arriving at Carlisle, Spotted Tail was unhappy "because we were using soldier uniforms for the

7   Spotted Tail's delegation to Washington in 1880. Standing, left to right: identity of bearded man is unknown; Louis Roubedeaux, interpreter. Seated, left to right: Black Crow, Iron Wing, Spotted Tail, Coarse Voice, White Thunder. Photograph by Charles Milton Bell. Courtesy National Archives and Records Administration, NARA 523823.

boys" (237), and because the young Lakotas had to perform military drills. "He also found fault with the sleeping accommodations and the food," Pratt wrote, and he objected to the fact "that his youngest boy [Pollock] had been in the guardhouse for a week" (237). Pratt claims that upon the chiefs' return from Washington, Spotted Tail asked that his son-in-law Charles Tackett,[30] an interpreter for the school, receive a salary increase for his work (238). Pratt wrote that he not only refused but told Spotted Tail to take his son-in-law home with him, because it was important for the children to be using English all the time. (Although other interpreters would of course be retained.) It was in reaction to this, according to Pratt, that "Spotted Tail then said that I would have to keep his son-in-law or he would take all the Sioux children away" (298). He is once more told that he can take his own children but no others—and only if he bears the expense for their travel home.

Jeffrey Ostler makes clear that the issue of Tackett's salary, if it did indeed come up, was hardly the main concern. "What bothered Pratt's visitors," Ostler writes, "was the discrepancy between the description he had given the previous fall and what they now saw before their very eyes. In his recruitment speech, Pratt had said much about education's practical benefits, but not a word about haircuts, guardhouses, or military drills" (157).

George Hyde writes that Spotted Tail was also disappointed to find that in his family's nine months at the school, "None of them had learned English or to read and write" (322), and he too finds Pratt's claim about the request to increase Tackett's pay false (324). Hyde makes the further point that Pratt simply did not understand that these boys "were the sons of chiefs and headmen," and, from the perspective of his visitors, shouldn't be made "to do farm work and other manual labor like common white workmen" (324). The Indians' perspective on this matter undercut the very aim of Pratt's system.

Ending one paragraph with Spotted Tail's departure, Standing Bear begins the next by announcing: "During the early part of 1881, while we were still in school, news came that Chief Spotted Tail had been assassinated" (157).[31] He writes, "Of course we imagined he had been killed by the white people and we began to think of war again" (157), some of the "big boys" fearing that if there was war they would "all be killed at this school." Standing Bear himself, however, reverting to his earliest reason for going east, feels that the prospect of warfare "suited [him], as [he] was willing to die right there, just as [he] had promised when leaving home." In any case, the students "soon were advised that Spotted Tail had been shot and killed by an Indian named Crow Dog" (157), and Standing Bear next provides a highly partisan account of the "occurrence" (157), as he calls Spotted Tail's murder. Spotted Tail's death at the hands of Crow Dog, as Standing Bear represents it, showed that "swift justice had overtaken the man who had ... wanted to keep friendly to the whites himself, and yet keep his people in ignorance of his duplicity" (158). The charges Standing Bear levels against Spotted Tail are those alleged by Crow Dog's faction, to which, as I have said, the elder Standing Bear belonged. The truth, however, is more complex.[32]

Standing Bear next relates the swift decline and death at the school of a fellow Lakota student, "Wica-karpa, or Knocked-It-Off," and the refusal of the school, even when the boy's father requests it, either to send his body home or "at least to place a headstone over his grave" (159). Knocked-It-Off is Earnest or Ernest White Thunder, a young man who had tried to leave the school with Spotted Tail.[33] Standing Bear writes poignantly that this "was one of the hard things about our education—we had to get used to so many things we had never known before that it worked on our nerves to such an extent that it told on our bodies" (159). This was and would be the case for a great many boarding-school students.

In 1882 Standing Bear was asked by Pratt to return to the reservation in order "to induce more Indian children to come to the school" (161). Maggie Stands Looking and Robert American Horse, her cousin, would go as well, and the three would serve as interpreters for Mariana Burgess, who "was also going with [them]." He says, "Although we knew but little of the English language, we were ready to do anything for Miss Burgess" (161), a high compliment indeed—although in almost three years at Carlisle their English should have been better. Standing Bear writes that the recruiting party "met old Chief Sitting Bull and his followers" (161) at Fort Randall, in South Dakota, and although the young Sioux students, "did not talk much with the old chief . . . , Miss Burgess, through an interpreter, had quite a little conversation with him." This was despite the fact—or perhaps it was enabled by the fact—that soldiers "with guns on their shoulders, were marching around the camp constantly" (161).

The American Horse cousins go to Pine Ridge, their agency, and Standing Bear to Rosebud, his. There he "was soon put to work in the blacksmith shop, making stovepipes and elbows, as a demonstration of [his] education acquired in the school" (162). The "Indians . . . were very proud of [his] work," he notes, which suggests that several of them now had houses with stoves. Despite Standing Bear's desire "to interest more of the children to go back to Carlisle School," because "so many had died there . . . the parents of the Indian boys and girls did not want them to go" (162). While his people "were proud of [him], yet they were afraid to send their children away, fearing that they would never see them again" (163).

A council was held to "settle the matter," and Standing Bear "was delegated to speak." This makes him feel "very important, as many leading chiefs were to be present" (163). He is about fourteen years old. After he delivers his address, his father "arose and told of his visit to Carlisle, laying particular stress on the kindness he had received from Captain Pratt," of "his trips to the various large cities and what a numerous people the whites were" (163). To show his confidence that "this learning of the white man's way is good for [his] children," the elder Standing Bear announces that when Luther is

8 The elder Standing Bear with his children and a friend at Carlisle. Front row, left to right: Henry Standing Bear, Standing Bear, Red Fish, and (probably) Victor Standing Bear. Back row: Victoria Standing Bear, Luther Standing Bear, and an unidentified daughter of Standing Bear. Undated photo attributed to John Choate. Courtesy Cumberland County Historical Society.

ready to return to school, he will send his "daughter, Zintkaziwin, and [his] two sons, Totola and Wopotapi" (163–64) along with Luther. Standing Bear returns to Carlisle with "fifty-two boys and girls." "Captain Pratt," he writes, "was greatly pleased when we arrived *home* with so many students" (164, my emphasis).

Shortly after, because Pratt still "wanted more students for *our* school" (164, my emphasis), Standing Bear is asked to return to the reservation once more. He does so, and this time meets with resistance. A council is again convened, and "a man named Sitting Around came forward" (165). His only daughter has died at the school and he tells Standing Bear that if anyone other than he had come recruiting, he would have killed that person (165). Then Sorrel Horse, "one of our brave old men," forcefully states, "don't send any more of our children to school to die" (165), and "the council broke up right there, before either the agent or [Standing Bear himself] had a chance to explain matters" (165). Standing Bear writes, "It made me feel very bad;

but my business was to get more scholars for the school, and I determined not to get discouraged too quickly" (165).

The following day he explains to another gathering that although "it was true that many of the children had died at the school ... now everything was fixed up better" (166). Just as he had referred to Carlisle as "our school," he now tells the people, "*We* had a good medicine man" and "*we* were much better prepared to give all the children good attention" (166, my emphasis). Young Standing Bear heads back to Carlisle this time with "more than fifty" (166) Lakota boys and girls. Again, "Captain Pratt was greatly pleased" (166).

Standing Bear next serves his superintendent and his school by leading the Carlisle Indian Band "to play at the opening of the Brooklyn Bridge, and ... to march across it," "the first *real American band* to cross the Brooklyn Bridge" (171, emphasis in original).[34] He proudly and very specifically notes that "this was on the 24th of May, 1883," adding that his "three years [at school] were now drawing to a close."[35] (171) It is after recounting this event of May 1883 that Standing Bear describes the arrival at the school of Henry Teller, secretary of the interior, who meets with the students to remind them that the government had promised their parents to send them home at the end of three years, and that "the three years are up" (174). But Standing Bear's chronology is off; Teller had visited Carlisle a year earlier, in June 1882, when the Lakota students' three years at the school were indeed up.

In Standing Bear's account, Teller asked all those who "would like to go home right now" to raise their hands,[36] and Standing Bear writes, "Of course all raised their hands" (174). But he did not raise his. One might guess that he wished to remain because he had come to identify with the values Pratt had relentlessly inculcated, but this is not at all the explanation Standing Bear himself provides. Consistent with his self-presentation from the start, he writes that his choice to stay was in order further to please his father. He now quite clearly recalls his father's admonition to "learn all you can of the ways" (174) of the white people, and he writes, "I wanted to be brave and stay to please my father" (174). Once he announces his desire to remain at the school, "Robert American Horse said he would also like to stay.... Maggie Stands Looking, Frank Twist, Clarence Three Stars, and one other boy [he] cannot remember" all say that they, too, would like to stay. "This made five Sioux who wished to remain in the East" (174).

Standing Bear's next chapter begins: "Sometime later in the year we were all called into the chapel one Saturday evening" (177). There the students hear Superintendent Pratt announce a very special outing assignment:

two boys will be selected to "represent this school in John Wanamaker's immense Philadelphia store," to "work in the store as clerks" (177). This causes Standing Bear to wonder, "Who were the two best boys in Carlisle School?" The boys bet on the matter and Standing Bear puts his money ("about fourteen cents") "on a half-breed Creek Indian boy named Robert Stuart" (177).[37] On the following Saturday, in chapel, "After the usual prayer meeting was over," Pratt announces that the school has decided to send only one boy, not two, and it probably comes as no surprise to the reader that that boy is Luther Standing Bear (178).

Standing Bear then reproduces Pratt's speech to him. Before the assembled students, Pratt tells Standing Bear that he will be "going away" not only "to work for this school" but "in fact for your whole race." He offers his sense that the "majority of white people think the Indian is a lazy good-for-nothing," who "can neither work nor learn anything; that he is very dirty," saying to Standing Bear that he wants him to "to do [his] best." If he is a failure, Pratt adds, "then we might as well close up this school. You are to be an example of what this school can turn out." Exhorting him to "Go, ... and do your best," he states dramatically, "Die there if necessary, but do not fail" (179). What Standing Bear claims to recall Pratt saying, of course, resembles closely words he says he had heard from his father. The meeting concludes with Pratt asking "all the school to say a silent prayer that [Standing Bear] would not fail [his] people." Committed to "try and lift up a race of people before another race that had tried to hold us down," Standing Bear will also work "to prove that Carlisle School was the best place for the Indian boy" (179). Further conflating Pratt's words with his father's, he repeats to himself "that expression of Captain Pratt's: 'To die there if necessary'" (180).[38]

Although only one boy was to go to Wanamaker's, days later Pratt asks Standing Bear to pick another boy to be his "companion in the city" of Philadelphia. Standing Bear chooses Clarence Three Stars, who agrees to accompany him (180). Both boys go to work at the Wanamaker department store in March of 1884.[39] Three Stars finds the clerks there insulting him, and he writes to Pratt asking to return to the school. Pratt responds that he'd "better stay where he was and do his best" (183), but Three Stars decides to return home to the reservation.[40] Standing Bear, however, despite some difficulties, thrives at Wanamaker's.

Learning that Sitting Bull is "to appear at one of the Philadelphia theaters" (184), he attends, and listens as Sitting Bull "addressed the audience in the Sioux tongue" (185). He reports Sitting Bull saying "that it makes [him] glad to know that some day [his] children will be educated" (185). Although his audience might well be pleased to hear this, Sitting Bull's interpreter instead "started in telling the audience all about the battle of the Little Big Horn, generally spoken of [by whites, obviously] as the 'Custer massacre,'" despite the fact, as Standing Bear notes, that Sitting Bull had "never even mentioned General Custer's name" (185). Joining a line of people waiting to shake Sitting Bull's hand, Standing Bear is engaged by a woman who speaks to him in Lakota. She says that she is Sitting Bull's sister, and when Standing Bear tells her who his father is, she says that that makes him her nephew.[41] When she brings him to Sitting Bull, "He was pleased to see me again." Standing Bear also observes that he "had been working in [Wanamaker's] store so long that [he] had become lighter in complexion" (186). This does not mean that he was becoming what he had called "an imitation white man" (133). Although he is surely dressed like any Philadelphia theater-goer; and probably—after his "immersion" in this unusual outing at Wanamaker's—he speaks passable English, he is accepted by Sitting Bull and those traveling with him as unquestionably one of them, and he joins them at their hotel for a meal.

    Standing Bear stayed on at Wanamaker's during the school year, and, wished to remain through the summer of 1885, but found difficulty obtaining what he calls "a suitable place" to board in Philadelphia. Whenever he "would find something that seemed suitable, and the people discovered [his] nationality"—this is a curious reference in that, typical of the time, he more usually speaks of "race"—"they would look at [him] in a surprised sort of way," he writes, "and say that they had no place for an Indian boy" (189). Apparently race prejudice is substantial in the City of Brotherly Love. When he tells William Wanamaker, John Wanamaker's brother, "of the difficulty [he] had to find a decent place to board," making it necessary for him "to go back to Carlisle," Wanamaker assures him that he can come back to the store at any time, but he offers no help whatever in his present difficulty (189).

    Back at Carlisle, he tells Pratt he "wanted to go home to [his] people." Pratt urges him to stay on at the school, but Standing Bear is firm in his resolve. He tells Pratt, however, "I want to go in the right way. Several of the boys have run away from you"—this is the first and only occasion on which he mentions runaways during his time at the school—"but I do not want to do that." Pratt responds, "You may go, but I want you to promise that you will come back." "I answered," Standing Bear writes, "that if I cared to come back I would do so" (190). This would seem to demonstrate a good deal of independence from the man who had previously seemed like a second father to him and, indeed, from the school whose mission he had made his own. More impressed, perhaps, by Standing Bear's desire to leave "the right way" than by his refusal to promise to come back, Pratt provided Standing Bear with "a recommendation ... which led to immediate employment as an assistant teacher [at the agency school] at a salary of three hundred dollars a year" (Ellis 1985 147).

Pratt would have been correct in estimating that Luther Standing Bear remained staunchly in support of the school. Writing almost forty years later, Standing Bear says nothing about the strict military regimen, the marching, and the jail that had so upset Spotted Tail. Once regular food service commenced, he either found the fare satisfactory or chose not to register any complaints about it. Corporal punishment was administered, but if Standing Bear ever suffered or witnessed it, he does not say; he records no student resistance of any kind. If the reader wonders whether Luther Standing Bear ever did "care" to go back Carlisle, the conclusion of this chapter provides a definitive answer. Standing Bear writes: "So I said farewell to the school life and started back to my people, but with a better understanding of life. There would be no more hunting—we would have to work now for our food and clothing. It was like the Garden of Eden after the Fall of Man" (190), a poignant reflection, perhaps more nearly from the perspective of the mature author, than from the seventeen-year-old he was in the summer of 1885.

ᏦᏋ

The trip home, he writes "was very lonesome." His father meets his train in Valentine, Nebraska, and having prospered, it would seem, drives him home with "a team of pretty spotted ponies and a nice buggy" (191). The trip in no way reveals a paradise lost: "All along the road," Standing Bear writes, "everything looked so beautiful to me—the flowers, the singing birds, the herds of cattle and horses" (191). Surely the flowers and the birds would always have looked beautiful to a young Lakota, although the "herds of cattle and horses" would have been less numerous among them some years before. Almost half of the book remains, but Standing Bear's boarding-school days are over.

His first evening home, he writes, he was kept "busy telling [his] people all they wanted to know" about his experiences among the whites, and he "heard some of them remark that [he] looked more like a white boy, because [his] skin had become lighter from [his] work inside" the department store (191), something that had come up earlier, when Standing Bear had met Sitting Bull in Philadelphia. Whatever he may have thought on that occasion, he notes this time that "it made [him] feel very proud to have them compare me to a white boy" (191). Standing Bear "proudly" writes:

> The clothes I wore were the latest style at that time, and I felt quite "swell" in them. But I have to laugh now at my appearance. I looked like one of these Jew comedians on the stage. I wore a black suit with a cutaway coat which had quite a tail, a small derby hat, a standing collar, and my cuffs stuck out about half an inch below my coat sleeves, and I had on one of those "dirty-shirt hiders" known as a necktie at that time. All I lacked to resemble Charlie Chaplin was a cane (191–92).[42]

So he recalls himself in the summer of 1885! The young man will marry, become a father, and teach school for a time, gradually shedding his Chaplinesque appearance and his pride in being compared to a white boy. It is only in *Land of the Spotted Eagle* that he takes up the issue of "the returned student" in explicit detail, but before turning to that I want to look at some further observations Standing Bear offered about his identity later in *My People*. They come after an extraordinary event, the Wounded Knee massacre of late December 1890.

Standing Bear writes that although the whites refer to Wounded Knee as a "battle," it "was not a battle—it was a slaughter, a massacre" (224). "There I was," he writes, "doing my best to teach my people to follow in the white man's road—and even trying to get them to believe in their religion—and this was my reward for it all!" (224) This is a curious view of the carnage, taking it personally, as it were, as an affront to his choice of values. "The very people I was following—and getting my people to follow," he writes, referring to the government soldiers, "had no respect for motherhood, old age, or babyhood. Where was all their civilized training?" He also seems exasperated by the fact that "after the Wounded Knee affair," as he calls it, "more of the Indians joined the [Ghost] dancers" (224). When, however, he hears a rumor that the soldiers "were going to kill all the Indians, regardless of education" (224), there is something of a turn.

His "house surrounded by soldiers" (224), and not knowing "whether [his] own family were alive or dead" (225)—his "wife and children had gone to her father's before the trouble started" (225)[43]—Standing Bear "talked the situation over with [his] two friends, Julian Whistler and Frank Janis." Having no weapons, they "went out and each bought a gun and plenty of ammunition," determined to defend themselves if necessary against the soldiers or any hostile whites. "While we three were Carlisle graduates," Standing Bear writes, "we determined to stick by our race" (225). In fact, Standing Bear and Julian Whistler, whom we have already met, were not Carlisle *graduates*, both having left the school without graduating, Whistler in February 1884 and Standing Bear, as we have seen, the following summer. The student file for Frank Janis indicates that he had left Carlisle in 1889 but had not graduated. Calling the group "graduates" serves to strengthen the meaning of his and his two friends' choice of allegiance: Carlisle "graduates" and Christians as well, their allegiance is to their People. Only a few years later, in *Land of the Spotted Eagle*, Standing Bear affirms this in an even more rich and complex manner, and I'll close with his late observations.

In the eighth and next-to-last chapter of *Land*, called "Later Days," Standing Bear provides a condensed account of his decision to attend Carlisle and of his time there. He writes: "I returned from the East at about the age of sixteen, after five years' contact with the white people, to resume life upon the reservation. But I returned, to spend some thirty years before again leaving, just as I had gone—a Lakota" (235). He then makes clear what it means for him to be "a Lakota." "While I had learned all that I could of the white man's culture," he writes, "I never forgot that of my people. I kept the language, tribal manners and usages, sang the songs and danced the dances.[44] I still listened to and respected the advice of the older people of the tribe. I did not come home so 'progressive' that I could not speak the language of my father and mother" (235).

He knows he is fortunate in these respects, for he has seen "the sad sight, so common today, of returned students who could not speak their native tongue, or, worse yet, some who pretended they could no longer converse in the mother tongue" (235). In a few extraordinary pages, Standing Bear deplores the boys who "came home wearing stiff paper collars, tight patent-leather boots, and derby hats on their heads" (235)—exactly as he himself had done. It pains him to see the returned Indian schoolgirls "trying to squeeze their feet into heeled shoes ... and their waists into binding apparatuses that were not garments" (236). Looking at these returned students, Standing Bear realizes that "we went to school to copy, to imitate; not to exchange languages and ideas, and not to develop the best traits that had come out of uncountable experiences of hundreds and thousands of years living upon this continent" (236).

Standing Bear calls for a mutual or dialogic acculturation, writing, "while the white people had much to teach us, we had much to teach them, and what a school could have been established upon that idea" (236).[45] Although "the teachers were sympathetic and kind, and some came to be my lifelong friends," he continues, "in the main, Indian qualities were undivined and Indian virtues not conceded. And I can well remember when Indians in those days were stoned upon the streets as were the dogs that roamed them" (236).

Further to establish the "undivined" qualities of the Indians, Standing Bear speaks for the importance of Indian languages and culture generally—subjects Pratt had disdained—and goes on to reclaim the scorned Indian blanket. Earlier in *Land* he had written, "According to the white man, the Indian, choosing to return to his tribal manners and dress, 'goes back to the blanket'" (190). Assuming his readers fully understand this phrase as denoting a fall from civilized grace, Standing Bear insists that " 'Going back to the blanket' is the factor that has saved [the Indian] from, or at least stayed, his final destruction" (190). Further, "many an Indian has accomplished his own personal salvation by 'going back to the blanket.' The Indian blanket or buffalo robe, a true American garment ... covered beneath it the prototype of the American Indian, one of the bravest attempts made by man on this continent to rise to the heights of true humanity" (191).

To achieve his "own personal salvation," Standing Bear affirms, "though my hair had been cut and I wore civilian clothes, I never forsook the blanket" (237). So far as everyday attire in the United States of the late 1920s is concerned, he means this figuratively rather than literally—although he does insist: "For convenience, no coat I have ever worn can take the place of the blanket robe; and the same with the moccasins, which are sensible, comfortable, and beautiful" (237). So far as identity is concerned, the young man who came back to the reservation from Carlisle in "a black suit with a cutaway coat which had quite a tail, a small derby hat, a standing collar, ... and one of those 'dirty-shirt hiders' known as a necktie," is, finally, an Indian (*My People* 192).

On the final pages of *Land* Standing Bear declares: "If today I had a young mind to direct in the journey of life and I was faced with the duty of choosing between the natural way of my forefathers and that of the white man's present way of civilization, I would, for its welfare, unhesitatingly set that child's feet in the path of my forefathers. I would raise him to be an Indian" (258–59). Thus spake a former student of the Carlisle Indian School. Luther Standing Bear was surely changed forever by his education, but it did not in the least "kill the Indian" in him.

3

Zitkala-Sa's "Impressions of an Indian Childhood," "The School Days of an Indian Girl," and "An Indian Teacher among Indians"

GERTRUDE SIMMONS, ALSO KNOWN AS GERTRUDE SIMMONS BONNIN, OR Zitkala-Sa (Red Bird), the name she gave herself in 1898, had a good deal more education than Luther Standing Bear, although not nearly so many years of schooling as Dr. Charles Eastman. Born on the Yankton reservation in 1876, she went to the reservation day school for about two years, starting when she was six, and later spent part of 1889 at the Santee Normal School, the same bi-lingual Indian boarding school Eastman had attended earlier. But these were the only Indian schools she attended, and only Santee was a boarding school. Writing about her education, Zitkala-Sa had not a word to say about either of them.

But she did write about her first stay, from 1884 to 1887, at White's Manual Labor Institute, a Quaker school in Wabash, Indiana. White's had been established "to take boys and girls without distinction of color, White, Indian, or Negro" (Green 7), and, while it received modest government support for its Indian students for a time, they were never in the majority of the student body; the school was not an Indian boarding school. After some time back home at the Yankton Agency, Zitkala-Sa returned to White's in 1891, and she delivered the commencement address at her graduation in 1894. These school years are represented by only a single sentence in her autobiographical texts.

Zitkala-Sa next studied at Earlham College, also a Quaker school in Indiana, attending despite her mother's disapproval. She says little about Earlham as well, restricting herself to her triumphs at the college and state oratorical competitions. She did not graduate from Earlham, leaving the school in 1897 because of ill health. She next went on to a position as clerk and then teacher at Carlisle from 1897 to 1899, and she did indeed write about Carlisle. But she was not and had never been a student at the school. She concluded her formal schooling with violin study in Boston in 1899, although she wrote nothing of that experience either.

Just a year after her departure from Carlisle, Zitkala-Sa published three autobiographical pieces in the January, February, and March 1900 issues of the prestigious *Atlantic Monthly*: "Impressions of an Indian Childhood," "The School Days of an Indian Girl," and "An Indian Teacher among Indians." A fourth autobiographical essay, "Why I am a Pagan," would appear in the magazine in February 1902, and I agree with Penelope Kelsey that this can be taken "as the ending to Bonnin's autobiography" (64). These four essays are the sum total of her autobiographical writing, and only the second and third of them, "The School Days of an Indian Girl," and "An Indian Teacher among Indians," published when she was twenty-four, offer the young woman's reflections on her schooling.

Zitkala-Sa, as Ruth Spack has written, "blurs the distinction between fact and fiction" (2002 152), and she does so a good deal more than Charles Eastman, Luther Standing Bear, and other boarding-school autobiographers. This has led a number of her critics to debate whether her essays are best read as autobiography or autobiographical fiction. Given the titles of the three pieces—"Impressions of an Indian Childhood," "The School Days of an Indian Girl," "An Indian Teacher among Indians"—the author's name, and the use of the first-person pronoun, readers' likeliest assumption would be that these are indeed autobiographical texts. That is how I consider them—although as autobiography they are often misleading,[1] so that I will sometimes distinguish between the historical Zitkala-Sa, the author, and "Zitkala-Sa," the character who bears her name in the essays.

Whatever the proportion of factual reportage to imaginative invention in Zitkala-Sa's early texts, there is no question that they were intended to be read as literary art. As far back as 1902, Elizabeth Luther Cary read them in just that way, opining that Zitkala-Sa's "phrases burn themselves into the reader's consciousness. . . . And not alone by isolated metaphors does she attest to the richness of her style" (Cary 25).[2] Moreover, Zitkala-Sa engaged in literary art-making at roughly the same time as she sought to make art with her voice (she sang and gave dramatic recitations), her violin, and her piano, also posing for photographs that were in every way meant to be viewed (and were sold) as works of art.

I'll mention just a few other matters raised by the critics on the early work of this Dakota woman.[3] Amelia Katanski reminded readers that Zitkala-Sa was "very conscious of the politics of self-representation and quite comfortable with representing herself differently in different situations" (113). Penelope Kelsey suggested we see in Zitkala-Sa's literary writing an attempt to create "a Dakota self-determination analogous to the one she sought as an activist" (75), and Tadeusz Lewandowski has seen her as a forerunner of "Red Power." I find the latter two judgments mostly wishful thinking. I will review the three *Atlantic Monthly* essays of 1900, in particular "The School Days of an Indian Girl" and "An Indian Teacher among Indians," in the context of what a great many other Indian boarding-school students have written about their schooling.

ᘏᘏ

"Impressions of an Indian Childhood" is the first of Zitkala-Sa's *Atlantic Monthly* essays, and its final section is called "The Big Red Apples." In it "Zitkala-Sa" says: "The first turning away from the easy, natural flow of my life occurred in an early spring. It was in my eighth year; in the month of March, I afterward learned." She states: "At this age I knew but one language, and that was my mother's native tongue" (83).[4] It may be true, as "Zitkala-Sa" says, that she had not yet learned that the month in question was called March by the Americans, but Zitkala-Sa had been enrolled at the bilingual Yankton Presbyterian day school,[5] for all or most of the two years prior to this moment, and she would have learned a bit of English—perhaps the names of the months, or, indeed, perhaps not.

The speaker says she learned from "some of [her] playmates that two paleface missionaries were in our village" (83). When "Zitkala-Sa" asks her mother why "these two strangers were among us," she is told that "they had come to take away Indian boys and girls to the East" (83). When Luther Standing Bear had heard that white strangers wished to take Indian children to the east, his only thought was that they meant to kill the children.

But Zitkala-Sa's older brother, David, had studied at the Santee School and at Hampton Institute, and she has no anticipation of danger.[6] To the contrary, a friend of hers, Judewin, had already committed to going east with the missionaries, envisioning the trip as travel "to a more beautiful country than ours" (83). Of course the young narrator wishes to go as well.

Mother does not immediately respond, and "Zitkala-Sa" informs us that "big brother Dawee had returned from a three years' education in the East" (83), at the Hampton Institute.[7] His return, we are told, "influenced ... mother to take a farther step from her native way of living" (83), in that after first having adopted "the white man's canvas" (83–84) rather than buffalo skin for her "wigwam"—that term is Algonquian; more accurate here would be "tipi"—she now moves into "a home of clumsy logs" (84). But Ellen Simmons "apparently had become a Christian even before she moved to the Yankton Agency in 1874" (Spack 2002 152), and, having been married to three white men (Pierre St. Pierre; John Haystings Simmons, David's father; and a man known only as Felker,[8] Zitkala-Sa's father), it seems likely that she would have lived in some type of house before David Simmons's return in 1882. Ellen Simmons is not in favor of her daughter going to the east. Despite her son's generally positive experience, she persists in doubting the value of white schooling, and her doubts will shadow her daughter's feelings about the education she chooses.

Mother passionately warns her daughter of "the white man's lies. Don't believe a word they say!" (84) Then, on "the following day," the two white missionaries appear with "a young interpreter ... a paleface who had a smattering of the Indian language" (84). "Zitkala-Sa's" friend has relayed to her the missionaries' tales of a land of apple trees where the Indian children could "pick all the red apples [they] could eat" (84). "Zitkala-Sa" had indeed tasted "a dozen red apples in [her] life" (84), and like Eve, she is tempted by an apple now. She is avid to have the chance to eat apples in the east, as the missionaries have promised, after a "ride on the iron horse" (85). The little girl pleads to go, and her mother promises to send her answer to the missionaries the following day (85). For all her misgivings, mother assents, offering the very reasonable observation so many Native parents had, that it will be useful for the child to know the language and the ways of the whites.

"Impressions of an Indian Childhood" concludes with "Zitkala-Sa," "in the hands of strangers," crying into her blanket as she separates from her mother. The party drives "thirty miles to the ferryboat," and crosses "the

Missouri in the evening," a symbolic as well as a literal passage, the boat carrying the narrator to the farther shore, leaving her "Indian Childhood" in the west behind. The next *Atlantic Monthly* essay, "The School Days of an Indian Girl," does not pick up just where the first had left off but, rather, begins a little before the journey east that had just been recounted. Section I of "School Days," is called "The Land of Red Apples," and it opens by informing the reader that there were "eight in our party of bronzed [sic] children," two older boys, two older girls, and "three little ones, Judewin, Thowin, and I" (87). There is no mention here of a drive to the ferryboat nor a crossing of the wide Missouri before the children board the much-anticipated "iron horse" (87).

Like Luther Standing Bear's group on the train trip east, "Zitkala-Sa's" party is subjected to rude stares by the whites and their children, something the narrator "resented" (87). At one point, "Zitkala-Sa" hears her name called and finds "the missionary very near, tossing candies and gums into our midst"; this, she says, "amused us all" (88). Otherwise, the narrator reports, "Though we rode several days inside of the iron horse, I do not recall a single thing about our luncheons" (88)—and nothing is said of them, of other mealtimes, stops made by the train, or further incidents along the journey. "Zitkala-Sa" and her companions reach White's at night, again much as Standing Bear's party had reached Carlisle.

It was "in the spring of 1861," Alice Green writes, that "the first superintendent and matron were employed and the first children, three in number, were received" at White's Manual Labor Institute. The school had been established, as earlier noted, to "take boys and girls without distinction of color, White, Indian, or Negro" (7), and although I do not know whether the school's first three students were white or black, they were not Native children. Green writes that the "records show that the fourth and fifth children received by the school were Indians" (9), Sac and Fox (11). The "government was under contract to pay for the care and education of these [Indian] children," the school initially receiving $167 a year, a sum that was reduced to $150 annually for each child in 1885, the last year of Zitkala-Sa's first stay at White's. The "Indian work came to a close in 1895," the year of her graduation, because there was "a question about using funds for denominational work" (Green 15), work important to the Quaker school but apparently problematic for the government. (But as we will see, the government funded many religious "contract" schools.)

"Zitkala-Sa" says that the new arrivals were "led to the open door, where the brightest of the lights within flooded out over the heads of the excited palefaces who blocked [?] our way" (88). As it happens, Wabash, Indiana, the location of the school, was the first city in the world to have electric lights, having installed four on the town courthouse in March 1880, four years earlier. The speaker once more remarks the "strong glaring light," especially bright because the large room she has entered is "whitewashed" (88). White-washing Indian children is of course the purpose of this school, as it was the purpose of the Indian boarding schools generally.

"Zitkala-Sa" then describes being seized by "two warm hands" that toss her "high in midair [sic]" (88). The hands belong to a "rosy-cheeked paleface woman," who then proceeds to "jump [… her] up and down with increasing enthusiasm" (88), treatment that leaves the child "frightened and insulted by such trifling." Her "mother had never made a plaything of her wee [sic] daughter," and the child responds by "cry[ing] out loud" (88). While I can't say this never happened, I can say that no other Indian boarding-school student in the many accounts I have read described such treatment.

The little girl's tears are "misunderstood" as arising from hunger, so she is "placed" (88) at "a *white* table loaded with food" (89, my emphasis). Although White's—given the attention to whiteness, one would think the author would play on the name of the school—was usually in or near financial difficulties, the school at this moment seems to have been able to provide plenty of food for its students. Missing her mother, brother, and aunt, "Zitkala-Sa" persists in her weeping and is told by an older student "to wait until you are alone in the night" to cry (89). That would be in the dormitory, where many a homesick Indian boarding-school student would weep, alone among others. "Zitkala-Sa" is indeed "taken along an upward incline of wooden boxes, which [she] learned afterward to call a stairway," to the dormitory where there are many "narrow beds … in one straight line" in which "lay sleeping brown faces, which peeped just out of the coverings," one of her more vivid descriptions. "Zitkala-Sa" is "tucked into bed with one of the tall girls," who, she says, "talked to me in my mother tongue and seemed to soothe me" (89).

The morning introduces clock time as a "large bell rang for breakfast, its loud metallic voice" adding to the noise, as shoes "clatter … on bare floors," and a "constant clash of harsh noises," and "many voices murmuring an unknown tongue, made a bedlam" (89). A "paleface woman" whose whiteness includes "white hair" (89), places the newcomers "in a line of girls who were marching into the dining room" (90), a familiar action and a familiar *locus* of boarding-school life.

As at the Indian boarding schools generally, so too at White's do the girls march in one door of the dining room while the boys "entered at an opposite door" (90). Then "a small bell was tapped, and each of the pupils drew a chair from under the table" (90). The speaker assumes the children are now to be seated, but as she realizes only after seating herself, it is necessary for "a second bell" to be rung for all to sit. Then grace is said. "Zitkala-Sa" "heard a man's voice at one end of the hall," at the sound of which "all the others hung their heads over their plates." A "third bell is tapped," and "every one picked up his knife and fork and began eating." What they are given to eat—a subject of considerable interest among the boarding-school students—is not indicated. Nor does she mention any difficulty handling a knife and fork, as some students did; perhaps she had already used such utensils at home. She later finds that "this eating by formula was not the hardest trial in that first day," as her friend Judewin "had overheard the paleface woman talk about cutting [their] long, heavy hair." Noting that "among our people, short hair was worn by mourners, and shingled hair by cowards,"[9] the young girl vows to "struggle first!"—a recourse to resistance (90).

By now her moccasins have been exchanged for "squeaking shoes" (91); no other change of attire is reported. Disregarding the squeak, "Zitkala-Sa" climbs the stairs, enters an empty room, and hides "in a dark corner" under one of three beds. She is discovered, and although she resists "by kicking and scratching wildly," she is nonetheless "carried downstairs and tied fast in a chair" (91). Then her "thick braids" are cut off, something she, like a great many boarding-school students, takes as a painful indignity. She says, "Not a soul reasoned quietly with me, as my own mother used to do; for now I was only one of many little animals driven by a herder" (91). The young narrator records these things not merely as gross affronts to her personal and cultural integrity—being thrown in the air "like a wooden puppet" (91), having her "long hair shingled" like that of "cowards" (90)—but also as insults to her individuality, as she objects to being treated like "only one of many little animals driven by a herder" (91). Her "individuality" will become a significant issue as "Zitkala-Sa" makes her way through school.

Section III, "The Snow Episode," has received much comment. The "three Dakotas," "Zitkala-Sa" and her friends, are playing in the snow. They have been told not to lie down and make snow angels. They disobey and are called in by a female employee of the school. Judewin, who knows some English, provides the unfortunate advice that when the woman questions them, they must respond by saying, "No." Thowin is first to be interrogated, and when apparently asked if she is sorry or promises to obey in the future, she replies, "No." For this response she receives a spanking (92). Asked once more, she makes the only reply she knows, and she is beaten once again, and "This time," the narrator says, "the woman meant her blows to smart" (93). When "the blows ceased abruptly," and the woman asked yet again, "Thowin gave her bad passwood [sic] another trial.[10] We heard her say feebly, 'No! No!'" (93). But now, instead of punishing Thowin further, the woman "led the child out, stroking her black shorn head." "Perhaps it occurred to her that brute force is not the solution for such a problem," the narrator speculates. She also notes that the woman "did nothing to Judewin nor to me" (93).

The "brute force" observation would not have been that of the eight-year-old "Zitkala-Sa," and coming from the twenty-four-year-old Zitkala-Sa it is a bit puzzling. The woman did spank the little girl and then hit her harder—only to stop, when "perhaps" what "occurred" to the woman had nothing to do with the presumptive efficacy of "brute force," but rather with the recognition that this child simply did not understand what was being said to her and had no idea what the single syllable she repeated actually meant. In any case, stroking the girl's head and pardoning her two companions are hardly the actions of someone given to brutality. Be that as it may, "Zitkala-Sa" wants "revenge." She writes, "As soon as I comprehended what was said and done, a mischievous spirit of revenge possessed me" (93). Sent into "the kitchen to mash the turnips for dinner" as punishment "for some misconduct" she does not describe—perhaps it is the snow incident, after all—she engages once more in resistance. She "worked [her] vengeance upon them," mashing with such fury that she "sent the masher into the bottom of the jar" (93), breaking it. She writes that she "was a wee [sic] bit sorry to have broken the jar," although when she sees no turnips served for dinner, she says that she "whooped in my heart for having asserted the rebellion within me" (94). The next part of the essay, section IV, has her taking further "revenge," this time "upon the devil," as she defaced the pages of a book called *The Stories of the Bible,* in which pictures of the devil appear (95).

Before going further, let me offer here a brief excursus on turnips; Zitkala-Sa, had she chosen to do so, could have provided one far better than I can. It is a curious coincidence that the root vegetable upon which

"Zitkala-Sa" expressed her anger was, as she says, a turnip and not, for example, a potato or some other tuber. The turnips White's kitchen had planned to serve on the evening described were cultivated turnips, what most of us know as looking like a large, white beet. But the young girl would have been very familiar with wild turnips or prairie turnips, *tinpsila* (Buechel 305), *thinpsinla* (*New Lakota Dictionary* 1127), also called breadroot or *pomme blanche*, white apple, by the many French who had lived among the Dakotas.

Much smaller than the cultivated turnip, prairie turnips must be peeled before being cooked and mashed, or else roasted or boiled. They could also be dried and ground into flour, sliced and dried, or braided to dry for winter use. (Braids of dried prairie turnips are currently available for sale online.) Leonard Bruguier in his study of the Yankton people observes that "*tipsinna* (turnips) [were] indigenous to the prairies" (97), and Susan Dominguez affirms that turnips were once a staple of the Yankton diet (87). Dominguez also cites a *Washington Evening Post* interview with Zitkala-Sa in 1936 in which she said that even then she kept a string of dried *tipsina* for cooking (88), so she clearly valued the prairie turnip

So important a source of food was the wild turnip on the Plains that, as Buechel notes, "*tin.psin.la i.tka.hca wi*," is the name for the month of June, "when the seedpods of the wild turnip blossom" (305), the flowers a very attractive bright blue or blueish purple. Women would harvest the tubers using digging sticks in June, sometimes into July, before the blossoms fell, after which it was much harder to locate the plants. Elders claimed that the blossoms of each plant pointed to other plants, and children, mostly young girls, would accompany their mothers and, as their mothers dug one up, run to scout out the next plant. This is surely an activity in which Zitkala-Sa and her mother had engaged, and it was likely to have been a happy memory for a young Dakota girl, had she chosen to share it.

To return: section V of "The School Days of an Indian Girl," called "Iron Routine," does not develop the portrait of "Zitkala-Sa" the passionate resister but turns instead to an account of the regimented day at White's. It is very much like those we have seen at the Indian boarding schools. Clock time comes in the form of "a loud-clamoring bell awaken[ing] us at half-past six in the cold winter mornings." The sleepy children "stumbled out upon chilly bare floors back again into a paleface day." They dress, "wet [their] eyes with icy water," and, at the ringing of "a small hand bell," they descend to the "assembly room" (96). There a "paleface woman, with a yellow-covered roll book ... and a gnawed pencil in her hand" (96) calls the names of the

students. "Zitkala-Sa" says: "It was next to impossible to leave the iron routine after the civilizing machine had once begun its day's buzzing," adding
that "as it was inbred in [her] to suffer in silence rather than to appeal to
the ears of one whose open eyes could not see [her] pain," she "many times
trudged in the day's harness heavy-footed, like a dumb sick brute" (96). This
is a poignant reflection by Zitkala-Sa, but it is not consistent with what she
has reported thus far. For although no one of "Zitkala-Sa's" earlier acts of
resistance had sought to "appeal" to the "ears of [those] whose … eyes could
not see [her] pain," they were substantial enough to make one question her
description of herself as suffering in silence like "a dumb sick brute." In any
case, she testifies further to the contrary in the following paragraph.

The occasion is the death of a classmate. At the death-bed, "Zitkala-Sa"
finds a "paleface woman … moistening the dry lips…. The dying Indian girl
talked disconnectedly of Jesus the Christ and the paleface who was cooling
her swollen hands and feet" (96). It's not clear what illness had swollen the
young woman's hands and feet. Tuberculosis, pneumonia, and infections of
a variety of kinds were most usually responsible for fatalities at the boarding
schools. In any case, "Zitkala-Sa" says observing the scene made her grow
"bitter, and [she] censured the woman for cruel neglect of our physical ills"
(96–97), going on to blame "the hard-working, well-meaning, ignorant
woman who was inculcating in our hearts her superstitious ideas" (97).[11]
She continues that although she "was sullen in all [her] little troubles, as
soon as [she] felt better [she] was ready to smile upon the cruel woman"
(97). Although a change of mood makes her ready to "smile upon" this
"hard-working, well-meaning, ignorant woman," as she had called her, it
is not clear why she had called her a "cruel woman," and "censured" her for
her "cruel neglect of our physical ills" in the first place. Her description of
the woman as "cooling [the] swollen hands and feet" of her dying classmate
hardly portrays cruelty and neglect.

Her moods rapidly changing—this is a character trait that several critics have noted—"Zitkala-Sa" says, "Within a week [she] was again actively
testing the chains which tightly bound [her] individuality like a mummy for
burial" (97). She had earlier objected to her "individuality" being violated by
her treatment as "only one of many little animals driven by a herder" (91),
and "Zitkala-Sa" highly values her "individuality." Admirable as this may
seem, it is not something that derives from her Dakota upbringing,[12] her
reservation day school experience, or from her first stay at White's. I would
tentatively date its beginning from her second stay at White's, 1891–95,

perhaps the first years during which her school experience began to change her significantly, something about which I will have more to say.

Here, let me note the concluding paragraph of this fifth section of "The School Days of an Indian Girl." It is a set piece, almost a formal coda, packed with metaphors and sense impressions—sounds and colors—self-consciously attempting a thoroughly literary lyricism. "The melancholy of those black days," Zitkala-Sa writes, "has left so long a shadow that it darkens the path of years that have since gone by" (97). Those would be the thirteen years that have "gone by," from the end of her first attendance at White's as a girl of eleven in 1887 to the 1900 publication of this piece when she is twenty-four. "These sad memories," she continues, "rise above those of smoothly grinding school days," a curious sentence. The speaker next employs a dominant-culture stereotype—"Perhaps my Indian nature is the moaning wind which stirs them now for their present record," the assignment of things "Indian" to the realm of nature (perhaps her nature is like nature, "the moaning wind")—using it strategically to appeal for the reader's sympathy: "But, however tempestuous this is within me, it comes out as the low voice of a curiously colored seashell, which is only for those ears that are bent with compassion to hear it" (97). She had earlier written of her unwillingness "to appeal to the ears of one whose open eyes could not see [her] pain" (96). Now she willingly appeals to her (mostly) paleface readers to bend their "ears ... with compassion to hear" the speaker's "low voice" like that "of a curiously colored seashell" (97).

Section six, "Four Strange Summers" provides an impressionistic account of the four years between Zitkala-Sa's first and second stays at White's. It is likely, as I have said, that she attended the Santee Normal School not far from Yankton for at least part of 1889, but if so, she says nothing at all about those "school days of an Indian girl." Back home, in her early teens, she notes that she is too young to participate in the social events on the reservation that her brother, Dawee—David Simmons—some ten years older than she, attends.[13] Nor can her mother, who "had never gone inside of a schoolhouse," aid "her daughter who could read and write" (97)—although her mother is aware of and "troubled by [her] unhappiness" (99). In an attempt to comfort her educated daughter, Ellen Simmons offers her "the only printed matter [they] had in [their] home ... an Indian Bible, given her some years ago by a missionary" (99). Simmons, as noted, had by now been a Christian for more than fifteen years, having converted before moving to Yankton in 1874, although one would not know this from the way her daughter represents her here.[14] "Zitkala-Sa" rejects the Dakota Bible—she would probably have learned to read it at the Santee school—and her mother leaves the house. Then, "After an uncertain [?] solitude," the girl hears her "mother's voice wailing among the barren hills which held the bones of buried warriors." Her "unrestrained tears," "Zitkala-Sa" writes, had revealed her "suffering to her [mother], and she was grieving" for her daughter (100).

In the time of the warriors the Sioux had generally practiced scaffold or platform burial, something the missionaries had eventually persuaded them to abandon for the practice of burial underground. One can hardly expect Zitkala-Sa to have brought that to the attention of her largely white audience; but if cultural accuracy were in any way a concern, she might simply have written "the bones of *many* warriors," or some such.[15] Also, one may wonder whether this is the same hill as the one to which "Zitkala-Sa's" mother had pointed earlier, in "Impressions of an Indian Childhood," the hill where the narrator's "uncle and ... only sister lay buried" (69). At that point in the narrative, the mother had added a strong condemnation of the whites saying, "Since then your father too has been buried in a hill nearer the rising sun" (69). But of course her father was a paleface, one who had probably left his Indian wife before their child was born. Whether he had since died and been buried somewhere in the east is not something any researcher has thus far determined.

Mother returns home, but "Zitkala-Sa" remains unhappy. "Many schemes of running away from my surroundings," she writes, "hovered about in my mind. A few more moons"—rather a cliché to represent how Indians mark time—"of such a turmoil drove me away to the Eastern school" (100). She will return to White's despite having represented the school in anything but a positive manner. This section closes: "I rode on [not "inside," as earlier] the white man's iron steed, thinking it would bring me back to my mother in a few winters, when I should be grown tall, and there would be congenial friends awaiting me" (100). "Moons," "iron steed," and "winters" are word choices that self-consciously if stereotypically affirm the author's Indianness to her white audience—although she doesn't use any Dakota words. She embarks now on another stage of "paleface" education, one marked by the sense of separation from her mother, and also by the "turmoil" of this last stay with her on the reservation.

The seventh section of "School Days" begins with "Zitkala-Sa's" "second journey to the east," as she returns to White's. She treats "this second term of three years" (100)—almost four, until her graduation in 1895—in only a single sentence that announces her as "the proud owner of [her] first diploma" (100–1). Her next sentence reads, "The following autumn I ventured upon a college career against my mother's will" (101). After graduating from White's, Zitkala-Sa did attend nearby Earlham College, by her account against her mother's wishes. But what of those three or four further years at White's? Zitkala-Sa wrote not a word about them, but there is much that is worth noting.

Zitkala-Sa arrived for her second stay at White's in mid-December 1890, about the time, as Tadeusz Lewandowski has reminded us (2016 21), when Sitting Bull was killed and then Big Foot's band massacred at Wounded Knee, northwest of Zitkala-Sa's Yankton home.[16] I would guess that it was not long after her arrival at the school that her "individuality," earlier stifled, began to be appreciated and cultivated. This is to note that it was in these years that Zitkala-Sa learned to play the piano and violin and to sing. Although the extensive archival research of Susan Dominguez, Ruth Spack, and Tadeusz Lewandowski has not been able to establish exactly how this came about, as Lewandowski has written, Zitkala-Sa's "abilities in voice, violin, and piano were likely discovered by a local Quaker woman, Susan B. Unthank, and fostered by private study" (21), study almost surely paid for by Unthank and her husband, Joseph. Zitkala-Sa would keep in touch with them, referring to them in her letters as Aunt Sue and Uncle Joe (Lewandowski 2016 206 n.37).

Soon after Zitkala-Sa's return to White's, a young Lakota from Pine Ridge named Thomas Marshall came to the school, and in 1894 a Yankton man named Raymond Bonnin arrived. A few years later Zitkala-Sa would become engaged to Marshall, and after he died from the measles in 1899, she would marry Bonnin in 1902. It is also worth noting that, as Lewandowski writes, "At the start of 1893 school officials sent Gertrude on a recruiting mission to the Yankton and Pine Ridge Reservations, where she managed to sign up twenty-nine new students." He adds that "there is no record of how she felt about removing them from their parents" (21)—nor of "how she felt" about consigning them to the regimentation, disdain, and coldness that she would claim to have experienced at White's.

In any case Zitkala-Sa enjoyed great success at the school, and on her return from recruiting on the reservation was selected to give the commencement address at her graduation, making her not only the "proud owner of

[her] first diploma" ("School Days" 100), but also the valedictorian of her class. She would continue her education at nearby Earlham College, also a Quaker institution, her tuition and expenses almost surely paid by the Quaker Unthank couple (Lewandowski 206 n.38).[17] But her decision to attend the school, she tells the reader, comes at an emotional cost.

The seventh and final section of "The School Days of an Indian Girl" is titled "Incurring my Mother's Displeasure," and at the close of its first paragraph "Zitkala-Sa" informs the reader that she had "ventured upon a college career against [her] mother's will" (101). She says she had written to request her mother's approval to attend Earlham, but the answer she received "hinted that I had better give up my slow attempt to learn the white man's ways, and be content to roam over the prairies and find my living upon wild roots." She does not, of course, heed her mother but, she writes, instead "silenced" her "by deliberate disobedience" (101). The price she pays for this, we are told, is that "Zitkala-Sa" was "homeless and heavy-hearted," as she "began anew [her] life among strangers" at Earlham College (101). The only Native student in attendance, she describes her time there as consistently marked by feelings of homelessness and heavy-heartedness.

Before continuing, I want to consider further "Zitkala-Sa's" statement, just quoted, of the options available to her after her graduation from White's. In particular I want to observe that while her mother may well have "hinted" that she would do well to "give up [her] slow attempt to learn the white man's ways," I am certain that she did *not* say that the alternative would be for her daughter to come home "and be content to roam over the prairies and find [her] living upon wild roots" (among them prairie turnips, perhaps). These are the words of Zitkala-Sa, an accomplished woman of twenty-four, writing about herself as she was some five years earlier. They express, if only fleetingly, an exasperation that is never revisited or developed in these essays, but it is an exasperation, I suggest, that co-exists with or arises from a measure of guilt for which she will try to atone.

If she were to go home, Zitkala-Sa writes, she would have to "find her living"—to sustain herself both physically and culturally—"upon [the] wild roots" of the "prairies." This is youthful exaggeration. Conditions among her Yankton people varied, but their diet was no longer substantially made up of "wild roots," although these might still be gathered. Whatever of the old ways her mother adhered to, she was nonetheless a Christian who lived in a log house that contained a Bible in Dakota. David Simmons, her older brother, had attended the Santee Normal School and Hampton Institute, worked briefly for the government, and would go on to become a successful farmer; all of the family had taken allotments after the Dawes Act of 1887, Zitkala-Sa included. By the time she had to choose between attending Earlham and heeding her mother's wishes that she come home, home had already not been "wild" for some years. (This is not, of course, to say that traditional ways and traditional stories—several of which she would collect and publish—did not persist.)

Nonetheless, had she gone home, it is unlikely that she would have been able to take further instruction in violin and piano or that her oratorical skills would have been developed by addressing either traditional tribal councils or councils of a parliamentary sort. In Zitkala-Sa's time it was not possible for her to go home and also continue her studies at, for example, a nearby Sinte Gleske University or Oglala Lakota Community College. Those were not founded until the early 1970s. Had Zitkala-Sa returned home for the summer of 1895, she certainly would not have "roam[ed] over the prairies" searching for "wild roots." But she just as certainly would not have been able to stay "with the Unthanks while teaching music to earn money" (Lewandowski 2016 22), and then go on to Earlham College.

Many years later, in May 1913, she would write to Dr. Carlos Montezuma—she had been briefly engaged to him after Thomas Marshall's death, breaking the engagement to marry Bonnin—"I seem to be in a spiritual unrest. I hate this eternal tug of war between being wild or becoming civilized. The transition is an endless evolution—that keeps me in eternal Purgatory" (in Lewandowski 2018 100). I suggest that she first felt called upon to make such a choice, "between being wild or becoming civilized," when responding to her mother's entreaties that she come home. As the young writer posed it, she would either have had to return home and, in effect, live "by wild roots," or instead to accept what was probably the Unthanks' offer to her to become even more "civilized" by attending Earlham. Although she would put it this way only later—she and Montezuma were not in touch for many years after her marriage—her sense of being the subject of a "tug of war" begins to be prominent in her letters to Montezuma during their engagement. Those letters show Zitkala-Sa expressing strongly differing emotions and considering life choices more complex than the simple either/or binary of "savage/civilized."

This is not to suggest that this "tug of war" between being "savage" or "civilized" derives only from what was, in Zitkala-Sa's youth, a volatile temperament. Rather, it was a form of Du Boisian "double consciousness,"

a consciousness that in greater or lesser degree every boarding-school student—and, as we have seen with Eastman and Standing Bear, every educated
Native person—regardless of temperament, experienced as a consequence of
the colonial situation they inhabited. It was not only Zitkala-Sa's particular
subjectivity, but an objective material reality that framed her options as a
Native woman at a specific historical moment.

ഗ്ന

Beginning "anew [her] life among strangers" at Earlham, "Zitkala-Sa's"
feelings of homelessness and heavy-heartedness are the price she pays for
disobeying her mother, and they color her descriptions of her new life. She
represents only the negative aspects of Earlham—she will later represent only
the negative aspects of Carlisle—as if doing penance, suffering, as it were,
for her decision to pursue her "individuality" by means of highly "civilized"
modes of art making—letters, music, recitation, pose, and performance—and
leaving mother, motherland, and mother tongue behind.

"Zitkala-Sa" says she "hid [herself] in [her] little room in the college
dormitory, away from the scornful and yet curious eyes of the students." It is
true that when she "arrived at Earlham College in the autumn of 1895," she
was indeed "the sole Indian student on ... campus" (Lewandowski 2016 22),
and thus found herself in a situation very different from what she had known
at White's, where she could count Thomas Marshall and Raymond Bonnin
as Dakota friends, among other Native students. She "pined for sympathy,"
and claims to wish she "had gone West, to be nourished by [her] mother's
love, instead of remaining among a cold race whose hearts were frozen hard
with prejudice" (101). "During the fall and winter seasons," "Zitkala-Sa" says,
"I scarcely had a real friend, though by that time several classmates were
courteous to me at a safe distance" (101).

She is, to be sure, expressing how she felt. But there is a good deal
of evidence suggesting that "sympathy" for Zitkala-Sa was not lacking at
Earlham; that the "hearts" of the "cold race" were not all "frozen hard with
prejudice"; and that she was met with more than distant courtesy. Tadeusz
Lewandowski has examined the college newspaper, the *Earlhamite*, and from
its contents concluded that while Zitkala-Sa "likely felt a certain isolation
on campus, she was an extremely active and popular student." He notes that
she joined a campus music club and appeared "in school recitals, on and off

campus" (23); she was also a member of the literary club "at whose meetings she played piano" (23). Nonetheless, "Zitkala-Sa" represents her time at Earlham almost exclusively through the lens of her pain.[18]

She informs readers that her "mother had not yet forgiven [her] rudeness," that lack of forgiveness apparently conveyed by letters Ellen Simmons had sent her daughter. But "Zitkala-Sa" observes that she herself had "had no moment for letter-writing" (101), for all that not responding to her mother's letters might certainly be construed as further "rudeness." The reason why there was no "moment for letter-writing" comes in a bitterly poetic sentence: "By daylight and lamplight, I spun with reeds and thistles, until my hands were tired from their weaving the magic design which promised me the white man's respect" (101). This is purely metaphorical, of course, and it is strictly a Western literary metaphor; Dakota women did fine quill- and beadwork, but they did not spin or weave.

Of course, much of "Zitkala-Sa's" time was devoted to her studies: "English and elocution ... biology, zoology, Greek, and Latin" (Lewandowski 2016 22), a curriculum hardly inferior to that the older Charles Eastman was pursuing at just this time at Dartmouth. "For her thesis," Lewandowski writes, "Simmons planned to translate a series of traditional Sioux stories into Latin. In her spare time, she took up tennis" (2016 22), a sport in which Eastman participated as well. "Zitkala-Sa" mentions none of this, noting only that "in the spring term [she] entered an oratorical contest among the various classes" (101) at the college.

She then describes her performance and subsequent victory at that contest, writing that after her "concluding words, [she] heard the same applause that the others had called out" (102), no prejudice against her demonstrated by the Earlhamites.[19] When she receives from her "fellow students a large bouquet of roses tied with flowing ribbons," she forthrightly acknowledges that "this friendly token was a rebuke to [her] for the hard feelings [she] had borne them" (102). She will go on to represent Earlham at the state oratorical contest, and there it is not Earlham's students but the students from a rival institution who behave in a thoroughly prejudiced manner.

At the statewide competition, she reports hearing "slurs against the Indian" before she speaks, but it is only "after the orations were delivered" (102) that she finds "some college rowdies" displaying a "large white flag, with a drawing of a most forlorn Indian girl on it" (102), under which "they had printed in bold black letters words that ridiculed the college which was represented by a 'squaw'" (102–3). This of course embitters her, and when she is awarded second prize,[20] she confesses that "the evil spirit laughed within me when the white flag dropped out of sight" (103), although it might have been left in place as a flag of surrender. "Leaving the crowd as quickly as possible," "Zitkala-Sa" says, she "was soon in [her] room,"[21] where the "rest of the night [she] sat in an armchair and gazed into the crackling fire" (103), very comfortably accommodated—as was Eastman, also at a fine private college—as she reflects on the events that have just transpired.

In spite of the fact that Earlham students, staff, and administration have once more bestowed upon her abundant tokens of their appreciation, "Zitkala-Sa" says she "laughed no more in triumph when thus alone. The little taste of victory did not satisfy a hunger in my heart. In my mind I saw my mother far away on the Western plains, and she was holding a charge against me" (103). This is the very last sentence of "School Days of an Indian Girl." Readers of the *Atlantic Monthly* would have to wait for the following month's installment, when Part I of "An Indian Teacher among Indians" began by telling readers that "an illness left ["Zitkala-Sa"] unable to continue her college course," and that her "pride kept [her] from returning to [her] mother," who would rebuke her for trading "the freedom and health [she] had lost" for "the white man's papers" (104).

It has been speculated that the "periods of illness with lung infections, fatigue, and stomach illnesses" (Lewandowski 2016 27) that Zitkala-Sa had begun to experience at Earlham and that would affect her throughout her life were stress-related, the stress caused by the intensity of her experience with the oratorical contests, by her continued sense of isolation at the college, and, to be sure, by her ongoing sense of her mother's disapproval (which, however, she does nothing to dispel). Although she sang at Earlham College's commencement ceremonies in June 1897 (Lewandowski 2016 209 n.71), she did not return to complete the requirements for her own graduation. It is not clear how she obtained an appointment at Carlisle, but, once more without returning home to Yankton to face any "rebuke" from her mother or attempt a reconciliation, Zitkala-Sa boarded the eastbound train for Pennsylvania in the summer of 1897.

"An Indian Teacher among Indians," treats the time (1897–1900) Zitkala-Sa spent at Carlisle—which she refers to only as "an Eastern Indian School" (104). "An Indian Teacher" is a brief, impressionistic, and somewhat odd text. It is odd, for example, that in it readers never encounter a single one of the "Indians" the young "Indian Teacher" is "among" at the school in question, neither students, faculty, nor staff. So, too, do I find it odd that readers do not even once see that "Indian teacher" teaching. And, although the setting is an "Eastern Indian School," much of the piece takes place in the West—five of its thirteen pages in the paperback reprint—as "Zitkala-Sa" describes returning home on another recruiting expedition (she had, as noted, earlier recruited for White's), which includes a meeting with her mother and brother.

The opening section of "An Indian Teacher" is called "My First Day," and it begins with what I have cited, the narrator's statement of her ill health and her sense of the "rebuke" she would receive from her mother were she to see her daughter in her weakened condition. The second paragraph, however, contains a strong statement of purpose, and one that comes as a surprise: "Since the winter when I had my first dreams about red apples," the young woman states, "I had been traveling slowly toward the morning horizon," and, she asserts, "There had been no doubt about the direction in which I wished to go to spend my energies in a work for the Indian race [sic]" (104).[22] Looking back to that time, "Zitkala-Sa" claims to have known from the first that her education was not preparation for literary writing, music making, or oratorical performance but, rather, for the activism she would pursue most of her life.

Now, writing when she is only twenty-four, her words are extraordinary in their prescience—as they are also somewhat premature: it would be several years more before she would actually have "no doubt about the direction in which [she] wished to go to spend [her] energies." At this point in time, these words may be read in some measure as a statement of purpose that might please her mother—as her very next sentence suggests. "Thus," she says, "I had written my mother briefly, saying my plan for the year was to teach in an Eastern Indian school" (104). The implication, I think, is that her mother would approve of this teaching as "work for the Indian race." (Zitkala-Sa might also have engaged in this work by teaching at the Yankton day school, as she would briefly do later.)

The young woman arrives at the Carlisle school and finds it at first "a quaint little village, much more interesting than the town itself." It is pleasantly green, she notices: trees, grass, and "a low green pump" (104). But all the vibrant, green color disappears as she is "shown to [her] room—a small, carpeted room, with ghastly walls and ceiling," and "heavy muslin [curtains] yellowed with age" (105). Almost immediately upon entering her room, the young woman hears "a heavy tread at [her] door." She opens it to find "the imposing figure of a stately gray-haired man. With a light straw hat in one hand, and the right hand extended for greeting, he smiled kindly upon" her (105). This is her "employer," the head of the Carlisle Indian Industrial School (105), and, as Zitkala-Sa's contemporary readers probably knew, Captain Richard Henry Pratt. Despite his "kindly" smile, "Zitkala-Sa" finds herself "awed by his wondrous height and his strong square shoulders, which [she] felt were a finger's length above her head" (105). His "wondrous height" makes her conscious of being "slight" herself and also conscious of the fact that her "serious illness in the early spring had made [her] look rather frail and languid." Her self-consciousness is made more acute by her sense that Pratt, with a "quick eye measured [her] height and breadth" (105).

She reports his first words to her as, "Ah ha! so you are the little Indian girl who created the excitement among the college orators!" This is presented as patronizing, as it doubtless was, the manner in which Pratt, like most men of his time in positions of authority spoke to women, to employees, and perhaps to Native people generally. "Zitkala-Sa" insightfully suspects that his words are addressed "more to himself than to [her]," and she also finds "a subtle note of disappointment in his voice" (105). Perhaps he had not imagined that a champion college orator might be "slight" and "frail," or perhaps she is only projecting her feelings about herself onto him. Before leaving, Pratt inquires "if [she] lacked anything for [her] room," a question to which we are left to guess the answer. Immediately upon his departure, depression—"Zitkala-Sa" calls it "leaden weakness"—afflicts her (105).

The narrator says that "for a short moment [her] spirit laughed at [her] ill fortune," which, to this point, can only consist of the "ghastliness" of her room and Pratt's condescending manner. In that "short moment," she "entertained the idea of exerting [herself] to make an improvement," only to find that idea met by "leaden weakness ... as if years of weariness"—she was then twenty-one—"lay like water-soaked logs upon" her (105–6). She says she "threw [herself] upon the bed, and, closing [her] eyes, forgot [her] good intention" (106), the intention, I believe, "to make an improvement" (105). So ends "Zitkala-Sa's" "First Day" at the Carlisle Indian Industrial School.

The author does not provide an account of "Zitkala-Sa's" second, third, or subsequent days. Rather, section II of "An Indian Teacher," "A Trip Westward," begins a month later in August 1897. "One sultry month,"

"Zitkala-Sa" says, "I sat at a desk heaped up with work" (106). The work can't be student papers in need of grading because classes are not in session during the summer and she has not begun her teaching. What, then, is her work? The *Indian Helper*, a weekly periodical published at Carlisle by and for the school's students, teachers, and staff—edited and printed by Mariana Burgess, who also wrote some of it—provides the answer. I adduce this supplementary material to contextualize "Zitkala-Sa's" reportage.

The issue of the *Helper* for July 9, 1897, records that "Miss Gertrude Simmons is the latest addition" to the school and that she is a clerk in Miss Ely's office.[23] This is Anne Ely, Marianna Burgess's older partner, who teaches and also supervises the Carlisle outing program. The *Helper* of the following week, July 16, notes that "Miss Simmons is pianist for chapel services."

After informing the reader that she "sat at a desk heaped up with work," "Zitkala-Sa" wonders "how [she] could have dared to disregard nature's warning with such recklessness" (106). This would seem to mean her recognition that she should be outdoors rather than indoors and, apparently, not doing clerical work for Anne Ely or playing piano at chapel, both indoor activities. "Fortunately," the narrator continues, "my inheritance of a marvelous endurance enabled me to bend without breaking" (106). It hardly needs pointing out that "Zitkala-Sa" has just been presenting herself as "frail and languid" (105), rather than endowed with "a marvelous endurance."

"Zitkala-Sa" speaks next of being summoned to Pratt's office, where although she listened to him for "a half-hour," she "remembered one sentence above the rest: 'I am going to turn you loose to pasture!'" (106). Mocking this sort of euphemistic, male banter, she translates: "He was sending me West to gather Indian pupils for the school, and this was his way of expressing it" (106). Despite her strong negative feelings for White's, she had, as we have seen, gone to Yankton to recruit for the school. Now, despite the negative feelings she seems already to have developed for Carlisle, she will again undertake a recruiting mission among her people. "Zitkala-Sa" tells readers—she would not have said this to Pratt—that searching "the hot prairies for overconfident parents who would intrust their children to strangers was a lean pasturage." Nonetheless, she agrees to go "on the hope of seeing [her] mother" (106).

All the rest of "A Trip Westward" does indeed deal with the narrator's visit to her mother. Zitkala-Sa offers a gratuitously lengthy account of the "paleface" wagon driver who takes her from the train station to her mother's home, a "log cabin," with "a little canvas-covered wigwam [sic]" close by (107). Many readers will know that her mother's initial response upon seeing her daughter with the driver is shock, as she mistakenly assumes him to be her daughter's fiancé, or perhaps even her husband. But as "Zitkala-Sa" quickly makes clear, he is only someone who "has brought [her]! He is a driver!" (108).

Her mother's log cabin, the daughter observes, is not well fortified against wind and rain, and her mother cites her age and a decline in family fortune as reasons for this. She says she is "old," that she can no longer do bead work for sale, and that her son David has lost his government employment because he "tried to secure justice for our tribe in a small matter" (109). Tadeusz Lewandowski writes: "While David Simmons apparently did work intermittently as an assistant issue clerk, it seems farming was his true profession" (2016 210 n.19). Ruth Spack affirms that he was "an unquestioned success at it" (2002 152); that he had married, "and by 1897 had two children, a girl named Irene and a boy named Raymond" (Levandowski 2016 32).[24] Now, "Zitkala-Sa" says, "poverty-stricken white settlers" (110) were encroaching upon reservation lands in increasing numbers, and her mother felt their onslaught bitterly.

In section III, "My Mother's Curse upon White Settlers," "Zitkala-Sa" reports her mother once again warning her against the destructive, hypocritical "paleface" and even sending "a curse upon those who sat around the hated white man's light" (110). This does not take into account the possibility that some of those white men had Indian wives sitting around their "light" with them, something her mother, having been married to three white men, might have guessed. Meanwhile, "Zitkala-Sa" says nothing whatever about any recruiting activities. Unlike Luther Standing Bear, who had also recruited for Carlisle, she does not say a word about any contact she had with prospective Carlisle students and their parents at Yankton.

The fourth and final section of "An Indian Teacher" is called "Retrospection," and it begins, as the last section has ended, with "Zitkala-Sa's" mother: "Leaving my mother, I returned to the school in the East" (111). The young writer has had something less than a year for "retrospection," in that she had only recently left Carlisle and was writing these autobiographical pieces toward the end of 1899 and the beginning of 1900, when she would tour with the school's band. The recollection of her mother's vilification of the whites, however, is recent in her memory, and it strongly influences the "retrospection" presented here. As "months passed over [her]," "Zitkala-Sa" says, she "slowly comprehended that the large army of white teachers in Indian schools had a larger missionary creed than [she] had suspected" (111). A reader might well expect a strong critique of the boarding schools' "missionary creed," the ethnocidal ideology underlying their attack on Native peoples' languages, beliefs, and practices, to follow. But there is no such thing.

Rather, "Zitkala-Sa" says that the "larger missionary creed" of "white teachers in Indian schools" was "one which included self-preservation quite as much as Indian education" (111). To illustrate, she points to "an opium-eater holding a position as teacher of Indians"; an "inebriate paleface [who] sat stupid in a doctor's chair";[25] and a "white man ... who tortured an ambitious Indian youth by frequently reminding the brave changeling [sic] that he was nothing but a 'government pauper'" (111). The first two of these people are kept on, we are told, because the "pumpkin-colored creature had a feeble mother to support," and the doctor had a "fair wife ... dependent upon him for her daily food" (111). But this has absolutely nothing to do with the "creed"—the ideology or rationale—of the boarding schools. Rather, so far as staffing like this occurred, it is an abdication of responsibility on the part of the "imposing" and "stately" superintendent, Richard Pratt (105). This would, of course, apply as well to the utterly unfit white teacher "who tortured an ambitious Indian youth" (111). "Zitkala-Sa" offers a further critique of the Indian boarding schools based exclusively on the personnel employed, but I want to stop and examine the critique she has offered thus far. Once again, the intention is to contextualize the account offered, in the interest of a more balanced view of her early work.

There is no question that substance abusers of alcohol or opium were sometimes employed by the boarding schools or that there were miserable teachers who shamefully solaced themselves for their poor pay and often difficult working conditions by calling their charges "government paupers." Nor is it possible to deny that the people "Zitkala-Sa" singles out may have served as teachers or staff at Carlisle during the brief period she was there. But Carlisle was the flagship of the government boarding schools; to teach there was far more prestigious than to teach at other boarding schools, and Pratt had a number of well-qualified applicants for employment—both white and Native—from among whom he might choose.[26] To the end of his life Pratt considered himself a military man—he and his wife (like Zitkala-Sa and her husband) are buried at Arlington National Cemetery—and he expected discipline and good order from teachers, staff, and students. Substance abusers and disparagers of students were not likely to last at Carlisle for long.

But what of Carlisle's ethnocidal ideology—its "creed?" That deserved the harshest criticism. And what of some of its "savage" practices? Zitkala-Sa had chosen an Indian name for herself in 1898 while employed by the school, but a great many young people had had their Indian names obscured or obliterated, something Zitkala-Sa might have described for her readers, perhaps explaining to them just how much significance there was in an Indian name. She had been terribly upset when her long hair had been cut at White's. What of all those whose hair was cut at Carlisle? And the military drills, and the corporal punishment; and, too, the runaways and the acts of resistance: she knew of these things. Why not bring them to the attention of her readers? What of the guardhouse where Spotted Tail had been outraged to find his young son incarcerated? Why is this not described and denounced as part of a critique of Carlisle's "creed?"

Zitkala-Sa further observes of staffing at Carlisle that "even the few rare ones who have worked nobly for my race were powerless to choose workmen like themselves" (111). This may or may not be related to the fact, as she further notes, that the man sent "by the Great Father to inspect Indian schools" was "hoodwinked" by the "sly cunning of the workmen"—members of the faculty and staff other than, I assume, the noble "workmen." The "cunning … workmen" saw to it that the inspector did not get to observe the norm but, rather, managed things so that "what he saw was usually the students' sample work *made* for exhibition" (111, emphasis in original). I think it is merely realistic, not cynical, to note that schools—and other institutions—around the world have followed much the same practice, deplorable as it is.[27]

Several critics have credited Zitkala-Sa with presenting a far stronger case against Carlisle's ideology and practices than any she actually made. Jessica Enoch, for example, has called Zitkala-Sa's account in "An Indian Teacher" a "strategic rhetoric of pedagogical resistance" (118). Ruth Spack terms it "a scathing indictment of an unnamed boarding school that looked suspiciously like Carlisle" (2002 176). There are other similarly exaggerated estimates. But Zitkala-Sa's autobiographical texts contain nothing whatsoever that could be called a "rhetoric of pedagogical resistance," or "a scathing indictment" of Carlisle, something that would have been of great importance at the turn of the twentieth century.[28] Pratt's ethnocidal goals were morally repugnant and psychologically damaging. The Carlisle experience, like the government boarding-school experience generally, *hurt* a great many young

Indian people, some of whom did not survive it and many of whom suffered lifelong damage from it. We may add to this the bitter irony that Pratt's commitment to ethnocide, in retrospect, was totally unnecessary to his pedagogical aims. As the Presbyterian bi-lingual schools and some reservation day schools demonstrated, Native students could learn English along with other grammar- and middle-school subjects perfectly well while "remaining Indian." And indeed, all the Native students who survived did "remain Indian," for all the relentless assault on their languages and cultures. But a critique of Carlisle's "missionary creed" simply does not exist in Zitkala-Ša's early literary autobiographies.

In Zitkala-Ša's brief time at the school, there were not only noble and venal whites on staff at Carlisle but Native people as well. William Hailmann, appointed superintendent of the Indian School Service in 1894, had "adopted policies that favored the hiring of Native teachers" (Gere 48), so that "in 1899 ... Native Americans comprised 45 per cent of the staff of the Indian School Services," and "more than 15 per cent ... were teachers" (Gere 39). Although she was at Carlisle a bit too late to meet Dr. Montezuma there and a bit too early to meet Dr. Eastman, Zitkala-Ša would have had a number of Native colleagues, not one of whom she mentions.

For example, the *Indian Helper* for October 1, 1897, noted a performance by James Wheelock on the clarinet "accompanied on piano by Miss Simmons." James Riley Wheelock and his brother, Dennison, Wisconsin Oneidas, had both been students at the school. Dennison, the elder, entered at the age of fourteen in 1885, graduated in 1890, and became the Carlisle bandmaster only two years later. As a student, he, like Zitkala-Ša, had been a debater, and he also sang—tenor. James came to the school in 1889 and graduated in 1896; he would take over as bandmaster when his brother left Carlisle to become bandmaster at the Haskell Indian School in 1903. Later, during World War I, James Wheelock would be the conductor of a black regimental band. Both Wheelocks also taught music at the school. James, as noted, was a clarinetist, and Dennison was a virtuoso cornetist; in 1900 he led the Carlisle Band on a tour of the northeast that was meant to culminate in a trip to the Paris Exposition, although a lack of funds prevented the band from traveling abroad.[29] Zitkala-Ša performed and recited on that tour with great success.

Compared in his day to John Phillip Sousa, Dennison Wheelock was also interested in classical music. He had composed "a symphony in three parts" (Hauptman 127) titled "Aboriginal Suite" that was to have debuted

9 Dennison Wheelock, cornetist, and conductor of the Carlisle Band, 1890. Photo by John Choate. Courtesy Cumberland County Historical Society.

during the Carlisle band's trip to Paris. Although that did not come about, the symphony nonetheless premiered at New York's Carnegie Hall near the end of March 1900. In 1911 Wheelock would be among the founders of the Society of American Indians—to which Zitkala-Sa belonged. Although the very substantial egos of the Wheelocks and Zitkala-Sa might have been an obstacle to their developing any close relations, it would, of course, have been fascinating for her at least to have mentioned them in discussing her time at Carlisle.[30]

Nor does Zitkala-Sa record anything about the Native students she taught, not even the one whom she knew outside the classroom. On February 22, 1898, the *Indian Helper* reported the celebration of "Miss Simmons'" twenty-second birthday, on which occasion "Miss Seonia quietly invited to the parlor a host of Miss Simmons' friends, who joined in laughter, songs, and games and other merriment," while enjoying "cream and cake." "Miss Seonia" is Howice Seonia, a fourteen-year-old student from Laguna Pueblo who had entered the school two years earlier and would leave in 1902. Zitkala-Sa had met Indians from tribal nations other than her own at White's, but not, perhaps, from any of the Pueblos.[31] In any case, Zitkala-Sa's autobiographical writing about Carlisle did not report the merry "host" of her friends, students, faculty, and staff, both Indian and white, at the birthday celebration Miss Seonia had arranged for her.

Nor did she say a word about Thomas Marshall, the Pine Ridge Lakota man she had first met at White's Institute. Marshall had come east to enroll at nearby Dickinson College in 1897, about the time Zitkala-Sa came to Carlisle. But he resided at Carlisle, "where he supervised the boys' dormitories" (Lewandowski 2016 32). If Lewandowski is correct that he and Zitkala-Sa had become engaged "sometime between October [1898] and January [1899]" (2016 34), Marshall might have joined the birthday celebration either as her fiancé or just as her friend, if the two had decided not to make the engagement public—she and Carlos Montezuma would keep their engagement a secret. When Marshall died of the measles in the spring of 1899, the announcement of his death in the *Indian Helper* included the information that he and Miss Simmons had been engaged—and also that Miss Simmons had sent roses to his funeral from Boston, where she had gone to study violin in January of that year.[32]

This final section of "An Indian Teacher among Indians" continues with "Zitkala-Sa's" observation that the "illness, which prevented the conclusion of my college course, together with my mother's stories of the encroaching frontier settlers, left me in no mood to strain my eyes in searching for latent good in my white co-workers" (111). Nor, as I have noted, did her "mood" permit her to search for or report any "latent good" in her Native "co-workers" or students. Shifting attention from conditions at Carlisle, "Zitkala-Sa" informs readers: "At this stage of my own evolution, I was ready to curse men of small capacity for being the dwarfs their God had made them" (111). It is difficult to know what this means. Is it a further development of her scorn for the self-preserving incompetents she has condemned at the school? Is it an echo of the concern for individuality she had earlier expressed? Whatever she may have had in mind, it is not developed, as the subject once more shifts abruptly.

"Zitkala-Sa" now says that, "In the process of my education I had lost all consciousness of the natural world about me. Thus, when a hidden rage took me to the small white-walled prison which I then called my room, I unknowingly turned away from my one salvation" (111–12). The "natural world" she claims to have "forgotten" refers to "the healing in trees and brooks." She thus finds herself "Like a slender tree ... uprooted from [her] mother, nature, and God," now only "a cold bare pole ... planted in a strange earth" (112).

Then, perhaps thinking not so much about her last days at Carlisle as of her current situation—she is in Boston and writing for the *Atlantic Monthly* with many influential people supporting her, and with excellent prospects for both performance and publication—she tells us that although she felt herself "a cold bare pole ... planted in a strange earth" (112), she nonetheless "seemed to hope a day would come when [her] mute [sic] aching head, reared upward to the sky, would flash a zigzag lightning across the heavens." This odd image is a "dream of vent for a long-pent consciousness," and it permits her to walk "again amid the crowds" (112).

"At last, one weary day in the schoolroom," she continues, "a new idea presented itself to me. It was a new way of solving the problem of my inner self.[33] I liked it" (112). It is something of a surprise to learn that this young woman, "An Indian Teacher among Indians," presently at Carlisle to "work for her race," proudly admits that her attention, "in the schoolroom"—this is the only time she has represented herself as being *in* the schoolroom—is not focused on her Native students but rather on "solving the problem of [her] inner self!"[34] And the solution to the problem of her inner self? It is to go to "an Eastern city, following the long course of study I had set for myself" (112), in other words, to move to Boston to study violin.[35] Perhaps further study of the violin will indeed adequately "vent" her "long pent consciousness" and solve "the problem" of her "inner self." But it most certainly will not provide her with "the healing in trees and brooks" (112).

Once in that "Eastern city," Zitkala-Sa had the opportunity to write at the summer home of Joseph Edward Chamberlain, editor of the *Youth's Companion* and a prominent journalist.[36] Looking "back upon the recent past," she claims to see "it from a distance, as a whole" (112). But her final two paragraphs hardly offer a distant view of anything "whole." Rather, they turn back to offer a variation on the partial—in all senses of the word—account of the boarding school she had offered earlier. Once more she notes that all sorts of "civilized people visited the Indian school ... in an ignorant curiosity ... astounded at seeing the children of savage warriors so docile and industrious" (112). There is, to be sure, a reasonable enough irony in the use of "civilized" here—although it is less reasonable and more than a little arrogant to assert that the "curiosity" that prompted visitors to "the Indian school" was in every case an "ignorant curiosity."

The penultimate paragraph warns visitors to Carlisle, or I suppose to any of the Indian schools, to look beneath the surface and be suspicious of appearances.[37] And she continues to sound the single note that what the visitor, official or otherwise, gets to see is merely a show, not the norm. In her final paragraph she observes, "In this fashion many have passed idly through the Indian schools during the last decade," concluding anti-climactically: "But few there are who have paused to question whether real life or long-lasting [sic] death lies beneath this semblance of civilization" (113).

There is much to unpack in this final sentence. Zitkala-Sa is surely correct in stating that in 1900 "few [had] paused to question" what the actual effects of the boarding schools were on the Indian students who attended them, and she may indeed number herself among the "few" who had. And she quite properly alerts her readers to the fact that should they visit the schools and see the Indian children diligently at work, they must realize that there may be more to that than meets the eye. Meanwhile, her autobiographical essays have hardly raised the many questions needing to be asked about the government boarding schools.

10 Zitkala-Sa posing in "traditional" dress. Photograph by Gertrude Kasebier, New York, 1898. Courtesy of Visual Culture, Media and Communications, National Museum of American History, Smithsonian Institution, 69.236.103.

11 Zitkala-Sa with her violin. Photograph by Gertrude Kasebier, New York, 1898. Courtesy of Visual Culture, Media and Communications, National Museum of American History, Smithsonian Institution, 69.236.108.

Is it indeed the case that the "docile and industrious" (112) Indian children in the classroom represent only the "*semblance* of civilization" (113, my emphasis)? Or that the reality presents a choice between "real life" or what she termed "long-lasting death?" The truth here is much more complex, and it is a complexity that Zitkala-Sa herself in every way embodies, for all that it remains unarticulated in her essay. Zitkala-Sa had been photographed by Kasebier and Keiley in the summer of 1898 in stereotypical "Indian" garb and gesture. And, as noted, she also posed as a proper Victorian maiden with violin and book. The former of these poses was indeed only the "semblance" of a late nineteenth-century Dakota woman, but the latter did not offer merely a "semblance of civilization." Zitkala-Sa with violin and book was both a living Dakota woman and also a "civilized" woman of her time, a vivid example of Native modernity. Like many Indian people who had attended the boarding schools, she presented to mainstream America a powerful image of "Indians in Unexpected Places," in Philip Deloria's felicitous phrase.

Richard Pratt, of course, was not pleased by his young employee's depiction of Indian education at Carlisle, vague and general though it was. But to say, as Amelia Katanski has, that her account "shook Pratt and his cohorts to the core" (123) is simply not true; nor is there any evidence for Jessica Enoch's assertion that Pratt "reacted vehemently" (118) to it.[38] After Zitkala-Sa's essay appeared, Pratt wrote to her in February, March, and April of 1900 about the upcoming Carlisle band performances in which she would participate. He suggested that she perform a recitation of "The Famine" from Longfellow's *Hiawatha*; sent her a copy of Alice Fletcher's book on Indian music as a source she might use for violin encores (February 2, 1900); and urged her to borrow a buckskin dress that he had previously donated to the Smithsonian to wear for her recitations (February 24, 1900). On April 26 he sent a check to her in Boston. These are not "vehement" reactions.

Earlier, in a March 20, 1900, letter responding to J. M. Chamberlin's criticism of her *Atlantic Monthly* publications, Pratt offered a response at very much the same level as Zitkala-Sa's critique. Rather than defend the Carlisle "creed," he simply said of her commentary, "It is not at all true to the facts," and said he regretted "her shortsightedness and the shortsightedness of the people who inspired and encouraged what she has done," and, as he did in other letters of that period, he accused Zitkala-Sa of ingratitude to those who had sought to benefit her, a charge to which she was certainly open.[39] But she had decidedly let Pratt and Carlisle off easily, writing about none of the practices I have listed.[40]

Responding in turn to Pratt, Zitkala-Sa wrote in the *Red Man*—also in what seems a "relatively soft and temperate" manner (Katanski 123)—that in publishing the essays she had "hoped … to work a benefit for [her] people" (in Lewandowski 2016 46), something I would not doubt. Nor would I doubt what she adds next: "No one can dispute my own impressions and bitterness." Her "bitterness" is indeed beyond "dispute," as are her "impressions." But the old soldier Pratt and the young musician, orator, and author Zitkala-Sa appear to have been equally adept at negotiating representational politics for their own purposes. Neither was so bitter nor so impractical as to sever a connection that might still be useful to both. Thus, despite what Lewandowski calls the "tensions" between the two (2016 46), Zitkala-Sa returned to Carlisle in March 1900 to participate in the school band's tour of the northeast, a tour that, as noted, had been intended to go on to Paris.

"The Carlisle band's performances," Lewandowski writes, "featured violin solos by Zitkala-Sa and a charged dramatic recitation of 'The Famine' from Longfellow's *The Song of Hiawatha*," which she delivered dressed in "fringed and beaded buckskin" (2016 46).[41] Following her recitation she was introduced to Longfellow's daughter, Alice, who was in attendance. She was then invited to give a command performance at the White House, receiving flowers from First Lady Ida McKinley (Lewandowski 2016 48). It was on this tour that Zitkala-Sa first met Dr. Carlos Montezuma, some ten years her senior, who was traveling with the Carlisle band as physician and "caretaker for the boys in the band" (Spack 2001 178).[42]

Montezuma had known Pratt for some time by then, having first contacted him in 1887 "for advice and friendship," according to Peter Iverson, his first biographer, his letter initiating "a lifelong correspondence between the two men" (9). After some largely unhappy years in the Indian Service, he served as school physician at Carlisle from 1893 to 1896, leaving to establish a private practice in Chicago. Lewandowski cites two letters Zitkala-Sa sent Montezuma on February 9 and 20, 1901 (2018 19 and 22–23), that indicate it was in Chicago that she met him for a second time. By the next month they were secretly engaged, but in the summer of that year Zitkala-Sa began to see Raymond Bonnin, whom she had known earlier; by August she seems to have broken the engagement with Montezuma. Nonetheless, according to Iverson, she "kept a door open to a closer relationship in the future" (34), and after a time the two continued to exchange letters. None of Montezuma's letters to her have been preserved[43]—Zitkala-Sa did not keep them—but almost all of hers to him have. It is my strong sense that it is in her passionate letters to Montezuma that Zitkala-Sa first begins to offer developed defenses of women's rights and Indian rights, and outlines powerful critiques of colonialism and "civilizationist" arrogance, critiques that very much include the boarding schools' assaults on Indian languages and cultures.[44]

In part she may have been able to do this because—again for the very first time—she was writing not for an imagined public ("dominant white society," "people back home," "artists," "journalists," and the like)—but privately, to an older, educated Native man as strong-willed as she. Montezuma, as Zitkala-Sa knew well, was close to Pratt, and as she would soon discover, he shared the masculinist biases of the mainstream society of their time (as did Bonnin). Montezuma was also a man who felt deeply for her, as one can tell from her letters alone—and as she sometimes did for him. She writes to him expressing wild swings of emotion but also exploring a range of ideas with greater depth, sophistication, and passion than in any writing she had done thus far.[45]

In the February 9, 1901, letter to Montezuma just prior to their second meeting, Zitkala-Sa informed him that "two little books" of hers were soon to be published (only one, *Old Indian Stories*, was actually published), and, importantly, that she was "expecting to teach in the government school in Yankton Agency," South Dakota (Lewandowski 2018 19). As subsequent letters show, she had indeed determined by this time to work on behalf of Indian people from "home," at the Yankton Agency. Montezuma, however, had had only unpleasant experiences on the reservations where he had worked and wanted her to join him in Chicago. Although there were a sufficient number of other reasons for their breakup, this was a substantial one, as is generally agreed. As the wife of Raymond Bonnin, Zitkala-Sa would work in the Indian Service on western reservations (although not among the Dakota people) for the next fourteen years.

She nonetheless continued to write as she performed her Indian service duties, publishing poems and polemics in the periodicals of the Indian Rights groups of the day, in particular those of the Society of American Indians. In 1913 she contributed the libretto to *The Sun Dance Opera*, for which William Hanson wrote the music. Reading it today is no easy task, with its archaic "thees" and "thous." The opera premiered in Vernal, Utah, in 1913, and would be performed in New York in 1938, just after Zitkala-Sa's death.

Within a week of each other, on Christmas 1914 and New Year's 1915, Zitkala-Sa's mother, Ellen Simmons, and Raymond Bonnin's father, Joseph Bonnin, died (Lewandowski 2016 102). By that time Zitkala-Sa, as Gertrude Simmons Bonnin, had become prominent in Native Rights organizations. Her fortieth birthday was in the year 1916, and the following year the Bonnins moved to Washington, D.C., where they would spend the rest of their lives. When the U.S. entered the First World War in April 1917, Raymond Bonnin enlisted in the military. Because of his age—he was thirty-seven—he was not sent overseas but instead served in the Quarter Masters Corps in Washington (Lewandowski 2016 126).[46]

Zitkala-Sa had indeed been "changed forever" by her education, an education that had both caused her pain and also presented her with many opportunities. In her early writing we see those changes having produced a very talented, often conflicted, sometimes willful and self-serving young woman. As a mature woman, however, what we find for the most part is someone earnestly seeking to carry out her early decision to "work for the Indian race" (104). To describe that work is beyond the scope of this book, but having brought Zitkala-Sa to Washington, and to America's entry into World War I in 1917, I will close this discussion with an incident from the following year, 1918. On July 25, 1918, Gertrude Bonnin wrote the following to Arthur Parker of the Society of American Indians:

> I have an unusual tax upon my own strength, for after successfully getting a Non-English speaking Indian out of the Army with an honorable discharge, finding suitable work for him here in the city; I have had to make a "camp bed" for him on the SAI office floor; and give him his breakfast and evening dinners. When you remember I have no maid, you know I am putting myself out quite a bit for my unfortunate brother. However, I am a strong believer in backing up one's convictions with every ounce of life that the good God gives (Lewandowski 2018 173–74).

The soldier's name was Madoniawaybay, from Fort Peck, Montana, thirty-two years old. With the help of his benefactor, he learned English, obtained work as a railroad brakeman, and apparently did well (Lewandowski 2016 130). Later in 1918, Gertrude Bonnin joined Richard Pratt and the Eastmans to testify before Congress against the Indians' religious use of peyote.[47]

4

Walter Littlemoon's *They Called Me Uncivilized*, Tim Giago's *The Children Left Behind*, Lydia Whirlwind Soldier's "Memories," and Mary Crow Dog's *Lakota Woman*

I TURN HERE TO THE BOARDING-SCHOOL AUTOBIOGRAPHIES OF THREE Lakota people born fewer than ten years apart, not far from one another in south-central South Dakota, and a fourth from the same region born just over a decade later. Tim Giago, born in Kyle on the Pine Ridge reservation in 1934, was a student at the Holy Rosary Mission School (HRMS), known since 1969 as Red Cloud Indian School. He published *Children Left Behind: The Dark Legacy of Indian Mission Boarding Schools* in 2006. Lydia Whirlwind Soldier, one of three people to whom *Children Left Behind* is dedicated, was born in Bad Nation on the Rosebud reservation in 1942 and attended the nearby Saint Francis Mission School (SFMS). Her boarding-school recollections were published in 2001 in an extraordinary essay called "Memories." Also born in 1942, at Mouse Creek, about sixteen miles from Pine Ridge village, Walter Littlemoon at the age of five went to board at the Oglala Community High School (OCHS), which, despite the name, went from kindergarten to twelfth grade. (It is now Pine Ridge High School.) After ten years of work with his wife, Jane Ridgway, Littlemoon published *They Called Me Uncivilized: The Memoir of an Everyday Lakota Man from Wounded Knee* in 2009. Mary Ellen Moore-Richard was born in 1954 on the Rosebud reservation, and she attended St. Francis Mission School in the 1960s. Although she is the youngest of these writers, her autobiography, *Lakota Woman*, written with Richard Erdoes,[1] and published in 1990 under her married name, Mary Crow Dog, was the first of these four accounts to appear.

Although Littlemoon boarded at a government school like those we have considered thus far, Giago, Whirlwind Soldier, and Crow Dog went to Catholic Indian boarding schools; a few words about the similarities and differences between the two kinds of institution are in order. Gregory Gagnon has written that "the Catholic schools followed the same curriculum and rules as the off-reservation boarding schools" (51), but this was only generally the case. The "Peace Policy" of President Ulysses S. Grant, beginning in 1869, was in part an attempt to curb corruption in the administration of the reservations by placing them under the control of various religious denominations. The Roman Catholics were assigned seven reservations, a number with which they were dissatisfied. In 1874 the Church formed the Bureau of Catholic Indian Missions to administer its reservation schools and to lobby for access to more. The bureau's "mandate [was] evangelization and education" (Carroll 66).

Some of the Catholic reservation schools, like those at Fort Totten and Fort Yates in North Dakota, were overseen directly by the Office of Indian Affairs—it did not become the Bureau of Indian Affairs until 1947—and were thus funded by and run in the same way as the government boarding schools, except of course for the substantial amount of Catholic religious practice and instruction they provided. Others, like Holy Rosary Mission and Saint Francis Mission in South Dakota, the schools Tim Giago, Lydia Whirlwind Soldier, and Mary Crow Dog attended, were "contract" schools. This meant that they were "under the aegis of the Bureau of Catholic Indian Missions," which had made a contract with "the government [to give] financial aid on a per capita basis" (Carroll xvii). This allowed them somewhat more independence than the Catholic schools directly under the commissioner of Indian Affairs, but exactly what this meant varied considerably over the years and from school to school.[2]

Responding to anti-Catholic pressure from the influential "Friends of the Indian" movement in the northeast, Indian Commissioner T. J. Morgan in 1889 decided to issue no further "contracts" to the Bureau of Catholic Indian Missions for its schools. To make up for the financial aid the government withheld, the Catholic bureau in 1900 and then again in 1904 arranged with those tribes who favored Catholic education on their reservations to use the federal trust funds set aside for them to finance the schools. This was contested by the government and the issue was not decided—in favor of the tribes' right to use the funds as they saw fit—until a unanimous decision by the Supreme Court in *Quick Bear v. Leupp* (1908).

The Church was supportive of the 1934 Indian Reorganization Act and of John Collier's reforms, and that support seems to have been mutual; by 1935 thirty-five Catholic boarding schools had government contracts. Important to our discussion is the fact that although the government had banned corporal punishment in the Indian schools in 1929, and Collier had permitted the use of Native languages and cultural materials in the government boarding schools from 1934 to 1945, in the reaction that followed, at least in the mission schools of south-central South Dakota, physical brutality was rampant (as also in the South Dakota BIA school that Littlemoon attended), and no attempt "to remain an Indian," as the 1928 Meriam Report had stated (86), was permitted.[3]

ରର

Readers may well know Tim Giago's name from his work as an award-winning journalist, an editor, and a poet; the name comes from his mixed Lakota-Pueblo background and the misspelling of his grandfather's name, Gallego. *Children* includes revisions of the poems he had published in his 1978 volume, *The Aboriginal Sin*, many of which treated his boarding-school experiences, and it adds passages of historical and autobiographical prose along with many photographs. The "book is intended," Giago writes, "to bring back the memories of the boarding schools to those who have survived them. It is also intended to cause those memories, good and bad, to bring about a process of healing that has long been denied" (12). Giago here unself-consciously employs the idiom I noted in the introduction; that is, the treatment of boarding-school memories as survivor discourse, and the articulation of those memories as vital to the process of healing. This is the case, in varying degrees, with all four of these boarding-school students.

"Memories" is the title of Lydia Whirlwind Soldier's narrative. Professionally known as an educator, Lydia Whirlwind Soldier is also an award-winning craftsperson, a quilter, and a poet.[4] She writes: "I am writing my story for the children who suffered in the boarding schools. I speak for those children whose stories will never be told, for those of us who still suffer from post-traumatic stress, for the lost generations who stand on the street corners and dig in trash for aluminum cans to sell, for those who deaden their pain with alcohol and drugs" (159).

Walter Littlemoon was, for a time, one of those described by Whirlwind Soldier. For much of his life, he writes, he lived "as if a thick, dark fog covered [his] mind and heart" (34).[5] After school and service in the military he returned home and "drank for thirteen years" (68), the consequence, he says, of "the years of torture [he] had received in boarding school" (86). For Littlemoon, as Brenda Child has said for many Native people, boarding school was "the reason for the epidemic social problems" (2014 268) that he and others in his community suffered. With his wife's help, Littlemoon "sought counsel from mental health professionals at the Victims of Violence program in Boston, Massachusetts" (Littlemoon 86), and one of those professionals, Jayme Shorin, would write the foreword to his autobiography. Littlemoon writes that "finally, a breakthrough in [his] understanding came" when he got "the name of what [he] was suffering from—complex post-traumatic stress disorder" (86).[6] This refers to the intense, repeated, and prolonged trauma he endured at OCHS, much like what Giago and Whirlwind Soldier had suffered at their schools, and what the latter had called simply "post-traumatic stress" (159). Littlemoon writes that "once [his] fear had a name [he] could battle it and win" (86), retrieving buried memories, and emerging from the "thick dark fog" that had enveloped him for so long.

The fifth and central chapter of Walter Littlemoon's book bears the title "Learning to be Civilized." That is meant ironically, and a similar irony pervades Mary Crow Dog's chapter "Civilize Them with a Stick," in which she names the principal means by which she, like Littlemoon earlier, had "learned to be civilized." For her, the "civilizing" process took place at Saint Francis Mission School, the school Lydia Whirlwind Soldier had attended years before. Crow Dog achieved a measure of recovery from the trauma of Catholic boarding school through a mix of spiritual and political means. She was involved with the Native American Church, participated in the Lakota Sun Dance, and was a member of the American Indian Movement (AIM), active in the occupation of Wounded Knee in 1973.[7] As with the others, remembering and writing—making her painful memories public—was part of the process of healing.

Tim Giago, Lydia Whirlwind Soldier, and Mary Crow Dog were not the first of their families to attend these Catholic boarding schools, as Walter Littlemoon was not the first of his family to attend OCHS. Whirlwind Soldier writes that she "was the third generation of Whirlwind Soldiers who had attended St. Francis" (169), and Crow Dog was also the third generation of her family to attend. Giago's parents, "Tim Sr., and [his] mother, Lupe, also attended Holy Rosary Mission." They attended, he writes, at a time when "attendance at the boarding schools was mandatory" (Giago 7). Walter Littlemoon also believed that boarding school attendance was mandatory, but that was not strictly true. As Carole Barrett and Marcia Britton write, "In 1920 Congress made school attendance for Indian children compulsory and authorized the Bureau of Indian Affairs to enforce the law" (11). But an Indian child's parents had a choice between a nearby day school—if one was available—and a boarding school, although many were probably not aware of that.

Parental permission for Native children to attend boarding school had been required since 1893. Nonetheless, in 1896 Indian Commissioner Daniel Browning, wishing to build up attendance at government day schools, wrote to the agent at Pine Ridge that "the Indian parents have no right to designate which school their children shall attend" (in Carroll 120 n.124). As with so many official pronouncements, it is not clear whether this policy was communicated to reservation agents generally at the time, or whether, if they were aware of it, they carried it out. Policy changed often; it was frequently communicated poorly and acted upon arbitrarily, so that on any given occasion neither the Indian parents nor even the relevant authorities seem to have been certain whether boarding-school attendance was in fact mandatory or open to parental choice.

☙

At the end of the summer of 1940 Tim Giago's parents drove him to the Holy Rosary Mission School. While his parents visit with the school superintendent, Giago waits in the back seat of the car and observes something both terrible and portentous. He sees "two young boys pulling a red wagon. A larger boy was seated in the wagon" (25). The big boy is called Omaha, and he "was riding in the wagon because his feet had been amputated at the ankles." This, Giago will learn, is the consequence of his having run away from the school, getting "caught in one of the year's first blizzards," and having his feet freeze (25). Giago will find Omaha an angry and violent young man; he will also find conditions at the school so oppressive that he, too, will eventually run away.

His parents return, put him in the charge of a Mr. Burger, and drive off. When the boy runs after them, he is overtaken by Burger, who gives him "a cuff behind the ear. This," Giago writes, "was [his] introduction to life at the Indian Mission" (26), a life that would be filled with "an excess of unwarranted brutality from the administrators" (27), the teaching staff, and some of the students as well. Sister Carol Berg has expressed her sense that those employed at the Catholic schools were "more likely to give a greater amount of love and concern for their Indian charges" than employees of the secular schools (1989 27). This was most certainly not the case at HRMS.

Along with the callous attitude and rough physical treatment Giago encounters, he also finds an abundance of sexual abuse at the school. Had this been present when his parents had attended? If so, why did Giago's parents send him, his brother, and his sisters to the Mission School (23)? Giago writes: "When I was a boy we were in the middle of the Great Depression. Even though my parents had been products of the boarding schools, the extreme poverty on the reservation made the schools an alternative to starvation. They felt that we would at least have a roof over our heads and three meals a day" (6). Giago's memories of life at home, as we will see, do not reference any likelihood of starvation. Nonetheless, there is no doubt that his parents sent him and his siblings away to school in the hope that they would indeed be adequately sheltered and fed. As Brenda Child has noted, "demand for the schools by impoverished American Indians was high throughout the Great Depression" (Child 2014 271), and also for some years afterward, an important factor in the boarding-school attendance of many Native people.

Lydia Whirlwind Soldier is not driven to school by her parents. Rather, her introduction to boarding school begins when she returns home one late summer day to find that "in the yard a dusty car idled noisily" (160). The car is from the Bureau of Indian Affairs (BIA), and it is driven by an "Indian man [who] stood by ..., nervously smoking, raking his fingers through his short dark hair" (160). She, her brother, and a young uncle are put in the back seat of the car. Her mother protests to the Indian man that she is only four years old, but although school is not compulsory for four-year-olds, he is not to be deterred.[8] Whirlwind Soldier writes that "today, when [her] uncle talks about that day, he talks about being kidnapped" (161). Although there is no choice as to *whether* the children—Lydia only four, the others older—will go to school, she recalls that "the man asked [her] mother *where* they wanted to go to school" (162, my emphasis). Since her "father and grandfather had gone to St. Francis Mission," her parents, like Giago's, decide "it would be better if [they] were taken to a school [they] were familiar with" (162). This familiarity, however, would have included awareness of the brutality and abuse likely to be meted out by the nuns, priests, and lay people at the school.

Many years later, painfully aware that she "had left a vital part of [her] self behind in boarding school," Whirlwind Soldier asks her father "if he remembered how old [she] was when [she] first went to school. After thinking about it for a moment, he said he didn't remember" (207). She tells him, "'Dad, I was four years old!'" Then, he "sat looking down at his hands and when he finally looked at [her], he had tears in his eyes." It's her sense that "maybe [her parents] thought that [she] would at least have enough to eat and a warm place to stay at the school" (207), as indeed Tim Giago's and other Indian parents had thought. While Giago recalled the name of the man who welcomed him to school with a "cuff behind the ear," Lydia Whirlwind Soldier does not "remember the name of the Catholic nun who opened the door to take us into the building." Nonetheless, she "will never forget her grim lips and her hardened narrow blue eyes" (162–63).[9]

In chapter 6, "Learning to be Civilized," Walter Littlemoon does not speculate as to why his mother sent him to OCHS, the boarding school at Pine Ridge, instead of to the "community public school, run by the state of South Dakota—just yards from … home" (55), a school he would attend later. It is likely his mother chose to send him to the boarding school—as she had sent her older children—for the same reason that the Giagos and the Whirlwind Soldiers had sent their children: the hope that he would be safely sheltered and well fed. Littlemoon, in a manner similar to Whirlwind Soldier, writes that "shortly after [his] fifth birthday in 1947, a shiny gray car pulled up to [his] home with two strangers in it" (37). His mother, he recalls, "was crying. She told [him he] had to go with those people in the car." He recalls that he "had no warning, no preparation. Perhaps," he reflects, "she thought it was best that way or perhaps she wasn't expecting them" (37). Perhaps she did think it was best that way, or "perhaps she wasn't expecting them" at just the moment they arrived. But she would have filled out application forms for her son to go to the school—as she had filled out forms allowing her older children to attend—and she would have expected school officials to come for him at some point.

Walter Littlemoon's first day at OCHS submits him in short order to several of the *topoi* and *loci* of the boarding schools. First come the hair cutting and the cleanup: "Within minutes" of his arrival, Littlemoon was "abruptly sat ... in a chair," and "all [his] hair was cut off; [he] was stripped naked and scrubbed with harsh yellow soap and a stiff brush until [his] skin was raw."[10] This haircut, like almost everything at OCHS, is more violent than what most boarding-school students reported. Later Littlemoon tells us that "twice a month [the boys'] heads would be shaved" (43), probably in the interest of preventing lice, although there are far less harsh means of doing that.[11] Tim Giago tells us that shaving the head was a punishment meted out to runaways. When Littlemoon "questioned them in Lakota," he writes, he has his back "slammed ... with an open hand." Then "one woman tossed [his] clothes from home into a box, and the other threw a different set at [him]" (38). These consist of "grayish blue coveralls with a trapdoor in the back, a shirt, a set of underwear and great big brownish shoes." He also receives a pair of pants, "heavy denim, baggy around [his] waist and much too short," and a shirt with "ragged elbows, and ... sleeves [that] didn't reach [his] wrists" (38).

He is then left to sit for a time with other new arrivals until "the women led [them] all to another room where [they] were given sheets and two dark blue or grey blankets with big letters in the center that read: U.S." (38). Next he is taken to the dormitory, "up a flight of stairs to a large room with two rows of metal beds lining the walls." In attendance are more women, these holding "sticks in their hands" with which they "began whipping some of the other boys" in the dorm. It is not clear what these boys have done to merit their punishment, although we will find out that in the mornings bedwetters are whipped (40).[12] A contemporary reader may find this scene reminiscent of Kafka; and one may easily believe that young Walter Littlemoon "was unable to comprehend what [he] was witnessing." In particular, he "had never seen an adult beat a child" (38). The scene in the dormitory continues, but let me stop for a moment here.

In volume 1 of *Changed Forever* I pointed out that although the evidence is overwhelming that systematic corporal punishment was not part of traditional Native American child-rearing practices generally, a swat with a hand or a belt was occasionally practiced. Tim Giago, for example, writes that he had hid when his father was ready to drive him to school, and when he was discovered, he was told "in no uncertain terms that [he'd] better get [his] behind to the car, or [he'd] be using a pillow for a chair for the next two weeks" (23). Obviously his father did sometimes spank him. Curiously, a study of Lakota communities like that of the Giagos in the 1940s that I will reference further had observed: "Full-bloods say that spanking will make a child crazy and are contemptuous of parents who slap or whip" (MacGregor 128). Giago's family was mixed-blood—Pueblo, Lakota, and white—as was Littlemoon's family—Lakota, Cheyenne, and white—but Littlemoon states that he had not, in fact, seen children hit by grown-ups.

After the onslaught by the female attendants, Littlemoon's further experience of the dormitory consists of being shown by one of the older boys how to make his bed. The next boarding-school *locus* he encounters is the dining room. There he learns to take a tray and line up to be served food that "was green, red, and yellow. It smelled awful" (39). Just as on the Hopi mesas a half century earlier, he too will be served "the mush"—with one unfortunate addition: "Every morning we had oatmeal for breakfast. It always had mealy bugs in it." He says, "I remember the butter smelling worse than sour milk" (42). The boys "sneak out … to steal apples from the storeroom or vegetables from the garden," he writes. "We were always hungry" (43). At night he returns to the dormitory, where with clock time marked by a bell (39), he goes to bed: "The silence of the long, dark night was broken only by sounds of quiet weeping. That," he says, "was my first day of many years at the U.S. government boarding school in Pine Ridge, Oglala Community High School" (39).

෪

Giago, Whirlwind Soldier, and Crow Dog recall some of the *topoi* and *loci*—haircuts, cleanup, clock time, dormitory, dining room—at their schools in ways both similar to and slightly different from Littlemoon. Giago, for example, reports no initial cleanup nor any cutting of his hair—although he would himself later become "the school's barber" (18). He writes that the dormitory at Holy Rosary Mission had rows of army cots (16) and that he usually "fell asleep listening to the squeaky shoes of the prefect as he attempted to walk silently up and down the aisles between the rows of bunks" (17). The beginning of the day is announced by "a splash of cold water thrown in our faces," after which "the shocking clang, clang, clang of the large bell carried in the hand of the prefect" (17) submits them to clock time. For cleanup the boys "stagger sleepily from [their] beds and wash [their] faces from a row of metal basins. Then," he writes, they "would walk down the flights of stairs to the little boys' gym and fall into ranks, awaiting the command to start marching [the school, however, does not operate on a military model] to the chapel for morning Mass. [They] repeated this scenario seven days a week and twice on Sunday for nine solid months of the year" (17).

As for the dining room, Giago observes that, "after a summer of my mom's good home cooking"—this does not suggest the post-Depression scarcity he had mentioned earlier—"the first meal in the dining room was almost nauseating. For dinner we usually got a plate of strange-looking soup, bread and a cup of watery tea" (24). He too would write of the "mush." He says—again with no suggestion of scarcity: "We had to leave the good meals our mothers prepared for us and then adjust to the yellow mush and boiled, stringy meat prepared for us by the school cooks. It seems," he recalls, "that we were not just lonely, but always hungry" (33). In the dining room Giago finds himself supervised not only by the school staff but by a student monitor called "Boob," whose "favorite method" of enforcing his authority "was a slap across the face with an open hand or a punch in the stomach or arm with his fist" (33). This is tolerated and perhaps encouraged by those in charge.

On her first day at St. Francis Mission, Lydia Whirlwind Soldier remembers "two older girls and a nun" taking her and some other new arrivals "down dark musky concrete steps, down into a washroom that smelled stale and humid" for an initial cleanup. Its bathtubs and showers are lit by "Bare light bulbs [that] hung from the ceiling, glaring down on the drains in the concrete floor caked with dirt and hair, culturing mold" (164). The reader may note here that Whirlwind Soldier writes in a more literary manner than Giago—a journalist who employs a concise and paratactic style—or than Littlemoon or Crow Dog, both of whom worked with intermediaries. Whirlwind Soldier shifts between the perspective she had as a child and her present perspective; and her prose is richer and more detailed than that of the others. The "bare," the "glare," and the "hair," for example, may all have been noticed by the child, although rhyming them is the act of the mature writer—who, for emphasis, repeats "down," and "concrete." That hair and dirt *culture* mold is not a child's observation, nor would the child use *culture* as a verb.

The little girls are "told to undress and get into the tub, and then [they] were given a large bar of yellow soap that stung [Whirlwind Soldier's] skin" (164–65). It is only later that she finds out "it was lye soap" that "sucked the oil and moisture out of the skin, causing it to dry out and crack" (165).[13] This would seem to have been the only soap used at the school—probably because it was the cheapest available—and by "mid-year, most of the children had chapped, cracked, and bleeding hands" (165). Next the girls "were given clean clothes, underwear, socks, and uniforms ... made from a cotton canvas-type material with matching print blouses" (165). She clings to the clothes she has come in as "her last connection to home," but they are forcibly taken from her. Once dressed, the girls are "placed on stools while [their] hair was cut in a blunt Dutch boy style." As one might expect, she wonders what her "relatives would think when they saw her short hair," for her "hair had never been cut. Short hair," as we have several times seen, "was a sign of mourning" (165) for the Lakota. She then has "white powder" sprinkled on her head, "DDT for head lice" (165). Ironically, she had never seen head lice, "but we would all eventually catch them." This condition, endemic to the school, necessitates that the children's heads be regularly "sprinkled with the white powder or soaked with kerosene, which was not washed out until a week later" (165).

On her first night at the school Whirlwind Soldier is assigned a bed "in a large dormitory," "several aisles away" from her cousin, whom she could still at least see (165). Once more she provides fine detail, describing something unusual. "The mattresses on the beds," she writes, "were stuffed with corn husks," and "covered with blue and white-striped cotton material."[14] The children are "each given a pillow, white cotton sheets, and an olive green woolen army blanket," (166) war surplus, very likely. As Littlemoon had been helped by one of the boys, so "an older girl showed [her] how to make [her] bed" (166). Later, watching the other girls, she mimes saying prayers and climbs into her bed (166). Lying awake, Whirlwind Soldier thinks of her grandmother "always having spoken ... in Lakota about kindness, but the adults in this place showed no kindness." Later she writes about the way the "children at the school would learn to compete for affection" (166), also something she would not have learned from her grandmother, whose "Lakota society ... valued cooperation" (166). The students learn to compete on occasion for food as well.

Clock time rules: "We lived," she writes, "by the sounds of the bell and whistle. The bell woke us every morning, and the whistle signaled us to quietly line up in straight lines." Although there is no military system in place, like Giago, she writes: "We marched to every activity: class, meals, and church, twice on Sundays," and "We kneeled and sat to the sound of the bell and whistle" (170). A typical day at St. Francis Mission School "began around six A.M. We were awakened by a nun clanging a bell as she walked through the dormitory. I remember the anger and impatience etched on her face as she deliberately rang the bell in someone's ear" (170).   This is not the worst of it: "If we didn't get out of bed before the nun reached the end of the dormitory, we were jerked out, sometimes by the hair.... We also got into trouble if we did not make our beds properly. The nun tore apart the improperly made bed and the offender would have to make it over" (170–71). It is no wonder that "today, images of boot camp come to [her] mind when [she] think[s] of the little girls' dormitory" (171). She knew no kindness there.

After the girls "washed [their] hands and faces, combed [their] hair, and made [their] beds, [they] were in neat little lines quietly marching to church" (171). She notes: "The meals were very sparse at St. Francis. Every morning big bowls of mush, milk, and bread were placed on each table by the older girls. Some mornings we got soup that was left over from the day before. At lunch time we had a variety of foods, and every evening we had some type of watery soup with barley or vegetables and a few slivers of meat. Bread, butter, and milk were passed around the table" (173). Whatever her parents might have hoped for, the "mush" and all the rest she describes is not adequate nourishment: "Hunger made some of the children faint in church. Dropping here and there, they were picked up, shaken by the nun, and sat on the benches until mass was over." Then, "The children who passed out from hunger were helped to their feet by other children" (173), a grim scene.

The school, Whirlwind Soldier writes, "grew most of the food needed for the children," and in the fall they are sent to pick potatoes. "Teams of three to four children competed against each other, dragging and filling the heavy gunny sacks with potatoes. The team that picked the most potatoes received candy bars" (176), the desire for them overcoming traditional Lakota reluctance to compete rather than co-operate.[15] Hunger, as the following examples illustrate, could lead the girls into uncomfortable situations. Whirlwind Soldier recalls a "brother who was in charge of the greenhouse" coming "out into the girls' playground carrying a bushel basket of carrots, throwing them on the ground like he was feeding chickens. We scrambled for this treat" (177). If this was meant as an act of Christian charity, it is one that is thoughtlessly and arrogantly carried out.

But in fact it is not charity that motivates this brother. A friend of Whirlwind Soldier's sees him "working around the vegetable garden," and says, "Let's go over and see him; he'll give us candy if we sit on his lap" (177), something she knows from personal experience, or something she has heard. "When we approached," Whirlwind Soldier writes, "I saw the look on his face and decided it was not safe to be around him." Her friend, however, proceeds. "Later, when she came back with candy she offered me some." But Whirlwind Soldier refused. Somehow she "knew something was wrong" (177). We will hear of other things of this nature that are also "wrong."

In the 1960s, when the time came for her to go to school, Mary Crow Dog observes that she "was not taken to one of the better, modern schools. [She] was taken to the old-fashioned mission school at St. Francis, run by the nuns and Catholic fathers, built sometime around the turn of the century [it opened in 1886] and not improved a bit when [she] arrived as far as the buildings, the food, the teachers, or their methods were concerned" (29–30). It is unclear why she was not "taken" to "one of the better, modern schools" (29), boarding schools or perhaps day schools. She knows they exist, and they seem to have been an option. But despite the pain her mother—and before her, her mother's mother—had suffered at the school, Saint Francis is their choice. Crow Dog's older sister, Barbara, had previously been sent to SFMS and was still there when the younger girl arrived. She might—or, to be sure, she might not—have reported on her experience there.

While it is unlikely that *nothing* at the school had changed since its founding, Crow Dog's description of the place does sound more like what one would expect in 1886 than in 1966. Indeed, she begins by recounting an incident from times past, when, she informs us, her grandmother had been found playing with jacks in the church rather than praying. She was punished by being locked in a dark cell in the attic and "left ... there for a whole week with only bread and water....After she came out, she promptly ran away together with three other girls" (32). "They were found and brought back," and the "nuns stripped them naked and whipped them. They used a horse buggy whip on [her] grandmother. Then she was put back into the attic—for two weeks" (32). Crow Dog says that her "mother had much the same experiences but never wanted to talk about them" (32), as many survivors have not wanted to talk about their suffering.

Richard Erdoes, Crow Dog's editor, has presented the narrative in a somewhat rambling manner, presumably aiming to preserve the way she narrated her story. Following are some of the *topoi* and *loci* she describes. Crow

Dog remembers the "girls' wing" of the school as "built like an F and ... run like a penal institution" (32). In the first paragraph of her account she had used another extreme but telling comparison, one that would become fairly common. Crow Dog says that boarding-school survivors were not only like the inmates of a prison but "like the victims of Nazi concentration camps," and it was very difficult "to tell average, middle-class Americans what their experience had been like" (28).[16]

Clock time rules: "Every morning at five o'clock the sisters would come into our large dormitory to wake us up." Then, at "six o'clock we were herded into the church" (32). Like so many others, she notes that she "did not take kindly to the discipline and to the marching by the clock" (32). In the church there was "kneeling ... for an hour or so; seven o'clock, breakfast; eight o'clock, scrub the floor, peel spuds, make classes" (34). In the dining room, "Monday mornings we had cornmeal mush. Tuesday oatmeal, Wednesday rice and raisins, Thursday cornflakes, and Friday all the leftovers mixed together or sometimes fish" (34). As other students had found, the food sometimes had unsavory additives, "bugs or rocks in it." Nor was it fresh: "We were eating hot dogs that were weeks old," she recalls, "while the nuns were dining on ham, whipped potatoes, sweet peas, and cranberry sauce" (34). Crow Dog also notes that "in winter, [the girls'] dorm was icy cold while the nuns' rooms were always warm" (34) something she may know from experience or from hearsay.

She does not describe her own hair cutting—if, indeed, her hair had been cut—nor any cleanup. But she says that she has "seen little girls arrive at the school, first-graders, just fresh from home and totally unprepared for what awaited them" (34). What "awaited them" was the nuns assaulting their "pretty braids;" they would "chop their hair off and tie up what was left behind the ears" (34), a hairstyle somewhat hard to envision. Next comes an unusual hygienic practice: "they would dump the children into tubs of alcohol, a sort of rubbing alcohol, 'to get the germs off'" (34–35). Crow Dog writes: "Many of the nuns were German immigrants, some from Bavaria" (35), so one might guess that the alcohol bath was a Teutonic tradition, although I doubt it.[17] Whether Crow Dog herself had been immersed in alcohol we are not told.

Tim Giago titles one section of his book, "PUNISHMENT, NOT EDUCATION" (31), essentially a summing up of his experience at Holy Rosary Mission School. Mary Crow Dog's chapter about her time at Saint Francis Mission School also records a good deal of the former and almost nothing of the latter. In that all four of these autobiographers obviously learned to read and write—indeed, Giago and Whirlwind Soldier spent a good part of their professional lives as writers—it is clear that the schools must have provided some education.[18] But their accounts make clear that the education provided was subordinate to the infliction of pain. In the Catholic schools that Tim Giago, Lydia Whirlwind Soldier, and Mary Crow Dog attended and the government school Walter Littlemoon attended, learning seems to have taken place only in the context of and accompanied by violent and abusive punishment.

This makes for grim reading. I have already cited some of the brutalities these four boarding-school students endured, and I will quote them further and at some length. Their texts bear witness to one of the twentieth century's crimes against humanity,[19] and attention must be paid. In saying this I have not forgotten that in the introduction and at various points in these studies I have again and again insisted that the story of the boarding schools was complex; that as abhorrent as some of their practices were, we have testimony from many of their Indian students that significant learning did take place, and that there was at least some good as well as bad. Carole Barrett and Marcia Britton, for example, found that the twelve Dakota and Lakota students and the one Mandan/Hidatsa student whose oral histories of the boarding schools they recorded all had "bittersweet memories" of their time in school (8).

But Kathie Bowker's interviews with ten Lakota women who had attended boarding school for at least four years, and were between the ages of forty-five and fifty-five at the time of Bowker's research (2007), elicited predominantly bitter memories with no tempering sweetness. Tim Giago acknowledges that there were "some good and happy days" (36) at HRMS, and both he and Lydia Whirlwind Soldier remember weekend movie nights as enjoyable. But any happy recollections for them in no way balance— indeed, they are overwhelmed by—terrible memories that, again, they have been able to recall only through great and prolonged effort. Teachers and staff at these schools *hurt* them both physically and emotionally, and this includes sexual abuse beyond what I have thus far referenced.

പ്പം

Walter Littlemoon first went to OCHS in 1947, only two years after John Collier's resignation and thus early in the reaction against his pluralist educational policies. Littlemoon had had five older siblings go to the school before him, of whom two—his sister Pauline and his brother Ben—were still at the school when he arrived; we are not told whether their experience of the school earlier was any better than what he encountered. But Gordon MacGregor's *Warriors without Weapons* includes an account of conditions in the area at just that time, providing some context for Littlemoon's experience.

MacGregor's study was carried out in 1943 at the request of the government's Pine Ridge Agency in order to gauge "problems of acceptance and adjustment" to federal "economic rehabilitation" and education programs during Collier's tenure as Indian commissioner (10). Families and children from the communities at Kyle, Wanblee, and Pine Ridge were interviewed, and the children were administered a number of tests. Researchers included members of the Committee on Human Development of the University of Chicago, and the United States Office of Indian Affairs, all of whom had a good deal of experience with Plains people and Plains cultures, although most were non-Natives. The 1946 volume that resulted is dedicated "To the School Children of Pine Ridge Reservation," and one of the people thanked in the acknowledgments is "Albert Pyles, principal of Oglala Community High School" (13). He was surely in charge of OCHS when Walter Littlemoon's older siblings began school, although I have not discovered when he left the school.

Pyles had been a day school teacher before going on to become assistant principal of OCHS in 1941; he was principal in 1943, at the time of the government study, and perhaps as well in 1946 when he was thanked in the government study. The government and academic researchers in MacGregor's study concluded that "most Dakota children like going to school" (132). Considered in relation to Littlemoon's account of his experience only a few years later, it may indeed seem as if that statement of "fact" resembles some of Gerald Vizenor's fictions, a real-life example of social scientists missing the point entirely or being utterly unaware that they are being mocked. Because the researchers also state, recognizing no contradiction, that OCHS "has a high proportion of runaways who leave school for a short time or for good" (146). Corporal punishment, still officially banned in 1943, should not have been one of the reasons for this, although it may well have taken place and, in the post-Collier reaction, perhaps intensified. Certainly unrelieved brutality is what Walter Littlemoon describes having endured there.

After an unpalatable first breakfast, Littlemoon is met by his nine-year-old brother Ben, who "led [him] to a building he called the 'Primary,'" and took him to a classroom (40), where he finds a "teacher ... very tall and scary." This teacher shows him to a room where there is "a sandbox and a lot of toys." These do not appear to be "scary," but he does not care to touch them (40). Then "one afternoon, that day or perhaps the next"—the vagueness of chronology may in part be the effect of these events being shrouded in "a thick dark fog"—"we were led to yet another classroom" (41). There, "a man wearing a long black dress came up suddenly behind [him]." We are told that he grabbed the boy by his shirt collar and the seat of his pants "and threw [him] into the middle of the floor" so hard that he "still can feel the searing pain on the side of [his] face when [he] came crashing down." The man's attire identifies him as a priest, thus his presence in the classroom of a government school comes as a surprise. But Carole Barrett and Marcia Britton note: "It was not uncommon for religious orders to teach in federal schools" (5), although those teachers were usually nuns. Barrett and Britton also state that priests or nuns, "once hired, ... were subject to all federal Indian school regulations" (5), and surely this priest's actions are excessive. On "that day or perhaps the next," Littlemoon—he is only five years old—notes that he had been assaulted because he "hadn't sat down quickly enough" (41). But in one form or another, "Punishment came at least two or three times every day in the classroom and even more frequently in the dormitory" (41).

Further, "If we spoke out of turn, especially if we spoke Lakota, we were hit with whatever the matrons found handy: a belt, a stick, a book, a shoe, sometimes an open hand or a closed fist. Other times we had to pull our pants and underwear down, 'just to make sure' we didn't have any protection stuffed in there ... they would beat us with a belt doubled over, a strap, or a thick board" (42). In the classroom, Littlemoon's account continues, "The teacher liked to grab us by the ears, twist them, and pull us off the floor by them. Our fingers would be bent backward. We'd be made to kneel on a pencil holding our arms straight out for a long time until our bodies cried in pain" (44). He recalls "getting slapped with an open hand on [his] face and head ... the slapping went on and on, for at least two or three minutes. [His] mouth and nose bled, [his] ears rang, and [his] face felt hot.... There were times when they'd cup both hands and slam them simultaneously together over [his] ears. It would make a popping sound" (44). He states, "The teachers, the matrons, the Boys' Advisor, they all beat us" (44).

What to make of this? A priest—again, this was not a Catholic school— grabbed a five-year-old boy "and threw [him] into the middle of the floor" so hard that he felt "searing pain on the side of [his] face when [he] came crashing down" (41)? A teacher who "liked to grab [students] by the ears, twist them, and pull them off the floor" by their ears (44)? Boxing a child's ears hard enough to damage the eardrums? Slapping a child "with an open hand on [the] face and head" so that the child's "mouth and nose bled, [his] ears rang, and [his] face felt hot" (44)? Can that child have been left in the classroom, bleeding from mouth and nose? Wouldn't that child have been sent to a nurse or some medical attendant? And how would that attendant have reacted? Would he or she have been shocked and concerned to discover the cause of such substantial injuries? Or would he or she have been complicit, perhaps even saying: so what bad thing have you been doing now?

And what of the Kafkaesque matrons dashing about with sticks? In the study of conditions at Pine Ridge in 1943 Gordon MacGregor had written that prior to Collier's reforms, "student behavior was controlled by the boys' and girls' disciplinarians, who were allowed to employ severe physical punishment" (144). But he also wrote: "This type of discipline has now been banned, and the milder penalties invoked today take the form of deprivation of privileges and loss of prestige" (144–45). Albert Pyles, as noted, had been in charge of a school where such abuses were prohibited by government policy. He might have been transferred by 1947, when Walter Littlemoon arrived, just two years into the reversal of Collier's reforms. But can there have been, in that short time, such a complete turn-around of policy, administration, and personnel, so that the lower school was now staffed entirely by sadists and child abusers?

Littlemoon's wife, Jane Ridgway, writing in response to three reviews of *They Called Me Uncivilized*, speaks of her husband, after the publication of his book, having come "across a few classmates," some of whom "shared their memories with us." Among these, she says, was a boy who "had his head submerged in a bucket of ammonia for speaking his native tongue. Another had his eyes glued shut after he was discovered practicing a small ceremony. Still another had his back peppered with buckshot as he attempted to run away" (53). We know all too well that persons in authority have inflicted atrocities on their powerless charges, but one may yet wonder at the accuracy of these recollections. The effect of ammonia on the skin of a child's face, for example, is very serious, and would affect the child's eyes as well. Surely these injuries would be noticed by many—and judged acceptable practice? Gluing shut the eyes of a child? Would no one have raised strong objection to that? Would the community not have been outraged to learn such a thing had been done? Further, no single boarding-school runaway I have encountered in the literature reports the attempt to escape being thwarted at the outset. Most had carefully planned their escape and, so far as I know, every single student who tried to run off succeeded in getting beyond school boundaries. If an escape attempt was discovered immediately, as it would have to have been here, it is a unique instance. But preventing a child from running away by shooting him in the back? How would that have been explained to the person who removed the buckshot? What Ridgway reports as memories of harsh discipline surely rise to the level of felonious abuse of a child. These considerations lead me to offer a few words about what Dr. James Chu calls "The Nature of Traumatic Memories of Childhood Abuse" (78).

A great many instances of childhood abuse are forgotten by its victims, an adaptive mechanism that goes by many names, like "dissociative amnesia" (Herman 256, Chu 78) or "traumatic amnesia" (Chu 80), these terms largely replacing what Freud had called repression. But as Dr. Chu writes: "The idea that overwhelming experiences can be forgotten and then recalled has a long tradition," and "Dissociative amnesia is at the core of the controversy concerning traumatic memory of childhood abuse" (78). He provides a useful summary of recent historical periods when, initially, belated recollections of childhood trauma were dismissed outright as fanciful inventions; later most were taken as completely accurate; and later yet came a strong reaction against their accuracy, leading to the establishment in 1992 of the False Memory Syndrome Foundation (79). Chu states that "in the current [2011] clinical arena, clinicians generally accept that some recovered memories of childhood abuse are essentially valid reports of repressed or dissociated early experience" (79), but that a "balanced view" must acknowledge "that it is also possible that some people may construct pseudomemories of having been abused" (80).

My intention in raising this matter is not in the least to deny that these boarding-school students were horribly abused. Nor is it to doubt that Walter Littlemoon, along with the student who reported his or her head being soaked in ammonia; the student who said his eyes were glued shut, and the one shot in the back with buckshot may all have suffered terribly. I do not believe they have intentionally constructed "pseudomemories," nor that any one of them is lying. Nonetheless, a "balanced view" of what they report must allow for the possibility—or perhaps only the vain hope—that their recollections may not always be accurate in every detail.

ᏣᎳ

Littlemoon says: "If we got an 'A' we were beaten for cheating. If we got an 'F' we were beaten for being stupid" (44). This must mean that at the least assignments or exams were given and graded. He writes that "reading became [his] favorite activity. Through stories like 'The Adventures of Tom Sawyer', [he] could glimpse freedom" (48). "By fourth grade," he "was able to read fast and answer any questions given to [him] about the book [he] was reading." This achievement, however, is not rewarded: "Again and again, the teacher would insist that [he] must have cheated and she would order [him] to sit off by [him]self" (48). He tells of other things to which I will return; here, I cite only the conclusion to Littlemoon's present testimony.

He describes a boy who accidentally fell from a window being "whipped for the accident"; "No matter what we did we got punished" (49). The punishments include what he calls the "gauntlet." This, in Littlemoon's time, would be initiated by "the Boys' Adviser" on occasions when he decided "a particular punishment hadn't been enough" (49).[20] Then the older boys would form a line with their legs spread, through which "the little boy being punished had to crawl.... As he crawled, they'd beat him with straps and sticks. Sometimes the Boys' Adviser would get angry with an older boy for not hitting hard enough" (49–50). Littlemoon does not say whether he had endured this particular punishment. He describes other brutalities and humiliations suffered by his fellow students and mentions a boy who was not "able to find relief from [his] memories of the cruelty [he] had experienced at boarding school," and who, "overwhelmed by the painful memories, took his own life" (50). Most students who suffered as these children did suppressed many of their memories, consigning them to an amnesiac state in order to survive. The degree to which they could regain access to them and integrate them as adults, with or without professional help, was significant in determining their ability to function.

ᴥ

In his chapter "Punishment, Not Education" (31), Tim Giago recalls the punishments his mother's generation had endured for speaking Lakota at HRMS and describes a bitterly ironic example in his own time. He recalls a "Mr. John Bryde" who "made it his business to learn the Lakota language, even though the language was forbidden to the Lakota students." Giago writes, "Well, John Bryde learned the language all right, but he continued to mete out severe whippings with a leather belt to any boy caught speaking the language he, himself, was trying to learn" (32). Elsewhere—the book's structure is roughly free-associational—Giago tells of other abuses, and unlike Littlemoon or Whirlwind Soldier, he regularly names their perpetrators.

Thus there is Father Edwards, who "would make all of the students within reach line up to observe" a beating he was about to administer. Offenders were to "'assume the position,'" that is, to bend over, "grabbing and holding on to [their] ankles so he could have better access to [their] posteriors." Surely some homo-eroticism is involved here. Giago writes, "The flaying with 'The Cat' began." After "the pain and shame, he demanded that we say through our tears, 'Thank you Father Edwards'" (73). Many years later, Giago says he actually heard the man boast at a conference that "he beat more Sioux behinds than any white man in history." This was in 1974, and Giago understandably reports, "I couldn't believe my ears" (73).

Some further cruelties were perpetrated by Father Edwards. At some point, Giago writes, "a stray puppy wandered on to the Mission grounds. Several of the older boys immediately took him as a pet." This is forbidden, and it is Father Edwards who discovers the dog. "He called all the boys together"—he likes to publicize the corrections he inflicts—"and then he went to his office and returned with his favorite hunting rifle." Admonishing the boys for breaking the rules he "told [them] they had to be punished," and he immediately shoots the dog (75). All the boys are shocked and horrified, but Giago recalls the reaction of one in particular. This is Melvin White Magpie, one "of the quietest, nicest, and friendliest kids at Holy Rosary" (73), whose "hands and head started to shake as he fought back the tears" (75) after the animal had been shot. On an earlier occasion, for having improperly helped himself to a handful of chocolate cake (74), White Magpie had had that cake smashed into his face by Father Edwards, who then made him "assume the position" to be "beaten across the backside with a leather strap" (74). Giago notes that "Melvin White Magpie died, many years later, in the state prison in Lincoln, Nebraska" (76), one of those remembered as well by Lydia Whirlwind Soldier, persons who could not overcome the damage done by the abuse they had endured at boarding school.

It comes as almost a brutal anticlimax when Giago next informs us that a "few months after Father Edwards shot the puppy," a kitten wandered on to the grounds. When the priest discovered it, he "took the cat by the tail, spun it around his head several times and then crashed its head into a tree"

(77). We are not informed whether Melvin White Magpie was a witness to this further gratuitous violence. (Lydia Whirlwind Soldier would also witness the destruction of forbidden felines.) Above this sentence Giago has placed a large photograph captioned, "Father Edwards (Eddie Boy) stands amidst Indian students at Holy Rosary Mission" (77). A typical Catholic Indian boarding-school priest?

Lydia Whirlwind Soldier also suffered at St. Francis Mission School. Early in her account she offers a broad summation. "Whippings," she writes, "raised welts on my legs … and I was jerked around by my hair. I was slapped in the mouth and I had bruises on my cheeks from being pinched and shaken. We would learn over the years that raw knuckles and cracked hands were not something that one cried over" (170).[21] "Corporal punishment," she continues, "was being slapped in the face, a twisting pinch on the cheek, having one's hair pulled, or a whipping with a strap or a paddle," and she describes the "two types of paddle" (180) used for this purpose. She writes of third grade when her teacher, a "cruel charade of a woman," "walked around with a red switch, whipping it in the air, telling us what she expected." She remembers: "The first time she used that switch on me it caught me at an angle across my forehead and my eyelid. The swelling nearly closed my eye" (194). "That year," she writes, "we had many welts on our faces and legs from that red switch" (193), a switch used on third graders.

Whirlwind Soldier is not only the most literary of the four but also the most insightfully analytical, describing not just the immediate physical harm done to the children and visible to all—hair pulled, whippings, welts on the face and legs made by a switch—but also the internal damage inflicted, the hurt that could not be seen at the time and the effects of which would not fully appear until later. This particular teacher does not seem to have been a nun, although no one at the school, servants of Jesus, mitigated or checked her cruelty. "When there was a wild angry look on her face"—surely this woman, who also rants and raves (193), is not a person to be allowed around children!—"we found out," Whirlwind Soldier writes, "that switch could talk. It searched out all our misdeeds and it told us that we were evil children" (193).[22] Looking back, she knows that not only her body but also her "spirit was beaten and tattered in the third grade" (194). She will spend many more years at SFMS, and it will be a very long time before that "beaten and tattered" spirit can heal and perhaps be made whole

There is a great deal more sadistic violence addressed to children by the SFMS staff that might be cited, like that of the priest who "especially seemed to delight in thumping boys on the head, leaving welts on their foreheads" (172), but I will note only two further instances. Whirlwind Soldier writes that her father "was a talented musician, [who] wanted his children to learn about music," and so he managed to pay for piano lessons for her at the school (177). She "started out by playing the scales," only to discover that she would be struck with a "ruler across her knuckles [that] drew blood with every wrong note [she] played.... Sometimes the ruler ended up making welts on the top of [her] head" (177). Comment seems almost superfluous, and in any case, one hardly knows where to begin. Hitting the head and the *hands* of a young child trying to learn to play the piano? As Tim Giago had reported at HRMS, Lydia Whirlwind Soldier reports an incident with forbidden pets at SFMS. Two girls on kitchen detail, sent for potatoes in the cellar, discover a litter of kittens. "When the nun found the girls cuddling the kittens, she placed the kittens into a gunny sack and drowned them in a bucket of water. The girls became hysterical" (175).

ॐ

Mary Crow Dog began at HRMS in the lower school, and she too mentions students being struck with great regularity. She recalls that when she was thirteen, she once refused to go to mass because she "did not feel well" (33). Whether it was because she did not believe the child or because she did not care, a "nun grabbed [her] by the hair, dragged [her] upstairs, made [her] stoop over, pulled [her] dress up ... pulled [her] panties down, and gave [her] what they called 'swats'—twenty-five swats with a board around which Scotch tape had been wound. She hurt me badly" (33–34). This is in 1967. She says her "classroom was right next to the principal's office and almost every day [she] could hear him swatting the boys. Beating was the common punishment for not doing one's homework or for being late to school" (34). (Perhaps there were also day students, for it is not clear just how a student who boarded at the school could be late.) On another occasion Crow Dog writes that she and a friend played ball "three extra minutes, only three minutes more than we were supposed to," for which they received "twenty-five swats" (37). As the girls grow older, Crow Dog describes acts of resistance. "The nuns and the girls in the two top grades were constantly battling it out physically," she says, "with fists, nails, and hair-pulling." As for herself, she writes, "My claws were getting bigger and were itching for action" (35). Shortly after receiving "swats" for playing ball too long, she says to a friend,

"We are getting too old to have our bare asses whipped that way. We are old enough to have babies. Enough of this shit. Next time we fight back" (37). An occasion to do so comes when a nun is about to swat a little girl. Crow Dog says, "I went up to the sister, pushed her veil off, and knocked her down. I told her that if she wanted to hit a little girl she should pick on me, pick one her own size" (37). Interestingly, Crow dog receives no punishment for her defiance; rather, this particular nun "got herself transferred out of the dorm a week later" (37).

On another occasion Crow Dog talks back to "a new priest" in English class, and when he tells her to stay after school, grabs her arm, and pushes her against the blackboard, she "turned around and hit him in the face, giving him a bloody nose" (40). After this she runs to the office of Sister Bernard, perhaps the nun in charge, announcing to her, "Today I quit school. I'm not taking any more of this, none of this shit any more. None of this treatment. Better give me my diploma. I can't waste any more time on you people" (40). In what seems a surprising response, the nun says, "'All right, Mary Ellen, go home today. Come back in a few days and get your diploma'" (40). Thus Mary Crow Dog's education at Saint Francis Mission School concludes not with an actual graduation but, apparently, with a diploma nonetheless.

Crow Dog's account of her many years at SFMS references some sexual abuse as well. She notes the arrival of a "priest they sent here from Holy Rosary in Pine Ridge because he molested a little girl.... All he does is watch young women and girls with that funny smile on his face" (39). Whether this particular father did something more than "watch" at Saint Francis we are not told.[23] It would seem to have been another priest, a photography teacher, who invited a friend of hers into the darkroom, "to teach her developing" (39). This friend, as Erdoes's text has it, apparently with no pun intended, is "developed already ... nicely built." Very quickly the young woman comes rushing out of the darkroom, "yelling ... 'He's trying to feel me up. That priest is nasty'" (39).[24]

Lydia Whirlwind Soldier, in attendance at Saint Francis years earlier, also speaks out on this topic. We have noted her mention of the priest who would give the girls candy if they would sit on his lap, and along with the "physical, mental, [and] emotional ... abuse that occurred within those walls ... by these apostles of St. Francis Mission," she writes of the "sexual abuse" as well.[25] She recalls seeing "a nun leading a little girl by the hand into her room in the middle of the night several times," and also "how a girl would be summoned by a priest or nun, returning withdrawn and with swollen eyes from crying, refusing to speak to anyone" (203).[26] Like her grandmother, these priests and nuns "spoke of kindness and patience," she writes, but unlike with her grandmother, "their behaviors were contrary to their teachings" (203). She makes a point Tim Giago makes as well: that the "behaviors [these priests and nuns] demonstrated were eventually emulated and have become family tradition for many," so that, sadly, their "voices still echo in the adults who verbally abuse their children" (203).[27]

Sexual abuse is addressed by Giago very early in his book. He writes that the "sexual abuse of many students became a part of their [the Catholic boarding schools'] normal routine," and that his younger sister Shirley "was raped at Holy Rosary Mission" (4). As adults, these boarding-school students' behaviors testify to the fact that people often do unto others not as they would have done to themselves but, sadly, as has been done to them. This is because "the capacity to care for and raise children is substantially learned through having been adequately nurtured in childhood; that is, those who have had positive parenting are more likely to become good parents. In cases where parents have been the victims of childhood abuse or neglect, their parenting skills may be massively flawed" (Chu 10). Of his sister, Giago writes, "She was violent and cruel to her own children all her life" (4).

As he had named some of the brutal teachers, Giago likewise names some of the sexual abusers. A section called "Albert Rokey and My Sister" identifies his sister's rapist. Giago writes, "Albert Rokey—I am not sure of the spelling of his name, but that is the way it was pronounced—was the white all-around maintenance man for the Mission boarding school." The man had "a small house on the campus," and Giago says he "had easy access to the little girls at the school," in particular girls "who were between the ages of nine and twelve." He "enticed young girls to his room with promises of candy and then sexually assaulted them" (71).

Giago notes that he found out about this only years later, when, because he "was a writer and an editor of an Indian newspaper," he met with some of these girls who "wanted to talk to [him] about what happened to them. One of them was [his] little sister, Shirley" (71). It is his "contention that the Jesuit priests, Franciscan nuns, and the brothers and prefects of the Mission had the ultimate responsibility for the safety of the boys and girls who boarded nine months of the year at their school. It was their duty to protect the innocent children from predators and pedophiles. But they didn't" (72).

Giago recalls Sunday mornings when he would see Rokey "seated amongst the nuns and brothers in the chapel with his head bowed, hands folded, and praying intently" (135). Did they not know what the man was doing? Surely it is reasonable to suppose they should have known. Giago writes that "one day Rokey was no longer at the Mission," but whether "he was fired or just moved to another Indian Mission"—as Mary Crow Dog had found a pedophile priest later moved from HRMS to her school, SFMS—he does not know (71).

Giago also speaks of "one Catholic priest at the school" whom he does not name, who, according "to some of the girls . . . loved to make them sit on his lap while he felt around in inappropriate places on their bodies" (135). He can testify to sexual abuse not only from hearsay. Giago writes, "Some of the older boys often forced themselves upon the younger, smaller and most vulnerable boys," and that he "wasn't the only one who witnessed this." Not only did he witness it, but as "a boy small for [his] age, [he] had to fight off some of the older boys," adding, "why our guardians never saw this happening around them escapes me." He wonders all the more about the "guardians'" failure to protect the innocent children in that some of this occurred "right on the floor of the little boys' gym in full view of everyone" (136). Moreover, he "had [his] own experience with improper touching from a prefect named Mr. Price, who went on to become a priest." This was "a terrible experience," one he has "never forgotten" (72). But "nothing was ever done about the dormitory prefect who tried to sexually molest [him]" (135). "I name names here," Giago writes, "because I want those who believe there was never abuse at the boarding schools to know that the offenders are real, live people" (72).

Walter Littlemoon records nothing whatever of sexual abuse at OCHS, but it is my strong suspicion that it occurred. Considering the regular, unchecked physical abuse meted out by teachers, dormitory attendants, and an oddly placed priest; the encouragement to the older boys to inflict punishment on the younger; and the apparent lack of oversight or account-ability, it is difficult to believe that these excesses did not also include forcible touching and other acts by both staff and older students.

ᛞᚱᛞ

Having looked at some few acts of resistance on the part of these four writ-ers against cruel and abusive treatment, I turn now to instances of running away, a form of resistance found at all the boarding schools in every period. The subject of running away was raised for Tim Giago, as noted earlier, on his first day at school. Just a few pages after seeing Omaha, the boy who had fled HRMS with such dire consequences, he writes, "We were in our third-floor dormitory when 'Gabby' Brewer came up to us" (34). The boy asks whether his hair will grow out more quickly if he washes it every night. He is concerned because "the Jesuit prefects at Holy Rosary had ordered that his head be shaved to the skull" (34) as part of his punishment for having run away. The winter before, Giago explains, the boy's father and brother had drowned in a tragic fishing accident. After that, "Gabby became very quiet. He turned inward." He receives no help or consolation from those in authority: "There was no compassion, comforting or counseling by the priests, nuns, brothers, or prefects at Holy Rosary," and soon the boy runs off "for his home in Pine Ridge Village" (35). He is caught, returned to the school, "greeted upon his return with a razor strap and beaten until he had bruises on his legs and buttocks.... The next day he was taken to the barbershop and his head was shaved clean." This is not the end of Catholic charity. He is made to wear a sign "from morning until bedtime" on which was written, "'I am a runaway'" (35).

Although he knows what will be in store for him if he is caught, Giago, as a fourth grader, also attempts to run away. Along with a friend, he decides to make the attempt on a Friday in April. Unlike Gabby Brewer, who had sought to go only four miles to Pine Ridge Village, Giago hopes to make it 120 miles to Rapid City. "We made our getaway," he writes, "and for the first time in months we felt free" (55). Any freedom they may have felt does not last long. They meet a man on horseback coming toward them and, seeing that he is Lakota, "thought maybe he could help us." But he is the father of one of their friends at school, and he says he must take them back "for [their] own good" (56). We are not told whether the boys' heads were shaved, or whether they had to wear a sign identifying them as runaways, but they are beaten badly by none other than Father Edwards and the "leather whip he called 'The Cat'" (56).

Some years later, after learning that two boys from the school have escaped successfully, Giago runs away once more. It is now 1951, he is "in the eleventh grade, a much older and wiser guy" than on his last attempt, and, with his "anger at the school, the system and the priests [having] reached a boiling point" (128), he makes off on a Sunday night. He is now headed for Pine Ridge Village and the home of Glen Three Stars, once an outstanding athlete at OCHS, Walter Littlemoon's school, who "had become a fac-simile of the Underground Railroad for escaped students from HRMS" (129).[28]

Three Stars would indeed hide him until they could raise the price of bus fare to Rapid City. That trip completes his own "successful escape," which, as Giago soon finds out, leads to his being "expelled forever from Holy Rosary Mission" (129). He feels enormous "relief ... that [he] would never have to go back to that school again," nor has he "once in [his] life ever regretted running away from the Mission school." We are not told of his parents' reaction to what he had done; like the escaped slave, however, he sees his running away "as a new beginning" (129). A "year later," Giago writes, he "was in the United States Navy and traveling the world" (129). "After the military [he] went to college under the GI Bill" (130) and eventu-ally settled on journalism as a profession. He does not discuss in detail how he healed himself of the trauma of Catholic boarding school, although, as we will see, an engagement with Lakota history and culture was involved.

Lydia Whirlwind Soldier did not run away from Saint Francis Mission School. As she writes, if she "had decided to run, [she] didn't know which direction to go," and recalling "the long hours of driving it took [her] grand-father to come to St. Francis" (188), she knew she would have a great distance to cover in order to reach home. Like others earlier, she too had been warned that if she "ran away [she] would get lost in the canyons and would be eaten by the bobcats." She also had heard of "a boy who ran away at Christmas time during a winter storm." Nothing was heard of him "until the follow-ing spring," when his skeleton was "identified by a bag of marbles clutched in his hand" (188). Moreover, Whirlwind Soldier's father had warned her against running away, wanting her to remain and develop "the courage to face difficult things in [her] life." He had made clear that if she did manage to reach home, he would take her back (188).[29] Whirlwind Soldier reports the fate of runaways who "were caught [and] brought back" (187), and what she describes is perhaps even worse than what Tim Giago had reported.

"Their hair was cut with scissors," she writes, "snipped here and there, chopped at different lengths in spiky disorder." These would seem to be the girls. "Then "they were dressed in rummage clothes ... misshapen black crepe dresses, or dresses splashed with bright flowers, large and ugly, faded woolen sweaters shrunk with hot water and stretched out of shape, mismatched socks and high-heeled shoes. The runaways' faces were painted with exaggerated black eyebrows, and bright red lips and rouge on their cheeks. Signs hung around their necks that simply read, 'I ran away'" (187).

This, of course, is to equate the sin of running away with the sin of female immodesty and to dissuade the girls from the latter as well as to punish them for the former. Because this "was done to humiliate them, and to discourage the rest of us from running away," the offenders "were put on display: they stood in the halls as we marched through to the dining room, and we were told to look at them. They stood against the wall of the dining room eating so that they could be seen. They had been locked in the attic for several days before they were brought down for viewing" (187–88).

Although she did not run away, Whirlwind Soldier did resist, most particularly when, at the age of eleven, she became friends with a girl named May, whom "the nuns didn't like ... because she was not one of the willing flock and did not appear weak" (189). After May strikes one of the nuns and is badly beaten in return, Whirlwind Soldier recalls that she "felt like screaming, 'I hate this place, I hate everything about this place'" (191). As it happens, that very year turns out to be her last at SFMS. This is because her parents, having divorced, are "excommunicated," and she is expelled from "St. Francis in disgrace" (195). She will go to several other schools—eighth grade in a public school in California, then "a wonderful year" (196) at Rosebud boarding school in Mission, and time at the Flandreau Indian School, from which she graduates (201). Although each of these schools was far superior to Saint Francis, nonetheless, she writes, she "experienced institutional racism in every school [she] attended" (201).

Walter Littlemoon ran away several times, and, "after a few escape attempts,"—he does not specify how many—the tribal police kept him "in jail at night for a week" (50). The last time he runs away is in winter, a dangerous time in South Dakota. His "shoes kept falling off because they were too big," yet he continues for sixteen miles until he reaches home. His "feet had become so swollen [he] couldn't walk," but his mother and his brothers care for him (51). "Three or four days" later "the tribal police came to take [him] back," and, he writes, his mother, with a "firmness" in her voice and in "a tone filled with power," says simply, "'No, you will not'" (51). Is it that his injuries after this attempt at flight are much more serious than after other runaway attempts? She seems not to have resisted his being returned on prior occasions.

Littlemoon now goes to board at the Holy Rosary Mission School, the school Tim Giago had attended. The "atmosphere there," he writes, "was no

different" (52). "For a year," he says, he "struggled within its oppressive confines," already living "day by day in a thick dark fog, governed by stern men
in long black robes" (55). He does not describe what took place within the
"oppressive confines" of HRMS as he had at OCHS. Then finally, "whether
through a change in laws or circumstances"—the relevant laws had not
changed—his mother got him in "to the community school, run by the
state of South Dakota—just yards from [their] home" (55). As I have said,
I believe he could have gone there earlier. In any case, after two years at the
public school he "graduated from eighth grade and quit" (55).

In 1959 he traveled to San Francisco "to attend a vocational training program in cabinetmaking" (56) offered by the BIA, and, he writes, he
"finished the courses in 1961 just in time to join a declining job market
for cabinetmakers" (60). Reluctant to return home, he enlists in the army,
"unaware of the mental and emotional baggage [he] was carrying with [him]
from boarding school" (61). He begins drinking but manages nonetheless to
function at a high level. During the Cuban Missile Crisis of 1962 he is at
a base "on Red Alert" (66) and is later sent on various assignments for the
army. He volunteers for Viet Nam (67), and is honorably discharged in 1965,
when he returns home with "no self-confidence," and feeling "like a stranger
within [his] community" (68). It is at this point that his drinking becomes
worse, and as noted, he writes: "All together, I drank for thirteen years" (68).

During that time he lived through the AIM occupation of Wounded
Knee, an event he describes in detail (71–78) and one he found devastating
to the local Indian community. As he approaches the age of sixty, "there came
a turning point" (80), one that involves thoughts of the older Lakota people
he had known and a keen awareness of their values. That is when memories of what he had suffered begin "to come up to the surface" (80). Soon "a
breakthrough in [his] understanding came when [he] sought counsel … at
the Victims of Violence program, in Boston, Massachusetts," (86) where he
receives the name for his condition, complex post-traumatic stress disorder,
a name, as noted, that helped him considerably. Aided by the insights of the
mental health professionals, he more fully and more consciously re-engages
with Lakota culture and continues to heal.

Mary Crow Dog's escape from Saint Francis came about, as we have
seen, through an act of physical resistance. Although she described no
attempt on her part to run away, she does report her older sister Barb's
attempt to run off "during [Crow Dog's] first year or two" (33). Barb, then a
seventh grader, makes the attempt "early in the morning before sunrise" with

five other girls (33). It is winter, and when the girls are brought back in the evening, "hungry and cold, frozen through," they are made to wait two hours "in front of the mother superior's office." Asked if they would make any further attempts to run off—their response is not reported—they are told, first, that as punishment for what they had done they would not be allowed to visit home for a month, and then that they would be kept for a long period on work detail. Finally, they are made to bend over, lift their skirts, and pull down their underpants. Crow Dog observes sharply that these are "not little girls either, but teenagers" (33). She does not speculate as to whether there is a measure of eroticism mixed in with the sadism soon to be displayed as one of the nuns uses "a leather strap about a foot long and four inches wide fastened to a stick" (33) to beat each of the girls, singling out one in particular whom she assaults "until her arm got tired" (33).

ㅇㅇ

The traumas all four of these boarding-school students suffered affected their lives for many years after they had left boarding school. Walter Littlemoon and Lydia Whirlwind Soldier are the fullest and most eloquent in describing their healing, with Whirlwind Soldier offering as well something of the pedagogical critique of the schools that Zitkala-Sa did not even attempt. Important to all of them was the ability, as Tim Giago had also said (12), to bring back the memories of what they had endured, to achieve a reconnection to the culture the schools had assaulted, and thus to recuperate and reassert their identity as Indian people in community with others.

We can construct aspects of Tim Giago's healing process from bits and pieces he offers at various points in his book. In his introduction, for example, he writes: "In a traditional Lakota ceremony held many years ago, after I returned from Korea, I was given the name Nanwica Kciji by Enos Poor Bear and Grover Horned Antelope. The name means, "Stands Up for Them," and it is a name I carry with great pride since it was given to me long before I became a journalist" (12). This was not, of course, a name that he had lost at boarding school; rather, the new name is an honor name, and it means that in answer to the Lakota question, "In what manner do they say of you?" (E. Deloria 154) he can now answer, "Stands Up for Them."

Much later in the book, reflecting on the ethnocidal assaults of the school, he raises the question, "*If we were not Indian, what were we?*" (138, italics in original). As he becomes increasingly able to affirm that he and his classmates were and are indeed Indian, he recognizes that being Indian means being part of a family and a community. Less than a page after raising the question I have quoted, Giago reestablishes his own Indian family, describing how he reunited with the two daughters he had lost touch with as a consequence of an early divorce. After an appearance on national television, he writes, he received a phone call, and when he answers the phone, "The voice on the line said, 'My name is Theresa and I am your daughter'" (139). He also reunites with his other daughter Denise, who, he writes, "immediately identified with her Indian side" (139). (Their mother was not Native.)

In addition to family, he looks to Lakota people whom he knows only from history as well as to some he knew personally. Thus, at a gathering in March 2005 at the Holy Rosary Mission School, now called Red Cloud Indian School, he meets Lydia Whirlwind Soldier, a number of priests, and Robert Brave Heart, "the first Lakota ever to serve as superintendent at the school" (167). The seventy-one-year-old Tim Giago recalls that Robert Brave Heart's "father, Basil, was a classmate of [his] at the Mission School" (167). Giago writes: "If the school is willing to put away its denial and admit to its past wrongdoing," then "in the spirit of Red Cloud, Sitting Bull, Crazy Horse, Little Wound, Bull Bear, Young Man Afraid of his Horses, American Horse, Gall and all the other courageous and wise chiefs of the Great Sioux Nation, I ceremoniously bury the hatchet of contention between Holy Rosary Mission and myself" (160). Along with these eminent world-historical Lakotas whose names flood Giago's memory, the recollection of his former classmate, Basil Brave Heart, brings to mind the names of other contemporaries: "Sague (Walking Stick) [who] died a couple of years ago of throat cancer. His real name was G. Wayne Tapio," and "Charles Trimble, known as 'Wobbie', ... [his] classmate and friend ... P-2 [who] was really Aloysius Black Tail Deer, ... Buck Jones ...[and] Tiny Tim [who] was really Leo Wounded Foot" (181–82). Just as Lydia Whirlwind Soldier had, he too thinks of those who did not recover from what they had suffered at Holy Rosary Mission. He again names "Magpie, Melvin White Magpie, [who] died in prison," and recalls the boy he saw on the day of his arrival at the school, "Omaha, Louis Pretty Boy." He "was roaming the streets of Pine Ridge bumming money for alcohol the last time I saw him. He died about six years ago" (182).[30] And there are others, some of whom, like Giago himself, have managed well.

"As an adult," Lydia Whirlwind Soldier writes, "decades after I left St. Francis Mission School, I struggled through seasonal bouts of depression.

Every fall a subtle change came over me.... I felt a kind of numbness. As days went by those colors resurrected sadness, anger, and despair" (206). It is a bitter achievement of the Catholic school to have "resurrected" not hope but "despair." "Eventually," she writes, "I began to go into deep grieving purges, but my losses were so devastating and so pervasive that I didn't know where my mourning began and where it ended" (208). The title of Whirlwind Soldier's text is "Memories," and she makes explicit just why "memories" are so important: "I knew I could not heal without inviting those boarding school memories that I had totally ignored" (208) or, as one might say, dissociatively forgotten. While the forgetting was once a useful adaptive mechanism, now she must remember.

Whirlwind Soldier also pursued political activism on behalf of Indian people and, like Mary Crow Dog, participated in the occupation of Wounded Knee by AIM. (Littlemoon and Giago were critical of this action.) This was important to her, but "there were still the recurring nightmares" of boarding-school horrors, like "suffocating in a locked storage closet, of shouting voices that rang in [her] ears, and of evil spirits dressed in black habits waiting and searching for [her]" (209). Now a married woman with children of her own, she writes that at "thirty years old ... the imprinted memories still remained.... In order to heal, [she] had to validate the trauma [she] had suffered in the boarding schools" (209). An important part of that validation involves cultural reclamation. "At last," she writes, "the profound teachings of the Lakota came back to me. Being Lakota was not a temporary illusion" (210). Nor is it something that has been "killed," despite the massively destructive assault on "being Lakota" she had experienced at SFMS. Her account of cultural recuperation as a major step in healing is the fullest of any of these four boarding-school autobiographers' narratives, far more detailed and richly nuanced than my bare summary can convey.

Whirlwind Soldier writes: "I know the healing began with the trees. The rustling trees of Grass Mountain whispered to me. They drew me into their embrace, pulled at my heart, and rescued me" (210–11). Yielding to the embrace of the trees of Grass Mountain, Lydia Whirlwind Soldier "tied prayer ties into an old, old Rosebud pine, and the trees became my prayer partners again, and I began to make my peace." She "cut [her] hair in the ritual of the Lakota grieving process," and began to participate in Lakota ceremonies, entering the sweat lodge, and attending a Sun Dance, during which she "touched the Sundance tree" (211). Just as Walter Littlemoon had described his sense of living in a "thick dark fog," Whirlwind Soldier recognizes that "anger had been like ... [a] mist, cloudy and unclear around [her] soul." As she "worked through this anger, [she] began to enjoy long walks with [her] own children" (212)—who, through her efforts in conjunction with others, will now have "Lakota culture and language taught in the school" (213). All of this, she concludes, is part of a story that "will never be forgotten, it will be recorded, it will be told by my children to their children and passed on to the coming generations and it will become part of our oral tradition" (214), not less an "oral tradition" because it has been preserved in writing.

Walter Littlemoon's healing also began "with the trees" or, rather, with one ancient tree in particular. Early in his narrative, he had described seeing a hawk resting on an enormous tree, "Its girth ... wider than three men can reach around." One morning, he says—it is not clear just when this took place—"the Tree began again to speak to me in the old way known to the Lakota. Its words came through as strong, heartfelt feelings," and, he says, he has since "repeatedly sought its counsel" (20). Later in his story he returns to this moment. It is after the 1973 AIM occupation of Wounded Knee, a time, he writes, when "everything lay in ruins" (79). One morning "there came a turning point. I hiked up the dirt trail to my father's homestead at Mouse Creek." He is "looking for something with a little meaning that [he] could hold on to and get strength from." He sits in "the shade of the cottonwood for a long time"—this is the enormous tree that had addressed him earlier—and it speaks to him again: "Out of nowhere, [he] seemed to hear the word 'remember,'" and he wonders "where it had come from." "My eyes were drawn to that immense tree and I felt a glimmer of hope" (80), he writes. Littlemoon puts in quotation marks what next he "heard":

"Remembering is a basic ingredient for living."

"Remember to act these lessons out, and you will always have room in your mind for something new."

"All these things are part of being Lakota" (80).

The first of these dicta he will find reinforced by the professionals at the Victims of Violence program in Boston, with whose help he worked to overcome what they named as his condition, complex post-traumatic stress disorder.

Littlemoon takes a further step toward reclaiming his cultural heritage as "slowly memories from [his] childhood began to come up to the surface." "Voices of the elderly Lakota" he had known "began to return to [him] in fragmented bits and pieces." They are a rich and varied group of people, and like Tim Giago he remembers their names. First, he "saw Good Lance appear … his hair neatly held in two thick braids" (80–81). "Then came Left-Handed Jimmy, the storyteller," and as "Jimmy's image faded, Tall Charlie Shot-to-Pieces appeared riding his horse.… Next there was Lincoln Looking Horse in his long black coat that nearly touched the ground," and finally "Tall Jenny with her big pack on her back" (81). He does not know "how long [he] sat there hearing and seeing those people who had colored [his] childhood summers with their distinctive personalities and their loving ways" (81), but their vivid recall—his ability to integrate memories of them to restructure his Indian identity—constitutes an important step in his healing.

Mary Crow Dog, as mentioned, also participated in the Sun Dance: "The Sun Dance at Rosebud in the late summer of 1972 [when she was just eighteen] will forever remain in my memory" (82), she writes. She also was involved with the Native American Church. She recalls having been taken to her first peyote meeting by "Grandpa Fool Bull" (95) and remembers the peyote tasting like earth. In consuming it, she feels that "the earth was in me and I in it. Indian earth making me more Indian. And to me Peyote was people, was alive, was a remembrance of things long forgotten" (96).

Crow Dog married Leonard Crow Dog, a Peyote Church (Native American Church) "road man. He is showing the people the road of life" (98); having managed not to attend government or Catholic schools, he could not read or write. As I have said, Mary participated in the occupation of Wounded Knee in 1973, where, she writes, "Crow Dog was the spiritual leader" (129). In *Ohitika Woman*, published three years after her *Lakota Woman*, she describes running away from Leonard Crow Dog—"Illiteracy will get us nowhere" (Brave Bird 1993 268)—and acknowledges that she was drinking when her first book came out (133). I would not presume to gauge the degree to which, in the twenty more years she lived, she did or did not heal from the abuse inflicted on her at boarding school. It is clear, however, that despite all they had suffered at boarding school, Mary Crow Dog, Lydia Whirlwind Soldier, Tim Giago, and Walter Littlemoon not only preserved but strengthened their sense of Indian identity.

Part II

Ojibwe Boarding-School Autobiographies

5

John Rogers's
Red World and White

JOHN ROGERS, OR WAYQUAHGISHIG—"DAWN OF DAY," AS HE WOULD TRANS-
late his name (8)[1]—was born in 1890 and died some time "between 1959
and 1972" (Meyer iv). Not only the exact date of his death but much else is
not known about Rogers. He originally self-published his autobiography as
A Chippewa Speaks, in Hollywood, California, in 1957 with the author listed
as "Chief Snow Cloud (John Rogers)." That first edition had an attractive
hardcover binding, with the title in gold lettering and endpapers marked
with what I take to be Anishinaabe decorative figures.[2] Snow Cloud, readers
learn, was the name of Rogers's uncle, but Uncle Snow Cloud is not represented as a chief, nor does Rogers himself seem to have held a leadership
position among his people;[3] it is likely that he calls himself a chief to appeal
to a white audience. Consistent with this appeal is the illustration of him
in a feathered war bonnet on the title page of the first edition, with another
photograph of him in this headdress serving as a frontispiece to the book.
The first edition contained a brief foreword by Eric Heath, an illustrator and
cartoonist from New Zealand, who also did the illustrations for the book.
Rogers dedicated it to his "loving wife, [his] father, his relatives, and friends."

Just who that wife was, however, is also unclear. "In 1973," Melissa
Meyer writes, Rogers's "widow Edwardina assigned the copyright [for the
1957 original] to the University of Oklahoma Press, which reissued the
book in 1974 under a new title, *Red World and White*" (Meyer iv). Edwardina
could have been with Rogers when he first published the book in 1957, and
it may well be dedicated to her, although the couple did not marry until
1959 (Meyer iv), two years after the book and its dedication appeared. The

Oklahoma edition removed the illustrations and the other photographs from the original edition and added a subtitle, *Memories of a Chippewa Boyhood.* Because the type was reset, the pagination differs from that in the original publication. A second edition published in 1996 retains the pagination of the 1974 edition.

∞

Although Rogers does not begin with the date or place of his birth, he was born, as I have said, in 1890 in Bagley, Minnesota, on the White Earth reservation.[4] The book begins: "I, Way Quah Gishig, was six years old when my two sisters, Bishiu and Min di, accompanied me to Flandreau, South Dakota to attend an Indian boarding school" (3). Flandreau is almost three hundred miles away, and he doesn't explain why he and his sisters did not attend a school nearer to them—as they will do later. He writes that school was difficult for him at first because, as was usually the case at the boarding schools, "students were not allowed to speak the language of the Indians," and he "understood nothing else." Addressing some of the *topoi* and *loci* of the schools, he notes that because he was so young he was "forced to remain with [his] sisters in the girls' building," rather than in a boys' dormitory, something that does not please him. Soon, however, he "learned to speak and understand a little of the white man's language; and gradually the boys began coaxing [him] to play with them." He has come to school with his "hair in two braids, Indian fashion," and, "at last [his] sisters gave in and allowed it to be cut"—this implies that the choice was theirs—"so that [he] would be like the other boys" (3). He does not register his response to having his braids cut, and just as one eagerly anticipates further narration of his experiences at the Flandreau School, he writes, "My many happy years at the school have no place in this volume, so I will begin at the time Min di, Bishiu, and I took the train to return home" (3). If he arrived at age six and spent six years at Flandreau, his time there would have been 1896–1902.[5] But there are indeed no further details of what the boy experienced at the Flandreau boarding school before leaving as a youth of twelve.

The children return home to their mother, and we soon find out that she and their father have separated. Unfortunately, as a result of his "many happy years" (3) at school, the young man can no longer understand or speak his Native language. Although he has given no account of his renaming, he writes that at "school [he] was known as John." It's not clear what new names the other children might have received, but it is mother's wish that all three of her returned children use their Indian names at home. Mother has a new baby and Wayquahgishig learns for "the first time" that he has another "brother and sister who were away at school in Morris, Minnesota" (10). Their mother tells the children stories, and instructs the boy in various necessary skills, taking him for his "first ride in a boat made of birch bark" (9), and for a visit to the grandmother he has not seen during the years he has been away.

He soon meets a young man named Wagoosh, a would-be suitor of his sister Mindi, who extends an invitation for their mother to attend "the church of the white man, for a prayer meeting" (12)—the mother seems to be nominally Episcopalian—but he also invites them to a "squaw dance" (13). In the summer Wayquahgishig's brother and sister return from school, and, as had happened to him, "Neither could talk Indian" (15). Although he has now regained his own language skills, and is no longer called "John," it would seem that he is still wearing his school clothes—or perhaps he has merely brought them out to show—for he says he and his brother, a boy of ten, admired "each other's coats ... and found them very much alike, both having breast buttons and buttoned right up to the neck" (15). The rest of his brother's "costume"—his brother's name is Oshkin—"was a lot like [Rogers's] too—blue-gray short trousers, high shoes and black stockings" (15). His sister, about his age, is also wearing a school uniform, "a jumper skirt of blue, high shoes, and black stockings" (15). Chapter 4 presents an important Anishinaabe activity that takes place in late summer or early fall: gathering rice, something Rogers calls "very interesting work" (25). Then after a long winter, it is time to collect maple sap to make sugar. Following the seasons, Rogers tells us that it is in summer when mother's baby, Ahmeek, becomes very ill. This serves as an occasion to return to the subject of the white man's religion, which had earlier come up only briefly.

Rogers writes that he "had gone to the church of the white man" (45)—this would have been mandatory during his six years at the Flandreau School—where he "had learned much that was different from his mother's belief"—although his mother seems also to attend church—and "it was all very confusing" (45). He will resolve this confusion only near the end of the book. Mother gathers "healing herbs so that [the baby] might get well," and he is told to remember where medicinal roots are, in case he has to gather more.[6] The natural medicines do not help, leading mother to send for Raven Feather, "the Indian who had been taught the ways of the white man and was now a preacher to the Chippewas" (47). The man attends the baby—the degree to which his practice remains traditional or is that of the white man is not clear—but cannot cure him. The following day Raven Feather returns to lead "a prayer meeting" and Rogers says, "the Indians ... gathered for the last rites" (48), singing hymns and visiting until dawn. He means the phrase "last rites" only generally, in that Episcopalians—as the family seems to be—do not offer "last rites" as a sacrament. One of the hymns sung is "Lead Kindly Light," which Rogers prints "in [the] Chippewa tongue" (48).

In the next several chapters Rogers provides, in effect, a participant-observer's ethnographic account of his people's lifeways and a chronicle of family events that includes the death of a younger sister. Chapter 8 begins, "As we had missed school during the year, the authorities looked us up and sent Indian policemen to see that we didn't stay out another year. We had the choice of two schools: White Earth or Beaulieu" (68). It was not made clear why the children had gone to Flandreau, but now they will attend the boarding school at White Earth, "about thirty-five miles from home" (68). Rogers notes that one of the boys going to White Earth is "Joe Bush, who lived across the lake" (69), and because he "had attended the previous year," he "knew all the boys," in particular two bullies Rogers's age, about whom Bush warns him.

Rogers does indeed encounter and then defeat these two shortly after his arrival at school, and the battles are described in detail. One learns, for example, that in boarding-school fights about 1903 the boys actually put bark chips on the shoulders of those they mean to fight, which they then knock off. In passing, we are told that the students wear uniforms (69) and go to school for half a day and work half a day (71), the usual situation at the Indian boarding schools. Thanksgiving is celebrated, and after Rogers and his sister go home for Christmas, feeling badly about their "home being broken up, because the other children kept telling [them] what their fathers had done for them" (72). He says that because he was so young when he first went off to school, he doesn't "remember ever having seen" his father (72–73), who will later play an important part in his life. Rogers says that he is fifteen years old, which makes the year 1905.

With his "return to the classroom" Rogers introduces a theme that will run through the book: the difference between nature, the Indians' chief source of knowledge, and books, the source of the white man's. Learning "much that never would have been taught to [him] by continuing the ways of [his] Indian people," Rogers at this point in his life is gaining "knowledge ... from books supplied by the white man, not from Nature, which many of the Chippewas still thought was the best teacher" (73). Repeating the upper case N for Nature, Rogers states that he "knew then" as he has known since, that book-learning would never separate him from "loving the things of Nature," and that "Always would [he]"—the inversion is quite bookish—"long for the lakes and rivers and the hills" (74). Now, however, he will do "as the white man said, and ... not rebel." School goes on "as usual"; the students do their "drilling and he became accustomed to the bugle calls" (74), the school being run, it would seem, on the usual military model of the off-reservation boarding-schools. Nor does he "rebel": he mentions no act of resistance on his part, or on the part of anyone else; and there is no word of runaways.

Almost immediately upon returning home for the summer, Rogers informs readers that next "year we had to go to school in Beaulieu" (76). This is his mother's choice, because Beaulieu "was much nearer to our home, and so it was possible for Mother to come and visit us throughout the holidays." Many others "who had been going to school at White Earth changed with us to Beaulieu" (76), including his friend, Joe Bush. Little is said of either the routine or the education at Beaulieu, as Rogers instead describes the work duty he and Joe Bush were assigned. As "good students," he writes, "we had nice jobs" (77). He also joins the "wonderful baseball team," which has an unbeaten spring season (78).

When next he is home for the summer—school years pass quickly in his account—Rogers reports his mother receiving a letter "from a well-to-do white man" who also knew his father. Mother does not read English, and it is sister Mindi who reads the letter to her. The letter announces this man's desire to adopt Wayquahgishig and "send [him] to college and give [him] all the advantages of the white boys" (82). The man is not named, and who he is or why he would want to do this is not explained. The boy refuses the offer because he understands that accepting it would sadden his mother.

The family moves into a new home and "all too soon ... it was school time again" (83). For reasons not given, the unnamed white man, now along with his wife, "all through school ... continued to send [him] gifts" (82). Although he "had learned to love the primitive [!] life which had for many generations influenced and shaped the existence of [his] ancestors," Wayquahgishig will once more "return to the life that the white man had chosen for the Indian to follow." He will "read from books instead of from Nature" (83). "This," he writes, "was what the white man said [he] should do, and [he] could do nothing but obey" (84). It would be some time before he changed course.

Rogers has new and important jobs at Beaulieu, one of which is "drilling the boys." Learning there "was a good baseball team," he once more engages in the sport and he also plays football. In one of the football games, he writes, "he was severely hurt; that is, [his] shoulder was injured." Far worse, however, is "a sickness that did not come altogether from [his] shoulder." The "matron there at the school was always very good and kind to me" (86–87), Rogers writes, but his condition worsens, to the point where the school doctor says he "would die" (86). Wayquahgishig prays "to the Great Spirit, which [he] felt would understand better than would the God of the white man," and his prayers seem to be answered when his mother suddenly arrives to take him home in a sleigh. His sister Mindi had been attending him at school, and with his mother, "picked up the mattress with [him] on it and carried [him] down to the waiting sleigh." He says he remembered nothing until waking up "in the home of Wah cha ni, the medicine man" (88). There, with sweats and herbs and prayers, the young man is cured and able to return to his mother's home (89).

Once recovered, he is soon back at school, where he "was welcomed with open arms by the children and teachers alike," and quickly "caught up to the others in [his] studies" (90). But before his studies or his relations with the welcoming students and teachers can be discussed further, Wayquahgishig receives an unexpected visit from his father. Rogers writes that his "father's joy was great" upon seeing his children, and observes that his father is a very handsome man (91), but he says nothing about his own feelings upon suddenly meeting this man whom he had said he did not remember. They talk in their own language, and his father—we are not told his name at this point in the narrative—writes down his home address; obviously he is literate. The young man sees that his father's address is near that of the "people who for so long had wanted to adopt [him]" (91), but there is still no information provided as to what the connection between the white couple and his father might be. The children are told not to tell their mother about his visit, and then their father leaves.

Although no unpleasantness of any kind has been described at the school—nor, to be sure, any lessons, any meals, any friendships, any further sports or drilling, among many other matters—Rogers announces that his "heart sang with joy as the end of the school year drew near" (92), for he longs for nature and "the ways of the Indian" (92). Whether he knows it or not, he has now completed his formal education. Arriving home, he learns that his sister Mindi has married not Wagoosh but "John Chompson [sic] (Chaney), a half-blood"

(93), who seems a fine fellow. In chapter 11 we learn that instead of returning to school in the fall, the young man "got [his] first job. Ten dollars a month and room and board ... on a farm" (99). A few paragraphs later news arrives of the sudden death of his sister Bishiu, whom he "had loved very deeply." "We had been inseparable all these years" (100), Rogers writes. The family had been out ricing and they believed the girl may have eaten a poisonous root or plant, which quickly led to her death. He learns that she was buried on the island where they had camped, with his uncle Snow Cloud conducting the burial in a traditional manner (100).

Shortly before Christmas, Snow Cloud, who has lost his wife, comes to spend the winter with the family. When spring arrives and he prepares to return home, he asks if Rogers would like to come and live with him. The invitation pleases him greatly, and after a time of preparation, the two depart. On the way Rogers asks his uncle to take him to the place where his sister is buried (102). He does this, and the visit to his sister's grave is both moving and restorative (103). The young man knows "that Bishiu would always be by [his] side until [he] joined her in the spirit world" (104). A vision of Bishiu will conclude the narrative.

Not long after Rogers is established at his uncle's, a "trapping, hunting, and fishing" trip is projected with some friends (105). Before the party sets off, however, an unknown white man appears, and, Rogers writes, he "became frightened. Perhaps it was because of a guilty conscience that I was not in school where I belonged. Maybe this white man had come to take me back!" (108). This moves him to offer some strong opinions about his current commitment to "nature" rather than to "books." As if to re-assure himself that he need not have a "guilty conscience" about leaving school, he writes: "Nothing the white man could teach me, would take the place of what I was learning from the forest, the lakes, and the river. I could read more in the swaying of the trees ... than I could read in any books they had at school" (108). The man, however, has nothing to do with school; he is a watchman for a nearby lumber camp, his occupation leading Rogers to the disturbing thought that the loggers would soon be destroying "these beautiful trees that the Indian loved so much" (111).[7]

Life with uncle Snow Cloud provides abundant opportunities to learn traditional skills as well as to hear many stories, among them one about "Nana bush," identified as "a superman of the Chippewas" (113).[8] Rogers himself narrates a story that begins, "There was a little girl called Red Riding Hood" (124). The story pleases its audience, his school years proving useful on at least this occasion. Rogers continues to benefit from his uncle's "guidance," and he finds himself gaining "experience that [he] might not otherwise have acquired. Gradually [he] was departing from the way of the white man and reverting again more and more to the habits and customs of [his] people" (127–28). This reversion will soon develop further.

Rogers meets an Indian man named Fairweather who asks whether he has any relatives around Cass Lake. He wonders, he says, because "there is a man there who looks just like you" (131). Informing Fairweather that his name is "Way quah gisgig," he asks whether the man he is thinking of is called "Pin de gay gisgig" (132),[9] and is told that this is indeed the man's name, and he is a supervisor at a logging camp. The concern Rogers has expressed about the destructive activities of commercial loggers does not recur upon his learning that his father is also involved in this work. Happy as he has been living with his uncle, he is nonetheless responsive to Fairweather's suggestion that he go and work for his father, and Fairweather is willing to alert the father to his son's interest in joining him.

It is not long before a letter from Rogers's father arrives with money for train fare—which he immediately uses to buy groceries for his mother. It is not clear—as I have said, a great many things in the book are not clear—just when he had left his uncle or how long he has been back with his mother. When she asks where he got the grocery money, he lies, perhaps recalling that his father had told the children on his single visit to them at school not to mention him to their mother. The young man is reluctant to leave his mother, but nonetheless feels "Father had called me and I should go" (133). That is not exactly the case, but nonetheless he goes. Having spent the train fare, he imitates the behavior of white men he has seen and hitches a ride on a freight train. Before long he is with his father.

Father is a very interesting man. He clearly is successful, immediately purchasing "a complete outfit, from cap to shoes, and extra warm under-wear" for his bedraggled son; taking him "to the restaurant where [he] always eat[s]" (135); and driving a "beautiful team of horses" of which the young man is "proud" (136). He lives in a "two-story log building" (137), where Rogers meets his father's new wife and no fewer than five young chil-dren.[10] Inside, "a cylinder gramophone" (138) plays a song he can identify as "'Back to Mother's Knee'" (139).[11] But his father's full-blown modernity coexists with a deep and abiding traditionalism. "From the beginning," Rogers writes, "Father and I had many talks that had to do with the deeper things of life" (139).

Thus, only "a few days after" his son's arrival his father asked what church he attends. The young man answers that he has been "going to the Episcopal Church," but "only because he was told to go there," and he has "never been able to accept many of the teachings of this church or of any other church of the white man" (139). This pleases his father, who says, "Now that you are to live with me ... you can worship the Great Spirit with the rest of us" (140). That evening he brings out "a special kind of drum" (140); it will play an important part in the ceremony to which his father will soon introduce him. Rogers is also shown a birchbark chart "said to be fully six hundred years old" (142).[12] Among the "strange drawings" on the chart is "a symbol of the cross, and this seemed to resemble a man with his arms outstretched" (142). Rogers explains that the outstretched "arms denoted the act of embracing, to accept anything that the Great Spirit had put on earth" (142). But Rogers does not identify this symbol with Christ. This may well be because the Europeans and their God had not yet come to the Ojibwa six hundred years earlier, when this scroll is said to have been inscribed. Michael Angel makes the important point that the symbols do not have a fixed meaning: "The only way to know the correct interpretation was to be told by the person who owned the chart" (141). Thus if Rogers's father, the owner of the scroll, did not identify images of a cross as Christian, they would not properly be interpreted as Christian.

On the chart is "a figure that would be a steamboat," although, of course, as his father explains, this is something "the Indian could not know about until a steamboat appeared on one of the lakes and rivers" (143). The chart also predicts airplanes (143), and "a war between the white man and the Indians, for Bear Island, about the year 1893" (143).[13] Unfortunately, Rogers writes, this chart was "stolen and until this day it had not been recovered" (144), so any contemporary request to view it could not be honored. It is possible, however, that the loss of the chart had a far greater and more personal consequence, as I will consider in closing this discussion.

In early spring the family collects maple sap and boils it down to sugar; in midsummer, they collect a large supply of berries; and in early fall they go rice gathering on the lake (146). The book ends with a late fall Medicine Dance, near the shore of Cass Lake, of which "Father was to be the leader (Grand Medicine Man)" (147). This is a Midewiwin ceremony, and Rogers describes it in some detail.[14] Father is indeed in charge. He picks the spot where the ceremony is to be held and then oversees the construction of the Medicine Lodge. During the ceremony his father sends several participants "to the cross with this thought: 'Can you face the cross, believing it is a human being, with your arms outstretched to embrace the world?'" (150). There is again no reference here to Christ, nor is there on another occasion when participants "go to the cross" (151).

When the ceremony has been completed the family heads home, and the book ends with Rogers describing his strong sense of the presence of the Great Spirit and of a vision of his dead sister. "Never before," Rogers writes, "had I felt so near to my beloved Bishiu and the others who had passed on" (152). As he "passed [his] hand across [his] brow," and "looked over again the vision was gone" (153). These words are the last words of the book, and, so far as I can discover, they are the last words published by John Rogers.

Did he play a part in tribal affairs? When and why did he move from Cass Lake, Minnesota, to Hollywood, California, and then to Las Vegas, Nevada? What else did he do, over a long life, besides interior decorating to earn a living and playing golf for recreation? As for what part his boarding-school education played in what he did and did not do with his life, we know far too little about Wayquahgishig/John Rogers to say.

12   An Ojibwa chief outside a Medicine Lodge on the White Earth Reservation in Minnesota. Photo taken in 1910 by Robert Beaulieu of White Earth. Courtesy of the Minnesota Historical Society.

6

George Morrison's
Turning the Feather Around

GEORGE MORRISON (1919–2000), AN ENROLLED MEMBER OF THE GRAND
Portage (Lake Superior) Chippewa Tribe of eastern Minnesota, was an
important modernist artist. In the 1980s Morrison, who had "had problems
with health most of [his] life," wrote that he had a curing ceremony performed by Walter Caribou, a cousin, and "an elder who believes very strongly
in the spiritual side of the Indian psyche" (17). It was at this time that Caribou
"sang and chanted and gave [Morrison] two Indian names—Standing in
the Northern Lights, translated from the Chippewa Wa-wah-ta-ga-nah-
gah-boo, and Turning the Feather Around, Gwe-ki-ge-nah-gah-boo" (17).
These were two names that Caribou "dreamed, one dream, two names" (18),
engaging in traditional Anishinaabe naming practice—although for an adult
in this instance, not a child. Morrison used the second of these names as
the title for an autobiographical text subtitled *My Life in Art*, "as told to"
Margot Fortunato Galt.[1]

George Morrison's "life in art" was importantly influenced by his studies in the 1940s at the Art Students League on West 57th Street in New
York City, which he attended on scholarship while living in Greenwich
Village. In the Village, at the Cedar Street Tavern on University Place, he
would have lively discussions with Franz Kline, "Jack" (Jackson) Pollock, and
"Bill" (Willem) de Kooning (97), all of whom were working passionately on
their art. He would later live and work among the artists in Provincetown
on Cape Cod and study in Paris and Aix-en-Provence. He also taught art
at several institutions, Cornell University and the Rhode Island School of
Design among them, before returning to Minnesota to teach and work.

143

Always identified as Indian, he nonetheless found his work unwelcome at Native art shows until the 1980s, he says, because before that time "they wanted things related more to tribal art, Indian themes" (95), which were not overtly present in his work. Nor has his interesting autobiography received the attention it deserves.[2]

Born in Chippewa City, Minnesota,[3] just off the Grand Portage reservation, Morrison was the third of twelve children. His father had a fifth grade education and was completely bilingual; his mother could not write. She was fervently Catholic, Morrison says, while he considered himself only "tongue in cheek Catholic" because "We had certain Indian beliefs that were inherent" (29). His education began at a public school in nearby Grand Marais, and he would return to graduate from the public high school in Grand Marais in 1938. But in 1928, at the age of nine, he transferred to the Hayward Indian School, a boarding school in Wisconsin, which he attended for only two years. (The school closed in 1934.)

During the Depression Morrison's father got work through President Franklin Roosevelt's Works Progress Administration, but, Morrison says, he "could feel prejudice. A lot of people were down on Indians because ... the Indians were poor and more shabbily dressed ... A lot of us, of course, were darker in skin.... This is a racist country. People ... are prejudiced against anyone who is dark-skinned" (32). He says, "The Hayward, Wisconsin, Indian school helped people with big families. It was available to a lot of poorer families during the Depression" (37), as were several of the Indian boarding schools in that period. Morrison was not at the school long, and wrote little about it; nonetheless, I will note what he recalled about his experience there.

He says students stayed at the school for a full nine months, going home only for summer vacation. "Many of the kids probably spoke Indian," Morrison writes, and the "school did not repress it or stop it the way [he's] heard was done in some schools." He recalls that a "counselor in charge of the boys' dormitory was Indian" and that he "was strict but not mean." Similarly, he says, "I've heard stories of the teachers in certain schools being very cruel to Indians. But as I recall, the teachers at Hayward were fairly decent" (38). In his second year at Hayward he begins to have problems with his leg. The diagnosis is tuberculosis of the hip, currently referred to as tubercular arthritis. He is transferred to the Gillette Crippled Children's Hospital in St. Paul (today Gillette Children's Specialty Healthcare), where bed rest for six months is prescribed, after which he undergoes an operation, followed by eight months with both legs in casts (39). Morrison continues his education at the hospital during his long convalescence, no longer at an Indian boarding school. Sometimes, he says, the children had their beds wheeled to "the auditorium where [they] saw circus performers, movie stars, even the prizefighter Jack Dempsey." At the time, he "was eleven, doing a lot of reading" (40).

When he is able to walk again, he attends the public high school in Grand Marais, where the "principal was also [the] English teacher, a good one. She made us aware of literature as an art. We read Dickens, *Oliver Twist, David Copperfield*" (43). At age seventeen he "got into a CCC camp for Indians in Grand Portage" (46),[4] and in 1938, after he "graduated high school, [he] entered the Minneapolis School of Art" aided by "some loans from the Consolidated Chippewa Indian Agency and, along the way, some scholarships from the school" (47). He notes that the Second World War began while he was in art school, and that "a lot of men, some relatives from Grand Portage, ... got into the war" (56). But the condition of his legs made it impossible for him even to consider military service, and at that time many "of us art students were beginning to look to New York, the art capital of the world" (56). Upon his graduation "from the Minneapolis School of Art in 1943," he receives a scholarship that will allow him to go to New York and the Art Students League—and as mentioned go on to Provincetown, Paris, and a successful career as an artist. Before all this, for a short time George Morrison was a student at a government-run Indian boarding school.

7

Peter Razor's
While the Locust Slept

PETER RAZOR, A SHINNOB (ANISHINAABE) AND A "FONDJALACKER" (FROM Fond du Lac in Jim Northrup's parlance, like Northrup himself, as discussed later), was born in November 1928.[1] As was the case for Charles Eastman and George Morrison, Razor's education mostly did not take place at boarding schools for Indians. Very much unlike Charles Eastman and George Morrison, however, Razor did not attend such institutions as Beloit College and Dartmouth, or the Minneapolis School of Art, and the Art Students League. Rather, he spent seventeen years at the School for Dependent and Neglected Children in Owatonna, Minnesota, entering in April 1929 at the age of only seventeen months. Although his account of his time at Owatonna and at several different public high schools is different from those given by students of the government Indian schools, it is well worth considering. Razor's dedication of the book, "For all the children in the cemetery at the Owatonna State School and for all those who survived but in silence," is very much in keeping with this study's attention to those Native people who "spoke the breath of boarding school life."[2]

Although this is Razor's only published book—he has said in interviews that he had previously written poetry and nearly completed three historical novels—it is artfully constructed and vividly written.[3] Made up of twelve parts and an epilogue with each of the parts preceded by epigraphs of different kinds, the first part of the book references Razor's title invoking the locust that "*slept seventeen years in darkness before soaring into the summer light*" (4, italics in original).[4] At this early point, a reader might or might not understand this as a metaphor for Razor's experience: his seventeen years at

Owatonna and his emergence as an Ojibwe artisan and a writer. The image of the locust reappears in the epigraph to the final section of the book.

Serving as an epigraph to the book as a whole is an exchange quoted by Razor between a Miss Wittman, probably a social worker, and a judge in the juvenile division of the district court in Ramsey County, Minnesota. It provides the information that in October 1929 Razor had been in a foster home since he was eleven months old and was now to be remanded to Owatonna. In April 1930 now seventeen months old and classified as a dependent child, he became a ward of the state. This had come about because his mother had been sent to an "asylum," and his father had abandoned him and his siblings when he was only ten months old (6).

Ideally, the Owatonna school would find adoptive parents for the children as soon as possible.[5] But as children grew older without having been adopted,[6] they were "placed-out" on indenture contracts with families that had presumably been vetted for fitness, and Razor begins his book in September 1944, when he is sent from the home on an indenture contract to the farm of John and Emma Schaul. He is to work for them and attend the local public high school, much like Carlisle's students on "outing" assignments. Razor believes that the fact he had run away two years earlier and been "gone over a week" (9)—he does not provide details for this attempt to run away—"set the stage to hand [him] over to farmers" (9).[7] He writes, that having been an "institutional state ward for fifteen years, [he] would now be a farm-indentured state ward. The state would not be responsible any more for [his] room, board, or clothing. Now they would only pay for major medical expenses or burial costs" (9).

He later learned that the institution's psychologist, Dr. Yager, had opposed the farm placement. He had written that Razor "*communicates intelligently, scores very high in science, art and mechanical intricacies*" (35), and that while he was only "*average in math,*" he was nonetheless, "*creative in areas that are difficult to assess*" (35–36). The doctor's recommendation was: "*No farm placement for this boy. It will end in failure and be just another unfortunate experience for him*" (36, italics in original). The doctor's advice is ignored. Razor is "uneasy" (5) on first meeting John Schaul, and the man will turn out to be a vicious, drunken brute who beats both his wife and the boy. Razor will nonetheless live with them for several years.

He tells us of the school that the children live in cottages, "numbered one to sixteen," some for boys and some for girls, who "transferred, as they grew, to cottages for older children" (7). There they are overseen by full-time matrons "called *house mothers*," who, while "on duty, . . . ate with the children and slept in small private rooms" (7, italics in original). During the time Razor lived at C-15—Cottage 15—the woman in charge was Miss Monson. "She was absent only once in five years," he writes, "but her diligence wasn't for love of the boys. Miss Monson's passion was punishment" (40). She beats her charges, to the point that Razor "was gripped by a secret fear that one day Miss Monson would cripple or kill me" (41). It is not long before she does indeed cripple him. Nor is she the only staff member who is brutal to the point of criminality. There are, for example, those Razor had earlier named as the "first four terrors of [his] childhood—Miss Monson, the two Krugers"—a house matron and her husband—"and Mr. Beaty" (22), the gardener. Mr. Beaty's attacks on the boy occur partly out of the man's prejudice against Indians—most of the children are German or Scandinavian with some Indians and some African Americans—and he takes particular pleasure in tormenting Razor, another Indian boy, and a black boy, as we will see further.[8]

In the epigraph to part 2 of the book Razor noted his treatment at the hands of "*Mr. Kruger, husband of Matron Kruger*," who "*was the first man to attack [him]. [He] was seven years old*" (17, italics in original). The description he gives is frightening. As the incident is presented, the man—no motive for his action is given—seems to have dragged the seven-year-old boy from his bed one night, carried him from the dorm into the apartment he and his wife shared, and then, holding him by the wrist and ankle spun him around "*in wide flying arcs*" (18, italics in original). The boy loses consciousness and wakes "*in the infirmary*" where he learns he has been for "*two days*" (18, italics in original). Only later would he discover that "*Hospital records describe treatment only, not cause*" (18, italics in original). Mrs. Kruger had been present and had witnessed her husband's violent attack on a seven-year-old boy, and it is very difficult to imagine what justification either of them might have given for it, had they been called upon to do so.[9]

Razor introduces us to Mr. Beaty's abuses in the epigraph to part 4 of the book. Beaty "paddles" Razor when he is ten, along with another boy, in concert it would seem, with Miss Monson and one of her assistants, the cruel Mrs. Burt (45–46). (Mrs. Burt specializes in assailing the boys with broomsticks (122), rather like the matrons Walter Littlemoon has described at OCHS.) Beaty has also beaten a boy named George Lawson so badly that "it seemed to take weeks before George healed. George was black" (106). When Razor accidentally cuts a bean plant while working in the school garden, he is savagely kicked in the lower back by Beaty, "violently wrench-ing [Razor's] spine." The blow is accompanied by the words, "'Dirty Injun bastard!'" after which Beaty kicks him in the chest (107) and would probably have assaulted him further but for the intervention of Razor's friend Dale.

The boy is badly injured. He is attended to by one of the more sympa-thetic matrons, to whom Dale reports what has happened. In response the woman says, "'I know the men sometimes slap boys, but it's hard to believe Mr. Beaty would almost cripple you'" (109). When Dale adds that Beaty had not only done this but also called Razor "a *dirty Injun bastard*," all she can do is to say weakly that "'Mr. Beaty is well respected, and I'm sure he didn't intentionally hurt you.'" Meanwhile, Razor's "ribs were sore for a week," while his "back injury prevented normal bending and lifting for a month" (110).[10]

As Beaty has crippled him on this occasion, so too would Miss Monson—just as Razor feared. Her assault upon him, as Razor presents it in detail, cannot be justified as the act of a strict disciplinarian; it is clearly the behavior of a violent psychopath, exactly the sort of person who should not be around children. The violence takes place at a time when Miss Monson is particularly on edge because a boy named Max had recently either been pushed or fallen through a dormitory window, crashing to the dining room floor below, where he lay in pools of blood. He was taken away, not to return, and the boys do not know whether Max has died or not.

On one of the following nights Razor finds himself extremely thirsty. He knows that walking "in the halls after bedtime," even to get a drink of water, "was forbidden," adding, "but some could, some couldn't. The rules, it seemed, were used to punish certain boys more than others and some not at all" (61). He doesn't develop this, although from what he has said thus far, it would suggest that black and Indian students were singled out for more abusive treatment than was meted out to other students, at least by some of the staff. (It is not clear which students were punished "not at all.")

The water fountain, unfortunately, is near the door of Miss Monson's room. Razor carefully makes his way to it, and then goes back to bed, believing he had been quiet enough to escape detection. But soon he hears footsteps. Miss Monson, Razor writes, "stepped to my bedside and struck me with something small and solid. I jerked and she hit me again before the weapon glinted in the glow from the hall. A hammer.... It thumped against my chest.... I doubled up, knees high to protect myself, but Miss Monson kept swinging. The hammer cracked against my right kneecap, strangely numbing my lower leg" (62). Razor writes that despite being struck multiple times—with a hammer!—he managed not only to get through the night and the next morning but even to scrub floors on his hands and knees with the other boys later in the day. By that time his knee is infected, swollen badly, and he has a fever. When a kindly assistant matron, Miss Crusely, offers help, Don, a boy who had witnessed Miss Monson's attack, tells the woman, "'Monson pounded him with a hammer! Look at his ribs'" (64). Razor notes that "Miss Crusely seemed to believe Don, but she was helpless, for fear of being fired, to say anything against Miss Monson" (64). Sent to the hospital and asked how the injury occurred, he too says nothing.

Razor is bedridden for a full four weeks, but during that time he has more favorable interaction with the hospital staff than he has had with any of the school's employees thus far. Several of the women play cards with him, and they bring him "*The Book of Knowledge*, a children's encyclopedia, Indian books, and novels." He observes: "No staff, including teachers, had shown interest in my thoughts before" (70), certainly not, it would seem, to encourage his awareness of things Indian. When he must be moved for the fifth week of his hospital stay, he learns that one of the male staff members will be carrying him to the new location. (Perhaps there are no wheel chairs?) This makes him "very uncomfortable" (70). The young man who arrives for the task is a large stranger named Dan. When he picks Razor up, Miss Pearl, one of the hospital staff who had been kind to the boy, suggests that he put his arms around the man's neck and hold on. He does so and is transported safely. He writes that "Teachers talked about the men we'd be when we grew up, about becoming fathers, soldiers, or inventors, but we never saw any of those people at our school. I couldn't picture them." Rather, of the men he knows, he "had nothing but fear and hatred for Beaty" and affection for none of the others. Razor writes poignantly of Dan, "It was the first time I was thankful to a man for anything" (72). It is a full three months before he can leave the hospital and return to the cottage and boarding-school life.

A runaway attempt in 1943 with two other boys is described as a rather haphazard effort; the boys had not really planned their escape. "Within moments of first discussing it," Razor writes, "we were walking west on the tracks and didn't look back. We had no idea where to go or how to get there" (120). They nonetheless remain away for three days before sheriff's deputies pick them up and hold them for return to Owatonna. Later that year, in midsummer, he again decides to run away, this time with his friend Dale and a new boy named Billy. The last attempt has taught him "a lesson that was never, in any form, taught at the State School—how to plan for [him]self" (122). Razor's plan is to get back to "the reservation in northern Minnesota," although he wonders "how one could possibly get to a place so far away" (123). (The Fond du Lac reservation is just over two hundred miles north of Owatonna, and slightly to the east.)

The boys hop freight trains and make it past Saint Paul, about sixty-nine miles north. They are hungry, dehydrated, and very badly sunburned. On several occasions someone they encounter singles Razor out as Indian but, for the most part, with no particular animus. After a variety of adventures mostly involving trains, the boys are apprehended and spend a night in the town jail. In the morning a state social worker arrives to collect them, complaining to the jailers about their condition; they are dirty, in threadbare clothing, and hungry. He puts them on a train to St. Paul, where they are picked up and taken back to Owatonna. Once there, the cottage matron greets them with the words, "'You'll certainly come to nothing when you're grown'" (160). But in general the boys are treated kindly on their return. They are cleaned up and well fed; "our punishment," Razor writes, was mostly on paper" (161). I assume that means extra assignments, but there are no beatings or the like.

For much of this time Razor has been working on the Schauls' farm, having his wages stolen, often being kept from school and other activities and regularly brutalized. A visit from a social worker who might terminate his stay uncovers nothing of the abusive nature of the situation. In part 12, the last of the book, a drunken John Schaul strikes Razor in the head, seriously injuring him. He describes this in detail, and indeed, some of the most vivid passages of the book are those in which he writes of his pain and suffering at the hands of one or another violent adult. Partially paralyzed by Schaul's assault, the boy sleeps outdoors and, in the morning, drags himself to the road, where he is picked up and driven to the home of a doctor, who attends to him carefully and calls "county juvenile services" (171). This time the boy makes quite clear who it is who has hurt him so badly, leading to his temporary placement in the nearby home of a retired nurse. She cares for and treats him well, and the doctor continues to look in on him. Finally Razor is able to return to the local high school he has sporadically attended, where he is heartily welcomed—except by the school bully, who offers, "'Dirty Injun!'" (174).

Permanently removed from the Schauls' farm, Razor boards with another German farm family, the Klugs. They are also a Catholic family—Razor on several occasions has said that his only possessions are a rosary and a Bible—and unlike his previous hosts, they are kind and thoughtful. At breakfast after his first night there, Mrs. Klug is concerned that Razor had "screamed last night. Must have been a nightmare" (184). His life to date has provided a good deal of material for nightmares. Safely lodged and boarded, Razor still must face the school bully, who once more calls him "Injun," and whom he will eventually have to fight. The bully, Bud Lange, is bigger than Razor, who nonetheless bests him. Razor describes the fight in such detail that one may wonder to what extent it is being re-created rather than actually remembered. This is the case, of course, with many of the scenes he has rendered vividly, or conversations reproduced verbatim, and he will speak to this matter in an epilogue.

Razor is brought before the school principal, who tells him that although fighting is not to be condoned, he believes Razor has nonetheless done "a wonderful thing for the school, and for Bud, too. Hopefully he'll stop to think now when he bullies smaller boys" (192). The epigraph to this section had concluded with Razor's recollection of the time when he "*first heard the name* locust, *and listened to the sound of its singing*" (184); an epilogue will indicate the degree to which Razor, like the locust, has "*soar[ed] into the summer light*" (4, italics in original) and perhaps begun to sing.

Although he is grateful for the kindness of the Klug family, his long-term experience has been such that he "suffered recurring bouts of anxiety and depression ... before the age of nineteen." He reproduces a record he obtained from the hospital to which he'd been sent, in which the doctors admit their "confusion" as to the cause of his condition, in that "*his entire childhood at the State Public School was such a stable and well-regulated environment*" (196, italics in original). The irony here is too obvious and too painful to require comment. Drafted into the army soon afterward and sent to Korea, Razor finds himself, "at the age of 21, ... made electrical supervisor of twenty Korean electricians and five GIs." War begins in June 1950, and although he does not write about it, he does say that he saw combat and "received three bronze stars ... before rotating back to the States ... after an armistice stopped the fighting" in July 1953 (196).

Tanya Cooper cites a 1997 study that found "children who turn age eighteen in [foster] care are overrepresented among welfare recipients, prison inmates, and the homeless" (241), and all the more so for children of color.

Harvey Ronglien writes of his childhood friends at Owatonna that "two hung themselves in prison, one escaped from Stillwater Prison and was shot down by police, another was gunned down in his apartment, one had a mental breakdown, one has completely blocked out his past, and four are alcoholic (including myself)" (67). If Peter Razor had problems with alcohol, relationships, or other such matters, unlike Ronglien and Walter Littlemoon, he does not say.

Sketching his subsequent life in the epilogue, Razor says he became an electrician, and "raised three children," who have given him "six grand-children" (196): "My children have been my joy, and they have saved me" (200). Although he had known no parenting himself, he seems to have been a good parent. Curiously, there is no mention of his children's mother. Razor notes that he has also explored his "roots" and "studied Indian culture," and although he has heard it disparaged as "terrible to so many," he "found it beautiful." He takes pride in discovering in Frances Densmore's *Chippewa*

13　Peter Razor in 2014. Photo by Jerry Olson for the *Minnesota Post Bulletin*. Courtesy of the *Minnesota Post Bulletin*.

Customs (1929) that his "great-grandmother, Mrs. Frank Razer of the White Earth Reservation, was well known for her beadwork" (197).[11]

At the encouragement of his daughter, he "made a list of memories and worked them into a rough sequence" (197), surely the basis for this book. Another daughter accompanies him to obtain his "childhood records" from "State Child Services," and a son-in-law "encouraged [him] to keep writing," so that his "children and grandchildren [might] understand what it was like for [him]." He explains that he "added dialogue and tried to bring each scene to life, as though [he] were reliving that childhood" (198). At the age of seventy-three Peter Razor concludes his book, "I'm still haunted by those seventeen years" (200), years of darkness, although like the locust, he seems to have lived the rest of his life in *"the summer light"* (4). For all its differences from other autobiographies we have considered, *While the Locust Slept* deserves consideration among the texts constituting "American Indian boarding-school literature."

8

Adam Fortunate Eagle's *Pipestone: My Life in an Indian Boarding School,* Dennis Banks's "Yellow Bus," and Jim Northrup's "FAMILIES— *Nindanawemanaaganag"*

THREE ANISHINAABE MEN WHO ATTENDED THE PIPESTONE INDIAN SCHOOL in western Minnesota and wrote of their experiences there are Adam Fortunate Eagle, born Adam Nordwall at Red Lake, Minnesota in 1929; Dennis Banks, born at Leech Lake, Minnesota, in 1937; and Jim Northrup, born in Sawyer, Minnesota, on the southern end of the Fond du Lac reservation, in 1943.[1] Fortunate Eagle's *Pipestone: My Life in an Indian Boarding School* (2010), is one of the very few book-length accounts of life at a boarding-school.[2] Banks's autobiography (with Richard Erdoes), *Ojibwa Warrior: Dennis Banks and the Rise of the American Indian Movement* (2004), treats his boarding-school experience much more briefly, in a single chapter of the book called "Yellow Bus." And Northrup's account, even briefer than Banks's, appears in "*Nindanawemaaganag*," the first chapter of his *The Rez Road Follies* (1997).

Fortunate Eagle attended Pipestone from 1935 until his graduation in 1945, and Banks from 1943 until 1948; Northrup entered in 1949 and left when the school closed in 1952. Fortunate Eagle went on to become one of the organizers of the 1969 occupation of the former federal prison on Alcatraz Island, the subject of his book *Heart of the Rock: the Indian Invasion of Alcatraz* (with Tim Findley, 2002). Banks was one of the founders of the American Indian Movement and prominent in the takeover of Wounded Knee in 1973 (of which Fortunate Eagle disapproved). Northrup served in Viet Nam and became an award-winning journalist, and the author of fiction and poetry. Banks and Northrup have entirely negative recollections of the Pipestone Indian School, very different from Fortunate Eagle's positive assessment of his time there.

Pipestone was in operation from 1893 to 1952, with classes up to the ninth grade. The years Fortunate Eagle was there were indeed a fortunate time for students in most of the Indian boarding schools, for those years encompassed the entirety of John Collier's tenure as commissioner of Indian Affairs (1933–45) and the official government abandonment of any notion of "killing the Indian." Banks's first two years at the school (1943–45) also fall within that period, although his last three (1945–48), saw the beginning of the reaction against Collier's reforms that I noted earlier. During the entirety of Fortunate Eagle's time at school, Pipestone was under the supervision of James Balmer, who had become superintendent in 1924. Balmer held the position until 1946 and thus was still in charge of the school for the first three years Banks attended. C. L. Crutcher was the principal at Pipestone for all of the time Northrup was a student, and I have been able to find out nothing about him or about how the school was run at a time when its imminent closing was known to teachers and staff.

Sally Southwick writes that "Balmer's supervision secured the school's place among the most respected government educational institutions," adding: "A 1931 publication that was otherwise critical of BIA policies labeled [Pipestone] 'undoubtedly the best school in the Indian Service,'" and called Balmer "'kind, jovial, patient, and constructive … a singular breeze of fresh air in a stagnant desert of disappointments'" (87). Gaylord Reynolds notes that "under his jurisdiction the annual budget was more than doubled," and "many new buildings were added" (31). After Balmer's departure, C. H. Beitzel headed the school from 1946 to 1948, the last year Banks was there. As previously acknowledged, it is simply not possible to generalize about the degree to which any particular government or contract school did or did not actually follow the official policies for any given period. But Balmer surely instituted the reformers' program at Pipestone, and I doubt there was a radical reversal of his generally benevolent oversight in the years immediately after his departure, although that is certainly possible.

Fortunate Eagle is aware of these issues, and he addresses them in his introduction to the autobiography as well as in the narrative itself. He offers a quotation from Collier that I think worth reproducing in full. He cites Collier as follows: "The cultural history of Indians is in all respects to be considered equal to that of any non-Indian group. And it is desirable that Indians be bilingual—fluent and literate in the English language, and fluent in their vital, beautiful, and efficient native languages"[3] (xvi). Admitting that he does not know the degree to which these reforms were carried out at the schools generally, he affirms "from personal experience ... that Pipestone Indian Training School was carrying out these federal mandates" (xvii). I believe that to be true, although there were some exceptions.

With the end of the Second World War and Collier's retirement as commissioner, the government moved toward a policy of "termination"—getting out of the Indian business, as it were—and Pipestone "was making strides toward closure" (Landrum 139), something Fortunate Eagle treats in an appendix to his book. Gaylord Reynolds explains that his history of the Pipestone School "was written because of the writer's interest in the education of underprivileged Indian children" (Preface n.p.), and Cynthia Landrum notes that the majority of Pipestone's students were indeed "those who were less fortunate" (135). This is to say that they were orphans or from families unable to care for them.[4] Late in the book Fortunate Eagle cites Mrs. Burns, a Peoria Indian house matron, saying of the school that "desperate parents want us to take in their children" (141), and Fortunate Eagle records the story of a student friend whose mother died, leaving seven boys and two girls for his father to care for, "so all his kids," he writes, "go to the boarding schools." He adds that this "story sounds a lot like my own family's story" (67). In an appendix, Fortunate Eagle cites twelve brief biographies of Pipestone students from Reynolds's study, all of whom came from precarious family situations.[5]

Fortunate Eagle writes that he kept two separate journals at Pipestone, but lost both long before he thought of writing his book (xiii). Nonetheless, his account is rich in precise detail. He names many staff members—almost no teachers—and a great many of his fellow students, and tells of all sorts of pranks and adventures he clearly relishes recalling. In many respects his story could be that of many an American boy growing up in a rural setting in those post-Depression and postwar years. That is to say, while *Pipestone* is certainly the narrative of an *Indian* boy and his life in an *Indian* boarding school, and while it touches upon most of the *topoi* and *loci* of Indian boarding-school life, these are not highlighted or emphasized so much as they are treated as incidents in the development of an energetic and talented boy.

This is not for a moment to forget that young Adam Nordwall was constantly aware that he was Indian and boarding at a government Indian school, the aims of which were not to deepen and enrich his Indian identity. But the places and topics of the boarding school, while certainly influencing him in a great many ways, did not define or even constrain him—at least not much. Rather than a narrative of incarceration and punishment, *Pipestone* reads more nearly like the story of a bright, creative, and brave Indian boy's mostly happy childhood, albeit a childhood largely spent far from home. He describes the school he attended as having some unusually sympathetic staff, from Superintendent James Balmer down, Indian and non-Indian. Nordwall's wonderfully resilient temperament responded well to his encounter with Indian boys and girls of many Native nations, and led to a strengthening of and pride in his Indian identity—something that was not inconsistent with federal Indian Service policy from about the mid-1920s to 1945, as I have observed.

കൗ

Although "there are schools on the reservation" (3), Fortunate Eagle writes, shortly after the premature death of his father, he and five of his siblings find themselves driven in a "big, black, government car" (4) more than three hundred miles from the Red Lake reservation in northern Minnesota west to the Indian Training School at Pipestone, Minnesota.[6] Once there, he notes his first breakfast and his first shower—"with cold and hot running water! It sure feels good" (6). His oldest brother, Stanley, "comes up to [him] with an Indian couple" he introduces as "your new parents, Mr. and Mrs. Burns" (6). These two will play an important part in the boy's many years at Pipestone.

Assignment to a dormitory is next, and his, unfortunately, is "Dormitory Five—the home of the bedwetters everybody calls the 'Stink Dormitory'" (6). Not yet six years old, he is put there only because of his age. On his first night in the dormitory, he cries himself to sleep, remembering happy times at home, especially his "last Christmas on the reservation" (6)—his family seems to be

Episcopalian. Then, abruptly, there is a space break, after which Fortunate Eagle writes: "I turn six years old on July 18, and the end of summer brings an end to school vacation" (7). Summer vacation, thus oddly comes immediately after the few events—shower, introduction to Mr. and Mrs. Burns, and the "stink dormitory"—that Nordwall[7] describes as occurring on his first day there, as though nothing happened during the intervening eight or so months. Nor is anything said about the summer vacation, after which we find Nordwall back at school. He is now in his second year at Pipestone, but the narrative treats all that he encounters as if for the first time.

Fortunate Eagle writes that the boys shed their clothes—the "old raggedy ones ... thrown away" (7)—and shower. After the showers, they go naked to the basement, where Mr. and Mrs. Burns use "bug rakes"—fine combs—"that pull out any nits or lice from [their] hair" (7). If anything is found, the boy is sent to have "all ... [his] hair cut off with hand clippers." It is Nordwall's fate to be sent to the assistant boys' advisor who serves as barber—this is Mr. Paul Smith, another Indian employee of the school—and he cries "as those hair clippers chomp off [his] hair" (7–8). Salve is then rubbed over his scalp, and a stocking cap put on. When he is seen to have a rash on his body, another salve is applied. He then dresses "in denim coveralls that're too big and high-top shoes that're too big." He is sent out to play in the yard, where he is joined by some "other little boys ... all crying. We're lonely," he writes, "bald-headed, our clothes don't fit and we smell awful" (8).

The children "learn a whole new way of life at the boarding school" (9), and Fortunate Eagle gives the daily schedule: up at 6:30, dress, make the beds, and "head down the hall to the lavatory to wash up" (9). At 7:00 the children line up in "Companies"—although the school is not run on the military model, and the denim coveralls Nordwall has been given are not military attire. They then go to the dining hall, where, as at most of the boarding schools, the boys enter from one side and the girls from another. The children "stand behind their chairs, eight to a table," with an older student "at the end of the table to keep us quiet" (9). The dining hall matron is "a Sioux Indian from South Dakota" (10). She rings a bell and the children say grace, apparently still standing, for when she rings the bell again they all sit. Nordwall, like several of the others, does not understand what is said. (But he does not speak Chippewa.) Breakfast is described in detail: there are hot and cold cereals, sometimes "corned beef hash or chipped beef and gravy on toast," which the boy says he likes, although he notes that the older boys do not. The children are also served "hot coffee with sugar and cream already added" (10).[8]

He writes that at "the beginning of the school day, all us kids line up in formation in front of the school building," where they "put up the American flag and salute it ... with our arms raised up, like the salute of the Nazis that we see in newsreels and pictures" (10). Fortunate Eagle includes a photo of this salute, which does indeed look like that of the Nazis (11); the children, although "in formation," are not in military dress. When one of the boys devises a makeshift Nazi uniform and shouts "'Heil Hitler!' when [they] said the Pledge of Allegiance"—Adolf Hitler had become chancellor of Germany in 1933—the superintendent, Mr. Balmer, changes "the flag salute to a three-fingered Boy Scout salute," accompanied by "putting [their] right hands over [their] hearts" (72). Years later Nordwall would hear of the Japanese bombing of Pearl Harbor on December 7, 1941, on the radio at school and "shout the news to all the boys like a town crier" (76). As the war progresses, schoolboys as young as thirteen try to join the military, Fortunate Eagle writes, and when they are of age, so will Nordwall's brothers join, two of them to become war heroes, and one to return with severe PTSD.

This school year is a very busy one, although nothing at all is said about classes. Nordwall plays a joke on Mrs. Burns, the housemother, made possible, we are told, because the boys catch and cook rabbits "out in the parching place" (12), of which we will hear more. Here readers may benefit from something the writer has learned at boarding school: that "cottontail rabbits taste better than jackrabbits" (13). Soon Nordwall observes his "first Thanksgiving" at the school, and although it does not include turkey, he finds the "fried chicken and mashed potatoes" served "wonderful." Christmas time reminds him once more of his "last Christmas on the Red Lake Reservation" (13). Enlisted to sing for the festivities, he offers a performance that is not entirely appropriate for the occasion (13–14). The boy suffers several accidents, once breaking his ribs; he will also have his tonsils removed (40), and at another time be kept in the school hospital more than a month for a burst appendix (87). Soon the year is up, and he learns that "all the Nordwall kids are going back to the reservation for summer vacation" (16). Whether children do or do not go home for the summer depends on whether there is anyone available to care for them.

Back home, he finds that his mother has a new husband, a Sioux, who is "strong and handsome, but when he gets drunk, he gets real mean" (16).

The summer with family and friends is full of adventure; then it is back to Pipestone for a third year, which once more is very rapidly sketched. This time all of the Nordwall boys "pass the awful 'bug rake' test," but because Adam is "lonesome and homesick," he joins "the little stinky boys wearing stocking caps and oversized clothes" and shares with them "a good cry" (22). During the school year he does a good deal of gardening, puts up root vegetables and preserves, learns something about hog butchering, and again says not a word about classes. Soon it is Christmas once more. He recognizes Mr. Balmer dressed up as Santa Claus and is pleased with the presents he receives. Although his mother has moved to South Dakota to be with her husband, the Nordwall children can still go home to the reservation because there are "family and friends to take care of us kids" (26). This would not always be the case.

The book continues in this manner: a year of school and then summer vacation, both full of adventure. For two summers—his mother still away, but family and friends now unable to care for the Nordwall children—he remains at the school, helping with farm and maintenance work. In his next year we belatedly learn that church is mandatory every Sunday (31), although government policy had made attendance at church services optional in these years. The lye soap in use when Nordwall had first come to the school—"so strong that it burned our skin" (32) (and painful to Lydia Whirlwind Soldier later at St. Francis Mission School)—has now been replaced with "big white bars of Ivory soap" that the boys carve into animals and boats with which to play in the showers (33). Observation of Thanksgiving, Christmas, and now also New Year's are once again remembered warmly, so much so that Fortunate Eagle writes, "We're like a great big family" (33), a feeling expressed by only a few boarding-school autobiographers.

The third year brings mention of a basement room "that the older boys say is where they keep the runaway boys locked up," although Nordwall hasn't "ever seen that room used like that" (34). Nordwall had earlier observed that Mrs. Burns "checks our bed, because boys always run away from school to go home" (11). Not only boys run away. Much later in the book, Mr. Burns announces that "we have some runaway girls," and calls for ten boys to volunteer "to help round them up." The boys are "eager to volunteer, because [they] know that whoever catches a runaway gets a twenty-five cent reward" (118); there is no hint whatever of rebel solidarity. Driven some distance in a pickup truck, the boys descend and very quickly find the girls in a corn field (120). While the boys will be rewarded, we are not told of the girls' punishment.

Still later we learn of a boy named Joe Bebeau who, "lonesome and homesick," runs off in "the middle of winter" with a friend nicknamed Cry Baby (144). Joe, like several other boarding-school students who run away in winter, winds up losing a limb. In his case, however, it was not frostbite that caused his arm to be "cut off at the elbow in the boarding school hospital" (144). Rather, as the boys tried to jump a train, Joe slipped, and had "the huge steel train wheels roll over and crush his right arm just below the elbow" (144). This may well have been punishment enough, for we do not hear of any penalty administered to him, or for that matter to his accomplice, Cry Baby.

But although corporal punishment has been officially proscribed, it is still practiced and several instances of it are recorded.[9] The Ivory soap adventures, for example, had led to a boy "being whipped with that leather strap" (33) by Mrs. Burns, who on a later occasion whacks the boys with her broom for a prank they play on her. This is followed by her husband's use of a leather strap on the boys' behinds. Then, when the same prank is played on Paul Smith, he also whips the boys (42). A later raid on a farmer's chickens a mile or so from the school—the boys fashion makeshift spears to kill them, and then cook them, along with some corn, at their "parching place behind the school" (66)[10]—leads to all being punished by Mrs. Burns, who "whacks the hell out of our little butts." To this point, the only infraction of which she is aware is their having gone AWOL. But when something about chickens is blurted out by one of the boys, they "have to stand in line again for a second whipping" (66). This is painful, and all but one cry (66).

There is, however, no suggestion that any of the punishments administered are unjust or excessive, and as it happens all those described in the book are administered by Indian staff.[11] The whipping, however, does not serve as a deterrent. That very night, the boys are off again, now to raid a bakery shed a mile and a half from the school, where "old pies, cake, cookies, and sweet rolls" (67) are kept. Still, it is noted that Mr. Burns often carries a bullwhip, "and practices snapping and cracking it all the time" (73). Later, when "Mr. Balmer hired Beulah Shields, a Chippewa woman, to be the assistant boys' advisor," we hear of her hitting one of the boys "with a steel ring full of keys so hard it cuts his head" (130). But even this does not provoke any criticism from Fortunate Eagle. Indeed, when Mrs. Burns again gives them "a good whipping," the boys "laugh about what happened" (94)—the laughter occasioned by the mischievous fun they had had, and in no way diminished by the pain they had suffered for it.

It is a discussion of corporal punishment that leads a new boy to ask whether one is allowed to speak an Indian language at the Pipestone School. This is Joe Crown, an Ojibwe from Leech Lake, who had previously gone to St. Mary's Mission School on the reservation. He reports that when he would talk "Chippewa at the mission school a nun would whack him across his fingers" because his language, she said, "'is the language of the devil'" (Fortunate Eagle 2010 46). For the same offense, another nun threw him down the stairs to the root cellar, and when he tried to prevent her from closing the door on him, smashed his fingers between the door and the door frame (47). It had been the sight of the boy's misshapen fingers that provoked the discussion of punishment at the St. Mary's School for speaking one's own language.

Others who had attended St. Mary's tell of a Father Causian who, finding a boy speaking Chippewa, "took him to his office, ripped off his shirt, … grabbed a buggy whip and lashed that boy until he had bloody welts all over his back" (47).[12] Knowing this, one can well understand why Joe Crown would ask whether students are punished at Pipestone for speaking their language. In answer to his question, "a boy from Red Lake," responds, "'No, never! … I've been here four years and I've never seen anybody punished for that.'" The boy says he speaks Chippewa with friends without interference or punishment and reports seeing "Sioux boys sitting in a circle on the lawn … speaking Sioux. Nobody's ever stopped them or punished them'" (48).[13] Mrs. Burns later tells the boys explicitly that while years ago "everything that was Indian was forbidden" at the schools, since then "the times and federal laws have changed. Now nobody is punished for speaking their language here at this school" (143), which clearly adheres to Collier's commitment to bilingualism, as Fortunate Eagle has quoted him. In a display of true Christian charity, Joe Crown and some of the other boys who had been to the mission school name the priests and nuns at St. Mary's and judge some of the former good guys and some of the latter "nice" (48). The conversation concludes with Joe Crown saying, "'Compared to the mission school, Pipestone is a little bit of heaven'" (48).

Nordwall learns carpentry, plastering, shoe repair, and even how to darn socks (62). He and some others ingeniously make themselves skis and sleds from barrel staves and put both to good use (75). At one point he gets a paying job unloading boxcars (86), and another roasting peanuts, something for which he shows considerable talent (86–87). Like John Rogers earlier, he has a number of fights (37, 137). The *topos* of sex is introduced when Fortunate Eagle informs us that quite early in his Pipestone years, he had formed the opinion that Delores Two Stars, two years older than he, was "the most beautiful girl at the boarding school" and was developing "beautiful bumps and curves" (72). He is not the only boy to notice the maturation of the girls, and soon a plan is hatched to release gophers into the girls' shower room so that the boys can enjoy the sight of them fleeing naked. Panic is indeed induced in the young ladies showering, although, much to the disappointment of the plotters, the girls find an alternate path of flight to the one anticipated.

Sex is again the issue just a few pages later, for all that the young boy is unaware that that is indeed the matter at issue. On a summer excursion—he has again remained behind at the school—Nordwall is walking with a girl named Mary, who has a slight limp. At some point, he tells us, they sit down to rest. Then Mary lies on her back, and "starts moaning and groaning." He fears she is "having some kind of fit," or that "it's something to do with her leg." Meaning to help, he grabs her hands and lifts her up from the grass (84). When he tells the other boys about this, he is informed that "Mary was bulling" (85), like a cow in heat, inviting him to intercourse—which, as it happens, he is still too young to perform. We hear no more of Mary or of any further sexual adventures at the school.

Although Fortunate Eagle is consistent in providing no descriptions of his classes, he does say that by the time he is in fifth grade he is an avid reader. He does not speak his language, but he has not for a moment thought of himself as anything other than an Indian boy, and his account makes clear that the school, whatever its commitment to assimilation, is not interested in altering his self-conception. Nonetheless, the history books he studies are all " about guys like Columbus, Ponce de Leon … and all that stuff they call Manifest Destiny.… I can't understand how all these white guys are given the credit for discovering different parts of our country when Indians were already here for thousands of years" (74). "Those stories upset me," he writes "'cause … Daniel Boone and Kit Carson are American heroes for fighting Indians" (74). Fortunately, those are not the only books available to him at the school. "Going into the school library," he writes, "is like going to another planet," for there is a section of books about Indians which he devours (74).

He also visits Roe's Trading Post, where there are "so many beautiful Indian things to see," and Mrs. Roe tells him "about the history and people who made these things … stories [he] can't find in our history books at school." A "very eager student," Nordwall appreciates that some "of the older boys at school tell [him] more stories like that" (94). He also benefits from a man he meets named "Old Charley Morrison" (94), a Chippewa who "speaks Chippewa real good and knows a lot of stories and legends." Everywhere he goes, Fortunate Eagle writes, he hears "the storytellers. They tell stories [he] can't find in books," and, he says, "I love all of it" (95). He also benefits from the fact that "every so often, Mr. Balmer invites [him] into his office and tells [him] stories, including the history of the boarding school." Of these stories as well, Nordwall says, "I love all of it" (125).

"Graduation day is May 18 and it's hard to believe my ten years at the boarding school are almost over," Fortunate Eagle writes. "I'm the sixth of the Nordwall kids to graduate," and, with the war not yet over, "all four of my brothers are serving in the military" (146). As the graduation ceremony ends, he says he feels "it's like leaving my family all over again." Mrs. Burns has tears in her eyes, and after ten years he feels that what his brother had told him on his first day was true: "Mrs. Burns will always be a second mother to me" (147). The school tradition is that every graduating ninth grade class "presents the school pipe to the new ninth graders.… It's a strong message for us Indian students to carry on the traditions, culture, and spirituality of our people, so we can pass it on to future generations" (147). The book ends with Nordwall saying, "Next fall I'm going to Lawrence, Kansas, to go to Haskell to continue my education" (147). He did indeed go to Haskell, where he met Bobbie Kills Among Many, a Shoshone woman who would become his wife. The two eventually moved to California, where he founded the First American Exterminating Company, eventually becoming active in the Indian Rights/Red Power movements of the time, and organizing the occupation of the abandoned federal prison on Alcatraz Island in 1969. In 1973 he traveled to Italy to claim it by right of discovery, as of course Columbus had claimed the New World. He visits the Pope, and when the Pontiff extended his right hand for his ring to be kissed, Fortunate Eagle—so the story goes—put forth his own ringed right hand. It is said to have been a Crow woman who gave him the name Fortunate Eagle. Adam Fortunate Eagle turned ninety on July 18, 2019.[14]

ᏧᏣ

In an autobiography (with Richard Erdoes) called *Ojibwa Warrior*, focused, as its subtitle makes clear, on *Dennis Banks and the Rise of the American Indian Movement* (2004), Banks, an Ojibwe from Leech Lake, devotes a single brief, early chapter to his attendance at the Pipestone Indian School from 1943 to 1948. The chapter opens with an epigraph:

> *The old boarding schools that Indian kids were forcibly taken to were concentration camps for children where we were forbidden to speak our language and were beaten if we prayed to our Native creator.* (24, italics in original)

The epigraph does not consist of words quoted from another writer, like epigraphs generally, but is instead by Banks himself, and it is meant to prepare readers for a narrative of victimization.

As discussed in the introduction and elsewhere, while it is true that at most of the schools—although for many years not Pipestone—Indian children were beaten for speaking their languages and until 1934 were required to worship as Christians, the schools were hardly "concentration camps." Rather, for Banks the "boarding school is … a useful and extraordinarily powerful metaphor for colonialism" (Child 2014 268), "the primary explanation for social dysfunction and adverse conditions on reservations and [Indian] communities" (Child 2014 271). Even so, as Child stated clearly, it is "impossible to view this history as one of simple victimization" (2014 269). Moreover, to view it in this way (I am thinking of much of the work of Gerald Vizenor) is counter-productive; even when deployed in the service of the contemporary "ethnopolitics of the disadvantaged" (Kenny 421), in that a narrative of pure victimization deprives Native boarding-school students of all creative agency.

Nonetheless, Banks begins, "There is one dark day in the lives of all Indian children: the day when they are forcibly taken away from those who love and care for them.… They are dragged, some screaming and weeping, others in silent terror, to a boarding school where they are to be remade into white kids" (24). Many Indian children had been "forcibly taken" to one school or another, but Banks's generalization is simply not true. Not a single student had been forced to attend Carlisle, for example, and every one of the families of Pipestone students had applied for their student's admission to the school—as had Banks's mother. He says that "dark day" came for him in 1942, when "an agent from the Bureau of Indian Affairs, a large-bellied man smelling of cheap cigars and beer, came into our home waving a bunch of papers" (24). Perhaps Banks does remember the appearance and the odor of the man from the BIA he saw more than fifty years earlier, or perhaps he has instead offered up a caricature villain. In any case, he, his brother, and his sister are taken off to school, and he remembers becoming frightened as he realizes they are going far away, "to Pipestone, Minnesota, a full two hundred fifty miles away" (25). (Actually, a bit more.)

The year the Banks children went to Pipestone was 1943, not 1942, and if they are indeed being taken "screaming and weeping," or "in silent terror," that would be because their mother had not told them that she had filled out and signed an "Application for Admission to Nonreservation Schools" for them in April that year. Although Banks was eligible to enter first grade at the Onigum public school two miles from his home (with transportation provided), B. A. Black, the local "Education Field Agent," had recommended enrollment for Dennis in "regular 1st grade" at the non-reservation school for reasons that have been redacted from his records but that are not hard to guess.[15] Black's recommendation was exactly that, a recommendation; it did not compel Mrs. Banks to send her children to a non-reservation school.

On the form she had filled out, Annie J. Banks noted that her only source of income was "Direct Relief," and there was no father to provide support. If the Banks children had gone to the local Onigum school, transportation for them would have been provided, but nothing for room, board, clothing, and medical attention. The form Mrs. Banks signed reads, "I hereby voluntarily consent and agree to this enrollment," and the reason she consented and agreed was surely because she hoped the off-reservation school would provide the best care for her children.

When he first arrives at the Pipestone school, Banks says, he sees children "dressed all the same—little soldiers in khaki uniforms" (25). Adam Fortunate Eagle had mentioned the very belated arrival at the school of some World War I surplus clothing—it could only have been worn by the older children—but no khaki uniforms or uniforms of any sort. It is, of course, possible that first graders in 1943, during World War II, were issued khaki uniforms, although I am skeptical. Banks says that the children were "fed … something," and the boys were then put "in barber chairs and dusted … all over with some awful smelling white stuff. It was DDT. They rubbed lots of it in [their] hair." He "suppose[s] it was to kill lice," asserting that "we didn't have any lice, but they assumed we did." He may know that he and his siblings did not have any lice, but he can't possibly have known about the other children. "Then," he writes, "they shaved our heads down to the skin." This removes the long hair young Dennis Banks had worn "down to [his] shoulders." He writes that he "felt uncomfortably naked without it" (25), as most Native children did after their hair was cut.

Adam Fortunate Eagle's description of the delousing and hair-cutting at Pipestone seems more accurate than Banks's account. Fortunate Eagle had described the school personnel first employing the "bug rake" (7) to see whether a particular child had lice or not, since experience would have shown that in fact some children did and some did not. It seems likely that if DDT was applied, as Banks states it was, that would have happened only *after* the children's heads had been shaved, not before.[16] The children then have their clothes taken from them and they are issued "a government khaki uniform and stiff black shoes which immediately started to chafe above [his] ankles and soon rubbed [him] raw" (25). They were probably given socks as well, although these might not have prevented the chafing. Banks's next observation is: "I remember the years of Pipestone as the years of blistered feet" (25). But the problem he had described had been ankles rubbed raw, not blistered feet. Perhaps he means raw ankles *and* blistered feet. It doesn't matter a great lot, to be sure, but this is careless writing—and careless editing on Erdoes's part.

After the clothing issue—no prior showers, such as Adam Nordwall had experienced, are mentioned—the new arrivals are "lined up to receive bedding" and then taken "to the dorms" (25). Finding himself "among strange kids in a large, stone-cold hall," he "quietly cried [himself] to sleep" (26), as so many other boarding-school students had done over the years. Banks says nothing more about dormitory life except to note later that on one occasion, having wet his bed, he was sent "to the stink dorm"—where Adam Nordwall had spent his early nights at Pipestone—for a humiliating seven days (28). In the morning Banks is introduced to "the dining hall where [he] had his first breakfast at Pipestone." He doesn't say what was served, but it can't have been too bad since, after finishing, he gets up to go for more. At this point he is admonished and told "to raise [his] hand and ask politely for seconds" (26). This, he writes, is "the beginning of a life of innumerable rules." When he sees his sister on the other side of the dining room, he runs toward her as the children are leaving, only to be driven back by "the advisors [who] had sticks.... One of those advisors thrashed [him] with a stick" (26). This was, to be sure, the sort of brutal treatment Walter Littlemoon suffered about this time at Oglala Community High School, as did Lydia Whirlwind Soldier and Tim Giago at the South Dakota mission schools. But Adam Fortunate Eagle had described nothing of the kind at Pipestone, nor do I believe that James Balmer, still superintendent at the time—this was 1943 and he did not leave until 1946—would have allowed such treatment, especially of the youngest students.

Banks recalls an advisor named Mr. Smith "who had been a drill sergeant in the army," and who "lectured [the boys] on how the army built character," and "made *men* out of dumb boys" (26, italics in original). Since this is war time, and Mr. Smith is at the school and no longer in the army, his military service must have been in an earlier period. Banks also remembers Smith's wife, who, "In contrast to her husband ... was a nice, kindly lady." He writes that she attempted to offer the children "a little comfort ... but the kids came from ... such a different world that she could not really communicate with [them]" (26). This is meant to establish the fact that Mrs. Smith is not a Native person, and that even "nice, kindly" non-Native people cannot "communicate" with Indian children. But if Mrs. Smith had been at Pipestone for some time, and was "a nice, kindly lady," might she not have learned to "communicate" with the children, at least to the point that some might accept "a little comfort" from her?

Banks describes the school schedule, with wake-up "at six in the morning," followed by "mess hall, then ... school [and] ... finally to dinner, and then the dorm again" (26), with cleaning chores in between. He is one of "thirty to forty first-graders" (26). His sister Audrey and his brother Mark receive letters from their mother, which they read to him, but, Banks writes, "not once in the nine years [he] was at Pipestone did [his] mother visit" (27). Banks, however, was at Pipestone from 1943 to 1948, five years, not nine—although he once more says nine years on the same page and repeats it on the following page (28). The Cass County Welfare Board in April 1948 had sent a letter to C. H. Beitzel, the new superintendent at Pipestone, recommending that Banks remain at the school because his mother's situation was not conducive to his return. The recommendation was not binding, for on September 3, 1948, Beitzel wrote to Banks care of his mother (who is addressed as Mrs. Bertha Mattson), enclosing a government check for $6.25, his "last check for the summer," probably payment for some work he had done. Beitzel hopes Banks "had a [good] trip home and that [he] arrived safely." The eleven-year-old Dennis Banks had arrived safely and he was never to return to Pipestone.

Comparison of Banks's account of his time at Pipestone to his student files indicates his carelessness as a writer. He accurately reports, for example, "When I was eleven years old I was transferred to another boarding school at Wahpeton, North Dakota, a junior high school" (30),[17] so that even if he had come to Pipestone in 1942 as he had said, if he left it for Wahpeton when he was eleven, he would have been at the school for six years, again not the nine years that he several times repeats. This treatment of chronology is not that of the traditional oral storyteller but rather of an autobiographer indifferent to matters of fact.

He says that not only did his mother not visit, but no family member ever came to take him and his siblings home for summer vacation—again surely because conditions were such that care for them could not be provided. Banks misses his grandparents and "the woods and the lakes, which remained vivid in [his] mind" (27), and he daydreams of flying home. For his "first year in school," he writes, "sleep was [his] only escape" (27). He makes some friends at school, "Indian kids [his] own age" who also "never had any visitors and could never go home for the summer," and for "nine [sic] years [they] were always together." Banks recalls that he "felt happy" with these other kids, and that they have remained friends for over fifty years (27).

But "even with their friendship, sometimes the yearning to be away from that stone-and-brick heap and the longing for home was so strong" (27) that "four times [he] ran away and four times [he] was brought back" (27). He contradicts this a few pages later, writing, "I ran away nine times, always heading north. Always they caught me" (30). He doesn't say when these four or nine attempts were made, although two of them are detailed later. His student file records four absences (A) from October 1943 to May 1944, his first year at the school, but no D for "Deserted," the boarding-school's term for running away. No absences at all are recorded for the following two years. Then, there are no fewer than ten absences in April 1947. Some of these might indicate times he ran away from the school, although again no D was entered, and Banks was "Promoted to Grade V," with the notation that he is an "Honor Student. Works diligently and applies himself well." To be sure, as Brenda Child observes in an essay about runaways at Flandreau and Haskell, "Runaways were frequently considered hard-working students who were well behaved while in school," so that "their first desertions often caught officials by surprise" (1996 51), and this may have been the case with Dennis Banks.

There are again no absences recorded for him for grade five, which went until May 14, 1948, and his file indicates that he was promoted to grade six, with the comment "Capable of doing *very* good work. Rather nice boy, has sweet kindly expression." Nonetheless, after the semester had ended, Superintendent Beitzel wrote on May 17,1948, to inform the Becker County Welfare Board that Dennis Banks and four others (names redacted) "were absent without permission from the Pipestone School," that they had "deserted" or run away. In a follow-up letter on May 22, the superintendent informed the Board that Banks and two of the others "were returned to the school as of same date"—the same day they had run off, it would seem. On this occasion, Banks reports a punishment for those runaways who were returned that Walter Littlemoon at OCHS, Tim Giago at HRMS, and a few other students elsewhere had called the "belt line."[18]

Banks calls it "the hot line," and he explains that the student to be punished had "to run between two rows of other kids, who held sticks and switches," with which they "lashed out at [him]" (27). Aware of this harsh punishment, Banks nonetheless makes two subsequent attempts to run away. He writes that in "the summer of [his] eighth year, Grandpa and Grandma came" to visit (29). As noted, he was not at Pipestone for eight years, but whatever year the visit did occur, he writes that it "triggered a rush of memories and longing to get back to Leech Lake," so that after his grandparents left, he "tried to run away. The authorities caught [him] two days later and threw [him] in jail." Perhaps the room Adam Nordwall had heard was once used as a jail had now come to serve that purpose again. Banks says only that when he was released from jail, he "had to go through the beatings again" (29), perhaps "the hot line," perhaps something else. "In spite of the beatings and the futility," he writes, he "was determined to try again." No fewer than seven friends would accompany him, and this time the boys had given their plan much thought. Some "of the older boys," he says, "told us which towns we would have to go through" (29) to get home.

Despite their planning, the runaways suffer from the cold and their food runs out. When the "school sent two cars out after us," Banks writes, "I was almost relieved to see them because, whatever the punishment, they would at least feed us when we got back" (29). They probably were fed and they were most certainly punished. Banks says that the boys were made to drop their pants before receiving ten lashes with a strap. Then they were made "to run through the hot line," at the end of which the authorities "shaved our heads and made us wear girls' dresses everywhere for three days" (30). Such punishments were common enough at some of the boarding schools of an earlier day, and Banks may indeed be accurate in saying they were in force at Pipestone just after World War II.

Banks recalls that in the classrooms there "were no pictures on the walls of Native American or Indian heroes," and that the history books "depicted Native people as murderous, mindless savages"; his "white teachers and their books taught [him] to despise [his] own people" (28). Adam Fortunate Eagle had also noted the school's texts as praising Indian fighters. Banks says that although he "could speak some Chippewa when [he] arrived at Pipestone," he forgot it in the years he spent there "because we were forbidden to speak our Native languages." As several times noted, this was not the policy at Pipestone, at least until 1946 (when Superintendent Balmer left), although the policy might have changed subsequently. Banks is surely correct when he writes, "Our teachers only allowed us to speak English" (28). But there were many other Chippewa students at the school, and Banks describes no attempt to speak the language with them outside the classroom, regardless of whether that was allowed or not. The matter of language loss is taken up further in the following chapter, which covers his first months home, as he describes "the shock" of realizing he "had forgotten most of [his] native Anishinaabe language. At school, English overpowered everything," he writes, adding that he "had to think in English to avoid being punished for accidentally speaking in [his] own language" (33).

In his time at boarding school Banks writes, he "began to hate himself for being Indian," and to "believe that [he] was really a white boy" (28). He sadly admits that at the movies the students attended once a week, he "sided with the cavalry cutting down Indians" (28), as did many another Native boarding-school student. The junior high school at Wahpeton where he was for "the seventh and eighth grades" (30), he writes, "was run like a military institution" (30), and he describes marching in uniforms with "wooden play guns over our shoulders, ... to the sound of the band," behind "the Stars and Stripes, our conquerors' flag" (30). This is an irony well worth noting, although it is also true that many Native men had joined the armed forces and fought in the war only recently ended, and Banks would also enlist in the military.

"After the eighth grade," Banks writes, "I was transferred again—this time to the big Indian boarding school at Flandreau, South Dakota, on the Santee Sioux reservation" (30). He says he was there "for about a year," and that he "was sixteen years old" (30). In "the ninth grade" (30–31), deciding finally "that enough was enough," he says, "I made my last escape" (31). With a friend, he walks from Flandreau to Pipestone, catches a freight train, and finally hitchhikes home to Leech Lake.

There, finding his mother remarried and with young children, he confronts his feeling of being "rejected" by her, the thought "that by sending [him] away to boarding school, [she] ... had tried to get rid of [him]" (31). This, too, is something many a boarding-school student had felt. Banks wants to understand "why she didn't come and get [him]" (31) for so long. He is sixteen years old, has not seen his mother for some nine years, and these would have been difficult conversations for the mother and her adolescent son to have at the time. From what Banks writes almost fifty years later, it appears that they never did have those conversations. To the question of why his mother had sent him away to school, Banks gives the answer, "I did not know then that it was government policy that forced Indian kids away from their families" (31). Yet what he might well have learned by this time is that the government had not forced him and his siblings to go "away from their families," but that his mother had accepted the recommendation that her children would be better provided for at Pipestone. He might have learned that she had sent them there not at all "to get rid" of them but rather to provide for them as best she could. As for why his mother didn't come and visit him, he also has a reductive and abstract answer: "She was a victim of the system. Her life consisted of unending hard work" (31). Had he at some point asked his mother about this, she probably would not have spoken of herself as only "a victim of the system," a categorical description that denies her agency and individuality.

A year and a half later, Banks writes, he "went into the military" (31), choosing, of his own volition, to march behind his "conquerors' flag" (31). Although he has affirmed that in spite of everything," he "loved" (31) his mother, he nonetheless "listed [his] grandparents first as [his] nearest kin to notify in case of injury or death," then his aunt, and his "mother after her" (31). After completing his service, he would go on to become "Dennis of Wounded Knee."[19]

∽

Jim Northrup and his older sister Judy took the yellow bus recalled by Dennis Banks to Pipestone in 1949, when Northrup was six years old. They are, in Northrup's parlance already noted, Shinnobs and Fonjalackers— Anishinaabe people from Fond du Lac. He and his sister had both spent "some months" in a sanatorium in Walker, Minnesota, for suspected tuberculosis (3–4), and Northrup had also had a year of kindergarten in Duluth. He would attend Pipestone from first through fourth grade. Although he was doing well and was promoted to the fifth grade in 1952, Pipestone's closing required him to go to school elsewhere. For an unspecified time he transferred to the Brainerd Indian Training School, a Methodist school in Hot Springs, South Dakota, and then graduated from Carlton Public High School in Minnesota in 1961, enlisting in the marines soon after. He tells us these things in his collection, *The Rez Road Follies: Canoes, Casinos, Computers, and Birch Bark Baskets* (1997), the first chapter of which is called "FAMILIES—*Nindanawemaaganag,*" one of the book's eight bi-lingually titled chapters. His account of his boarding-school experience is very brief but can to some extent be supplemented by at least one of his poems and by his student records.[20]

Northrup remembers asking his mother "why the white kids didn't have to leave home when they were in the first grade." "She couldn't answer," he writes, "she just looked away, but not before I could see the pain in her eyes" (4). Alice Northrup is pained because her two oldest children will indeed be leaving home to go to school three hundred miles away. But although it would have been difficult to explain to an eight-year-old girl and a six-year-old boy just why they had to go so far, nonetheless, Mrs. Northrup, like Mrs. Banks, could have answered. Her children were going to Pipestone for the same reason that Adam Nordwall and Dennis Banks (and many other Native children) traveled to Pipestone: because their family situation was such that their parents had decided the children could be better provided for at the boarding school than at home. The fact that this was so would surely have caused her "pain."

Alice Northrup had been very ill, and she was raising her four children on her own. The year before, she had had severe headaches; a tumor had been discovered, and the operation to remove it had kept her hospitalized long enough for her children to have been separated and temporarily put into foster care. In the summer of 1949 she anticipated needing another surgery, which would also require a lengthy convalescence, and she did not want her children to be separated again. Her mother could care for the two youngest but not the two oldest, and the Welfare Board of St. Louis County, Minnesota, had recommended Pipestone for them. As had been the case with Banks, this was a recommendation, not an order; these Indian children did not have "to leave home when they were in the first grade" (4) against their parents' wishes. Mrs. Northrup had signed the application form for the Pipestone School on August 19, 1949, and just a week later, on August 26, 1949, the U.S. Department of the Interior sent a letter addressed to six-year-old Jim Northrup informing him that he had been accepted to the school and requesting that he let them know whether he would be attending. It is reasonable to assume that Mrs. Northrup did not show—or read—that letter to her son but simply accepted the offer of admission on her own. It also appears that she did not tell him he would be going away very soon.[21]

The yellow bus, Northrup recalls, was filled with Anishinaabe kids from other reservations. Upon arrival at Pipestone, he and his sister were "separated as soon as [they] got off the bus" (4), and it seems that she went "to the girls' dorm," in that he writes, "We met our matron and were shown where we would sleep" (5). Northrup finds the "dormitory was a huge room with rows and rows of beds. I remember the smell of urine and disinfectant" (5). Because he is so young, it is quite possible that he is being placed—as Adam Nordwall had earlier been placed, and Dennis Banks for a brief period had been placed—in the "stink dorm," reserved for habitual bedwetters. It also may be that the dorms at Pipestone in its last years generally smelled of "urine and disinfectant."

Then "some adult washed our heads with kerosene and we were given a tablespoon of cod liver oil" (5). He does not say anything about his hair being cut, a major concern of most boarding-school students, nor does he speak of any further cleanup, or a change of clothes. Although the war had been over for several years, there was still marching at Pipestone. "As I recall," he writes, "our days went something like this. We woke up and made our beds. After that, we went downstairs to clean up and get dressed for the day" (5). Then, he says, "We formed squads and marched down the sidewalks to the dining hall" (5). "The first meal," he recalls, "was a brutal learning experience. While I was eating, a big guy reached across and took most of my food" (5). Thus the first lesson he learns at school is "how to eat while guarding [his] food" (5). There is no word about bells or bugles ordering his world according to clock time; if grace before meals was said, it is not mentioned.

After breakfast—he does not say what the food was like—the boys clean their dormitory, after which, Northrup writes, "we went to school." He finds school "easy," and he "quickly skipped a grade" (5). He did indeed skip a grade, although not "quickly." His file indicates that Northrup successfully completed first and second grade, and after the first semester of third grade, in November 1951 he was advanced to the fourth grade, skipping more than half of the third. As Northrup represents it, most of his time at Pipestone involved fighting other boys, some his own size and some a good deal bigger. He says he "was in thirty-seven fights by the time Halloween came," and that he "won two of them" (5). He offers more detail about some of those fights than about any other aspect of the school. That there were so many of them, apparently with no adult intervention, does not speak well of Pipestone in its last years.

"The nights in the boys' dormitory were the worst," he recalls. "After the night guard woke up the piss ants—those who usually wet their beds—we would try to sleep" (7).[22] Northrup writes, "Sometimes you could hear a big guy crawling into bed with a younger boy" (7). Then, "A young one on the little guys' side of the dormitory would begin quietly crying. Maybe he was crying because he was lonely and homesick, maybe he had been assaulted by a big guy" (7). This second "maybe" introduces a very serious possibility. But Northrup simply continues, "*Whatever the reason*, the boys on either side of him would tell him to be quiet" (7, my emphasis). But if "the reason" for the young boy's crying was that "a big guy" crawled into bed with him and "maybe ... assaulted" him, surely the nature of that assault would be sexual. The others may just "tell him to be quiet," but recalling this many years later, wouldn't Northrup want to offer some further thoughts? He is writing of a time when he himself was a "younger boy," only six. Had he perhaps been "assaulted" in his dorm bed by "a big guy" and told to be quiet? Is that why "The nights in the boys' dormitory were the worst"? (7).

What may well be a very painful memory is dismissed with the phrase I have emphasized, "*Whatever the reason*." Whatever the reason, "the little guy's crying became contagious, so that soon all the boys began to cry." Northrup writes, "I suspect all the boys were crying because it was the only thing we could do." Crying was indeed the only thing they could do to deal with their homesickness. But was crying the "only thing" the smaller boys could do in response to sexual abuse by the bigger boys? If so, this would again speak to an appalling lack of adult supervision at Pipestone in its last years.[23] "After a night like that," Northrup continues, "we all got up in the morning and pretended that it didn't happen" (7).

"After a couple of months in the first grade at Pipestone, I decided I'd had enough of this boarding school business," Northrup writes. "I wanted to go home" (7). In those "couple of months" he'd already heard "talk around the school about runaways so [he] thought [he'd] try" (7). He is now six and a half years old, and the time would be something like November in western Minnesota. It must be getting cold, and having traveled from Fond du Lac to Pipestone on the bus, he surely knows that home is a long way off. But he is a determined little boy. He tells his sister what he intends to do, and "she tried to talk [him] out of it but couldn't" (7). He has found school easy so far and has described no punishments; food, if you can protect it from the bigger boys, seems acceptable. Of course he is homesick, and he has had to do a great deal of fighting. But there is, of course, "the worst," those "nights in the boys' dormitory" (7).

His sister advises him to get on to Highway 23 and just head north. She then proceeds to walk him "to the rear gate of the school" (7) just after breakfast (8), and she waves goodbye as he goes off, surely one of the most casually public defections from boarding school in the literature.[24] Northrup writes that he enjoyed "the freedom of that bright, sunny day" (8), and walked until "close to dark" (8) when "a big, black car" comes up behind him. He runs into a cornfield—it probably wouldn't have provided much cover in November—but he is soon "caught … and dragged … to the car" (8). He says he doesn't "remember the beating [he] got back at the school"; there is no "belt line" or "hot line" to deal with, and no word of a jail. His sister is glad to see him, and she gives him "a big bite of our maple sugar cake," one that their grandmother had made and given them. "The taste always brought me home" (8), Northrup writes. He reports no further attempt on his part to run off.

Nor does he say anything more about that first year of boarding school: "Finally we were finished with school for the year. We rode home on the same yellow school bus" (8). That he and his sister could go home for the summer meant that their mother was well enough to receive them. "Once we were home," he writes, "I told my Ma how I got slapped for using an Ojibwe expression" (8–9).[25] His mother voices her outrage by swearing "in English at the white matron who was three hundred miles away." Northrup adds that "our parents and grandparents spoke only English during our summer at home" (9), something worth a moment's consideration. It is likely that Mrs. Northrup and her parents would want the boy to be able to speak his own language. But aware that it is now apparently forbidden, they all speak English during summer break, the colonial situation forcing them to make a difficult choice between speaking their Anishinaabe language and trying to make things a bit easier for the boy and his sister once they return to school. This is all that is said of the summer at home; the next paragraph has Northrup back at school.

Similarly condensed are the "second, third, and fourth grades," which, he says, "were easier because [his] cousin … transferred [to Pipestone] from another boarding school." This meant he "didn't have to fight so often" (9). Northrup does not mention the fact that he skipped a little more than the second half of the third grade—or, again, anything whatever about classes. Apart from his cousin, he doesn't name any of the other students. He does, however, speak of the attraction of the nearby Pipestone quarry, where "a red rock that can be carved into pipes and other objects" (9) is found.[26] He sums up, "Federal boarding school wasn't a totally negative experience. I learned to survive some terrible things. I learned how to fight even when scared. Most important, I learned how to read and write English" (9).

Of his further education Northrup writes, "In the 1950s, when I was a teen ager, my relatives and I went to a Christian boarding school in South Dakota. Brainerd Indian Training School was run by the Wesleyan Methodists" (10). Pipestone closed in 1952, when Northrup would have entered the fifth grade, and he would not be a teenager until 1956. This means either that he went to Brainerd earlier than he recalls or that several years of his schooling somewhere else are unmentioned. In any case he writes that Brainerd "was situated in the southern part of the Black Hills," and the "campus was in a valley between two hills." This allows for an important activity engaged in by Northrup and his "relatives," which was hauling tires to the top of one of the hills to see "whose tire would go the farthest, whose would jump the highest" when rolled down those hills. This was a pastime that was not approved of by the authorities, and the punishment, Northrup writes, required them to use "a pick and shovel to dig many ditches" (10).

Brainerd, as Northrup said, was a Methodist institution, but he is little inclined toward religious instruction. "It was fun outwitting the teachers and preachers," he writes. "We didn't respect those who gave their lives to minister to the godless heathens" (10). This is a bit puzzling. On the school application form for Pipestone, Mrs. Northrup had listed the children's religion as Methodist, and Northrup would have attended church services during his three years at Pipestone, Methodist services most likely. Can most or many of the Indian students at Brainerd have been "godless heathens" and not Methodists? Northrup and his sister would have been enrolled as Methodists. Nonetheless, Northrup proudly affirms himself "a heathen" (10), one who, along with his sister Judy—perhaps also a heathen—"ate with the Christians for a few months" (10). Whatever the disparity between the school's beliefs and Northrup's, "This boarding school," he writes, "was a lark compared to Pipestone" (10).

At the Brainerd school Northrup and his siblings "were given heavy doses of Christianity," which he describes in some detail, noting in particular that "we heathens went to church every night for three weeks," although "the Christianity didn't stick and we returned to the Reservation and our heathen ways" (10). Northrup returned to this subject in a column for Tim Giago's paper, *Indian Country Today*, one of a series of journalistic essays he referred to generally as "Fond du Lac Follies." In a piece titled "Thou shalt not use a siphon hose as a credit card," published on April 6, 2007, Northrup recalls the Brainerd school because William D. Gale, whom Northrup describes as "the lead dog" when he was a student there, has been in touch and asked to visit him in Minnesota. Noting again that the "school was operated by the Wesleyan Methodist Tribe," Northrup repeats the phrase he had earlier used when he states that its purpose was "to minister to the godless heathens" (n.p.). Northrup then makes clear that when Gale came to call, he managed not to be at home, and he refers to the man as "Chief Hugs Himself." He does not say what it was that led to an animus lasting some forty years.[27]

Northrup writes that he graduated "from Carlton Public high school in 1961" and then "enlisted in the United States Marine Corps," like the earlier Pipestone student Dennis Banks (along with many other Native boarding-school students) joining the military. He was sent to Viet Nam in 1965 (10), where he served for thirteen months (11). Jim Northrup returned to the Fond du Lac reservation to be with his "extended family" (1), to speak his Native language, to live in as traditional a manner as he could, and, of course, to write the newspaper columns, fiction, and poetry that brought him wide acclaim.

9

Edna Manitowabi's
"An Ojibwa Girl in the City"

EDNA MANITOWABI, AN OJIBWA/ODAWA WOMAN, WAS BORN IN 1941 AT THE
Wikwemikong Unceded Reserve on Manitoulin Island, Lake Huron
Province, Ontario. She is currently professor emerita of Indigenous Studies
at Trent University, a founder of the Nozhem Theatre, an actress, and Head
Woman for the Eastern Doorway of the Three Fires Midewiwin Lodge. In
1970, she published "An Ojibwa Girl in the City" in a progressive Toronto
journal called *This Magazine Is About Schools*. Perhaps a year later—there
is no publication date—this was reprinted as *An Indian Girl in the City*, in
Buffalo, New York, by a small press calling itself Friends of Malatesta, after
the Italian anarchist Errico Malatesta. The republication changes the title
from "An Ojibwa Girl in the City" to *An Indian Girl in the City*, making
it more general, and other specifics in the text are systematically general-
ized, as I'll note.[1]

The original essay was not long, and the reprint is an even shorter
free-standing book, only seventeen pages. The early pages briefly treat
Manitowabi's time at a Catholic boarding school in Canada,[2] and although
I have thus far only looked at the accounts of Indian boarding-school students in the United States, I think it is worth making an exception to consider
Manitowabi's account among the recollections of Ojibwe boarding-school
students. Several of the texts considered thus far are little known, and I have
stated my hope that they may become better known—as they deserve to
be. Edna Manitowabi's account, however, is practically unknown, at least in
the United States, for all that it is a very fine piece of writing well worth a
reader's attention.[3]

Manitowabi begins matter-of-factly: "I was born on a typical reserve ... located in an isolated area, the baby in a family of nine children ... in a two-room cottage" (8/1).[4] This "rather casual and cozy existence," she writes, "came to an end when I was six and was sent to a boarding school in a small town seventy miles from the reserve" (9/2). She notes that just off the reserve, three miles away, there was "a school in the village," but unfortunately "there was no school bus, and the roads were in a pretty bad condition" (9/2). Now Manitowabi finds herself in a "Catholic residential school, segregated by age and sex" (9/2). An older sister is also in attendance, and two of her brothers are at the nearby boarding school for boys. "I stayed there for four years," she writes, "and I don't think I ever stopped being scared and lonely" (11/2). Her fears are very much those experienced by young students at boarding schools elsewhere. She "was scared of being caught speaking Indian, scared because I didn't understand the English of the teachers and could not follow the lessons, scared that I would get punished for wetting my bed," and because this is a Catholic school, "scared that I would not wake up in time for the six o'clock mass." Clearly there was good reason to be scared, for she remembers "being beaten up for many of these things" (11/2).

She receives a visit from her parents at Easter time, not having seen them since she had left home in September (11–12/3–4), and her description of the visit vividly conveys the mix of anxiety, pleasure, and awkwardness of these occasions at the schools. She, her sisters, her brother, and also her parents "were all kind of confused about why we were there in that boarding school in the first place" (12/3), her parents telling the children only "that they had nothing to say about [their] going there. They were required by law to send [them]" (12/3). I would guess that in Canada, too, if there had been a school bus so that they could have traveled the three miles back and forth each day to the public school, that would have been acceptable, and the children would not have been sent to boarding school. Manitowabi writes that "the worst thing about the school was that I grew to resent my parents for having sent me there." She accurately notes: "A lot of the kids from reserves are sent to boarding schools, and they all go through the same thing, I suppose" (12/4).

She then provides an instance of a former boarding-school student who has gone "through the same thing." She is visiting her aunt when her cousin, a man in his thirties, "all of a sudden turned to his mother and said, 'Why the hell did you ever send me off to that bloody place, the boarding school?'" His mother says, as Manitowabi's parents had said, that it was the law. Her cousin has had a bit to drink, Manitowabi notes, and he repeats again and again his feeling that since his time in school his mother both is and is not his mother. Manitowabi writes, "I guess a lot of us feel that way about our parents" (13/5). Also like "a lot of us," Manitowabi on her first summer home insists "on speaking English ... although [she] knew that [her] parents didn't understand it" (12/4). The paragraph in which she muses on why she did this—because she had absorbed some of the school's values, because she was angry with her parents—is a powerful example of deeply insightful self-reflection, one of many such movingly "self-analytical" (Battaile and Sands 164) observations that Edna Manitowabi, not yet thirty years old, offers in her autobiographical essay.

What she does not offer is any details of her experience at the Catholic boarding school. We don't know the sleeping arrangements or what food, classes, or prayers were like. We know that she was beaten, but exactly why, when, or how is not recorded. Nor is any resistance on the part of students mentioned, nor instances of running off. Manitowabi writes only that when she "was eleven years old, a rural school was established near the reserve and [she] went back home to live." Like many another boarding-school student she "no longer felt at home there the way [she] used to." This is partly because two of her "sisters had had babies and brought them home," a situation that prompts her to begin "staying away from home more and more." Meanwhile, the "local school which [she] attended was not much of an improvement on the boarding school" (13/5), although for a somewhat different reason. "The teacher there"—perhaps the only teacher?—"was a distant relative, ... a middle class Indian who looked down upon me and my family for being poor." She stays out of school, falls behind in her work, and at age fifteen leaves "school without having completed grade nine." She writes that she was "fed up and ready to leave the reserve," deciding "to go to Toronto and get [herself] a job" (13/5).[5] Edna Manitowabi's formal schooling thus comes to an early close. She will have many other opportunities for learning, but these come only after she engages in some self-destructive and literally suicidal behavior that is very much related to her treatment and instruction at the Catholic boarding school she has attended.

She travels to Toronto with an older sister who "had already worked there as a domestic" (14/5), and with her sister's help, she gets work "as a mother's helper" in a "well-to-do Jewish home." Finding herself ill-suited for the job, she leaves it "and [drifts] in and out of several similar ones" (14/6). Meanwhile, she spends time with "other Indian kids who were working on shit jobs just like [hers]. We all felt equally lost." Manitowabi attempts to mitigate her sense of aimlessness and worthlessness in a ready-to-hand but self-destructive manner. "I got myself pregnant in a rather mechanical way by an Indian fellow who didn't mean anything to me," she writes insightfully and unsentimentally, and, "Remembering the situation at home ... didn't want to tell [her] parents about it and gave the child away for adoption" (14/6). But when she becomes pregnant again she returns home to the reservation, where her mother is ill and subsequently dies. Manitowabi has the child and makes arrangements for him to be cared for while she returns to Toronto. (The reprint again says "the City.")

She obtains work as a maid for a couple who are "both university teachers," and as she describes it, initially she "really felt at home" and found she "could talk about this whole Indian-White thing with them and tell them how confused [she] was, and they would try to understand." She has brought her son to Toronto, and it is not surprising, as she writes, that "the two of us had a great deal of difficulty in getting on with each other." The couple[6] is "really helpful when [she] needed somebody to talk to about these things" (14/6) as well. She is still seeing some of "the Indian kids [she] has known before," and "was always in danger of getting pregnant" (14/6). This is because she is not using any contraception, mostly, it would seem, because birth control is not permitted to Catholics, as abortion most certainly is not, something she will deal with soon.

At this point things become confusing on several levels. For one thing, Manitowabi finds it increasingly difficult to deal with "both being their [her employers'] friend and equal and their maid" (14/6). Planning to leave them, it would appear, she goes to St. Michael's Catholic hospital—its name is removed from the reprint—"looking for a job as a nurse's aide." She is "interviewed by a Sister Eileen"—name removed from the reprint—who tells her, "'we don't like to hire Indian girls, because they cannot be depended on, they are not reliable'" (15/7). This is surely similar to things she had heard from the sisters at the Catholic boarding school. Manitowabi writes that she can't remember what she said in response, although it seems to have made the sister feel "guilty," leading to her being "hired right then." But, as she acknowledges with the honesty that gives the writing great power, "I really felt at the time that she was right ... I was a person that could not be depended upon." (15/7).

She is still living with the university couple, however, and a further element of confusion is introduced when the wife—it is unclear what would prompt her to this—says that if Manitowabi is determined to get herself pregnant—apparently she has not hidden the fact that she is sexually active and using no contraception—she should have an affair with the husband and have his child. When she does sleep with the man, however, "all hell broke loose," and Manitowabi feels "guilty and miserable and became more and more apathetic and withdrawn." In this condition, she loses the hospital job, "proving again to Sister Eileen and myself that Indian girls could not be relied upon." "Finally things got so bad that Marsha [Gerta] arranged for [her] to get admitted to Toronto Psychiatric Hospital" (15/7). ("City Psychiatric Hospital" in the reprint.)

This is not, as it happens, a descent into hell. Quite the contrary, for, Manitowabi writes, at the hospital she felt "totally safe: doctors, nurses and other patients all seemed friendly and approachable" (15/8). For a long time she "stayed in [her] shell ... brooding about [her] Indianness and [her] isolation," but then she warily joined group therapy sessions where she "would begin to talk." She is extremely fortunate in having "a psychiatrist who was both gentle and tough in a right combination," but when she is discharged after ten months, she "felt totally helpless. It was like being born again. It was even worse than when [she] had first come from the reserve." A social worker gets her a place "at the Adult Retraining Centre," although she finds she "just couldn't cope with the situation at all." She is still on medication and feels "slowed down," and "like a zombie." Although she understands, again with great insight, that committing suicide "is a very selfish thing to do," she takes an overdose of sleeping pills nonetheless (16/9). But when she first feels their effect, she hurries to call Marsha [Gerta], with whom she is still in touch. The woman arrives to help her and she has apparently called the appropriate authorities, for Manitowabi finds herself waking "in a hospital" (17/9).

There she has a dream vision, but it is not filled with traditional symbolism that shows her a path forward. Rather, as she understands it, "It showed what a struggle it was for me to decide whether to go on living or not. Death was such a powerful temptation" (18/10). The place in which she now finds herself is very different from the hospital in which she earlier spent ten months. This is "a grubby old mental hospital in the outskirts of Toronto." Rather than everyone seeming "friendly and approachable," the place is "dark and crowded and staff were always in a hurry." She speaks of no treatment being offered, and, finally, "just to have something to do," she begins singing to herself, "old Indian songs and chants, and sometimes [she] would make up new words" (18/11). She continues to sing once out of the hospital—after a stay of four months—and finds that "people responded very well … it seemed like I had finally discovered something I could do and not be ashamed of" (18/11).

A social worker finds her "a job at a big downtown department store," and she goes to see a psychiatrist recommended to her by the one she earlier "had liked so much"—he has left town—at the Toronto Psychiatric Hospital. Manitowabi writes, "I went to see Dr. Jones and that was perhaps the most important event in my life." The doctor is "kind and unassuming, softspoken almost like an Indian. He never asked me any stupid questions or gave me any advice" (19/11). She "can't quite explain it, but it seemed like his liking me and accepting me the way I was gave me a new kind of energy." She still has difficulty keeping jobs, and when she tries to go back to school, "that didn't work out either" (19/12). Although she sees herself "'failing' again," she nonetheless "did not feel as badly about [her]self as [she] had in the past." The doctor recommends her for "an office job in a private art school," and once there, she "fell in love with the place right away." Before long, she says, she feels she has a "community" again "for the first time since [she] left TPH [Toronto Psychiatric Hospital]" (20/12), and of course this is a community in the wider world.

As Manitowabi poignantly describes it, feeling less "badly" about herself, and being in a position to do well are not without their own difficulties. She writes, "I wanted that job very much, yet I was scared of it. Part of me also felt that I didn't deserve it, that I was still 'no good'" (20/12–13). She had "done the mental hospital bit," and she "had tried suicide," neither of which she wanted to try again. "But there was also another way open for self-punishment and escape," she writes, "one that I had used many times before. The night I found out about the job I went out and slept with an Indian fellow I neither knew well nor cared about. I knew why I was doing it and I knew well what was going to happen. I became pregnant again" (20/13).

In the past, she observes with great self-awareness, "Pregnancy … meant that [she] had an excuse to withdraw." She would "feel too sick to do very much for the first few months, and then … move into a home for unwed mothers and vegetate there until the baby was born" (20/13). She does not want to do that now and decides to have an abortion so that she can keep the job she loves. And Dr. Jones informs her that he can help her "get a therapeutic abortion." After speaking to "a hospital psychiatrist whose recommendation was necessary" (20/13), however, he learns "that in view of [her] 'history' they could only recommend a therapeutic abortion if it went together with sterilization" 20–21/13), something she adamantly rejects.[7] "The alternatives left," she states, "were having an illegal abortion or having the baby" (21/13).

It is at this point that she begins "trying to figure out why sex had played such a destructive role in [her] life," and realizes that it "dated back to [her] Catholic schooling and the values [she] received there" (21/13–14). Her parents, she writes, were only casually Catholic, but they "did not have any other values that would have replaced the Catholic ones" (21/14). It would be interesting at this point to know more about the "values" of this Ojibwe family that spoke an Indian language at home, and also sang Indian chants and songs that Manitowabi remembered. Nothing further is said of this, however. She acknowledges here that for her, "birth control was out of the question," and it "seemed only just to [her] that [she] ran the risk of 'getting punished' every time [she] slept with somebody." She is once more acutely aware of the intensity of her low self-esteem, the fact that when she "started sleeping with guys [she] felt pretty badly about [herself] in general," and "would invariably pick an unemployed homesick Indian fellow who seemed to be in an even worse shape than [she] ... a kind of suicide" (21/14).

Only now does she inform readers that having been advised by a doctor at the Toronto Psychiatric Hospital to take birth control pills, her first response had been to consult with a priest, although she knew full well what the priest would say (22/14). As a result, she says, she took birth control pills randomly, not regularly, "So," as she realizes, "the Catholic values were pretty deep in me" (22/15). Although once more she does not discuss it, those values derive from her time at the Catholic boarding school. She obtains an abortion without incident and surprises herself "because [she] didn't feel guilty at all," something that makes her "really angry with [her]self for not feeling badly about the whole thing"—but also "relieved" (22/15). At this point she recognizes—the choice of metaphor is interesting in a discussion of pregnancy—that she has to "cut the cord with the Catholic church" (22–23/15). "And," as she triumphantly writes, "I never again got pregnant after that" (23/16).

The break with the church is a break with her painful boarding-school past, and things look up for Manitowabi from this point forward. Dr. Jones and the director of the art school direct her to a part-time position at the "university" (Trent University, not far from downtown Toronto) "for an Indian language consultant that could help graduate students in a practical way." Her response, understandably, is, "Working at the university with a school background like mine!" (23/16). But she takes the position, soon is given "a full-time appointment," and commences work on "an Ojibwa language manual, to be used by both graduate students and Ojibwa Indians who want to learn to read and write in their own language." She also takes courses toward a B.A. (23/16). Structurally to complete what is an essentially integrative comic narrative—see later discussion of comic, tragic, and ironic narratives—is the fact that Manitowabi is now earning enough to have her son live with her—and she has "fallen in love" with Jim Dumont, "an Ojibwa Indian … not brought up on a reserve." They are hoping to "go back to the old Indian ways" and planning to be married "by a medicine man." Their hope is to "set up a school for Indian kids where they are taught in their own language and where special attention is given to Indian values and Indian ways of life" (24/17), a school very different from the Catholic boarding school that had badly harmed Edna Manitowabi. She did marry Dumont, and she did "go back to the old Indian ways." Her Catholic boarding school had indeed changed Edna Manitowabi, but by no means forever.

PART III

A RANGE OF BOARDING-SCHOOL AUTOBIOGRAPHIES

10

Thomas Wildcat Alford's
Civilization

No literary importance attaches to the account; and Mr. Alford at 76 monotonously remembers only the fine qualities of his people. He and his amanuensis have not striven to make a drama of his life. The book takes its place without fanfare on one's shelf labeled "Contact of cultures."

—James G. Leyburn

THUS READS THE LAST PARAGRAPH OF A THREE-PARAGRAPH REVIEW BY Professor James Leyburn, a Yale sociologist, of Thomas Wildcat Alford's *Civilization* (1936) that appeared the same year as its publication (1039). One may wonder what other volumes stood on Leyburn's "Contact of cultures" shelf, and which of them, if any, had struck him as more worthy of "fanfare" than Alford's. Although I doubt that readers of the *American Sociological Review* in which Leyburn's estimate appeared were legion, the relative obscurity of Alford's autobiographical volume today makes one wonder. It is also the case that two other contemporary reviewers of the book, the anthropologists Frank Speck (1937) and Erminie Voegelin (1937), were only a little more enthusiastic than Leyburn. In 1979, when the University of Oklahoma Press reissued *Civilization* in a paperback edition, it chose a historian, Angie Debo, to write the introduction.[1] Nonetheless, reviews were no more numerous for the reprint than they had been for the original. I would agree with Leyburn that Alford's account is wanting in "drama," although his recollections strike me as far from "monotonous."

    Civilization had been considered by a literary scholar just two years after being reprinted, when David Brumble included brief mention of it in his 1981 *Annotated Bibliography of American Indian and Eskimo Autobiographies.*

Brumble found it "a very interesting book" (12), and he mentions it again in passing in his *American Indian Autobiography* (1988 138–39). In 1983 Jacqueline Fear had discussed it in detail in a French publication, and, writing as Jacqueline Fear-Segal, she returned to it almost a quarter century later in her book *White Man's Club* (2007), its title deriving from Alford.[2] A few years earlier Ruth Spack included a highly selective account of *Civilization* in her *America's Second Tongue* (2002), treating Alford's relation to the teaching of English, the subject of her book. Otherwise, apart from a few brief mentions, *Civilization* has very nearly sunk into the oblivion to which Leyburn wished to consign it. Alford has much to say about his boarding-school education, a sufficient reason to consider his book here.

ཚ

Born in 1860, Thomas Wildcat Alford, an Absentee Shawnee,[3] died in 1938, the same year as Zitkala-Sa, and just a year before the death of both Charles Eastman and Luther Standing Bear, his better-known contemporaries. The title of Eastman's autobiography was *From the Deep Woods to Civilization* (1916), a title suggesting a passage from relative darkness to light. Other "from-to" titles of the period, like that of Joseph Griffis's *Tahan: Out of Savagery into Civilization* (Tahan 1915), also highlighted the passage from the author's earlier condition to a later one. This, as I'd observed, was often the case as well with the titles of autobiographies by immigrants to the United States. Mary Antin's first autobiographical text, *From Plotzk to Boston* (1889), for example, uses the name of her city of origin in present-day Belarus—an awkward, unattractive, and distinctively *foreign* name to the tongues and ears of American English speakers—to contrast with the name of the city to which she has come, Boston, the acme of American civilization. But Antin titled her second autobiography *Promised Land* (1912), now naming only the wonderful place she finds herself at last.

One could read Alford's *Civilization* in much the same way, taking its title as simply referencing the height to which the author has ascended. Or one could read it as more nearly like the title of the Dutch immigrant Edward Bok's story, *The Americanization of Edward Bok* (1920). "Americanization," this is to say, while surely a fine thing, is nonetheless complex; the processual term allows for more nuanced consideration than does the nominal "promised land." Similarly, "civilization" would no doubt seem a good thing for a

Shawnee born in 1860 to have attained—but like "Americanization," it is available for interrogation. Although Alford did not participate in Indian rights organizations, or have a correspondence with his contemporary Native writers and activists, and although from the evidence of his book, he does not seem to have been a wide reader, by the time he wrote, words like "culture" and especially "civilization" had been lowercased and relativized, making it possible for them to take a plural: not Culture but cultures; not Civilization but civilizations. These developments provide useful context for consideration of his book.

Any attempt to recuperate Thomas Wildcat Alford as a visionary of the "progressive" era would be an exercise in misplaced critical ingenuity; his untroubled sense, near the end of his book, that the Shawnees are not "'dying out'" but "just gradually losing their identity" (198) would be only one of several obstacles to such an attempt.[4] Nonetheless, although Alford's education changed him forever, it did not diminish his sense of himself as a proud Shawnee, one who would spend his entire life working among his people for their benefit—as he understood it. His understanding was historically bound, and a good deal of it now seems mistaken. But it would be unwise simply to dismiss Alford as an assimilationist unworthy of critical attention.

Alford was indeed born in 1860, but he dates his birth more specifically than that. He writes that "according to [his] parents," he had been born "'about the time blackberries were ripe,' which probably would mean about July 15" (1), the old way of reckoning dates apparently aligning fairly well with the calendrical dating he would learn later and use throughout his book. At the time of his birth, Alford's family was living in Indian Territory, near what would become the town of Sasakwa, Oklahoma. This was then Creek country, the Creeks having allowed his people to settle among them "after the forcible removal of the Shawnees from their former reservation in the state of Texas" (1). Migrating as a result of white pressures, the Shawnees at one time or another had been settled not only in Texas but in Mexico, Kansas, and Ohio.

On the first page of the book he informs us that his father "was of mixed-blood, having had an English captive for his grandmother" (1). Captured by the Shawnees as a child, and living among them until she was fourteen, when his grandmother was returned "to her own family" (2), like many another returned white captive, she preferred life among the Indians, and soon ran off to rejoin them.[5] His mother's father, Alford writes, was the "son of the celebrated Shawnee warrior Tecumseh" (3), something of which he reminds us only once more late in the book, when he refers to his great-grandfather—parenthetically—as "(the noted Tecumseh)" (179).

His father's Indian name translated roughly as "lying-spotted-in-the brush," and he "was called Wildcat" (1). Shawnee custom does not ascribe the father's name to his son, and it is probably when Alford first goes to school that he is given Wildcat as a surname. He writes that when he was ten days old he was named "by an old friend of the family," to whose clan he then belongs.[6] The name he was given is "Gay-nwaw-piah-si-ka (one of long following or file, as the leader of a drove of wild horses) which soon was shortened to Gay-nwah" (3). He offers no other English equivalent.

The first years of his life, he writes, "were years of great agitation among all Indians of the Old Indian Territory, as well as among all the citizens of the nation" (5), as civil war seems imminent and soon breaks out among the states. His family's Creek neighbors would have his father join the Confederacy, which his father refuses to do, requiring the family to relocate to Kansas. There he is pressed to join the Union army, and, with other Shawnee men, he finally enlists in the Kansas cavalry and serves until the end of the war (12). Alford writes that it was "about the year 1868 when [his] father and mother with other members of their tribe returned to the country then known as Indian Territory ... to select their permanent home." "For eight years," he specifies, "they had wandered from place to place with no settled home" (18).

Alford's narrative was edited by Florence Drake, and one may wonder whether the fact that it consistently provides dates, exact or approximate, is the result of her influence. But Alford had a fair amount of formal education, and he had also taught at and been principal of a school. He had been employed in various capacities by the Indian Service, for which he wrote many letters, all of which bear the date of their composition, so that the Western clerk's or historian's use of chronological specificity might well have become habitual with him. Brumble (1981) and Fear-Segal (2007) have both raised the question of how and to what extent Drake influenced the published text of *Civilization*, and while I cannot answer that question as well as I would like, I can adduce a few facts on which to base some tentative speculation.

In 1960 Florence Drake published an essay called "Tecumseh at the Turn of the Century," describing the town of Tecumseh, Oklahoma—Oklahoma Territory until 1907—where both she and Alford lived. At the bottom of her essay's first page is a brief biography of the author. It notes that she was born near Coldwater, Mississippi, in 1872 (397), but it does not provide her name at birth. She was born Florence McNeely and married John Drake in 1889. She moved with him to Oklahoma Territory in 1898, had a large family, and published a number of historical articles. She had been a signer, with others, of the Articles of Incorporation for the Historical Society of Pottawatomie County in May 1937, and I have seen mention that she was a professor at the University of Oklahoma, something I have not been able to confirm. I suspect she was not an academic historian but, rather, a passionate amateur. Whether Alford had sought her help in writing his life story or whether Drake was the initiator of the project is unknown. She died in 1967 and was buried in the Tecumseh Cemetery where Alford had been buried almost twenty years earlier.

In a brief preface Drake expresses regret for her "inability to convey the ideas presented by Mr. Alford in exactly his own words" (n.p.), hoping "that the sympathetic understanding of the reader will give the interpretation which [she has] failed to convey" (n.p.). In that Alford narrated in English, it is difficult to understand why there would be any "inability" on her part "to convey the ideas presented by Mr. Alford in exactly his own words." His contributions to the *Southern Workman*[7] and his letters in the Hampton Archives that I have read are in nearly faultless standard English (a lengthy one appears as appendix A to the present volume), so it remains unclear why Drake would feel any "inability to convey" Alford's ideas in his own words. I believe her contribution to the book consisted of some modest editing and perhaps the addition of some dates and explanatory footnotes. *Civilization* most certainly represents Alford's ideas.

His family having ended their wanderings and returned to Indian Territory, Alford now offers a number of ethnographic details concerning Shawnee culture, with the desire like that of Eastman and Standing Bear to provide mainstream Americans with some accurate information about the beliefs and practices of his people. He begins with the subject of education, writing that although his family had indeed been unsettled for quite some time, often "with no roof to cover us" and "food ... scarce," nonetheless, "the care and training of the children had been given just as much thought as if we had lived happily in an established community." Of course there "were no schools, no paid teachers," and yet, he emphasizes, "Indian parents realized just as much responsibility for the training of their young as any other race of people" (18). "In fact," Alford asserts, "I now believe that the Indian family of fifty years ago paid more attention to the teaching of their children than does the average white family of today" (18).

This is from a chapter titled "Indian Child Life," and among the many things he tells readers is that while Indian children "were seldom punished," and punishments were rarely physical in nature, when a "severe punishment was deemed necessary, children's thighs and calves of their legs were scratched" with an implement he names and describes in detail. It was, he notes, "a very painful punishment and one that was seldom used." Familiar with corporal punishment among the whites, he acknowledges that among his people, "Sometimes parents used switches or sticks to beat their children," but he points out that this "was considered a disgrace to both the parent and the child" (22).

"As a boy," he continues, "I held just as much fear in my heart of a white man, as any white boy held fear of a 'wild Indian'" (26), and he reacts "with a terrible fear and awe" (26) on seeing a white man for the first time. This particular white man is a "licensed Indian trader" named McDonald, called Mac by the Indians. Alford says he and his young friends "used to go with [their] parents to Mac's store and gaze in wonder at the many interesting things he displayed," and since he "always was very kind" to them, they "learned not to fear him." Before his introduction to the white man's schools, the "first 'store shoes' [he] ever wore came from that store" (27).

About 1872, he writes, the Shawnee chiefs allowed the Quakers, who had formerly visited among them and gained the people's trust, to open a mission and a school. The mission "was built about one-third of a mile from [his] father's cabin." (Alford's mother had died some three years earlier.) His father "was one of the few Indians of the time who really believed in education, and he heartily endorsed the efforts of the Friends" (75). The Friends' missionary is a man named Thomas Stanley, "whose manner was very different from what we had been taught to expect from white men, for he was full of smiles and kindness" (75). "When the mission was finished, and a day school opened, six Indian children and I," Alford writes, "were admitted, and were given English names." Stanley suggests that the young man "be given his name, Thomas" (76), and—although nothing is said of this—it is probably at this point that his father's name is added as a surname, making the new student Thomas Wildcat.

Alford writes that he spoke "no word of English, except for the word 'soldier' which was [his] nickname" (76),[8] and it is at this point in the narrative—the beginning of his education in the white man's schools—that

Alford, looking back more than sixty years, recalls the intuitions that would determine the course of his life. He writes that he "no longer had any fear of white people, but had a great desire to learn their ways," adding, "In fact for a long time there had been a question in my heart for which I could find no answer." He doesn't put that question into words as yet, but writes, "I loved my people and I liked their ways," the second verb, I think, meant only to avoid repeating the first rather than to weaken it. Moreover, "I had a profound respect for and confidence in those men who were my father's friends, who had such a bitter hatred against the white race, or rather against those things which the white race represented. There were some warm friendships between Indians and white men, but generally the Indians hated the thought of civilization" (76). "Civilization" here means the ways of the whites and the power they have to impose those ways.

But looking back, he recalls: "Deep down in my nature however, there was a yearning desire for things which civilization represented. I hardly knew what it was that I desired, young as I was, yet I was conscious of a deep and unsatisfied longing. Something, some inner voice, told me there was a *better* life, a better way of living than my people knew" (76–77, my emphasis).

I've emphasized his use of "better" as a vague but powerful indicator of the growing appeal of "civilization" in a broader sense, and Alford will use it again. He offers here, of course, the retrospective view of a devout Christian, for it is unlikely that the twelve-year-old Thomas Wildcat would have expressed his feelings in just this way. That said, it would be a mistake to reject the portrait painted here as no more than the back-projection of a man in his seventies onto the pre-teen boy, for it is consistent with the sense of self that Alford presents all through the book. The attractiveness of some of what the United States Americans brought was felt by a great many indigenous individuals the world over. The "better way of living" that Alford—and, again, many others—felt might be theirs, as they came to know it more fully, does not inhibit sharp criticism of "civilization," nor does it undermine their Native identities. As Carlos Montezuma's poem put it, "Changing is not vanishing."

There is no cleanup at the school because it is a day school, and the children wear the clothes in which they have come. "We boys wore our hair short," Alford writes, but this is not because the school cut their hair. Rather, "This is the way Shawnee men always have worn their hair. Never did they braid it, as some other tribes do" (77). The girls, however, do wear their hair "long and braided," and the school makes no attempt to change that. In time, the children receive secondhand clothing "like white children wore," sent by "good friends in the East" (77). Alford does not recall "what books we studied at first," noting that the "teaching must have been mostly oral" (78). This "oral" teaching is effective in that the children, he states, can spell and read even before they receive "McGuffey's readers." These readers, he recalls, "opened to us many wonderful visions of the life of white people, especially white children" (78).

"In that school," Alford says, "we learned to read and to write, to spell and to cipher, and we were also taught a new idea of serving the Great Spirit—the personal way white people served him" (78), in particular the Quakers' manner of worship. (Zitkala-Sa was also first taught by Quakers.) Where religion has planted its banner, the flag of the state soon follows: "For two years the Friends held the day school in connection with the mission, then the government assumed control, added a new building and turned it into a boarding school" (79). This was in 1874, four years before the beginning of the Indian program at Hampton Institute, and five years before Richard Pratt would establish the Carlisle Indian Industrial School. "Although the opening of the mission had meant a great deal to our people," Alford writes, "government control of the school meant a great deal more," as the Shawnees "began to realize that civilization would be forced upon them" (79). "Civilization" here too refers not to something "better" but rather to the dictates of the government. As was the case whenever and wherever Native people "began to realize that civilization would be forced upon them," response to that realization was broadly of two kinds: "the more progressive ones," as Alford puts it, "accepted the fact," and "sent their children to school so they might learn to fight the white man with his own weapons—words" (79), the key to the "club of the white man's wisdom," as one of the chiefs had earlier put it (73).

Alford does not, at this point, offer a name for those Shawnees who disagreed with the "progressives," nor is it the government school itself that leads to "a division among the tribe" (81). This division is occasioned by an Act of Congress, which in 1872 had allotted tribal lands in the area, "giving the Pottawatomies just double the amount allowed the Shawnees" (80). (This is well before the Dawes General Allotment Act of 1887.) While the Shawnee progressives resign themselves to what the government in its wisdom had done, "nearly half the tribe ... known to the government as the non-progressives, refused to accept the allotments." Early in the spring of 1876 the "non-progressives," as he now calls them, "removed into the Kickapoo Reservation (which had not been allotted in severalty)" (81). By this time, as Alford had explained earlier, he had "attended the mission school two years" and then gone "to the government school two years." Unfortunately, he does not describe his experiences in either place, only stating proudly that he "learned rapidly."

He writes, "I believe it is a compliment to the old methods of teaching"—he means in the Indian day schools of the 1870s—"when we consider the advancement a student could make in so short a time." Thus, at the end of only four years, he tells us, " I could read and write reasonably well; I had mastered the first four rules of arithmetic to the complete satisfaction of my teachers, and I had a smattering knowledge of geography, physiology, grammar, and had taken a peep into the fascinating study of natural philosophy and other branches of higher learning and science" (80). All this in just two years of Quaker instruction and two more of government instruction! Admirable as these accomplishments are, Alford writes, "I learned what was far more important—that I had only glimpsed the wonders of education. I had only tasted the joy of knowing things, and I had a consuming thirst for more knowledge" (80). A very great deal is omitted from this general summary—there is no word, for example about his teachers, his fellow students, or discipline at the school; nor is there mention of whether other students were less willing or less successful pupils than he.

His father's health had been impaired by his military service, and by 1876 it had deteriorated to the point where the young man "had to quit school … and help … make a living for the family" (82). Alford provides a fascinating "inside" account, as it were, of the situation of his Shawnee family as white "civilization" encroaches. "As the people in the country increased in number, the game and wild animals decreased, while the price of pelts and furs was the same as before, or perhaps lower" (82). He and his siblings hunt, trap, fish, and for the most part work his father's land, which as he describes it, "was rich valley soil, but only about ten acres were cleared for cultivation, and our farming methods were crude indeed" (82). He gives a brief but fascinating description of just what those methods were, which I will not quote but recommend highly to the reader.

Alford's ambition while at school had been to gain employment as a government interpreter, and he was "deeply disappointed" to think that because he had to leave he "never would be able to prepare [himself] for such

a position" (83). He does, however, become interpreter for several local traders, and the position causes him to qualify the glowing account he had given
earlier of his scholastic accomplishments. He acknowledges that his "use of
English was somewhat limited," although it was sufficient "to interpret all
that was necessary in [his] position" (83). Unlike how they are depicted in
old western movies, these traders are, as Alford has found other whites thus
far, kind and decent men who encourage him to continue his education.

One, a Mr. Blossom, seeing the young man's "hunger for reading
matter"—"it was almost impossible to get books to read" and "very few
newspapers came into the country"—"suggested to [him] that he subscribe
to the *Youth's Companion*, a weekly magazine published in Boston" (85). This
he does, finding it at first "hard ... to read ... for there were so many words
and expressions used that [he] could not understand" (85). But he attends
eagerly to the illustrations in the magazine, and persists to the point that
"gradually [he] learned to understand the stories," thus gaining "not only
a *better* use of English, but a *better* knowledge of the conditions of life and
the ways of the world" (85, my emphasis), steps on the way to "civilization."

The earnest and curious Thomas Wildcat—he is about seventeen or
eighteen, and if he has participated in any Shawnee rituals for young men he
says nothing of them—is attentive not only to the ways of the world. "While
[he] had been in school [he] attended the mission services on Sundays" (85).
He would like to continue his attendance, although his present situation
does not permit it, inasmuch as "the trader's cattle ... needed grass on the
Sabbath as well as on other days" (85). Like many an Indian shepherd, the
young cattle herder finds that some days "sitting idly for hours on guard,
while the cattle grazed peacefully, were days of deep thought." And "daily the
conviction grew upon me that there was a *better* way to live than my people
knew" (86, my emphasis). His "visits with the teachers, [his] talks with the
missionaries, fired [his] ambition and strengthened [his] determination to
make something of himself." Like many an American country boy, he says
that "above all I wished to see the wonders of a large city" (86). His next page
begins a new chapter, and it is called "Planning for an Education."

In 1877 Alford's father dies, a sister marries, and his stepmother remar-
ries and takes her children to live with her new husband. This leaves Alford,
on the one hand, "free to make such plans and to undertake such things as
[he] pleased about [his] future," but on the other, "under the guardianship
of [his] uncle, his mother's brother, Chief Big Jim." Among the Shawnees,

as in many other tribal nations, the mother's brother is the authority figure, all the more so when his nephew's parents have died. Big Jim, however, is "the non-progressive leader of half of the tribe,"[9] "opposite to [Alford's] father in all his views," with "little sympathy for [Alford's] ambitions" (87). Nonetheless, even some of the non-progressive leaders "realized that times were changing." They are persuaded by the missionaries to "have some of their men educated so that they might understand the treaties and messages sent from Washington," and prospective students are "selected from the two principal clans" (88) by the chiefs. One is our narrator; the other is a friend named John King, eight years his senior. Alford is delighted at the opportunity to continue his education and notes that although both young men "hoped to lead a life that would be worthwhile," they "differed in [their] philosophy." King "longed for success in a business way, while [Alford] thought more about the mystery of life, the development of his mind, and the welfare of [his] people" (88). Charles Eastman had also been drawn to these latter dimensions of American "civilization," "rather than those of commerce, nationalism, or material efficiency" (*Deep Woods* 195).

To pay for the young Shawnees' education, their minister turns to the Philadelphia Society of Friends. Two "scholarships for Indian boys in the Hampton Institute" in Virginia are obtained, one donated by an unnamed "friend of the Indians" and one "given by Miss Alice Longfellow in memory of her father, Henry Wadsworth Longfellow" (89). Thus will Thomas Wildcat become the Longfellow scholar at Hampton.[10] Before they start for the East, the two friends receive a nocturnal visit from the chiefs, including Alford's non-progressive uncle, Big Jim. The prospective Hampton students are reminded that they are "not to go as individuals, but as representatives of the Shawnee tribe." They are to "learn the white man's wisdom. How to read in books, how to understand all that was written or spoken to or about [their] people and the government." Once they have done so, they are to return home and "assume the duties and positions of chiefs at the death of the present chiefs." To do this, Alford admits, is his "greatest ambition" (90), and the clans to which King and Alford belong are indeed the ones from which hereditary chiefs of the Shawnees were chosen.

There is, however, an important condition imposed by the chiefs, and that is that the young men "*should not accept the white man's religion;* [they] *must remain true to the Shawnee faith*" (90, italics in original). If they "did accept the new teachings, [they] would forfeit all hope of becoming chiefs.

Fired with ambition," Alford writes, "and not realizing the importance of the obligation ... [they] solemnly pledged [themselves] to remain true to the faith of [their] fathers" (90). The council "lasted most of the night," the chiefs affirming to the young men that they are to acquire the secular knowledge of the white man but to retain the religious beliefs of their people. Although the thoughtful and philosophically inclined Thomas Alford has gladly absorbed some of the teachings of the Friends, at this important moment his ambition to become a chief obscures any doubts he may have about holding true to his pledge.

The two young Shawnees set out "early in October, 1879." They have with them a paper addressed "'To Whom It May Concern,'" identifying them and their destination. This is deemed necessary in spite of what Alford has told us about his ability to read and write, and his service as interpreter for some Indian traders. Alford and King will travel by train, and they have been instructed "to show this paper to conductors ... and to policemen," because "policemen always were to be trusted" (92). In order to board the train, however, they must first ride "about one hundred twenty miles" (92) to Muscogee. Once there—the trip is not described—Alford, like many another young Indian headed for a distant boarding school, describes "the marvelous passenger train ... with its shrieking engine and grating noises," and the "sheer marvel of that coach," with its "softly cushioned seats," and its "carpeted aisles." Also on the train are many "strange people who stared at [them] so intently" (93).

The young men change trains in St. Louis, and the trip east produces in Alford a sense of wonderment at both the country—"The deep, swift rivers, the beautiful mountain scenery, awe inspiring, marvelous"—and its development—"well-cultivated fields, ... beautiful homes, ... busy, bustling cities, and small towns" (95). The train is late arriving in Baltimore and a carriage they hire to take them to the ship they must board to complete the journey delivers them to what Alford describes as a "big building." They enter the "building" which of course turns out to be their ship, something they realize only after hearing "the most terrible, ear-splitting sound ... somewhat like the whistle on the train, but even more terrible. Then the whole building began to move" (97). We are not told the duration of the voyage, only that they arrive "at Fortress Monroe about nine o'clock in the morning and were met there by General Armstrong, superintendent of Hampton Institute, with a carriage. A few minutes later [they] reached [their] destination, the school" (98).[11]

The next chapter is called "Hampton Institute," and Alford begins: "When John King and I enrolled at Hampton Institute it was as if we had entered a new world. Although we had been accustomed to the regulations and discipline at the Shawnee Indian boarding school, yet in reality we knew nothing about the regulations of such a school as Hampton Institute" (99). Hampton, he observes here, "was a semi-military and industrial school" (99), and perhaps contrary to what readers might expect, the young Shawnees are not treated harshly, or forced immediately to sink or swim. Rather, the "management [sic] was very lenient with us from the beginning," to the point that "for thirty days we were allowed absolute freedom from discipline and were encouraged to investigate the campus and in fact the whole surrounding country" (99).

The student body consisted of "four or five hundred ... young men and young women from all parts of the United States and Cuba." Of these, "fully one hundred were Indians" (99), although he and his friend are the only Shawnees. It is worth pausing to note that Alford makes no mention here or elsewhere of the fact that the three or four hundred "young men and women" who are not Indians are blacks: American freedmen and freedwomen, and others not only from Cuba but from Latin America and even Africa. Because many of the Native students did not speak English, they "were placed in the Indian Department"—which also served non-English speaking Cuban, Latin American, and African blacks—while "Indian entrants [who] were often somewhat acculturated"—like Alford and John King—"usually moved quickly 'out' of the Indian Department" (Lindsey 119), overseen, as noted, by Booker T. Washington. Although Alford is partly subsidized by the government and has Alice Longfellow's help, he must still work to cover his expenses. Unfortunately, these interesting and unique aspects of Indian education at Hampton are not engaged in Alford's book.[12]

Alford describes settling into the regular routine of the school in the first-person plural, sometimes using "we" to speak generally but often to speak for himself and his Shawnee friend, John King—who is not once quoted directly or paraphrased. Alford describes how "we" were "assigned to our places in Company C of our battalion," and then more generally, "awakened at five o'clock in the morning" (99) to march to the dining room, where "we would stand at attention, boys on one side of the table and girls on the other" (100). He says nothing about the quality or quantity of the food served, a subject of considerable importance to most boarding-school students.[13] There is "an hour of study" after breakfast, after which "we prepared our rooms for daily inspection. Our uniforms must be brushed properly and worn properly, and our shoes shined." A bugle "called us to fall in line for another roll call after which came the morning inspection and military drill before regular class work began" (100). Once more Alford says nothing about what "regular class work" was like, the grade or level to which he was assigned, or day-to-day events at the school in general. Nor does he name or refer specifically to a single one of the black students or to any Indian student other than King.

After supper—again with no mention of what was served—there was, Alford writes, "a short evening prayer, accompanied by an instructive talk from the principal, which took place in the assembly room." This is followed by "a period of study ... until nine o'clock, when we returned to our rooms to prepare for bed." Taps is sounded at nine thirty, "when lights must be out. This completed the day's work" (100). Speaking of himself and John King, he points out that the two had only "recently adopted the dress of the white man," and that "Tooth brushes and bath tubs were conveniences we had to learn to use."[14] As was the case for most Native students, "It was all very strange to us," but, he says simply, "we liked it. Only a short time elapsed before all these things came to us just as naturally as if we had practiced them always." Their Shawnee upbringing, he says, was such that they "had been trained to respect authority, and that is the secret of a successful apprenticeship to military life" (100). If there were moments when the two Shawnees, despite their prior cultural training, were less than "successful" in their "apprenticeship," or if they knew of other Native students who experienced greater difficulties, we are not told. Nothing about runaways, resistance, or punishment of any kind is mentioned.[15]

Alford, like Eastman, tells of enjoying "a certain amount of social activity between the boys and girls." The music and the dancing are, of course "entirely new to John King and [the author]" (101). But with "the sympathy and encouragement we"—the "we" now referring to the two young Shawnee men—"received from our teachers, their politeness and dignity, helped us to understand this phase of civilization, which was as delightful as it was new to us" (101).

New though it is, the "delightfulness" of what Alford calls "the usages of polite society in vogue at that time, the so-called Victorian era" (101), derives from the fact that these "usages," as he views it, were based upon "just the same principle as the simple teaching of our own people." One may well pause at the notion that American-Victorian and Shawnee "usages" were based upon the "same principle," although Alford's reasoning is interesting. The "principle" at issue in both cultures, he writes, is "consideration for the rights of others, respect for our superiors (elders), and unselfishness. In short," he continues, "etiquette is just an outward and uniform method of expressing courtesy" (102). This is not the first time he has expressed a possible congruence between the two "civilizations," "Victorian" and Shawnee. In any case, so courteous do Alford and King prove to be that "each found a young lady," and "the young lady who became [Alford's] partner was a beautiful Indian girl, a member of the Sioux tribe from South Dakota" (102). The two plan to marry.

He writes of his surprise upon receiving a letter one day "from one of the teachers at the Shawnee Mission school" containing an affidavit attesting that his "name was Alford" (103). He does not explain how it had come about that "his name was Alford," or even whether it is a name he recognized. He says that he had "liked the white man's way of taking his father's name," and thus "had enrolled under the name of Thomas Wildcat" (103), and he does not wish to part with either of those names. An advisor makes the fairly obvious recommendation that he simply add the new name to the ones he already has, so that from that point forward, "I signed my name Thomas Wildcat Alford" (103).

Chapter 15, almost at the middle of the book, is called "White Man's Religion," and it confronts a matter the reader has surely known would be important. Alford writes: "Hampton was not a sectarian school, yet there was a strong moral and religious influence ever working among the students" (104). There is a "short religious service ... held daily ... and attendance at some church on the Sabbath was compulsory." One teacher in particular engages Alford and King, "even detaining [them] after Sunday school to talk to [them] and tell [them] the advantages of Christianity." He says he and his friend "enjoyed the study of the Bible," and, Alford writes, they find "many instances where the teachings set forth in the great Book were similar to those of [their] own people" (104). This had been Charles Eastman's view as well. Until this point, Alford had not thought he "would ever care to break the promise [he] had made [his] uncle Big Jim concerning [his] acceptance of the Christian faith," but as "the interest of [his] teachers became stronger, their pleas more insistent, [he] could not ignore the subject" (105).

Although he feels "the continual pressure and interest of [his] friends and teachers" (106), he insists that it is his own "study of the Gospel of Jesus Christ" (105) that has the greatest influence upon him. He repeats that "this did not seem to be a different religion to our own," only "a *better* way of teaching or understanding the belief of my own people" (105, my emphasis). That

14 The first Indian graduates of the Hampton Institute in 1882. Left to right: Michael Oshkenenny (Menominee), Thomas Wildcat Alford (Absentee Shawnee), John Downing (Cherokee/adopted Wichita). Courtesy of the Hampton University Archives.

notion is not sustainable once he accepts "deep in [his] soul that Jesus Christ was [his] Savior" (106), nor does this acceptance bring him peace of mind. Rather, it agitates him, because he knows that when he accepted "this faith [he] renounced virtually all hope to be a ruler, a chief of his people," and he does not doubt that as a Christian, his people "never would accord to [him] the honor and respect they gave to their chief." From his present perspective, he writes, clearly with ongoing regret, "Time has proved this true" (107).[16] Nonetheless, he affirms that he "was happy in the love of God" (106). He does not say what denomination he joined—although this will soon prove to be important—nor does he describe any ceremony marking his conversion.[17]

Alford's conversion and the accompanying recognition that his ambition to become a hereditary chief will never be fulfilled mark the climactic moment of his education at Hampton. As mentioned, despite his scholarship he still had to work "to help pay [his] expenses," and he initially did so "at a sawmill that was operated by the school" (and overseen by Booker T. Washington, whom he mentions at no point in his book). When he cuts a finger very badly, he transfers "to the printing office," where he learns most "of the work that was to be done in the shop." He mentions that Alice Longfellow wrote to him on occasion, urging him to "to do something for [his] people," and in particular "to use [his] influence to improve the condition of Indian women and girls" (107). He does well in his studies, wins some honors (107), and at the end of three years he graduates, in 1882 (107).[18]

The trip home is very different from Alford's trip east. He is traveling alone—John King would graduate two years later, in 1884—but there is no need to carry a "paper" as his English is adequate for conversation with the conductors and other passengers. As the "train sped westward and the towns … became smaller and smaller, the country homes poorer and more isolated, [he] felt an odd sense of disappointment" (110). Alford repeats the word "disappointment" in describing a return similar to that experienced by at least some boarding-school students, and I will quote him at some length:

> My homecoming was a bitter disappointment to me. Noticing at once the change in my dress and manner, in my speech and conduct, my people received me coldly and with suspicion. Almost at once they suspected that I had taken up the white man's religion, along with his habits and manner of conduct. There was no happy gathering of family and friends.... Instead of being eager to learn the new ideas I had to teach them … they did not approve of me, … and my relatives did not welcome my presence (111).

His parents have been dead for some years, his stepmother has moved away, and like his uncle Big Jim, his other relations are still strongly "non-progressive." Also discouraging is the great difficulty he has in finding work, and it is only after considerable effort that he obtains an "assignment as teacher for a Pottawatomie Indian day school" (113). But although Hampton's mission was to prepare students for teaching, Alford had not intended to become a teacher.[19]

He had, however, intended to marry his Sioux sweetheart from Hampton, but this is not to be. He receives "a letter from the pastor of the young lady making a strong objection to [their] marriage on denominational grounds," "a terrible blow to all [his] plans and hopes" (118).[20] Although he would write that "after many years of close study of the scriptures," he is "still … unable to find anything to justify [the minister's] attitude" (118), neither Alford nor the young woman contested the pastor's objection at the time. It is nevertheless not long before he does marry and raise a family, and when his first and then his second wife become ill and die, he marries a third time. Two of his sons—the eldest, Pierrepont (called Pierre), and his second son, Charles Reece—also attended Hampton; his son Webster graduated from Haskell in 1914, and another son, Paul, traveled to Hampton in 1903 to deliver an address his father was too ill to present himself (*Southern Workman*, July 1903 290).[21] There were daughters as well.

Alford had begun to compile a Shawnee dictionary while at Hampton, and late in his book, he writes movingly: "The more that I read and studied the English language, the more my admiration grew for my own Shawnee language, and I was anxious to preserve it in all its purity and beauty. In the description of nature … and in the idea of things intangible, the inner man, the soul, the Spirit and God, the Shawnee language is peculiarly sweet and full" (166). Wondering "in what manner it was best to try to preserve the language" (166–67), he decides to do so by translating the gospels, and after great labor, in 1929 he published *The Four Gospels of Our Lord Jesus Christ Translated into the Shawnee Language.*[22]

In view of this extraordinary achievement, evidence of Alford's commitment "to preserve the language," it is sad to learn that he did not allow his children to speak Shawnee. He had written to the *Southern Workman* in 1890 stating, "I desire my children not to know any Indian language, for it breeds superstition" (in Fear-Segal 2007 156).[23] Although raised as Christian

Shawnees, Alford's children could not appreciate the gospels in their own language in the translation done by their father, nor could they know the "purity and beauty," the "sweetness" and "fullness" of Shawnee expression regarding "the inner man, the soul, the Spirit and God" (166).

Living among the people he knew and loved, Alford sought "to use [his] education and [his] life for the benefit of [his] people" (109). Today, just as one regrets the fact that he did not allow his children to speak Shawnee, we would also question some of his other efforts to "benefit ... [his] people." For example, Jacqueline Fear-Segal, cites a letter Alford wrote to a former teacher of his at Hampton, Miss A. E. Cleaveland, informing her that he had "secretly collected names of all heads of families and allotted them land against their wishes" (in Fear-Segal 2007 148).[24]

Alford continued to work in education and he was employed by the Indian Service on several occasions, always, as he writes, committed to "civilization and citizenship" (128). Citizenship for Native Americans, something desired as well by Eastman, Standing Bear, and Zitkala-Sa, had been granted in 1924, well before Alford wrote, so he would have had time to judge whether its achievement had been worth the effort. Luther Standing Bear, as I have said, thought it had not; Alford expresses no view of the matter. In addition, although he is writing just after John Collier became commissioner of Indian Affairs, and the Indian Reorganization Act had just been passed, he has not a single word to say about these important developments. Did he, for example, approve of the fact that Collier allowed some teaching of Indian languages and cultures in the government schools? Did he approve the newer, more lenient attitude regarding the practice of Indian religions?

If Alford was among the most "progressive" of the Red Progressives, and fully committed to assimilation, it should not be thought that he avoids or is incapable of criticism of the Americans. In the graduation address he had delivered at Hampton in 1882, he spoke of "civilization, which was raging and approaching on [sic] the Indian with strong irresistible force and would soon sweep over his reservation like prairie fire that consumes everything with which it comes in contact" (*Southern Workman* 78), hardly a development to welcome, and no compliment to "civilization."[25] In light of these remarks, it is not without irony that *Civilization* would become the title of his autobiography more than fifty years later—but again, the book also offers some modest critiques of "civilization." For example, early in the book, discussing the health and general well-being of his people in the past,

Alford writes, "It remained for civilization and the white man's system of living to breed discontent and to make invalids of a large number of our people" (42), and he engages in a brief but serious questioning of American "civilization" near the close of the book.

When President Cleveland declared Indian Territory "open" to settlement, Alford participated in the land rush of April 22, 1889, and obtained substantial holdings. In the penultimate chapter of his book he speaks of "those strenuous months and years" as a time "when Indian history was adding another chapter to its tragic history" (191), a history made tragic surely by the "raging" approach of "civilization." Then shortly before the end of his book Alford observes: "*Our young people are taking up the ways of the white people*" (italics in original), and in view of that fact, "one must ask, what is civilization?" This would seem to raise the question of whether "*the ways of the white people*" and "civilization" are indeed the same thing, and if so, are both really "better" than what he had known of Shawnee culture? Unlike Eastman, or even Standing Bear, Alford does not attempt to answer broad questions of this sort. Instead he simply wonders whether what he sees occurring among young Shawnee people "will lead them to a higher civilization or to a more flagrant vaunting of their freedom," admitting, "I do not know" (197). In the end *Civilization*, the title of his book, is open to interpretation.

In his brief summary of *Civilization* David Brumble called it "very interesting," and "not least because Alford is not always in control of the ambivalence that is at the heart of the book: he is a 'civilized' Indian yearning with a part of his being for primitive innocence" (12). I hardly think it is "primitive innocence" for which Alford "yearns," and I would substitute for Brumble's "ambivalence" the sort of Du Boisian "double consciousness" I have discussed in regard to Eastman: the "problem" of being both an "Indian" and an "American." In that regard, Alford is a Christian, literate Indian, who does indeed find Christianity and literacy, the pillars of western civilization, "better" than the old Shawnee ways he had known. Like Eastman, he is decidedly an "American." But again like Eastman, he is enduringly an "Indian." Thus in a book he titled *Civilization*, a condition his schooling enabled him to achieve, he demonstrates as well his continuing respect for Shawnee religious insights and ethics and the beautiful Native language in which these were expressed: his respect, that is, for Shawnee *civilization*.

11

Joe Blackbear's *Jim Whitewolf:*
The Life of a Kiowa Apache Indian,
and Carl Sweezy's *The Arapaho Way:*
Memoir of an Indian Boyhood

JOE BLACKBEAR (1878–1955), A PLAINS APACHE FROM OKLAHOMA,[1] WAS THE subject of *Jim Whitewolf: The Life of a Kiowa Apache Indian*, an ethnographic life history edited by anthropologist Charles Brant and published in 1969. "Jim Whitewolf," as Brant states in his preface, is a pseudonym (Whitewolf viii), for a man with whom Brant had worked for about five weeks in 1948–49 as part of his research for a PhD at Cornell with Morris Opler.[2] Carl Sweezy (1880/1–1953) was a Southern Arapaho, also from Oklahoma, and a painter whose reputation continues to grow. His autobiography, *The Arapaho Way: A Memoir of an Indian Boyhood* (1966), was produced with the help of Althea Bass, a University of Oklahoma history professor and the author of several books on Native and historical subjects, with whom Sweezy had become friendly in the years before his death. Blackbear and Sweezy were both boarding-school students in Oklahoma, with Sweezy also having attended Carlisle and the Chilocco Indian School.

Blackbear's date of birth accords his story a place just after Thomas Wildcat Alford's in this study, but Sweezy's, even if it were 1880 (possibly) rather than 1881 (probably), would place his account just after that of Ah-nen-la-de-ni, a Mohawk born in 1879, whom I will consider next. I am, therefore, making a slight exception here to the structuring principle observed thus far in order to consider Blackbear and Sweezy together. Almost

213

exact contemporaries, the two men spent most of their lives within roughly fifty miles of each other. They were from different tribal nations and their individual experiences differed as well. But the books representing those lives are not merely different from but effectively antithetical to each other. I argue that this is largely a function of their editors' strongly divergent perspectives on these men's lives and cultures. Charles Brant constructed Joe Blackbear's life as an ironic narrative of what, in Abigail Wightman's telling phrase, might be called "Disappointing Indigeneity." In contrast, Althea Bass represented Carl Sweezy's life as a comic story of integrative achievement.[3] I use "irony" and "comedy" as specifically literary terms naming two of the four master plots of Western narrative. Following is my understanding of these plots based on the work of Northrop Frye and Hayden White.

This means, to be sure, that I am claiming that Western narrative structures govern these autobiographies "by" Native American persons. This would not be true for the life stories of Charles Eastman, Luther Standing Bear, and Zitkala-Sa, for example, or of Adam Fortunate Eagle, Jim Northrup, and Edna Manitowabi, all of whom were responsible for the composition and arrangement of their own texts. But for a great many boarding-school autobiographers, it was their editors who, for the most part, shaped their narratives. While Charles Brant would probably have attended to any concerns Joe Blackbear expressed about their work together, there is little doubt that Brant was the one responsible for the selection, editing, and arrangement of the material. Althea Bass and Carl Sweezy seem to have had a closer and less formal relationship than Brant and Blackbear, and Bass too, I believe, would have been open to anything Sweezy, a painter with a sense of the interplay of Western and Southern Arapaho forms, desired in the final product of their work together. It is almost certain, however, that she, like Brant, was responsible for the "plot"—the narrative structure—of the book she and Sweezy made together.

In Brant's narrative, to borrow terms from Anthony Webster, the protagonist appears as a "victim ... and pawn ... in a world largely outside [his] understanding." In Bass's narrative—again borrowing from Webster—the protagonist is represented as an "intentional agent" (2007 302) and the story celebrates his "creativity" (2007 310). Carl Sweezy's narrative is comic in structure; Joe Blackbear's story is structured as an ironic tale.[4]

Comedy and irony, along with tragedy and romance, are the four types of Western master plots. Tragic plots show how formidable or noble (although flawed; that is, human) individuals battle heroically but succumb to forces greater than themselves. Their unfortunate fall is sad but inevitable, and we acknowledge it as just.[5] As readers or observers, we feel a stoic sadness, John Milton's "calm of mind all passion spent" (*Samson Agonistes*): they did their best; it could not be helped; God's will be done. Our pain and sorrow are assuaged in some measure by an awareness that we have attained a deeper consciousness of the order of things. Comic plots show ordinary or "normal" individuals achieving temporary resolutions (H. White 9), overcoming obstacles to a better life. "The reconciliations which occur at the end of Comedy," White writes, "are reconciliations of men with men [i.e., not gods], of men with their world and their society ... seemingly inalterably opposed elements in the world ... are revealed to be, in the long run, harmonizable with one another" (9). To cite Frye, "Comedy usually moves toward a happy ending, and the normal response of the audience to a happy ending is 'this should be'" (167). Comic endings produce a sense of modest satisfaction: at last they have figured out who is really who; she has come through all right; they will marry and live fairly happily ever after. Romantic plots are "the nearest of all literary forms to the wish-fulfilment dream" (Frye 186), or to certain kinds of fairy tales. The protagonists of romantic narratives are knights and princes, heroes, or persons with special gifts. The conclusion of a romantic narrative produces in the reader something like elation or joy: he's found the Holy Grail, hallelujah! They've made it to the Promised Land, behold!

White calls the fourth Western emplotment satire. For reasons I will not develop here, I think it is better called irony. Ironic narratives present "a drama dominated by the apprehension that man is ultimately a captive of the world rather than its master" (H. White 9). Irony's protagonists are "figure[s] of the low norm" (Frye 228), who tend, despite their efforts, to remain in place or sink somewhat lower. Where tragedy illustrates how even those persons capable of great agency may nonetheless fail, irony represents those without effective agency. Ironic protagonists are not so much victims as people to whom things just happen. And what usually happens? In the modern idiom, "Shit happens." Consider the opening of Franz Kafka's *The Trial*: "Someone must have been telling lies about Josef K., he knew he had done nothing wrong but, one morning, he was arrested" (1). After being arrested Josef K. will *do* many things, but he cannot *act* in such a way as to clear himself and see that justice is done. The feeling we have at the end of the ironic protagonist's tale is, to take an often-repeated phrase from Kurt

Vonnegut's *Slaughterhouse Five*, "So it goes." Or, to instantiate the very end
of Samuel Beckett's *Waiting for Godot*:

> VLADIMIR: Well? Shall we go?
>
> ESTRAGON: Yes, let's go.
>
> *They do not move* (61, italics in original).

By identifying a narrative's emplotment—recognizing the *kind* of story
being told—Hayden White writes, "one penetrates to that level of consciousness on which a world of experience is *constituted* prior to being analyzed"
(33, italics in original). This is easily granted for a Shakespeare, or indeed a
Kafka, Beckett, or Vonnegut: their stories are fictional, imaginative, creative,
invented. But the stories historians and ethnographers tell are about "the real
world," a world that would seem to be already "constituted." Isn't it, then,
empirical reality that determines the story each narrator tells? In fact, that
is not the case. White's monumental book is about the narratives offered by
historians who surely tell stories about "the real world," and it demonstrates
clearly that beyond the level of factual accuracy, or error, the "same" reality
leads historians (and also ethnographers, like Brant and Bittle) to tell very
different sorts of stories. The meanings of the stories they tell are importantly
conveyed by the *kind* of story—tragic, comic, romantic, or ironic—told about
a sequence of events (or a culture or culturally exemplary person).

Of course, "Historians in general," White writes—and ethnographers
in general—"tend to be naïve storytellers" (8), and unlike with literary masters, their plot "choices" are relatively simple. Charles Brant and Althea Bass
look at the "field," talk with their consultants, and record the material they
have offered. The editors then make a selection, and pre-cognitively—that is,
largely unconsciously—structure their story: as an *ironic* narrative in Brant's
case, a *comic* narrative for Bass.

ॐ

Jim Whitewolf is not a long book; Joe Blackbear's life story is told in just
a hundred pages. These are preceded by a three-page preface and a thirty-
nine-page introduction by Brant, who closes with a brief epilogue. Brant
introduces the narrative of Joe Blackbear's life—I'll use "Jim Whitewolf"
only when quoting—as serving to "convey some feeling for the reality of

a man's experiences under conditions of stressful culture contact and social disorganization" (vii), leading to the "breakdown of the aboriginal way of life" (12). He looks to the work of several distinguished predecessors—Paul Radin's *Crashing Thunder* (1926), Walter Dyk's *Son of Old Man Hat* (1938), and Leo Simmons's *Sun Chief* (1942)—as models of the life history as a vehicle for the representation not so much of individuals but, rather, of exemplary culture-bearers at a time when their cultures were threatened by the dominant Americans.

Brant dates the period of "social disorganization" for the Plains Apache from the people's confinement to the reservation after the Treaty of Medicine Lodge in 1867. "Within a period of three decades," he writes, "the very foundations of the old way of life of the Kiowa Apache were shattered" (16). He notes that in Blackbear's community, "None of the homes have running water or an inside toilet, and only a small minority have electricity. . . . None has a telephone" (19). Brant includes a note acknowledging that the "time referred to . . . is 1949–50," so that the "sociocultural situation here described should not, therefore, be regarded as obtaining in all particulars now" (1969 18 n.23). But he does not specify which "particulars" might have changed, and how those changes might bear on our understanding of the story presented.[6]

Brant says almost nothing about his work with Blackbear and how the final text was produced. He notes that Blackbear sometimes spoke an English which Brant found "moderately fluent" (viii), and he sometimes spoke in his own language.[7] When he used Apache, his nephew, "Wallace Whitebone," also a fictitious name, served as translator. There is no indication either in the introduction or in the notes as to which parts of the narrative were originally presented in English and which in Apache. I am fairly certain that Brant used a tape recorder, but he does not say. Nor does he say anything about the dynamics of performance, or indicate an awareness that Blackbear might have experienced his nephew's presence as that of an *audience* for the storyteller. In his preface Brant states that he made "certain rearrangements of the material" (viii) to "introduce some semblance of chronology," but as I will show, there are many places in the text where linear chronology does not pertain.

In Brant's ironic presentation Joe Blackbear appears as the only Native boarding-school student I have encountered of whom it can be said not only that his schooling did not change him but that it had almost no effect on him whatever. Brant's narrative represents him as having spent three years at an on-reservation Indian boarding school and then having gone on with his life almost as if he had not been to school at all. Although Blackbear recalls some of his time at school in great detail, in Brant's presentation he recalls it indifferently. That is, the school's practices and the lessons it sought to teach neither engaged him nor troubled him. In no way did they raise for him the important *topos* of identity; after boarding school he was, *ironically*, just the same person as he had been before. If one is willing to consider a text's literary interest apart from its attractiveness or excellence—this is, no doubt, a good deal to ask—*Jim Whitewolf* is an Indian autobiography that has much to offer.

∾

Born "about 1878," Joe Blackbear did not get his name until he was six years old; up until then, he says, "They just called me 'boy'" (39). Brant offers an explanatory note here referring to "the anxiety felt by the Kiowa Apache concerning survival of newborn," and to this particular family having lost two boys before Joe's birth. Because of "the strong tabu [sic] upon uttering the name of a deceased relative" (39), Blackbear was not named until his parents were sure he would live. The naming is described in detail, indicating either that the story was important to him—he was about seventy at the time of his narration—or that Brant pressed him on the matter. Blackbear speaks of being taken by his father[8] to a Kiowa Sun Dance when he "was about ten"—"the last time the Kiowas ever had that ceremony," he says—and a bit later to a "water-medicine ceremony" (41). He was taken to the Sun Dance because his father "wanted [him] to grow" (41). Brant offers a note on the life-enhancing powers of the Sun Dance but says nothing about the second ceremony. His practice in providing explanatory notes is inconsistent, a different sort of irony.

Two years later Blackbear saw his "first Ghost Dance." He says it had come to his people from "the Arapaho up north who had seen the Ghost Dance" (42). He is referring to the fact that the Arapahos, in the 1880s, had sent a delegation to the southwest to visit Wovoka, the Paiute prophet, resulting in great enthusiasm among them for the dance. Brant, the anthropologist, does not offer a historical footnote here, although he does two pages later. At this first Ghost Dance, Blackbear says, there "were Kiowas, Arapahoes and some ... Apaches" (42).[9] He next describes a Ghost Dance among his own people, and when he remarks that he "was a grown man then, so [he] went over there on horseback" (42), one realizes that this is another instance in which Brant's editing did not produce "some semblance of chronology" (viii) in the Western sense; I will point to several more cases.

Blackbear records the presence on the reservation of "some Catholic sisters," who gave out rosaries, and recalls his pleasure in receiving one although he had no sense whatever of its use or meaning. There are also Protestant missionaries in the community, a Mr. Methvin (we will hear more of him later),[10] and a Mr. Curtis, and Blackbear recounts anecdotes of the ways in which he and others gingerly tested the waters, as it were, of the white man's religion. He also tells of spending time with his grandfather who, along with some friends, "all old men" (46), told him stories. The stories he hears instruct the boy in tribal history and provide practical and ethical lessons (46–47). Blackbear tells Brant that his grandfather urged him to remember the stories, so that he could "tell them to [his] children and they can tell them to their children." Addressing Brant directly, Blackbear says: "Now I have told you all those old stories, I want you to give them to me so my grandchildren will read them and be able to tell them to their children, too" (47), and he affirms that he has himself "tried to teach [his] own grandson Willy some of the things [he] learned from [his] grandfather" (50). Had Brant so chosen, these strong statements of Blackbear's ongoing commitment to education by means of the oral tradition (preserved in writing), might have been emphasized to provide a perspective other than ironic.[11] Nor is this the only matter presented by Blackbear that might have motivated a very different narrative presentation.

∞

It is in the chapter called "Going to School" that Blackbear tells of his father taking him on horseback to the Kiowa School near Anadarko, north of the reservation, in 1891 when he was thirteen years old.[12] "Before [he] went," Blackbear says, his "mother's brother," who had been to school, "tried to teach [him] the ABC's," but all he managed to learn "was the letter 's'" (83). In just a few paragraphs, he touches upon many of the *topoi* and *loci* of the boarding schools. Arriving at school "with long hair and ... dressed in buckskin...really dressed up," he is taken by his father to meet the superintendent who "introduced [him] into the school" (83). Then "The first thing they did

15 Joe Blackbear, about age 71, at the American Indian Exposition, Anadarko, Oklahoma, 1948. Photo by Pierre Tartoue. Courtesy of the Archives and Manuscripts Division, Oklahoma Historical Society.

was to cut [his] hair. There were a lot of boys ... having that done." He notes that his "hair was long and braided," adding, "just like it is now," an indicator, I would suggest, that after attending school he would be just the same as he was on the day he first arrived. "They took a scissor and cut the braids off and gave them to my father," he says, "then they trimmed my hair short all around." This may or may not have come as a surprise—his younger brother and sister had already been to school—but in any case it is not troubling to him. Next he is taken by one of the boys "who spoke good English" to "a place where they gave me a bath. After I was all cleaned up and ready, I went back to the superintendent.... I was all dressed up in school clothes" (83). These consist of black pants and a blue shirt with stripes.

Not long after, Logan, the boy "who spoke good English," tells him "that when the first bell rang"—clock time—it meant "we would go to eat," although it was not until the ringing of a second bell that they could enter the dining room—of which Blackbear provides a detailed account. The boys line up "according to height"; then "Some fellow there gave a command that I didn't understand, and I saw all the others ... standing ... at attention with their arms at their sides. Then the fellow said something else and we all turned. This fellow would hit a bell he was carrying and we were supposed to march in time to it" (84). Finding marching awkward, he walks "to the eating place," where, "there were long tables ... in rows. Logan was still with me. When we got to a certain table he told me to just stand there. There was a lady there in charge who had a little bell and, when she hit it, everybody sat down" (84). The bell is rung once more, and "everybody had his head bowed," then the "bell rang again and we started eating" (84). Although "the sweet potatoes were cooked differently from what [he] was used to ... it was a good dinner ... bacon and beans, plums and dried peaches" (84). Another bell announces the meal is over, and the students march out, also "in time to a bell" (84). There is still one more bell to come, and this one announces playtime.

Then, playtime over, more bells signal a chapel service. The chapel, from Blackbear's description, looks like a classroom (85). The service is marked by much singing, and when that is over, "One lady after another came in and picked out her class and they all went off to another room. All that were left were us beginners" (85). When their teacher arrives, she escorts them to her classroom, where the young man takes a seat at a desk. Again, Blackbear offers a very detailed description of a day more than fifty years earlier. The

students have slates and erasers and also some "yellow-looking books."
He is given colored "wooden sticks, something like matches," and told to
"build things, like houses and a fence." It is Logan who explains all this to
Blackbear in their own language. Then there is recess, followed by a return
to the classroom, where he again plays with "blocks," by which he seems to
mean the objects he had earlier called "sticks." "Things went on like that day
after day" (85). Blackbear records nothing threatening about his first days at
school, nothing even unpleasant, save for mild boredom.

He does not recall "how long it was after [he] started school when
Logan came over and said they were going to take [his] blocks away and give
[him] a slate" (85–86). Along with the slate comes "something that looked
like a bone. That was a slate pencil" (86). He gives a detailed account of how
the teacher points at a picture of something with a "pointing stick" and the
students "call the names" of the things to which she has pointed: cat, dog,
bird. Next they are taught to spell the things they have named (86). This is
all we learn of Joe Blackbear's first year at school.

Almost all boarding-school students had something to say early in
their narratives about sleeping arrangements at their school; as we have seen
many times, the dormitory is an important *locus*. But Blackbear's brief summary of his first year at school does not mention this. That, however, is not
because it was a subject he omitted; rather, for reasons I cannot provide, Brant
included this material only after he has had Blackbear arrive at incidents at
the school in his "second or third year" (90). It is only then that Brant has
Blackbear say, "When I *first* got started in school they showed me where I
was to sleep" (93, my emphasis). This is certainly not consistent with "some
semblance of chronology" (viii), although it may be a trace of the order in
which Blackbear himself presented material.

Blackbear does not refer to the sleeping place as a dormitory, describing it only as a large room for all the boys who "were the same size as [he]
was." The boys have to double up and he "had to sleep with another boy,
named Earl." It is Logan who shows Blackbear "where he is to stay," telling
him that he "would find the bedclothes under the pillow" (93) on his bed.
Logan also made clear that he was to wait for the sound of the second bell
each morning before rising, because "the first bell in the morning was for
the boys who were to build fires in different parts of the school" (93–94).
"The second bell," Blackbear observes, "was the signal for us to get dressed"
(94). Each night someone checks that the boys "all had [their] nightshirts

on," before saying "Good night" and "turning out the lights (93). Blackbear reports: "The beds were made every day by women who worked there—we didn't have to do that" (93), a unique instance of such a service at an Indian boarding school.

"During the night," Blackbear explains, reporting on a matter that many student autobiographers mention, "we didn't go out to the toilet. They had buckets on the inside for us to use" (94). He does not say who empties and cleans them each day. The boys fold their nightshirts and return them to their place under the pillows; then they go to a playroom "where another fellow took charge"; after which they perform the daily cleanup, in a "big room with pans to wash in, and pitchers full of water" (94). Earlier in the narrative—another piece of the story out of chronological order—Blackbear had said that eye trouble eventually prevented him from returning to school, and it is likely that he had contracted trachoma from sharing wash basins and towels with the other boys. A far less serious problem, and one not reported by any other boarding-school student, concerns the fact that Blackbear "was supposed to part his hair on the left side," but "when they had first cut [his] hair they parted it in the middle, so that confused [him] at first" (94). It is a confusion he remembers more than fifty years later.

Like most Indian boarding-school students, Blackbear not only attends class but works at various tasks around the school. When he began, "these jobs were in addition to going to school all day. Later on I worked half a day and went to school half a day" (95), the usual schedule at the boarding schools. Unfortunately, "they"—he almost always uses the general third-person pronoun to identify teachers and authorities—gave him jobs that he "didn't like." He knew that if he "did them all right they wouldn't bother [him]. But if [he] didn't, they might whip [him]" (94). This is the first mention of corporal punishment. One of his jobs is washing dishes "over in the building where the teachers and employees ate." Regardless of whether he "liked" that job or not, it has its advantages. "We got to eat there, too," he says. "The food was much better" (95).

At the end of the school year Blackbear returns home for summer vacation and finds he "felt kind of funny toward those kids who hadn't gone to school. They still had long braids." He is not troubled by the contrast; to the contrary, "I combed my hair," he says—parting it on the left, perhaps—and as other boarding students had done, "kind of showed off to them." His showing off also involves telling the other boys "the names of things in English

that [he] learned in school," and singing songs he had learned; one of them
is a song that many an Indian boarding-school student had encountered,
"'Jesus Loves Me'" (95). "The old people thought I was smart," he recalls,
"but I didn't really know what I was singing about" (95)—also the situation of many another boarding-school student. He now repeats that "in the
second year of school I had jobs that took half days to do," also repeating:
"The best job I had in school was that one when I worked at the employees'
building washing dishes. There I got the best food to eat" (95). Repetitions
of this sort provide the reader some feel for Blackbear's oral narrative style,
although I suspect this was not so much Brant's intention as the result of
careless editing.

Blackbear's description of his second year at school is oddly placed,
appearing in the text before Blackbear had finished telling of his first year
there. "The next year," he had said, he "was given a little yellow book," but he
"had learned all of that chart already" (86). It is not clear what he means by
this. Occasionally Brant has Blackbear simply list experiences and events: "I
felt like a stranger. I never mixed with the other kids much … I stayed out
of all the mischief," and so on. At one point he is issued "paper and pencil,"
using a slate no longer, and, he reports, one of the girls in class began to tease
him. This leads to a lively response on his part and, shortly, a reprimand from
the teacher (86–87). When the banter between the two continues, Blackbear
and the unnamed girl are put in the corner for "about an hour, right through
the recess, until about noon" (87).

Immediately after this Blackbear reveals that he "ran away from school
three times." But it is not poor treatment or dissatisfaction with the school
that are the reasons. The first time, he and some other boys—one of them is
named Abraham Lincoln—run off because they are in a hurry to get home
to camp for "ration day," the government distribution of food and supplies
he had described earlier. Although the school releases the students for just
that purpose, the boys are unwilling to wait. The second time he runs off,
others "coaxed [him] into doing it," because "there was going to be a big
hand game at camp."[13] The third occasion involves going "down to the hog
lot"—this is off limits to the students—"and … hitting the hogs and chas-
ing them around" (89).

The punishments vary, and on two occasions Blackbear is given a choice
as to which he prefers to suffer. After his first offense, he has the option either
to "spend all the next Saturday, sitting alone in the chapel," or he "could take

a whipping on the palm of [his] hand." He chooses the former (87), but then realizes that will prohibit him from going home on Saturday evening as the other students do. (This is an on-reservation boarding school, and it does not keep students from home and family for long.) Logan continues to serve as benefactor, persuading the superintendent to let Blackbear help him in a work detail instead of remaining behind. The chronology of that particular weekend is not at all clear, but apparently both the boys and the superintendent are satisfied with how it turns out. For his next dereliction, the choice of punishments involves "taking a whipping or working for two days with the girls in the laundry" (89). He again chooses not to be struck, and once more describes the alternative in detail, in particular, the embarrassment of having to "put on an apron and wash clothes," and the "stink" of "those dirty socks and girl's [sic] underdrawers" (89).

The third time he is punished, he is given no choice but directly sentenced "to do this hard work for three days" in the barn, after which he is to get a whipping from a Mr. Bight, "who was in charge of all the boys who were out working" (90). At the end of the three-day period, however, Mr. Bight tells the superintendent, Mr. Larson, that the boys had worked very hard and "he wasn't going to beat [them] on top of it." This gives rise to what seems a quite comic physical battle between Bight (who is big) and Larson (who is small), the fight continuing until a "fellow by the name of Clark came by and said, 'That's enough'" (90). When the reservation agent hears about this affair, he takes it seriously enough to dismiss Larson—who was generally said to treat "the boys pretty badly at the school"—and appoint Clark as interim superintendent. Blackbear's father—exactly when this takes place is not given—scolds him for his part in "the trouble," and warns him not to run off again. And indeed, Blackbear says, "After that, I never ran away from school again" (90).

Blackbear introduces a special occasion at the Kiowa School with a phrase I have already cited, saying, "I don't remember if it was the second or third year in school" (90), a common feature of oral narration that Brant left intact. A girl gives Blackbear a note that he cannot read—in his "second or third year in school." When he learns that it says "she wanted [him] to be her sweetheart," he has someone write a note in response saying "it was all right with [him]" (90). Blackbear tells us that "whenever I would meet this girl, I would talk with her. She was a Comanche girl" (90). This suggests that the two spoke to each other in Comanche. The girl's note to him would have been in English, and if he couldn't read it, his spoken English—only "moderately fluent" some fifty years later—may also have been inadequate for the two to have conversed in English. Because the girl would not have understood Apache, and because many nineteenth-century Plains Apaches could understand and speak Comanche, that is likely the language they spoke to each other.[14] (We find out later that the school has Kiowa and Comanche interpreters.)

Blackbear's observation "She was a Comanche girl" also serves as a transition to what comes next. "One night in the school dining hall," Blackbear says, "they had an affair in which each of the boys was sitting with a girl" (90). "They played music, and we walked around in pairs.... The girls had done the inviting of the boys to this affair" (90–91). "They [those in charge] were going to pick out the best couple there" (91). But then, instead of continuing, Blackbear goes back in time, and this particular failure of Brant's to rearrange Blackbear's narrative chronologically is fortunate in that it provides an interesting example of oral narrative style.

Having already told us that the student couples were walking in time to the music, Blackbear goes back to say, "Before this affair took place, we boys were in the playroom and a fellow came there and read out the names of certain boys that had been invited by the girls." Finding that his "name was on the list" (91), he joins the others whose names have been called. The "fellow" told them "to put on [their] Sunday clothes for this event," so that in the "evening [they] all got haircuts and took baths and got dressed up and ready to go. They gave us shoe polish to shine our shoes with." Upon the ringing of a bell, the dressed-up boys enter the dining room two by two, and seat themselves on a bench, where they await the girls. The girls enter "dressed in white, with red flowers on. They sure were pretty" (91).

We are still at a point prior to that with which Blackbear had begun, because the boys are *not yet* each sitting with a girl, as they had been earlier in the text; music is *not yet* playing, as earlier, and nor have the boys and girls *as yet* begun to "walk ... around in pairs." All this will only now take place. Blackbear's further description of this event re-presents his Comanche "sweetheart," the mention of whom had prompted the narration. The details Blackbear recalls are once again many and vivid.

When the Comanche girl—she remains unnamed—enters with the other girls, she sits down next to him. The two will participate as a couple in a rhythmic walking competition to see who can best "keep in time with the music" (91). Blackbear and his partner, along with one other couple, are chosen as finalists, and although "the other couple could march better, ... the girl in that couple was chewing gum," and because the judges "didn't like her to be chewing gum, ... they gave [his] girl and [him] the first prize" (91). He concludes, "I was about fifteen years old at this time. It was the first time I ever had a date with a girl and talked with her like that" (92). Whether they ever saw each other again is not related.

With no transition nor any apparent reason for the shift in subject matter, the following paragraph announces that the young man's "eyes bothered [him]," something he had mentioned briefly earlier. Here Brant's editing reproduces Blackbear's style in the paratactic manner he had offered in 1963 (see note 33): "My eyes bothered me. Those days all the children seemed to have sore eyes. I lost the sight in my left eye. I was taken to the eye doctor and he said that I had bad eyes. They told the agent about it. After that they never bothered me about going back to school" (92). The eye doctor was unable to help him, and for "about two years [his] eyesight was very dim," and he "stayed close to home then." He is taken to an Indian doctor, a woman, who used "a piece of glass from a bottle and cut away some white substance that was growing over [his] left eye. After that [he] could see better" (92). She also gave him "some stuff, like salt, from the creek and something else to mix it with and told [him] to put this in [his] eye." He does so and soon his "eyesight was all right." Nonetheless, he says, "I never returned to school" (92). It is therefore something of a surprise when, immediately following these words we encounter a description of Blackbear's first Christmas at the school "in 1892 during his second school year" (92). He then goes further back in time to narrate an account of his introduction to the dormitory (already discussed); a description of several other jobs to which he was assigned; his first summer vacation at home (also discussed earlier); and, in "about 1893 while [he] was still in school ... a measles epidemic" (96). It is with the outbreak of measles that the chapter "Going to School" closes. For good or ill, Brant has once more failed to impose chronology.

Blackbear is quite certain that there was no Christmas celebrated in his first year—this is unlikely—and that it was only in his second year that he heard "people around school talking about having Christmas." He says he "didn't know what it meant" (92), but he describes the event nonetheless. Christmas morning the "parents of all the children came to the school," the children got "cleaned up," and at the sound of a bell, they entered the dining room, where he "saw the tables all lined up with food ... turkeys, chickens, beef, pork, and oranges and apples." He specifically notes: "It was at this dinner that I first heard a prayer at the mealtime" (92). This is also unlikely since he had noted that at his very first meal in the school dining room, "Everybody had his head down"—although he "didn't hear anyone giving the blessing" (84). Nonetheless, if all the students regularly bowed their heads before meals, he would surely on some occasion have heard someone "giving the blessing" before his second year and first Christmas. Blackbear notes that "the same old man that later married me was the one who prayed," although at the time Blackbear "didn't understand what he was praying about—he was just talking."[15]

When the prayer is finished, the meal begins. Later there is more singing and praying, and Santa Claus appears. Kiowa and Comanche interpreters—this is the first time they have been mentioned—announce, doubtless in Kiowa and Comanche (not Apache), that those who "are having [their] first Christmas" would get presents from Santa. Blackbear's gifts include "candy, cakes, nuts, and a scarf, gloves, and shirt" (93). Other children receive presents laid out under the Christmas tree (93). The following day the students go home for a vacation of "about fifteen days and then [they] were to come back to school" (93). It is here, after a space break, that Blackbear tells not about his return to school that second year but about his first encounter with the dormitory, incidents we have already considered.

After his belated account of his dormitory experiences, Blackbear observes that "by [his] third year in school, [he] was experienced at all the jobs and knew what to do" (96). As noted, the chapter ends with an 1893 measles epidemic, which seems to have originated when a boy who had run off—his name is Bill Day, and except for Abraham Lincoln, he is the only student whose full name is given[16]—is brought back sick with the disease. He is isolated, but nonetheless "several more boys got sick" (97). We are not told whether Bill Day recovered, but many children died before the school began to send the students home. Blackbear himself breaks out with the measles upon his arrival home, and although "his second younger brother died from the measles" (97), clearly he himself recovered. "Going to School" ends anticlimactically: "The old Indians said the measles was the white man's sickness and that they never had it before the white people came" (97).

The two remaining chapters of the book, chapters 4 and 5, are called "Sex, Marriage, and Divorce," and "Religions, Old and New," and they comprise incidents from Blackbear's life dealing with the subjects named. In his introduction, Brant had cited Leo Simmons's work with Don Talayesva, *Sun Chief*, as one of the models for his own work. Simmons had pressed Talayesva for details of his rich and varied sexual exploits (as seen in volume 1 of the present work). I suspect Brant also pressed Blackbear for such details, for "Sex, Marriage and Divorce" opens with an account of his first intercourse when he "was a young fellow, just beginning to think about sex" (99), and describes some other sexual escapades. In this chapter Blackbear marries Priscilla—called Louisa in the narrative—and then divorces her.

Although Brant has Blackbear occasionally employ the oral narrator's temporal manner—it was the second or third year, a couple of months or maybe more—sometimes he records him as being very precise, as here. He had earlier said, "It was in my third year at school that I met Louisa, the girl that I later married" (100), but now, in regard to his divorce, he speci-fies, "This was 1925"—and he adds, "I never did get married again" (107). Some time before his divorce he had begun to drink, and Brant concludes this penultimate chapter with the death of Blackbear's mother; the death of his father, who he says "never thought too well of [him]" (109); and with his wife leaving him. His mother provides the advice "to stay single" (109), and it is advice he has heeded. The placement of these unfortunate events at the chapter's end conveys Brant's ironic vision of dissolution and disinte-gration for Joe Blackbear and by extension for the Plains Apaches as people without effective agency.

The last chapter, "Religions, Old and New," tells of a vision quest and the use of special powers—although not by Blackbear (111–13); of a Kiowa Sun Dance (113–14); and of a hand game between some Cheyennes and Apaches, the outcome determined by the strength of the participants' "power" (114–16)—although not Blackbear's. If the Sun Dance was part of the old religion, the new religion involves peyote, and it is here (123–26) that Brant reprints the narrative he had earlier published as "Joe Blackbear's Story of the Origin of the Peyote Religion." Except for altering the paragraph breaks, Brant reproduces his 1963 publication exactly, and the reader may or may not remark the sudden return of a paratactic style for "Jim Whitewolf."

That style continues as Blackbear initially describes "the first time [he] ever took part in a peyote meeting" (126).[17] He says, "I heard that they were going to have a peyote meeting there that night. There I saw my cousin, my mother's brother's boy. His name was Carl. We went in and sat down on the south side" (126). At this point some of the sentences become a bit more complex. When the all-night meeting is over, "Everyone sat on the outside and told stories, and then at noon there was a big feast, after which everyone returned home" (128). This was 1896. Blackbear concludes, "From that day on I liked the peyote worship and even today I go to it and enjoy it.... I believe that it is because of going to that first meeting that I have lived to be an old man today" (128).

Blackbear notes that he later met James Mooney, sometime after 1903, when Mooney was sent by Washington "to investigate peyote" (130). Mooney participated in several peyote ceremonies and later held a meeting with a number of the participants, including Blackbear. Blackbear recalls that Mooney "told us to organize, choose officers, and name our church.... He said to call it the 'Native American Church'" (130), and he accurately reports that they would later get "a charter for the 'Native American Church' for Oklahoma in 1918" (131). Had Charles Brant so chosen, these passages might have served as a thematically meaningful climax for Blackbear's story, or perhaps even its conclusion.

Coincidentally, 1903, around the time Blackbear met Mooney, was also the year that his only son, Ray, was born. Brant knew that Old Man Blackbear, Joe's father, had been strongly committed to the peyote religion, and he also knew, from working with Joe in the late 1940s, that Ray Blackbear had grown up to become a committed member of the Native American Church as well. In March 1949, in Kay Schweinfurth's view, Joe Blackbear had "described his first sighting of [peyote]" to Brant "as a religious experience." Blackbear said, "When I saw my first one [peyote plant] ... I smoked and prayed," adding, "Now I have seen it growing, I will cut it and take it back so my people can eat it and pray for their relatives who are sick" (in Schweinfurth 174). Surely this is indicative of a sense of forceful agency on Joe Blackbear's part; indeed, as we have seen he had earlier told Brant, "I believe that it is because of going to that first [peyote] meeting that I have lived to be an old man today" (128). Had that statement, along with the fact of his son's continuing to follow the peyote road,[18] registered strongly with Brant it might once again have caused him to construct something other than an ironic narrative. But rather than seeing Joe Blackbear as a link between the commitment to the Native American Church of his father and his son, Brant undercuts that important continuity, making Joe Blackbear's religious belief in why he had managed to live to be an old man just one more thing among others.

Thus Brant continues this final chapter with Blackbear's memories of the influenza pandemic of 1918, and one may wonder why he places those memories in a chapter called "Religions, Old and New." More in keeping with the chapter title is the presentation of material about the encounters by Blackbear's wife, his mother, and other Apaches with varieties of Christian religion. All this is put in the context of his drinking. Indeed, the book works to its ironic conclusion by moving even further back in time to Blackbear's and his wife's baptism, events that took place a full forty years earlier, about 1909 (136). Do these events bring Blackbear's story to a close because they are of great significance? Not at all, and that is the ironic point. Here is the conclusion Brant chose for "Jim Whitewolf's" story: "I worked at the church like that for several years. Then one time I started drinking again. This was before the First World War. My wife started going around to the dances again. I began taking the old road again, drinking and running around with women. I quit my job at the church. This all led up to my wife and I quitting each other" (138). These are Joe Blackbear's last words in the narrative constructed by Charles Brant.

Although Blackbear narrated at the end of the 1940s, Brant—twenty years later!—chose to have him conclude his life story in the years "before the First World War," and 1925, the year of his divorce. His last words are of drink, dissolution, and disintegration—these things representing not only his condition but that of the Apache people whose cultural representative he is. Individually and collectively, Charles Brant has given us a bleakly ironic tale. One could not easily recognize this Joe Blackbear and his wife in Julia Jordan's description of Ray Blackbear's parents as "both traditionalists with strong nostalgia for the former way of life" (1968 9).

இஇ

Carl Sweezy was a Southern Arapaho artist born in 1880 or1881, and thus only a bit younger than Joe Blackbear. He too grew up on reservation lands determined by the 1867 Treaty of Medicine Lodge and later decimated by allotment. Charles Brant had set Blackbear's story in the context of "disintegrating" Plains Apache lifeways, and Althea Bass, Sweezy's editor, also saw Southern Arapaho ways as "disappearing" (viii), as did Sweezy himself. Nonetheless, the texts of their life stories could not be more different. Brant, as I have shown, emplotted Blackbear's story as an ironic tale of happenstance and failed agency in a largely dysfunctional world where things fall apart. But

Bass emplotted Sweezy's narrative as comic, as a more nearly hopeful story that tends "to include as many people as possible in its final society" (Frye 165). It is, to be sure, a somewhat melancholic comedy in that a measure of sadness for what has been lost suffuses the elements of successful integration.

I know no more about Althea Bass's work with Carl Sweezy than what she writes at the close of her foreword to the book: "The following pages give an account of what Carl Sweezy told me in our frequent visits together. Except to rearrange it by subject matter and to add a few dates, I have not altered it. These are Carl Sweezy's memoirs" (x). Those "visits" were not occasions on which, for example, she came to his home or he came to her office for the two to work on his memoirs. Rather, she writes, the visits consisted of going "together to places on the old Reservation that he remembered" (ix), and one is to infer that the book is largely composed of the things "he remembered" and imparted to her. Did Bass take notes as they talked? Did she carry a tape recorder? Did Sweezy write down some of his recollections and pass them on to her? It would be good to know the answers to such questions—but I do not raise them skeptically, to lay the groundwork for a charge that an editor has so managed the text that its "real" subject has not been allowed to speak fully or "authentically." Although there is little information about how the final manuscript was arrived at, it is my belief that it represents Carl Sweezy accurately and sympathetically and that indeed "These are Carl Sweezy's memoirs" (Bass x).

ολο

Although he had "never known the date of [his] birth," Sweezy gave it as 1881 because when he came to the Mennonite Mission School in 1888 his age was listed as seven (8). When he entered Carlisle in 1896, however, his age was recorded as sixteen. Birthdates of either 1880 or 1881 are obviously very close to each other and it may not matter which year is correct. Sweezy's mother died when he "was quite small" (64), and upon her death he was sent to board at the Mennonite Mission near his birthplace in Darlington, still Indian Territory. Almost nothing is said about his father.

In 1870 Brinton Darlington, a Quaker, had been sent to run the Upper Arkansas Agency under President Grant's "Peace Policy." Darlington had died in 1872, but Sweezy had heard good things about him and felt that "he believed many of the things that we believed." Although he "had not been trained in our religious societies and did not know our ceremonies ... he did not try to wipe them all out, as some white people believed in doing" (4). "Even today," Sweezy observes, "when the Arapaho think of Darlington"— he refers now to the town named after the man—"we think of a place where life was once happy and good" (5), a sort of second paradise lost, after the first paradise, the good life the Arapahos had led before the coming of the missionaries and government agents, was gone. That second lost paradise will be regained, if only in memory, toward the close of Sweezy's book.

The Mennonites had established a school at Darlington in 1880, which soon burned down. A new building was completed by 1882, and it was in that building that Sweezy was "proud to live" (64) from the time his mother died until he went to another Mennonite school in Halstead, Kansas, probably at age seven. Just as Sweezy had praised the religious tolerance of the Quaker Darlington, he praises that of the Mennonites, who, he writes, "were religious in a way that we Indian children could understand" (64). That the first Christians Sweezy encountered were sympathetic played an important part in establishing his general outlook.

Sweezy's name in Arapaho, he tells, us is "Black" (61), and, whatever he may have been called at the Darlington school, at the Halstead school he gets the name Carl.[19] He says that when his "older brother went to school at Halstead he took the name of the station agent there, Fieldie Sweezy. Then when I entered school I was given the name Carl Sweezy" (61).So much for the *topos* of naming. He remembers that he "was still a little boy wearing knee pants"—the abandonment of traditional attire seems to have come early for him, perhaps even before attendance at school—"when the Mennonites sent me up to Halstead to their school there." He seems to have had no problem adjusting: "Young as I was," Sweezy recalls, "I managed to fit in with the others" (65). At the school he "began to learn dairying and the care of livestock, along with more things out of books, and my training was so thorough that for years afterward I was able to earn my living and a living for my family after I married, in one or another of the Government schools for Indians or at some one of the Indian missions" (65). Unfortunately, he gives no particulars about this "thorough" "training" or about his learning "things out of books."

At the South Dakota Catholic schools, as we have seen, Indian students were often treated badly by some of the German nuns and priests who staffed those schools. That most of the Mennonites were Germans does not, however, seem to have been a problem for Sweezy. Indeed, as he describes it, the fact that their first language was German presented more nearly an opportunity than a difficulty. Sweezy notes that some "of the Indian students there, good at books and at languages, learned to talk German and to read and write German script." He says that for "fun they sometimes sent letters in that language back to people on the Reservation," and he recalls that "To be able to write it was an accomplishment for a Cheyenne or an Arapaho, who had already learned, besides his own language, to talk in the sign language and to read and write in English" (65). Apart from this, he says little about his experiences at the Halstead school—although he references his time there in order to date his first meeting with James Mooney, an encounter that importantly shaped his life.

Sweezy writes that Mooney had come to visit "many times between 1891 and 1918" (62), although "his longest visit must have been during the year 1895, when he stayed several months" (62). It was in the summer of that year that Sweezy, "a boy of fourteen ... just back from the Mennonite school in Kansas where [he] had been for five or six years" (63), first met Mooney. He was aware that Mooney had come "from the Smithsonian Institution in Washington to study the ways and the beliefs of the Plains Indians, just as he had already studied those of some other tribes" (62). Of the many white visitors to Darlington, it was Mooney, he says, whom he remembers "best of all, and who meant more to [him] than any outsider." Looking back, Sweezy explains that fifty years ago it "was hard for us to realize, when [Mooney] first came, that there were now people employed by the Government who believed that our art and history and religion had value, and that instead of stamping out everything Indian they must do what they could to understand and collect and record everything that belonged to our way of living" (62).

By the time Sweezy told this to Althea Bass—he died in 1953—he knew well that the reason the government had been collecting and recording the Arapahos' "way of living" and relocating its material contents to the Smithsonian was because it was certain that this "way of living" was no longer viable. Sweezy seems to have accepted the fact that the Arapaho "way," as he had known it in his childhood, was indeed "vanishing." But what he emphasizes is not so much the people's sense of loss but, rather, the degree to which Mooney's admiring attention "made us feel proud in the peculiar ways and dress and beliefs of the Cheyenne and Arapaho" (62), something of a recompense for what is gone.

 споки

Sweezy says he "had been trying to draw since [he] was a little fellow," and at some point, "a woman at the Agency had showed him how to use water colors." Apparently no one at school had helped him to develop this interest. Mooney, Sweezy recalls, "entertained many Indian visitors, especially old men and women who could answer his questions about the way things used to be" (62). At some point he learns that "Mr. Mooney ... wanted an artist to draw some of the designs on the handiwork that was brought in and to restore the paint on some of the old shields that had been dug up" (63). With characteristic modesty, he says, "I was the best they could offer him"—and the untrained and inexperienced young man does not disappoint.

He listens closely as Mooney discusses "with the Indians ... the shields and robes and leggings they brought in," and then he goes to work in a room Mooney has provided. The following day Mooney "laughed and seemed surprised when [Sweezy] showed him" some of what he had done, and he "praised it because the colors were true and the design was exactly like the original" (63). Sweezy continues to work for Mooney, and he makes the point that "Mr. Mooney was the only art teacher [he] ever had." The advice Mooney gave him before he left, Sweezy says, was: "Keep on painting, and don't paint rocks and trees and things that aren't there. Just paint Indian." He seems to have understood this advice and found Mooney's counsel to be of great value. "So I am still painting," Sweezy says, "and painting Indian. It is the only way I know. I call it the Mooney way" (63).

Before Mooney left, Sweezy tells us, he "gave a big party for everyone, white people, and Indians ... with everything on display that he had collected." He explained that these things would be on view at the Smithsonian Institution "where they would never be lost or destroyed" (63).[20] Sweezy observes that the elders present who had made some of these things "were proud of their handiwork," and in regarding it, "all of us had proof that the old road of the Arapaho had been a good one in its day and would not be forgotten" (64). It is his people's pride in the goodness of "the Arapaho Way," the title of his book, and the fact that it "would not be forgotten" to which he calls attention, rather than to any sadness (or anger) they might have felt that "its day" had passed. This gesture is typical of Carl Sweezy; his autobiographical text and his many fine paintings deserve much more attention from scholars than they have received.[21]

ಞಞ

It is "after [he] had been back from Halstead for a year or two," and was already painting "the Mooney way," that Sweezy says he "was sent to school at Carlisle, in Pennsylvania" (65).[22] He provides no information as to who had "sent" him. And as had been the case with the Mennonite school, he would have very little to say of Carlisle, giving it no more than two paragraphs,[23] which include his observation of how different that "part of the country was ... from what [he] had known on the Reservation and in Kansas" (65). As he often does, Sweezy generalizes here, remembering that "we had good teachers there, and Captain Pratt, who was in charge of the school, believed that if Indians had a chance they could learn anything that white people could learn" (65–66). He is well aware that this opinion was not universal among whites at the time (or since).

He describes his "outing" experience, "two summers ... with a farmer's family at Washington Crossing, New Jersey, close to the Delaware River" (66),[24] where he learns new methods of crop raising and demonstrates to the farmer that he "could be trusted with the full care of all the livestock on a farm" (66). He says he "would have liked to stay at Carlisle until [he] could graduate," but the cold and dampness of "the winters there [were] different from what [he] had always known," leading to his becoming ill and then being "sent back to the Reservation to get well" (66). Although he had wished to continue at Carlisle, he nonetheless finds it good to be home, and "to hear Arapaho spoken and take part in Arapaho ceremonies and eat Arapaho food" (66). In his short stay at school, his perspective has not so altered that he is disheartened, as many returned students were, upon re-encountering the life they had left behind.

When Sweezy is "well again," he is "sent back to school, but not so far away this time," to Chilocco Indian School, in "what was then Oklahoma Territory" (66).[25] Consistently reticent, Sweezy does not say with whom he stayed while recuperating in Darlington, or who cared for him, nor does he mention any contact he might have had with his father or brothers. For that matter, he says no more of his first year at Chilocco than he had said of his time at Carlisle. He does tell us that on his "way back to Darlington at the end of that school year"—the one he has just spent at Chilocco—he "met one of [his] old school friends in the railway station" (66). This fellow "had signed up to play baseball with the Enid[, Oklahoma,] team and he thought [Sweezy] was a good enough player to sign up too" (66).[26] He had earlier mentioned returning "from the Mennonite school in Kansas where [he] had been for five or six years," with "a baseball bat and a catcher's mitt" (63), about the time he met Mooney, and clearly he had become adept at the game. Now the people "in charge of the business" of playing baseball in Enid agree that he is indeed "good enough." Thus, much to his own surprise, he gets "to enjoy playing baseball every day and to be paid a salary for doing it" (66). Sweezy has, however briefly, attended two of the largest and most prestigious off-reservation boarding schools of the time, but he has nothing further to say about his education or the degree to which it did or did not change him.

Bass has structured the book so that there are three more brief chapters still to come: "Teachers, Travelers, Preachers," "Religion," and "The End of the Road." These will work toward an ending by having the narrator go back in time. So, too, had Charles Brant's final chapters of *Jim Whitewolf*, "Sex, Marriage and Divorce," and "Religions, Old and New," taken Joe Blackbear back in time. But the effect of this movement in *The Arapaho Way* is very different from what it had been in *Jim Whitewolf*.

In "Teachers, Travelers, Preachers" Sweezy recalls that "a few years after the Mennonites began their mission at Darlington, [they] extended their work by opening a branch mission ... sixty-five miles to the northwest" (66–67). At that time, "Another Mennonite missionary, H. R. Voth, came with his family to take charge ... and he and his wife were as faithful and as much interested in the school" (67) as those in charge earlier had been. Sweezy's baseball playing would have been about 1900, so Bass's placement of this material here does indeed take us back in time. Voth came to the Darlington school in 1882, became superintendent in 1884, and served until 1892. Both at Darlington and later at Hopi (see volume 1), Voth was in the paradoxical situation of being deeply interested in the Indian languages and cultures he encountered and also committed to wiping them out as essentially pagan. It is likely that Bass places Sweezy's recollection of Voth here because it is related to some of what he had just said about James Mooney's collecting for the Smithsonian. Sweezy says: "Mr. Voth made a large collection of our handcrafts and equipment, and I am told that some of these things are still to be seen in the display at the Smithsonian Institution" (67). He is correct. Voth had sold a number of Arapaho items to the Bureau of American Ethnology, among them pieces of Arapaho Ghost Dance paraphernalia, some of which are indeed on display at the Smithsonian. Moving from Mooney's collecting

16 The Reverend H.R. Voth, Mennonite Missionary, with a group of Arapaho girls. Photo taken by James Mooney of the Bureau of American Ethnology in 1893. Courtesy of the Museum of the Great Plains.

to Voth's, Sweezy's recollections of the past now lead him to think back more generally to the Mennonites he had known at Darlington.

The Mennonite missionaries of his childhood, as Sweezy remembers them, "laid the foundation for the kind of life we were to live when our tribal days were over" (67), he says, and he expresses no sadness here concerning the "end of the road," as the last chapter is called. Bass concludes this chapter with Sweezy describing Darlington at the end of the nineteenth century and providing a more detailed picture than he had given before of a cosmopolitan paradise lost—a second paradise lost, as I called it earlier, after the disappearance of traditional Arapaho ways. Because the book is little known, I quote this paragraph in full. Sweezy says:

> Germans and Americans and Indians, traders and farmers and soldiers and anthropologists, Quakers and Episcopalians and Mennonites and believers in the religion of the Indian, we were all mixed up together there at Darlington. We Arapaho learned something from them all, and kept the best of our own beliefs as well. And it is to the credit of those who sat down with us on our Reservation, for a short time or a long one, that in the end we learned to follow the white man's road and became good American citizens. (67)

Here, I would suggest, is the climactic moment of this narrative, and the sort of climax typical of a comic narrative. One of the important aspects of a narrative plotted in the comic mode is its movement "to include as many people as possible in its final society" (165), and this is a matter of some importance for Carl Sweezy's life story.

Of course in order to sustain and emphasize this positive movement, he must pass over the fact that there would not have been a "Reservation" on which all these Germans and Americans, missionaries and functionaries and even anthropologists might "sit down" with the Arapahos if not for the power of the colonial American state. Nor had Arapaho leaders agreed to "sit down" on the reservation strictly of their own accord; their abandonment of what Sweezy several times calls "the buffalo road" in order to adopt "the corn road" was hardly the people's free choice. These are things that Carl Sweezy obviously knew, and he may even have spoken further of them. If he did, and if Althea Bass had emphasized them, it would have produced a different sort of book, a tragic or even possibly an ironic narrative. She could, for example, have represented Sweezy's story as Brant did Joe Blackbear's, as one of dissolution and disintegration, had she emphasized what she had noted in her foreword:

17 Carl Sweezy. Date and photographer unknown.

Sweezy's "neat, if much worn, clothing" and the fact that "he carried a port-folio made of cartons from the grocery store and bound with rope that held the paintings he had come to sell" (vii). About midway through the book she quoted Sweezy as saying that since his wife's death he has had "no real home of [his] own" (41), but clearly Althea Bass did not—as Charles Brant did with Joe Blackbear's divorce—present this as determinative by way of conclusion.

The book's penultimate chapter is called "Religion," and it does not concern Mennonites or Episcopalians but rather several Arapaho religious practices, including one of which Sweezy strongly disapproves. He has praise for the traditional Arapaho Sun Dance and medicine lodge ceremonies but acknowledges: "It would be impossible for the Southern Arapaho to hold their full medicine-lodge ceremonies today"; nor could they practice the Sun Dance, outlawed by the government in 1904. Sweezy says when he "was a boy, a false religion sprang up that disturbed the Indians throughout the country for years. It was called the Ghost Dance" (72). Despite this estimate, in fact the Arapahos were active participants in the Ghost Dance for many years.

As we have seen, the peyote religion had come to the southern Plains about 1880, and as with Joe Blackbear, it was attractive to Carl Sweezy. He says: "A much simpler ceremony, with some of the same meaning, has taken place among many of the Arapaho and among other Indians as well. This is the ceremony of the Native American Church, the peyote ceremony" (76). Claiming here that the ceremonies of the peyote church have "some of the same meaning" as traditional Arapaho religious practices, Sweezy presents change as consistent with tradition. Unfortunately, he says, "white people have misun-derstood the Indians' worship and have tried to outlaw the Native American Church" (76). Oddly, he does not mention that James Mooney, a man he had known and continued to admire, had worked with Kiowas, Arapahos, and others to help get the Native American Church incorporated in Oklahoma in 1918. Bass concludes this short, penultimate chapter on a positive note, as Sweezy says of the peyote service, that when it "ends at sunrise, and the fast is broken with the water and the food that the women bring, those who have taken part face the day and the world before them with a new sense of beauty and hope in their hearts.... There are many ways to God" (76).

Bass's last chapter is a mere two pages long, and although it has the somewhat ominous-sounding title "The End of the Road," its tone is very different from that of Brant's ending to *Jim Whitewolf.* It is Carl Sweezy's sense that the "end" came into sight when the Arapaho chiefs in 1891 agreed to have their lands allotted. The Cheyennes made "the same sort of agreement, and in 1892 the surplus lands of the Southern Arapaho were opened to white settlement" (77). Whatever exceeds "the quarter section of land" assigned to each member of the tribe by the government constitutes "surplus" land available for sale, allotment once more serving as a means to transfer land from the Natives to the settlers.

Despite white settlement, Sweezy recalls that for a time, under a number of admirable Indian agents, "our lives went on in much the same way as before" (77). This changes in 1906 when a new agent named Shell arrives, a man who "seemed to be ready to do away with everything about our lives that was Indian" (77). One of Shell's first acts is to combine the Arapaho government school with a Cheyenne school at Caddo Spring—a place which now will be called Concho, the agent naming "it for himself in Spanish" (78). The book's final two paragraphs are of an elegiac nature, as Sweezy, in his last years—it is not clear just when he told these things to Althea Bass—looks to times past and things long gone. Typical of the Native American elegist, he responds to loss not only by mourning but by re-membering the past, so the People might live.

Sweezy observes that the "Agency grounds at Darlington are fenced and closed," and that "the fine brick Mennonite Mission building is falling into decay.... Fort Reno is no longer a fort.... There is nothing to be proud of there now." "Hardly a landmark is left of what was once the center of our lives," he says. But, he continues, "we still remember that it was once a place where we lived as Arapaho, and where good white people were friendly and kind and gave their lives to setting us on the new road of the white man" (78). Sweezy has been treated very much as a distinctive individual, but the pronoun here—it is impossible to say whether it came from him or from Althea Bass (and in Arapaho pronouns are indicated only by the form of the verb)—is not "I" but "we," referring to Carl Sweezy as an Arapaho. This, of course, is selective memory, for he has just told of Agent Shell, not a good white person at all, as he has also told of other whites who were not friendly and not kind.

Comic plots, as I have quoted Hayden White, conclude with the "reconciliations of men with men, of men with their world and their society"; ordinary or "normal" individuals achieving temporary resolutions, overcoming obstacles to a better life (9). Carl Sweezy's story ends with a modestly hopeful vision of a world in which persons and cultures are indeed reconciled, the proper conclusion, as Althea Bass has structured it, for a narrative in the comic mode.

12

Ah-nen-la-de-ni's
"An Indian Boy's Story"

AH-NEN-LA-DE-NI, ALSO KNOWN AS DANIEL LA FRANCE, WAS BORN IN 1879
in Gouverneur Village on the St. Regis Mohawk reservation in New York.
His brief account of his early life and his varied educational experiences was
published in the *Independent* as "An Indian Boy's Story" in 1903. The journal's
editor prefaced the piece by noting that the author "has been aided only to
the extent of some rewriting and rearranging" (1780).[1] It has been widely
noted that Zitkala-Sa's autobiographical essays appeared in the *Atlantic
Monthly* along with works by authors still renowned today, so it may also be
worth noting that Ah-nen-la-de-ni's essay was preceded in this issue of the
Independent by Rebecca Harding Davis's story, "A Great Object Lesson"—her
best-known work of fiction today is probably "Life in the Iron Mills"—and
it was followed by "Detached Thoughts," "fragments from the private journal of Count Leo Tolstoy here published for the first time" (1788).[2] Unlike
Zitkala-Sa, however, Ah-nen-la-de-ni was not a writer but a nurse, although
his essay does include some samples of his poetry. "An Indian Boy's Story"
is the only published work of his I have discovered. I suspect there may
be more.

Ah-nen-la-de-ni writes that his "father was an Indian medicine man"
(1780), but of a modern sort, a man who "made frequent journeys, taking
his family with him and selling his pills and physics in various towns along
the border line between Canada and the United States" (1780).[3] Father is
described as a "striking figure" whose hair "was long and black, and he wore
a long Prince Albert coat while in the winter quarters, and Indian costume,
fringed and beaded, while in the tent. His medicines were put up in pill boxes

and labeled bottles, and were the results of knowledge that had been handed down through many generations in our tribe" (1781), another example of the co-existence of tradition and modernity.

Apparently he was not alone among his tribesmen in this regard, for his son writes that on the reservation, "the people farmed and dressed somewhat after the fashion of the white man, [but] they still kept up their ancient tribal ceremonies, laws and customs, and preserved their language" (1781). Their children have formal education readily available to them, although apparently not of a useful kind. "There were four Indian day schools on the reservation," Ah-nen-la-de-ni writes, "all taught by young white women. I sometimes went to one of these, but learned practically nothing. The teachers did not understand our language and we knew nothing of theirs so much progress was not possible" (1781). Although he has announced his own attendance at school as sporadic, he nonetheless recalls clearly the method of instruction: "Our lessons consisted of learning to repeat all the English words in the books that were given us. Thus, after a time, some of us, myself included, became able to pronounce all the words in the Fifth and Sixth readers, and took great pride in the exercise. But we did not know what any of the words meant" (1781). Arithmetic "stopped at simple numeration," and the children "spent much of [their] time in the school in drawing pictures of each other and the teacher;" there was also "a great deal of fighting" (1782). In view of this it comes as no surprise that "the attendance at these schools was so poor and irregular ... that on many days the teachers sat alone in the schoolhouses because there were no scholars" (1782). There do not seem to be any disciplinarians, Indian police, or other officials maintaining attendance or order. He notes, however, that since "that time a great change has taken place, and there are now good schools on the reservation" (1782). But by the time he was thirteen, he "had been nominally a pupil of the school for six years," but "still so ignorant of English that [he] only knew one sentence, which was common property among [the] alleged pupils." That was: "'Please, ma'am, can I go out?' Pronounced: 'Peezumgannigowout!'" (1782).

It is at this time that "the honey-tongued agent of a new Government contract Indian school appeared on the reservation, drumming up boys and girls for his institution," promising "good food and teaching, ... fine uniforms, the playground and its sports and toys" (1782). Ah-nen-la-de-ni's father is away at the time, but his mother and grandmother "heard [the man] with growing wonder and interest, as [he] did [him]self." Although he has been "leading a very happy life, helping with the planting, trapping, fishing, basket making and playing all the games of [his] tribe"—especially lacrosse, for which his people are "famous"—nonetheless, "the desire to travel and see new things and the hope of finding an easy way to much knowledge in the wonderful school outweighed [his] regard for ... home and its joys" (1782). He imagined that if he went "to this wonderful school," he might "become a great man—perhaps at last a chief of our tribe" (1782).[4] Like a considerable number of bright young Native people, he is eager to attend the distant boarding school, and Ah-nen-la-de-ni becomes "one of the twelve boys who in 1892 left our reservation to go to the Government contract school for Indians, situated in a large Pennsylvania city and known as the———Institute" (1782).

Although he does not name it here, he later makes clear that the large city in Pennsylvania is Philadelphia; but he never does reveal the name of the school, the Lincoln Institute. In 1882 Richard Pratt had brought Carlisle students to Philadelphia to celebrate the city's bicentennial and they had stayed at the Lincoln Institute, which at that time was a children's charity home. Impressed with Pratt and his students, the institute's directors asked his aid in obtaining government funding to turn the institute into an Indian boarding school. They were successful, and the school opened in 1884, operating on the Carlisle model. I have found little information about it, although around the turn of the twentieth century it would become notorious for frauds perpetrated on Indian Service inspectors of just the sort Zitkala-Sa had alleged against Carlisle, and which Ah-nen-la-de-ni describes later in his narrative.

The young Mohawk finds the "journey to Philadelphia ... very enjoyable and interesting," in particular, his "first ride on the 'great steel horse,' as the Indians called the railway train" (1782). Far less enjoyable are his first encounters with the *topoi* and *loci* of government boarding school. He notes that although he and his fellows were used to spending a "good deal of time in the water" at home, "this first bath at the institution was different. For one thing, it was accompanied by plenty of soap," and it had been "preceded by a haircut that is better described as a crop" (1783). The cleanup is administered not by staff members but by "larger Indian boys of tribes different from his own," who wield not only soap but "very hard scrubbing brushes" (1782). He had earlier noted his "surprise" that the school had many "strange Indian boys belonging to tribes of which [he] had never heard" (1782). After "the astonishing bath," as he calls it, "the newcomer was freshly clothed from head to foot," and the clothing he had come in was "burned or buried" (1783). Just what sort of clothing he is given is not described.

Now comes a renaming, "a change," he writes, "which, though it might seem trifling to the teachers, was very important to me" (1783). His name, Ah-nen-la-de-ni, he explains, means "'Turning Crowd' or 'Turns the Crowd,' but [his] family had had the name 'La France' bestowed upon them by the French some generations before [his] birth" (1783), and that would be the name by which he was known at school. Although it is not an unfamiliar name, he nonetheless feels that "Daniel La France was … a stranger and a nobody with no possibilities. It seemed as if my prospect of a chiefship had vanished. I was," he writes, "very homesick for a long time" (1783), like many boarding-school students before him.

He is assigned to a dormitory with "twenty beds in it, … under a captain who was one of the advanced scholars. It was his duty to teach and enforce the rules of the place in this room, and to report to the white authorities all breaches of discipline" (1783). He notes the regular surveillance—"Whether at work or play, we were constantly watched" (1783)—as particularly displeasing to "us Mohawks, who were warriors at fourteen years of age" (1783), although no Mohawks of any age had engaged in battle recently. The "cramped quarters and the dull routine of the school were maddening," he writes. "There were endless rules for us to study and abide by, and hardest of all was the rule against speaking to each other in our own language." Like boarding-school students elsewhere, however, he says: "This last we did quite frequently, and were punished, when detected, by being made to stand in the 'public hall' for a long time or to march about the yard while the other boys were at play" (1783). He describes no corporal punishment, and, although he had called the older boy in charge of the dormitory a "captain," there is no mention of marching or drilling, as there were at Carlisle. He says nothing of religious observances, such as attendance at Sunday services and reciting grace before meals, although he does observe that when he "first went to the school the superintendent was a clergyman" (1784).

Like Carlisle, "this school contemplated every Indian boy learning a trade as well as getting a grammar school education," so that the students "went to school in the morning and to work in the afternoon, or the other way about." There are only Indian boys at the school, "about 115 boys," while "three miles from us was a similar Government school for Indian girls, which had nearly as many inmates" (1783). The use of the word "inmates" where one would have expected to find "students," suggests, of course, that these places are more nearly prisons than schools. That implication is merely a suggestion here, but later, as I will note, it is insisted upon. And, to be sure, the Lincoln Institute, like Carlisle and a great many of the boarding schools, also had a jail—in which Ah-nen-la-de-ni at one point finds himself.

As for the trades these student-inmate boys learn, Ah-nen-la-de-ni writes that there "were shoemakers, blacksmiths, tinsmiths, farmers, printers, all sorts of mechanics among us." He himself worked "to learn the tailoring trade," and "stuck at it for two and a half years," until he "began to cough" (1783). Tuberculosis was still common at the schools, and because "it was said that outdoor work would be better for [him]," he went, "during the vacation of 1895, up into Bucks County, Pa., and worked on a farm." This is at once an outing assignment—Ah-nen-la-de-ni does not use the term, although he describes other outings—and also a cure. And the farm work does provide a "benefit" to his health, although he "was not a very successful farmer—the methods of the people who employed me were quite different from those of my reservation" (1783–84).

The experience on the farm must have been satisfying in addition to being beneficial to his health, for Ah-nen-la-de-ni writes that although he had been "homesick soon after coming to the Institute," it was not long before he "did not care to go back to the reservation at vacation time," but preferred to spend his "vacations working for Quaker farmers" (1784), just as students on outing assignments from Carlisle sometimes chose to do. As with those students, "the money [he] earned at this and other occupations was turned in to the Institute bank credited to [his] account." He could draw on this for "expenses and for special occasions like Christmas and the Fourth of July" (1784). He tells us that although Indian parents on his reservation had agreed that their children were to remain at the Institute for five years, he stayed on for eight (1784). This was because after finishing "with the grammar school [he] got a situation in the office of a lawyer while still residing at the institution." During this time, he tells us, he "also took a course of stenography and typewriting at the Philadelphia Young Men's Christian Association," so "practically [he] was only a boarder at the Institute during the latter part of [his] eight year stay there" (1784).

He now reports that he "wanted to leave and go to Carlisle school, which [he] had heard was very good" (1784). But he "could not obtain permission" (1784). If he has been at the Lincoln Institute for eight years, his request to leave for Carlisle "during the latter part" of those years would have been made about 1900 (he had come to the institute in 1892). But as will become clear, both his request and its denial in fact occurred about 1898. For Ah-nen-la-de-ni reports that upon the outbreak of the Spanish-American War in 1898, the young lawyer for whom he worked wished "to go to it in the Red Cross service" (1785) and also to take him along. Ah-nen-la-de-ni writes that he "greatly desired" (1785) to go, but this was "not allowed." He speculates "that the lawyer could easily have obtained [his] liberty," but he "did not wish to antagonize the Lady Managers [of the Lincoln Institute], who considered any criticism of the institution as an attack on their own infallibility" (1785).[5]

Why might his departure from the institute, whether to attend Carlisle or to serve in the war, appear to be "an attack" upon the "infallibility" of the Lady Managers overseeing the institute? Ah-nen-la-de-ni had earlier somewhat cryptically noted that his request to go to Carlisle was denied because he "was valuable to the authorities there [at Lincoln Institute] for certain purposes" (1784). He now explains what those "purposes" were. He writes that the "reason why [he] and others like [him] were kept at the school was that [they] served as show scholars—as results of the system and evidences of the good work the Institute was doing" (1784). This had not always been the case. "When I first went to the school," he writes, "the superintendent was a clergyman, honest and well meaning, and during the first five years thereafter while he remained in charge the general administration was honest" (1784). This would have been from 1892 to 1897. But "when he went away the school entered upon a period of changing administrations and general demoralization." All of the new superintendents "seemed to us boys more or less dishonest." Their dishonesty is of the sort generally alleged by Zitkala-Sa at Carlisle.

Ah-nen-la-de-ni explains that boys like himself who had been at the school for eight years were displayed as examples of progress made in just two years; "shoes and other articles bought in Philadelphia stores were ... exhibited as the work of us boys." He himself "was good for various show purposes" in that he "could sing and play a musical instrument"—he doesn't say which one—"and ... wrote essays which were thought to be good" (1784). It is here that he includes two of the verses he had composed "that visitors admired" (1784).[6] About 1898 the superintendent was responsible to "a Board of Lady Managers with a Lady Directress, and these visited us occasionally, but there was no use laying any complaint before them. They were arbitrary and almost unapproachable" (1785). The lawyer who had employed him, he reasons, "did not wish to antagonize" (1785) them by removing one of their prize students, whose loss as a "show scholar" (1784) might diminish the reputation of the institute and thus constitute an "attack" on the "infallibility" of those in charge.

He says nothing further about his desire to attend Carlisle or to serve in some capacity in the Spanish-American War. Instead, while "waiting for a new situation after the young lawyer had gone away, [he] heard of the opportunities there were for young men who could become good nurses,[7] and of the place where such training could be secured , ... and [he] desired to go there." He presents "this ambition to the superintendent" (1785), who is encouraging. But when Ah-nen-la-de-ni completes "an application for admission ready to be sent ... to the authorities of the Nurses' Training School," the Head Directress "flatly refused its consideration without giving any good reason for doing so" (1785). He is not, this time, to be denied, and what he tells us about how he went about applying to the training school is very revealing.

He writes that because the Lady Directress "made the mistake of returning the application to [him]," he can contrive to get it sent to the training school which he now reveals is in Manhattan (1785). "It went out," he writes, "through a secret channel, as all the regular mail of the *institution's inmates* ... was opened and examined in the office of the superintendent" (1785, my emphasis). The words I have emphasized, the second of which we have noted earlier, here speak unmistakably. Ah-nen-la-de-ni substitutes "institution" for institute and once more writes "inmates" rather than "students" or "boarders," strongly suggesting that the school is more nearly a prison. The difficulties of this inmate, however, are not yet over. He learns that his application was acknowledged a "few days before the 4th of July, 1899," and it will soon be clear why he dates the event in its proximity to the Fourth, the day Frederick Douglass had called "*your* day of independence, not mine."[8] The response he has received requests him "to report at the [nursing] school for the entrance examination." The problem, however, is that this "communication found [him] in the school jail, where [he] had been placed for the first time in all [his] life at the institution" (1785)—once more "institution," not institute.

He is there, because he has been "framed," as we might say, charged with, of all things, "throwing a nightgown out of the dormitory window" (1785). Although the nightgown in question was indeed his, Ah-nen-la-de-ni states that he was not the one who had ejected it. Rather, he believes his nightgown was pitched out of the window by "one of the official underlings ... in order to found upon it a charge against [him]" (1785). In punishing him and "other boys of the institution [sic]" for this trifling matter, the authorities are actually punishing them for something he has not as yet mentioned, a bold act of resistance on their part. Ah-nen-la-de-ni writes that he and some others "had gone to members of the Indian Rights Association[9] and had made complaint of conditions in the school, and that an investigation was coming" (1785). The authorities are holding him in the school jail now in order "to disgrace and punish [him] as one of the leaders of those who were exposing them" (1785).

Wishing to get to Manhattan, he "was very anxious to get away, but [his] liberation in time to attend that entrance exam seemed impossible." He writes that the "days passed, and when the 4th of July arrived [he] was still in the school jail" (1785), no day of independence as yet for him. Fortunately, through the carelessness of "the guard detailed to look after [his] safe keeping," he manages to escape. An advantage of going to boarding school in a great city is that as "soon as [he] got out of the inclosure [he] dashed after and caught a trolley car, and a few hours later ... was in New York" (1785). Although this was the "last [he] saw of the Institute"—perhaps his getting free of it allows him to return to calling it by that name rather than an "institution"—he learns that the investigation of the school that he and the others had urged has in fact taken place. The "Superintendent of Indian Schools had descended upon it upon a given day and found everything beautiful—for her visit had been announced" (1785).[10] When she makes a surprise visit the following day, however, "things were not beautiful at all, and much that we had told about," he writes, "was proven" (1785). He will later note that the "school was closed in 1900 as the Government cut off all appropriations" (1786).

Ah-nen-la-de-ni is admitted to the training school, and studying nursing in Manhattan, he finds "this new life ... very much to [his] liking." He provides details of his pay and the cost for room and board at the school, but although he notes with satisfaction that now "he was free," he says nothing about life in turn of the twentieth-century Manhattan. After a year at the school he returns home to the reservation for a "ten days' vacation ... the first time in nine years that [he] had seen his old home," and as one would expect, he "found things much changed." His mother and grandmother have died—he had earlier learned of his mother's death but "was not allowed to go to her funeral" (1782)—as also has "a little sister whom [he] had never seen. [His] father was still alive and still wandering as of old," but his friends "had scattered and [he] felt like a stranger" (1786), as so many returned boarding-school students had also felt.

Unlike for some of them, however, his sense of estrangement quickly passes. He stays with his older brother and finds it "very pleasant to renew acquaintance with the places and objects that had been familiar in [his] childhood ... and with the friends who remained." Observing that the "past and its traditions were losing their hold ... and white man's ways were gaining," his judgment of that development is "that our people had progressed" (1786). But this hardly means he has become an assimilationist, Ah-nen-la-de-ni no more, and only Daniel La France. "What [he] saw in the reservation convinced him that [his] people are not yet ready for citizenship," a goal advocated for by the Indian Rights Association, and at this historical moment by Charles Eastman, Luther Standing Bear, Zitkala-Sa, Thomas Wildcat Alford, and many other Native activists.

What he saw also convinced him that his people "should be allowed to retain their reservation," so that they "are greatly obliged by those who have aided them in defeating the Vreeland bill" (1786).[11] He observes that the "old Indians ... will not and cannot change," and although to "the white man these old people may not seem important, ... to us young Indians they are very important" (1786). Here he offers some insightful observations about those students who have returned to the reservation to make their lives, a decision he himself has not yet made. "White people," he writes, "are aggravated because so many young Indians, after their schooling, go back to their reservations and are soon seen dressed and living just like the others" (1789–87). He explains that "they must do that if they desire to keep in touch with the others," noting shrewdly that if they did not do that, Native parents would refuse to send their children to school, fearing that if they did, "'They would never come back to us'" (1787).

Although it is brief, in my view his analysis of these matters is broader and deeper than that of some of his far better known contemporaries. Ah-nen-la-de-ni/Daniel La France—it seems accurate from this point forward to identify him by both names, despite a certain awkwardness—asserts: "The young Indians are right to go back to the reservation and right to dress and act like the others, to cherish the old folks and make their way easy, and not to forget their tribe" (1787). But, he explains, "It is a mistake to think that they"—the students who return to the reservation and take up their old manner of dress and comportment—"soon lose all that they have learned in school." Comparing them to "those who have not been to school" (1787), he finds them altogether "civilized," and whatever their dress, speech, and behavior, he sees them as "missionaries to the reservation" (1787), a term he means favorably.

Ah-nen-la-de-ni/La France also addresses another change he has observed: the fact that "on all the reservations the pure blooded Indians are becoming rarer." "On our reserve now," he writes, "you can see boys and girls with light hair and blue eyes.... They have the rosy cheeks of English children, but," he makes clear, "they cannot speak a word of English" (1787). Although he does not address the implications of this change, I think he regards it more nearly as full of promise rather than troubling. Insofar as one might traditionally have sought an unfamiliar Native person's tribal affiliation by asking, "What language do you speak?" clearly the rosy-cheeked Mohawk speakers are Mohawk, for all that their "rosy cheeks," mark them as a different kind of Mohawk than St. Regis had known before. To cite the title of Carlos Montezuma's poem once more, "Changing Is Not Vanishing."

Ah-nen-la-de-ni says no more about his visit to the reservation, turning to speak again of the training school, his subsequent nursing studies, and his present employment "principally in private practice" (1787). In regard to "prejudice against Indians among white people," like Dr. Eastman, Nurse La France doesn't "think it amounts to much," nor that he has "suffered anywhere from prejudice." He adds, however, that he has "suffered many times from being mistaken for a Japanese" (1787). "Some ask me whether or not I will ever return to my tribe," he writes by way of conclusion: "How can I tell? The call from the woods and fields is very clear and moving, especially in these pleasant summer days" (1787). I do not know whether Ah-nen-la-de-ni/Daniel La France ever returned to the reservation, but two recent Mohawk chiefs, perhaps no relation, were named La France, and the name is common enough at St. Regis today.[12]

13

Esther Burnett Horne's
Essie's Story

ESTHER BURNETT HORNE (1909–99), AN EASTERN SHOSHONE WOMAN FROM Wind River, Wyoming, was a graduate of the Haskell Institute (high school diploma 1928, then a year of junior college), where she studied with two accomplished Native teachers, Ruth Muskrat Bronson (Cherokee) and Ella Cara Deloria (Dakota), before going on herself to become an innovative and award-winning teacher. She collaborated with the anthropologist Sally McBeth in the production of *Essie's Story: The Life and Legacy of a Shoshone Teacher*, published in 1998. In her deeply thoughtful "Introduction: Methodological and Cultural Concerns of Collecting and Coauthoring a Life History," McBeth explains that she taped Horne's life story "from 1987 to 1997, but the majority ... was recorded and transcribed from 1987 to 1989" (xv). She says Horne "chose the chronological ordering; every word on every page has been reread to her so that errors could be remedied or re-remembered events included" (xviii).[1] McBeth considers Horne a "co-author rather than an informant" (xviii), and the book's spine has both their names. Sally McBeth's work with Esther Horne may well be the closest and most intimately respectful collaboration between a Native autobiographer and an ethnographic editor since David MacAllester and Charlotte Frisbie worked with Frank Mitchell on *Blessingway Singer* (see volume 1). McBeth did, however, precede each of the book's chapters with her own summary of its contents.

Horne was the great-great-granddaughter of Sacajawea, the Shoshone woman who served as guide to Lewis and Clark on their exploratory expedition of the West, and that relationship was an important part of her Indian identity. Indeed, the first chapter of her book is called "My Relationship to Sacajawea," and it concludes with her strong belief that the commonly acknowledged date of Sacajawea's death, 1812, is mistaken and that she lived until 1884. She says that "*we* know that she lived to be more than a hundred years old because she came back and lived among our people" (10, italics in original).[2] The second chapter, "Early Life at Home, 1909–922," introduces the chronological order the narrative will now follow.

Horne's "mother, Mildred Large was Shoshone Indian" (11–12), and her father, Finn Burnett, was Scotch-Irish. His father had been agricultural agent to the Shoshones on the Wind River reservation in west-central Wyoming, spoke their language, and "had learned to like the Indian people very much" (12). He did not, however, like the idea of his son marrying an Indian. As a consequence, Horne's father and the Indian woman he would take for his wife eloped, leaving the Wind River reservation for Idaho. Her father, Horne says, "spoke better Shoshone than [her] mother" (13) and "was a really good Indian dancer" (16); she recalls that both he and her mother "used to tell ... Indian legends" (18) in Shoshone. Initially, because there "was no school where [they] lived in Idaho" (19), she and her siblings were taught by their parents, and "sometime after that, [they] started attending a public school" (19). Horne mentions no prejudicial treatment at the public school, but she does emphasize the fact that her father was "teaching his part-Indian children and his Indian wife to be proud because they were Indians. Rather than trying to take the Indianness out of us," she says, "he always reminded us that our ancestors had given so much to the American way of life" (19). It was as a child, Horne says, that she became "an avid reader" (20), and at "not more than nine or ten ... [she] was reading all of these books that [her] dad had" (21). Those were an eclectic lot, she recalls, with Longfellow and Robert Burns, along with the more current Jack London and Zane Grey, among the authors represented.

During the 'flu pandemic of 1918 the whole family was stricken except for Horne's father, who cared for them by himself. Although many around them die, no one in the family succumbs. But only a short time after surviving the 'flu, her father is diagnosed with a brain tumor, which proves fatal in 1922. Shortly after his death Horne's mother gives birth to a boy. Horne and her sister Bernice then care for the baby, their mother, and an eighteen-month-old sister. They now return to Wind River, but the family situation is precarious. Horne writes that her mother's "new companions

were so different from ... dad. They were unschooled; they drank and par-
tied and were loud and raucous" (29). Although her mother works, there is
not enough money. The apartment they live in "became cluttered and dirty;"
the children—by now there are six—"were undisciplined," and when they
"enrolled in school in Wyoming, it was very difficult" (29). For the first time,
she notes, they "were discriminated against.... Kids would call us names
because we didn't dress very well and because we were Indian" (29). Relatives
intervene to help as best they can, and finally the "wheels were set in motion
through the Wind River Agency to enroll us at Haskell Institute" (31) in
1924. The three youngest children remain with their mother as Horne, her
sister Bernice, and her brother Gordon board the train for Haskell (31).
Admonished not to run away from school, they "clung tearfully to [their]
mother" (31). Because the mother is presently employed by the Union Pacific
Railroad and "knew most of the trainmen" (31), the children are fortunate
to have the conductor carefully look after them along the way.[3]

Haskell had opened in 1884 as the United States Indian Industrial
Training Institute, with twenty-two students. In 1887 its name was changed
to Haskell Institute to honor U.S. Representative Dudley Haskell, who had
been instrumental in bringing the school to Lawrence, Kansas. Since 1993
it has operated as Haskell Indian Nations University. Horne and her siblings
are met by "Haskell school personnel" (31), and Horne recalls, "One of the
first places they took us was to the dormitories," where she sees "the long
row of white cots on the sleeping porches in the dormitory at Haskell" (31).
In a note McBeth explains that the students slept in screened-in porches in
all but the coldest weather, on the assumption that fresh air was conducive
to good health (186 n.3). The cots remind Horne "of the crowded hospital
ward where [her] father died" (31), a grim recollection that makes her think,
"I hate this place; I will never be happy here" (31). Things quickly improve,
however, when she is sought out by a "couple of older Shoshone girls from
Wind River"; it also helps that she recalls that two of her uncles had been
to Carlisle, one of them proudly having played football with Jim Thorpe.

She will only later speak of the dormitories themselves, the "girls' dormitory on one side of the campus, and the boys' on the other" (38). "Five or
six girls would share a room" where clothes and night clothes were kept, but
as Horne confirms, they "slept on large sleeping porches ... where air could
circulate" (38). The girls' and boys' dormitories were "separated by a large
expanse of lawn that had a bandstand"—no doubt like Carlisle's—"and a

sidewalk down the middle" (38). It is only on Sunday afternoons that boys and girls can fraternize on the lawn "and listen to a band concert, or have a watermelon social"—this must be during the summer—one of the only times boys and girls are allowed to be together, because "the school feared that a girl might get pregnant without constant supervision." This, Horne notes, "did sometimes happen" (38). "In addition to the dormitories," she writes, "there was a chapel, a gym, a home economics building, a dining hall, a kitchen, a hospital, campus housing for the faculty and staff, a print shop, a carpentry shop, and other trades buildings" (38). Like Carlisle and a few of the larger off-reservation schools, Haskell was a substantial institution, akin to a small town or a village—and one that had rats! "There were rats at Haskell" (38), Horne remembers. "They were rather large" (39).

She mentions being "required to bathe several times a week," and remembers her old clothing being taken from her and new clothing being issued. There is a physical inspection of the newly arrived students, and "some kind of chemical treatment or solution" is put on her "hair every so often to make sure [she] didn't get lice" (32). Before describing other aspects of the boarding school, Horne and McBeth include a brief section called "Socialization." This introduces a subject Horne will develop at some length throughout her narrative: the importance to her at Haskell of a connection to students from many tribal nations. Horne notes—as other boarding-school students had not—the use of slang by the students, a kind of Indian-English neither known to nor taught by the teachers. It serves as a *lingua franca* for young Indian men and women who speak many different languages and, more important, as a subcultural formation constitutive of solidarity. Horne's recollection is that there were not "any intertribal hostilities" and that the students "were curious about one another's tribal culture and language" (32). She remarks again the students' ability to nurture "a sense of community among [themselves]. . . . Traditional values, such as sharing and cooperation," she writes, "helped us to survive culturally at Haskell, even though the schools were designed to erase our Indian culture, values, and identities" (33). Her time at Haskell clearly deepened Essie Horne's Shoshone identity while also allowing her to achieve a new sense of pan-Indian identity.

Horne knows that "all of the boarding schools had a military discipline" (33) in those days, and she describes that discipline at Haskell. Clock time prevails, with students rising at 6:00 a.m., to the sound of a bugle or a bell. The girls "combed [their] hair, brushed [their] teeth, and got dressed in [their] everyday clothes" (33). She later tells us that "everyday garb" consisted of "a plain, short-sleeved, light blue dress, that we called a 'hickory.'... Boys wore plain light blue shirts and dark pants. This clothing was used for work and school" (37), and during the week it was also worn for drill. "On Sundays," however, she notes, "we wore military uniforms. Girls wore navy blue skirts and capes and white middy blouses with ties, overseas caps,[4] plus dark hose and shoes." As for the boys, they "wore khaki-colored army uniforms and drilled with surplus army rifles" (37).

By 6:15, Horne writes, the students were "in formation,... divided into companies by grade and sex." She also notes that "there was competition between the companies" (33), and she later makes clear her awareness that fostering competitive behavior was part of the process of de-Indianization employed by the boarding schools. She nonetheless becomes "a commissioned officer by working [her] way up through the ranks," once more in spite of her understanding that "we officers were being used by the school." Here the dilemma of the boarding-school student, one of a great many dilemmas, is "to maintain a sense of responsibility to our fellow students," because a sense of "responsibility to community is part of the Indian way," despite the school's pressure on each individual student to attain and then to exploit privilege.

"The intention of military drill may have been to break down tribal values of cooperation," Horne writes, "but we found other avenues through which we ... nurtured a sense of community among ourselves." This helped her "not only to survive the boarding school experience but to grow in it and learn from it" (34). "Nevertheless," she writes, fully aware of the complexity of the students' situation, "it was an honor to be chosen as an officer, and most of us had great pride in the military" (34). She later writes that she and her husband-to-be, Robert Horne, a Hoopa from California, also a student at Haskell, "used to talk about the military regime in boarding school" (36). All in all, she says that both of them were "grateful for that military experience because it taught us self-discipline for our later lives" (37). She is well aware that "it may not have done that for everybody" (37).

Horne further details the school's morning routine, describing breakfast, "which usually consisted of bread and corn syrup, peanut butter, oatmeal, cooked dried fruit, and a cereal beverage [?]" (35). A bit later she describes the dining room—or, at Haskell, the dining rooms: "There were two dining rooms, the Prevo for grades one through six, and the Big Dining Room for the older students." As elsewhere, "The boys ate on one side of the dining room and the girls on the other." However, unlike what other boarding school students had described, Horne says that at Haskell, "We were assigned seats by company." The girls were "to serve the food, clear the tables, and wash the dishes;" other students, both boys and girls, were detailed "to work in the kitchen" (38). As for the food at Haskell, she observes, "we did not receive a well-balanced diet—it was top heavy with starch." Some of the food was not fresh and "the quality ... affected our health. Boils and pimples were common afflictions." The poor "student health" at the BIA schools, she writes, "provoked government investigations ... and home economists were hired to develop more nutritious diets" (38) Whatever the recommendations of these "home economists" might have been, improvements in the diet offered at Haskell or elsewhere were dependent on the willingness of Congress to allocate more money for the BIA and its schools.

After breakfast, Horne describes "detail," a group assignment to do cleaning, food preparation, laundry, "and all kinds of other chores," including work at the school dairy, garden, and orchard. This, as we have seen, was "a way to keep the government boarding schools self-sufficient" (35) to the extent possible. "The skills I learned have been beneficial to me all through my life," Horne writes, going on to state explicitly for the first time what is a concern of her book: "I make an effort to soften the point of view that government boarding schools were hellish places with harsh discipline and beatings," she says. "My recollections are that in general we were pretty happy; by and large we were like one big happy family" (36).[5] This is an opinion that also would be expressed by some of the students at the Pipestone School some ten years later in Adam Fortunate Eagle's recollections. Horne is well aware that this goes counter to what I have called the oral tradition's survivor rhetoric, in which the schools are a metaphor for all of colonialism's ills.

In this regard it is interesting to note that immediately after the "one big happy family" observation Horne references the "belt line," a "common punishment for going AWOL ... a serious disciplinary measure" (36).[6] Although Walter Littlemoon, Tim Giago, Dennis Banks, and others had described this as extremely harsh, Horne mitigates the severity of the punishment by observing that some students "were such good runners and good dodgers that they defeated the purpose of the punishment." She states that she "was never aware that any great harm was done to the culprit who went through a belt line" (36).[7] This may indeed be a reasonable conclusion based upon her experience, although it may also, perhaps, be a revision of memory to accommodate the positive orientation of the narrative. Still, Horne does include her recollection that she chose not to take piano lessons from a Miss Robbins, much as she wished to learn to play, "because she had the reputation of spanking hands if you didn't hit the right keys" (44). Such "spanking" recalls the later brutal assaults on Lydia Whirlwind Soldier's hands by her clerical piano teacher.

Horne writes that her own "academic instruction," "took place in the afternoon," and followed the "standard high school curriculum ... that one would have had in the public schools" (39). She recalls the "instruction" as "very intense," as a consequence of "the teachers' missionary zeal [which] stemmed from their purpose ... to take the Indianness out of the Indian in preparation for life in the dominant society" (39). Intensity in pursuit of that particular purpose, one might think, was not altogether a good thing, but once more Horne does not develop the negative aspect of her observation. Rather she goes on to state: "My personal evaluation is that I received a very good education at Haskell." She "felt that some of the BIA teachers were more effective in challenging and motivating students than any teachers [she] had in the public schools," and that she was "fortunate to have had some excellent teachers in [her] years at Haskell" (39).

Two of those teachers were accomplished Native women: Ruth Muskrat Bronson, a Cherokee graduate of Mount Holyoke College, and Ella Cara Deloria, a Dakota who studied at Oberlin College and Columbia University's Teachers College. Horne speaks of them in a section of the narrative called "Significant Teachers: The Decision to Become an Educator" (41). There Horne recalls that although Bronson and Deloria "taught non-Indian subject matter," each "had a very strong respect for Indian culture" (41–42). Both "had a wonderful sense of humor" (41), and "taught us about Indian values and kept them alive in us" (42). She once more observes of her teachers that "by and large they were a dedicated lot," for whom she has "the fondest memories.... They seemed to care about [her] and the other students" (44). Nonetheless, she herself had not then thought of becoming a teacher, preferring at the time "to go into the business department" at Haskell. Because it was oversubscribed, however, she was put "in the Normal Training Department," which engaged her sufficiently that when a place became available in business, she "refused to switch" (44).

18 Esther Burnett on the occasion of a talk on Sacajawea she gave at the Haskell Institute, about 1925. She is wearing a buckskin dress lent to her by her teacher, Ruth Muskrat Bronson. Courtesy of Sally McBeth.

Horne describes sports at Haskell, noting that the "football team was nationally renowned" and that although Haskell was "a high school-junior college," its team played and often won against college teams (as did Carlisle). "Basketball and baseball were also popular," she recalls, although during her time there, Horne writes, "girls did not participate in athletics outside of physical education class" (47). Although she mentions the national renown of the football team, one would not know from Horne's account that in 1926, during her time there, Haskell was "undefeated and the highest scoring team in the nation" (Buchowska 248).[8] This was possible because Haskell—again like Carlisle—although not a college, had players of college age and older. George Levi, for example, an Arapaho from Oklahoma born in 1899, was on the 1926 team. His brother John, who had last played for Haskell on the 1924 team, had been born in 1898.[9]

On Sundays "Haskell students were required to attend church," on the basis of their stated preference; for Horne that was the Episcopal Church (40). They attended in their "military dress clothes," and were "transported to church in an army truck" (40). She also enrolls "in a Bible history class taught by a professor from the University of Kansas" (40), in part because "Bob Horne, a California Hoopa student of whom [she] was quite fond, was signed up for it" (40). They would marry in 1929. For high school students like herself, Sundays after church might bring "watermelon socials"—farms in the vicinity of Lawrence, Kansas, then grew watermelons in abundance—"when the weather was good." Or one might take a ride into town "on the streetcar on some Saturdays, accompanied by chaperones." There students could attend the movies if they had the money—which might be earned by "odd jobs, such as housework or babysitting." Although "some of the students got money from home," her mother's situation was such that she "didn't usually send money" (47).[10] Other "Haskell Events" described by Horne are the October Halloween carnival and, of course, Christmas. Horne writes that "Haskell was our home away from home, and everybody stayed on campus during the holidays" (45).

The reason she gives for this is that there "were kids from all over the United States, including Alaska," and that there "would have been a great number of unhappy kids if some had gone home while others who couldn't afford to leave had had to stay" (45). This is no doubt true, but the matter is a bit more complex. Some students whose homes were far away, even those whose homes were not quite so far as Alaska, might have chosen not to make the trip home for other than financial reasons, as would also have been the case with some whose homes were closer to Lawrence, Kansas. That is, like the policy at Pipestone, students could only return home from Haskell if conditions there permitted. Horne's family situation, like that of Adam Fortunate Eagle and Dennis Banks, was such as sometimes to rule out the option of going home for Christmas—although, to be sure, the cost of travel was also prohibitive. She writes later that she and her brother and sister "didn't hear from home very often" (47), noting that her mother "had not gone to a government boarding school," and "was not a person who wrote many letters" (47)—although she did come for a visit "one time during [Horne's] high school years" (48). In any case, her memories of Christmas at Haskell are warm and she offers them in some detail.

She also reports that "several students came down with tuberculosis," and that two young women "in the last stages of the disease" were not sent to the Haskell hospital but, instead, remained in their cots until they could be sent to a sanatorium near their homes. It is not clear why their illness was handled that way. Horne later in her life discovered that she had "healed tubercular areas" (40) in her own lungs, and she believes she may have been infected by these two students. She describes minor derelictions concerning smoking (40) and beer drinking (41),[11] leading to her being "counseled" by her "company commander ... about [her] behavior ... [and her] association with the troublemakers." Soon she "began to do the right thing at the right time in the right place," and she is supported in her reformation by "the YMCA secretary," who "became a friend" (41).

Horne offers a section on "The Outing System and Summertime," which begins with the statement: "Since the intent of the BIA system was to Americanize the Indian, we stayed at school twelve months a year" (48). She is entirely correct that the preference of the boarding schools was to keep the students away from home for as long as possible in order to lessen the likelihood of backsliding. But again, students were permitted to return home for the summer if they wished to and if family or friends could pay for their travel and care for them. Haskell, as Horne explains, had a full summer program available for students who did not return home, and one in which it was hoped students would participate. But going home for the summer vacation was not prohibited.

For the girls, Horne writes, a YWCA camp was available "for about two weeks," with the boys attending "a different camp" (48). "If you were sixteen years or older and had been a good citizen, you could be included in the summer outing program," which was ably supervised by Ruth Muskrat Bronson (48). Horne spends two summers of outing work in Kansas City, Missouri, the first working "for a practical nurse," helping "her take care of two infants whom she was boarding in her home." Then in 1928, after her high school graduation, she works as a maid for a doctor and his wife. She is pleased to be helped with her work by "a black laundress" with whom she becomes friendly. One day, as the two are "eating lunch together and talking" in the kitchen, "the woman of the house ... informed her that [she] was not allowed to eat with the laundress," whom she sent "back to the basement" (49). This is 1928 in a southern city, and one may wonder whether Horne had experienced other instances of discrimination against blacks; she mentions no anti-Indian discrimination.[12] The incident, she writes, "saddened" her (49).

The rest of the summer of 1928 is spent back home. Horne's sister Bernice—she had left Haskell early—and her mother are "working at Y-Bings, a Chinese restaurant," and, although they think Horne should work there as well, she chooses to stay home, keep house, and care for the younger children. (One of them, her sister June, somehow gets taken to New Mexico, where she is "married by proxy" [?], and at the age of thirteen gives birth to a boy.) This leads to some disagreement with her mother, Horne observing, "I guess that the rigors of my Haskell training were not always in line with my mother's ideas" (50), something other returned students had sometimes found as well.

Horne writes that she had earlier decided to return to Haskell for junior college, and when the time approaches for her to go, she worries about her brother Finn and her sister Helen, "who were about five and seven years old." Recognizing that the "situation at home had worsened since [she] had been away at school" (51), she pleads with her mother to let her take them with her, eventually obtaining permission and procuring the fare. Horne says: "When the three of us arrived in Lawrence, [she] simply called the school to have them send someone to pick [them] up" (52). She knows, of course, that the superintendent, Clyde Blair, "was not expecting this entourage," nor did she have "completed applications from the tribe" for the young pair. Nonetheless, she writes, "he let them stay and did the paperwork with the agency to get them enrolled" (52). It was a challenge, she says, to accommodate a boy only five years old, who must be housed "in the girls' dormitory and ... cared for by the matrons" (52). Not only are the children "lonesome for Mother and for home," but as she is aware, "they didn't know [her] too well" either. Nonetheless, it is her sense that "they seemed to adjust quickly" (52). Horne's account of the treatment accorded her young brother and sister on their unexpected arrival at Haskell also serves to complicate the prevailing broadly negative view of the boarding schools.

Thus, in a somewhat awkward sentence, Horne says, "Heralding back to many of the harsh tales about the boarding schools, this occurrence is an example of the compassion and concern that was present among many of the employees" (52). She continues, "The boarding school provided a safe environment for me." After her father died, she says, "We didn't always have as much to eat as we needed ... and there wasn't much security in our house." Her mother "wasn't home much, and we were left to pretty much fend for ourselves" (52). This was the situation of Horne's family several years before the Great Depression, and it was a situation to become more common among Native and non-Native families as the effects of economic failure worsened and spread.

Perhaps most important is Horne's recollection "that the sense of community at Haskell was very strong. Among Indian people this is very important" (52). She asserts, "We were proud of our accomplishments and proud that we had retained so much of our Indianness. Critics dismiss boarding schools as assimilationist institutions whose intent was to destroy Native culture. While this may be a true generalization, the students and teachers at Haskell will forever be an integral part of who I am as an American Indian" (53). Esther Burnett Horne went on to be an effective and award-winning American Indian teacher at the Wahpeton Indian boarding school for thirty-five years, "retiring" to northwestern Minnesota, where she contributed further to Indian education in a variety of ways. In 1989 she was honored as Outstanding American Indian Elder by the Minnesota Indian Education Association.

14

Viola Martinez, *California Paiute:*
Living in Two Worlds

VIOLA MERONEY MARTINEZ, AN ENROLLED MEMBER OF THE BISHOP BAND of Paiutes of Owens Valley, California, today called the Bishop Paiute Tribe, was probably born in 1917.[1] Her mother died during the 'flu pandemic of 1918, and she barely knew her father, whom she believed to be half-Paiute. Her people's reservation had been established in 1912 at the foot of the Sierra Nevada Mountains, an area with an abundant water supply until the growing city of Los Angeles diverted the Owens River for its own needs in 1913. Martinez grew up speaking the Numic language of her people, a language of the Uto-Aztecan group, and as a child in the care of her maternal aunt, she learned many of the traditional subsistence practices of the Paiutes. She attended public school in Benton, California, a town originally founded by Indians, where she did well enough that one of her uncles arranged for her to attend the Sherman Institute in Riverside, California. Martinez arrived at Sherman in 1927, at the age of about ten, and spent twelve years there and at other schools in the area, returning home only once.[2] Her observations about her time at Sherman are relevant to this study.

But the book in which she offers those observations does not, strictly speaking, belong in this study. That is because *Viola Martinez, California Paiute* is not an autobiography, nor can it reasonably be considered Martinez's book. The book is a biography by Diana Meyers Bahr, and her name is the only one listed on the cover, spine, and title page. Bahr and Martinez apparently became close, and the book includes a lengthy chapter recording an automobile tour of the Owens Valley that they and another woman made in 1996. Bahr quotes Martinez often and at length, so that one certainly gets to hear her voice and her perspective on any number of matters. But the book is entirely Bahr's.

This is not Bahr's own view. Just before a brief afterword, she writes: "I tape-recorded each session. Viola directed the story, I provided the historical context. We reviewed each interview during the following session, both of us clarifying and enriching that segment of Vi's story. We used a similar procedure when Vi reviewed the first draft of the manuscript. When questions or uncertainty arose, Viola had ultimate authority. She owns the story" (170).

Bahr is thus entirely aware that these matters are of some concern. But she treats them in a less than satisfactory manner. What does it mean to say that Martinez "directed the story"? Did she choose the arrangement of the book? Did she decide what material from her interviews with Bahr to include and what to exclude—or to what extent did she do either of those things? I strongly suspect she did not choose the chapter titles. Most of the book consists of Bahr's words, not Martinez's (And to be precise, while Martinez may "own the story," it is the University of Oklahoma Press that owns the copyright to the book.) My sense is that any attempt to read *Viola Martinez, California Paiute* in even an approximately literary manner would be a study essentially of Bahr's competence as a biographer. Nonetheless, as I have said, Martinez has provided testimony to her experience at the Sherman Institute, and I present it as best I can.

Martinez recalls a car coming to her aunt's home, and she knew that "the only cars that they had in those days belonged to government people." This one is to take her and four other Indian children to Riverside, almost three hundred miles south (49). Founded in 1892 in Perris, California, the Perris Indian School was that state's first Indian boarding school. Five years later its superintendent, Harwood Hall, decided that the school needed to expand and that any expansion would require an improved water supply. He applied to Representative Joseph Schoolcraft Sherman of the House Committee on Indian Affairs for funds. Once funding was secured, the school moved some twenty-five miles south to Riverside. The new school's cornerstone was laid in 1901, and it opened two years later, named for Representative Sherman.

Upon first coming to Riverside, Martinez recalls her surprise on finding that "there were no mountains, nothing around ... only a few strange buildings and a different kind of trees" (49).[3] They are palms, and she had not seen palms before. She is assigned to what Bahr calls "an austere building, a dormitory named Minnie Ha Ha" (49).[4] "The thing that I remember," Martinez says, "the first morning I woke up, the sun came up in the wrong way." Bahr explains that Paiute dwellings face east, while Martinez's Sherman dorm faced west. "I wondered what kind of world I had come into because the sun came up in the wrong way, not in my face but behind me.... And it took me a long time to adjust to that" (17).

We do not get any information concerning the *locus* of the dining room, but Martinez does comment on the *topos*, food. She says, "We were very well fed" because "we had a farm, a school farm" (52). Apparently they were so well fed that "often the kids just left food.... I thought, 'Gosh, they waste so much food'" (53). There is thus no malnutrition, although sickness, in particular tuberculosis, is common, as at many of the other schools, and a cousin of Martinez's dies of the disease.[5] Along with the food, she appreciates the "inside bathroom facilities ... electricity ... running water.... I liked these changes. If you wanted to go get a drink, you didn't have to go down to the spring" (53).

She likes much less the rigid imposition of clock time, which brings with it the danger of being punished for lateness. If teeth weren't brushed or one was not in bed at the proper time each night, "you were punished," she says, "by having to stand outside for an indefinite time" (53); she does not speak of corporal punishment. Bahr then quotes Martinez at length about the rigors of the Sherman schedule. Martinez describes work in the morning and school in the afternoon for some students, while others attend class in the morning and work later; these schedules alternate. The girls' work, she explains, involved cooking, washing, ironing, general cleaning, and waiting on tables, while the boys worked at the farm and in the kitchen (54). She gives a typical day's schedule beginning when a "triangle thing" wakes them at 6:00 a.m. "It was good-sized and you could hear it throughout the dorms." It sounds again at 6:45, at which time the students go from the dorm to the dining room "which was quite a way from the dorm.... Breakfast at 7:00" (54).

Then, depending upon which schedule one was following, there was either work or class. At "11:30 a regular siren would go off to let everybody know that it would be time to eat in a half hour." At the siren's sound, the students would return to their dorms, and line up to go to the dining room for lunch at 12:00. I suspect they marched to the dining room and did a good deal more marching as well, but Martinez says nothing of this here.

Lunch is brief, for at 12:30 there is a line-up to return to the dorms, and at 1:00 either work or classes begin again. Dismissal is at 4:00, and "at 9:00 you had to be ready for bed" (55). It is only when she comes to describe school activities on Sundays that Martinez says, "You had to perform just like you would, I guess, in the military service" (55), describing the rigorous military regimen at the school.

Martinez had noted earlier that on Sundays outsiders came to watch the school's dress parade, which she describes somewhat oddly. She says that "there was definite regimentation [because (Bahr's addition)] people came to see the school." There is a "long parade ground, and if "you were in Company A you had to be in Company A. The companies started out, and the marching band was way up at the other end. The band started down the field and the companies came around to the front" (55). The picture given is not very clear. Nor do we hear—as we did from Esther Horne of her time only a little earlier at Haskell—how Martinez felt about the military regime and its competitive nature. Martinez notes that the girls "had uniforms of white tops and navy pleated skirts that we wore only for marching" (55).

Church on Sundays was required, and Bahr quotes Martinez at some length on her earlier experience of Christian religion. This involved an uncle whose "name was George Washington"—a name he surely was assigned at school somewhere—who taught the children to sing "Silent Night" and who "talked about God" (56). She says that back home, "Everybody went to church at the schoolhouse where there would be missionaries," who, as she recalls, told the people that everybody had either a black heart, a red heart, or a white heart, and that "you didn't want a black heart; you wanted a white heart" (56). Indian children apparently had black hearts, which they could replace "by becoming Christians" (56): but who then had a red heart?

At school Martinez finds that she must choose between the Protestant and the Catholic Church, a choice her previous religious instruction had not prepared her to make. Unsure, she mentions "the schoolhouse in Benton" (56), which is sufficient for the authorities to assign her to the Protestants. She marvels at how "all of a sudden, I go to Sherman, and the sun comes up in the wrong place, and then I'm told I have to pick a place to go to church." The Sherman students attend church in the middle of the week too, and also take Bible study, leaving Martinez "trying to understand about Jesus dying on the cross." She says, "all I knew was that this man had died for white people. I guess my thought was 'Who's dying for the Indians?'" (57). This is a very interesting question but it is not taken up further. Martinez would go on to become active in the Presbyterian Church.

The Sherman Institute adheres to the English-only policy of the boarding schools at that time, and Martinez says, "I did want to speak my language, my Paiute language. And every chance I got I did." Because this is forbidden, she and other Paiute speakers climb into the palm trees where they "wouldn't be seen or heard....We spent a lot of time in those palm trees," she says, although "we were finally told on. Someone heard us and told on us" (58). Her punishment is to scrub the bathroom, but that does not deter her from speaking her language. Although she had determined that she "was never going to forget" it (59), as time passes, she says, "getting the education and doing the things we were supposed to do" substantially curtails "the opportunity to talk" (59). Sadly, when she finally returns home, she finds "I wasn't understanding any of it" (60).

Sherman's students, like many of the federal boarding-school students, were sent on outing assignments. In regard to these Martinez is reasonably upset on hearing one of the matrons tell a prospective employer that the students are trained "to take care of other people's houses and toilets" (63). She is even more upset when she is mistakenly accused of taking a wristwatch from the home at which she worked. This does not, however, prevent her from getting an outing assignment for each of the summers she remained at Sherman. Fortunately, at some of these postings, she says, she was encouraged to use her mind and to get books from the local library. Her general estimate of her employers in the outing program is that "the majority were wonderful people" (63).

Bahr quotes Martinez as conceiving of her education in terms of becoming like a white person or being as good as a white person. This bears on the important boarding-school *topos* of identity, which Bahr theorizes not so much in terms of the "two worlds" metaphor of her title but, rather in terms of what she calls "marginality." Her understanding of "marginality" is roughly sketched in her introduction, and chapter 4 is given the title "The Creative Margin" (67). But Bahr quotes very little from Martinez on the subject. On the basis of what we do have, I would say that Viola Meroney Martinez's Indian identity was never in the least threatened by the boarding-school assault on her Indian culture and language, or by its aggressive assertion of Western superiority. She explored Mormonism (74), became a committed Presbyterian, and was proud of a great many "white" skills she had mastered, making her, in all these respects, as good as a white person. But she never considered herself anything but a Paiute woman,[6] nor did she lose touch with friends and family from the reservation.

After receiving her bachelor of science degree from Santa Barbara State College (76), she was urged to become a teacher in the Indian Field Service (78), but chose instead to return home and work with the Federal Housing Authority (90). Toward the end of World War II she was hired as a counselor at the Manzanar Japanese Internment Camp 220 miles north of Los Angeles (96). Finally, in 1968 she did begin to teach, continuing for eighteen years in the Los Angeles Unified School District (123). Viola Martinez died in February 2010.

15

Reuben Snake's
Your Humble Serpent

REUBEN SNAKE (1937–93) NEVER SOUGHT NOR ATTAINED THE BROAD VIS-
ibility of Dennis Banks, but he did play an important public role on behalf
of his Ho-Chunk or Winnebago People.[1] He was likewise a notable figure
in the Native American Church[2] into which he had been baptized, and he
was "ordained as a Roadman (spiritual leader)" in 1974 (Fikes 22).[3] In 1990
Justice Antonin Scalia had written the Supreme Court's majority decision in
Employment Division, Oregon v. Smith, which held that the Native American
Church's use of peyote for religious purposes was not protected under the
First Amendment. Following the Court's ruling, Reuben Snake—in spite
of two heart attacks, diabetes, and kidney failure—moved to the forefront
of the fight to overturn *Smith*, leading to passage of the Religious Freedom
Restoration Act of 1993, and the following year's American Indian Religious
Freedom Act Amendments, exempting peyote from the category of "rec-
reational drugs."

Snake had met the anthropologist Jay Fikes just after the 1990 *Smith*
decision. Fikes had been a student of Huichol Indian use of peyote,[4] and
he became an ally in the battle to overturn *Smith*. In the last two months of
his life Snake recorded interviews with Fikes for his autobiography, *Reuben
Snake: Your Humble Serpent, Indian Visionary and Activist*. The book is supported by—or one might say encumbered by—an introduction, a foreword
by James Botsford, a lawyer who had worked with Snake on behalf of Indian
religious freedom, and an afterword by Walter Echo-hawk, also a lawyer and
a longtime activist with the Native American Rights Fund. Reuben Snake

did not live to see the book's publication in 1996. The first five of the book's eighteen chapters record Snake's experiences at school.

Born in 1937 "at the Winnebago, Nebraska Indian Hospital" (Snake 33), Snake was "named and baptized" when he was "about three months old," on Easter Sunday morning. His grandmother's uncle, John Painter Sr., a Roadman of the Native American Church, "gave [him] an old Winnebago Snake Clan name, *Kikawa Unga,* which means 'to rise up,'"[5] and Snake says, "in telling of the crucifixion and resurrection of Jesus Christ, he put a Christian emphasis on [the] name" (35) as well. Snake spent much time with his grandmother, who wished her grandchildren to "learn something about this Winnebago way of life" and spoke to them in their "native tongue" (36). If the children also spoke to her in their native language, we learn later that their mother insisted they speak only English when at home with her.

He writes that when he was about four, his parents "broke up," his father having "developed a serious problem with alcohol" (41)—a problem that Reuben Snake, for a time, would have as well. A year later his mother remarried and the family moved to Sioux City, Iowa, "a boom town during the Second World War" (41). After his stepfather was drafted into the army, a variety of events resulted in Snake's being moved about a good deal, until his grandmother sent for him and he settled with her at the Indian Mission in Black River Falls, Wisconsin, "a settlement of probably a thousand Winnebagos" (42). Snake recalls that they "carried on the culture of our people as best they could even though they were being proselytized by the Evangelical Reformed Church" (42)—to which, as we will learn, his mother adheres. His grandmother "had left the Medicine Lodge Society to become a Native American Church member" (43).[6]

The third chapter of the book is called "Neillsville Mission School." It begins, "About 1942, my mother came to Wisconsin and took her children to a little town called Neillsville" (49). There, Snake will attend the Neillsville Indian Mission School, first opened in 1921. He boards at the school with his sister, two older brothers, and some cousins (49), and the book offers a detailed retrospective on his time there. Although it required some difficult adjustment, he writes that he "later appreciated ... getting used to a regimental lifestyle" (49). This involves clock time in the dormitory—"We all had to get up at a certain hour in the morning" (49)—and other of the *loci* and *topoi* of boarding school.[7] He and the other students "get cleaned up and march to breakfast.... Each of us had a specific place to sit at the breakfast table" (49). In the morning or the afternoon, "Each of us," Snake recalls, "had chores to do throughout the day: washing dishes, peeling vegetables, or mopping hallways" (49).

He writes that "the founder of the school had raised his children among the Winnebago so that they would all be fluent in the Winnebago language. But the rule enforced at the school was that we couldn't speak our own native language. We had to speak English" (49). This gives rise to an odd situation, for when his "grandmother came to visit, she and the headmaster would be laughing and carrying on a hilarious conversation in Winnebago."[8] It "used to bother [him] that he could do that but that when [the] students talked in Winnebago, [they] were breaking the rules." Snake calls this his "first experience of hypocrisy, of the Whites preaching one thing and doing another" (49). It is also the case in this Mission school that the Native students "couldn't practice any of [their] cultural activities because they were condemned as pagan, superstitious ritual" (49). "Life at that school," Snake writes, "was very rigid" (49). In spite of the rigidity, he remembers that an eighth grader "used to gather us younger guys together and he'd create some kind of drum sound, maybe by beating on a tin can. Next he'd start singing songs and get us all to dance. Then he'd talk to us in our own language and tell us things. He was really impressive" (50). Of course, he notes, "if we were caught doing this, we were punished" (50), recalling vividly that once when he was caught, the "housemother tied [him] to a stairwell post and beat him with a razor strap." This was in the early 1940s. He observes, "That kind of beating was standard practice at that school" (50), but offers no further comment on what seems extremely harsh punishment.[9] When Snake "talked with [his] grandmother and relatives about the unpleasant experiences at school," he says "they commiserated with us," but advised, "'do what they tell you and don't get into trouble'" (50).

Nonetheless, some "older guys would get truly upset and frustrated with the system and would run away" (50). When the runaways were caught and returned to the school, he writes, "they used to shave their heads. That was part of the punishment for running away, to be shaved bald-headed" (50). It is almost surely the case that another "part of the punishment" was a beating, although Snake does not mention that here. He does confirm: "That school was far more restrictive than any public school of today could be," and Snake describes some acts of resistance against the restrictions that are quite specific to the period. For example, students call a German-American housemother "Mrs. Hitler," addressing a "Japanese-American lady at the school … [as] Mrs. Tojo," thus insulting their pride in being Americans (50).[10] The punishment meted out in response to this, he says, was denial of food and having to "sit and read Holy Scriptures and think about our sinful ways" (50–51). But "whippings and denial of food were the standard forms of discipline" (51).

He tells readers, "I don't want to paint too bleak a picture. Some of these people had heartfelt feelings for us," but he makes clear that these "feelings" were subordinated to what he calls "the system," a term he'd used earlier (50). For Snake, unlike for Dennis Banks, this is not a vague abstraction. The "system … was designed to move us out of our culture into the Christian way of life" and also to "move" them toward Christianity as understood and practiced by members of the Evangelical Reformed Church. "That was the most difficult part," Snake writes, "to be denied our culture, our language, our music, and our ways. We were coerced and intimidated into adopting European, Christian values" (51). This is particularly jarring, he says, because "My first years were spent as a free spirit on the reservation, living with my grandmother and my parents and enjoying life. Then I was thrust into an environment where everything was controlled. We were told when to get up, when to eat, when to go to class, when to work and when to go to bed. It was quite a shock" (51).

As he had described them, his early years were not quite as edenic as recalled here, but there is no question that the life he encountered at the Neillsville School was much more restrictive and, indeed, "quite a shock." Nonetheless, "in retrospect," Snake writes, "I think that such early experiences helped me a whole lot later on in life" (51).[11] He had previously acknowledged the usefulness of the "regimental lifestyle" (49) at the school, particularly in regard to what he would encounter after joining the military. And fortunately, his attendance at the school allowed him "to get to know all these other Winnebago people my age. There were even some Oneidas and Menominees at the school. So I developed some lifelong friendships there" (51) and something of an inter-tribal or pan-Indian awareness. Snake's memories of boarding school can thus be placed somewhere between those of former students who regarded their school years as a positive experience, all things considered, and those who found them a nightmare from which—as Joyce's Stephen Dedalus said of history—they were still trying to awaken. Of course we don't know what some of those "Oneidas and Menominees" and "other Winnebago people" at the school with Reuben Snake thought of it in hindsight; surely their opinions would vary.[12]

Snake continues with an illustration not of the constraints he experienced at the Neillsville school but, rather, in spite of the restrictions, of a certain freedom. "When we got out of class each afternoon," he writes, "they gave us about an hour to do our chores. I was in a group that sat in the basement peeling vegetables for the next day's meal." But once done with that task, he writes, "I was free to run about outside" (51). It was not quite like the time at the reservation he remembers so fondly, but he says:

> It was a beautiful setting, a great big three-story building with a lot of beautiful lawns around it. The Black River ran close by the edge of the school. It was a pretty place. We used to run around and play outside until it was time for the evening meal [an abrupt end to freedom]. We'd have to go inside and wash up. Then we'd march into the dining room and take our assigned seats. We had our prayers and vespers and Bible readings. Then we sat down to eat. After the evening meal, certain people were responsible for washing the dishes and cleaning the kitchen. Then we had to do our studying until about 9:00 p.m., when they used to put us to bed (51–2).

This leads him to describe the dorms, separate ones, of course, for the boys and the girls, and also a "big dormitory for the little boys from the first to the fifth grade" (52).

As for his teachers, he remembers them "being pretty decent people. [He] got along better with some than with others." Thus although he "had a hard time" with the first and second grade teacher who "was an extreme disciplinarian," in the third grade, his teacher "was a real kind, gentle woman. She was truly a caring person ... more like a mother to us than a teacher" (52). He does not provide the names of any of these teachers. Later he tells us that he stayed at Neillsville only "halfway through the third grade" (56), leaving the "caring" teacher. Like most of the Indian schools, Neillsville "owned a farm," and young Reuben Snake participates in the planting and harvesting of vegetables; if he had stayed longer, he would have worked with the older boys "tending to the livestock" (54). He recalls many activities at the school, in particular, a Christmas play in which all the students get "assigned roles," and, he writes, his "relatives would come to performances."

Although he has described a good deal of marching, the students do not wear uniforms of any kind. Rather, the school was "supported by a variety of people and institutions that donated a great deal of used clothing." He recalls that once while he was there, a "truckload of used clothing" (52) arrived. When the truck was unloaded, the clothes were laid out and "class by class … we'd get to go through and pick out the things we wanted." Snake notes that because "this was during the war, … Everybody wanted to dress and look like a combat pilot" (52)—the boys, at any rate—who would "start looking for those leather flying helmets and silk scarves. We were going to look cool if we could find one of those" (52–53). The donations do not include shoes, however, military or otherwise, so they "used to issue us work shoes called 'Little Abners.' The manufacturer of these shoes donated rejects to the school. So everybody wore these brown stogies with big round toes like Little Abner wore in the comics.[13] Those were our weekday shoes. We saved our good shoes for going to Church on Sunday" (53). He does not say what "good shoes" were like in the early 1940s. Either anticipating a question a reader might ask or perhaps responding to a question Jay Fikes did ask, Snake says, "Getting those clothes was just part of the routine of life, part of the system we were involved in. I never felt any shame over it. I never felt deprived or anything. It was just something we did" (53).

After describing a sliding game one of his buddies invented to exploit the shiny leather heels and soles of those shoes, and noting the staff's attempts to thwart their playing it—the game rapidly wore out the shoes' soles—Snake writes, "Our teachers were puritanical. We could only have fun in a Christian way. For them, having a good time meant singing hymns" (53). Memorizing hymns, he recalls, was an important matter at the Neillsville Mission School (54).

Like many of the former boarding-school students who would record their experiences, Snake writes that "my favorite subject was reading. I developed a love for reading in that school." Among his favorites were "*Treasure Island* and all of Jack London's books about Alaska. And, oh, *The Black Stallion*. That kind of storytelling was really interesting to me." Although he "wasn't too hot in math … English and history courses interested [him]" (54). Similar to what Adam Nordwall had thought about the history lessons he received at the Pipestone School only a bit earlier, Snake wonders how it might be that George Washington, "this White guy with his big nose and his powdered wig could be [his] father" (54). At the Neillsville School, "Absolutely nothing about Native cultures was taught. There was nothing Indian in [the] schooling" (54). This is annoying and frustrating to Snake, but rather than undercutting his sense of his Indian identity, it enhances that in him.

When the school year was over, "All the children were sent home for the summer," and Snake "used to go back to [his] grandmother's" (54), which allowed him to keep up with the Indian language and culture that was not taught or allowed at the school. Snake writes that when "we stayed with my grandmother during the summer we were still involved with the traditional Winnebago ways" (54–55). These include hunting and trapping wild game and picking "cranberries and blueberries and a variety of things that grew in the forest." His grandmother also "knew about other kinds of natural foods like waterlily roots," and he describes how his grandmother gathered those roots and cooked them (55). He and a cousin also go to a local man "who had some milk cows," and from him they "buy a gallon of milk … every night." Snake's recollection is that "it cost ten cents" (55).

His grandmother's house, he says, "didn't have electricity. Everything was done by lamplight after the sun went down." Nor did the house have "any inside plumbing," so they hauled "water from a spring about 300 or 400 yards away" (55). Grandmother owns some land in Nebraska that she leases, receiving "a small land lease check" from the Bureau of Indian Affairs every month (55). When it arrives, she walks "from the Indian Mission to downtown Black River, about eight or nine miles," taking Reuben with her. After "a couple of miles," he recalls, "she would carry [him] on her back wrapped in her shawl" (55). Those times together, Snake writes, "had a lot to do with [his] feelings for [his] grandmother" (55–56). After cashing her check, grandmother stocks up on staples to supplement the foods they hunt or gather, always managing "to buy a little candy for all of us." Grandmother "would hire a taxi cab to drive [them] back to the mission with [their] monthly supply of staples" (56).

Native families around them lived much the same way, Snake remembers, so they "had a strong communal life," with, he says, "always some kind of social function going on, a moccasin game or a hand game." But even "the Evangelical Reform Church used to have gatherings." When he is midway through the third grade, his mother comes and takes the children with her to Hastings, Minnesota, "about twenty-five miles south of Saint Paul" (56). There are "very few Indians living in the area," he says, and ironically his mother's work, for which she enlists the aid of the children, is making "tourist trinkets ... little drums out of old inner tubes and tin cans" (57), ostensibly "Indian" drums, which go to a firm in Minneapolis for sale. At this time Snake and his siblings are "enrolled ... in the local school system" and, he writes, "carrying the name 'Snake' in a White society created a provocative situation," in which they "were often teased." Nonetheless, he says, they "were friendly with everybody and the non-Indian kids were friendly to us" (58), despite the teasing about their name.

At this point matters become a bit confusing. Continuing the account of his time with his mother in Minnesota, Snake says that when he attended public school there he "was about eight years old" (59), which would make the year about 1945. He describes a few further adventures with his siblings, concluding, "These were some of the fond memories I have of living in Hastings" (59). The next paragraph begins, "In 1941 or 1942 my mother and my grandmother took us up to Door County, Wisconsin" (59): this takes the narrative back in time, with no transition or explanation as to why we are leaving the events of 1945 to consider those of an earlier time. And for the next several pages of this fourth chapter, "Anglo Economics and Public Education," the chronology shifts about a good deal, raising questions about how the work between editor and subject was actually done and, in particular, how Fikes arrived at the book's final structure. .

Although Fikes's introduction and copious notes provide a great deal of useful historical and ethnographic material, they do not speak to this issue. Fikes did, however, responsibly deposit his taped interviews with Snake at the National Museum of the American Indian Archives, where they are available for study.[14] He also consulted with Snake's wife, his children, and other people close to him, both during their work together and after Snake died. But because Reuben Snake died three years before the book appeared, he could not have gone over any but the earliest drafts of it, if those. Did Fikes leave the confusing chronology as representative of Reuben Snake's narrative manner? Or is it rather a matter of editorial carelessness?

Regardless of its placement in the book, the account of Snake's trip with his mother and grandmother to Door County, Wisconsin, in "1941 or 1942" introduces the fact that, as Snake says, "Summer migrant work was a part of my life from the time I was four years old until I was about seventeen, ... [and] joined the service" (60), and he now describes picking cherries with his family in the orchards of Door County. For the young boy, the "work was very tiring.... I had to crawl on my hands and knees to pull weeds all day long, from six-thirty in the morning to six o'clock in the evening" (60–61). Snake's description of his time in the orchards runs for three pages, and concludes with his warm recollection that after so much hard work, "at the end of the week," his mother collected all the money the family had earned and took them into town "to dinner and a movie" (61).

Then he writes, "Summers were more fun than any other time of year because I was with my mother and my grandmother and my other relatives" (61). This would seem still to refer to the summers picking cherries—despite the fact that crawling "on his hands and knees" for almost twelve hours a day can't have been much fun. But when Snake next says, "I got to enjoy various aspects of our culture during the summer months. We could do those things which were denied us at the mission school during the school year" (61), the text would seem to have jumped forward from 1941 and picked up the Neillsville school years, 1943–45, a time when, as he had already made clear, he had been denied the opportunity to speak his language or practice any aspect of his culture.

Whatever his reason for having returned to Snake's time at the Neillsville School at this point, Fikes now introduces material that both repeats and also expands upon things Snake had said earlier. During the time spent with his mother in Minnesota in 1945, for example, Snake had noted that she had been so "strongly influenced by Reform Church missionaries in her formative years" (58) that she would only speak English to the children and required that they "use English" (58). She would speak to her husband and "brothers and other people in our Winnebago tongue," Snake had recalled, but "we couldn't join in." As a result the children "all knew a few phrases but ... could not carry on a conversation in [the] Winnebago language" (58). He adds, "I spoke English all the time even though I understood the Winnebago language" (61). This was not the situation of other Indian children, he observes, most of whom "at the mission school came from homes where Winnebago was the parent tongue," and where "everybody in their household spoke Winnebago." He adds, with what may be a note of regret, "A lot of children in my age group at the mission school were fluent in Winnebago" (61). Despite his lack of fluency in the language, he at no time thinks of himself as anything other than Winnebago.

Fikes has Snake repeat, "The Winnebago language and culture were suppressed at the mission school because anything Indian was considered inferior" (61), going on to re-emphasize—perhaps a bit more strongly than he had before—the fact that "to be 'saved' we had to forfeit our Indianness" (61) and "give up all of our Indian ways" (62). It is only here that Snake tells us that this involves the students at Neillsville having their "hair cut regularly," because they "couldn't go to school with long hair" (62)—the boys, it would seem—and, again, "Not a trace of our culture was allowed in the school. They denied us everything" (62).

Another chronological shift returns the narrative to 1945 and to Minnesota. We learn that with the war over, Snake's stepfather, discharged from service, comes to take the family "back to the reservation" (62). This is the Nebraska Winnebago reservation, not the one in Wisconsin where Snake had spent summers with his grandmother. Although the postwar economy is expanding, his mother and stepfather "couldn't find work on [the] reservation," and they leave the children to return to Minnesota "to find work again" (62). With his parents away, Snake, his brothers, and his sister "spent a couple of years" living at the Reformed Church Mission Home, while they attend public school (62).[15] Of the Mission Home, Snake says that this "second experience with the Reformed Church missionary people was a little more positive" (62), although it remains the case that the church was "dedicated to denying the spirituality of Indian people" (62). He and his siblings are fortunate in having a housemother who "was an extremely kind and loving individual" (62), although the director of the school "was very anti-Indian culture," and once hit "boys that he had caught doing this Indian thing with a ruler across the palms of [their] hands" (63). He does not say what this "thing" was. There are a great many church services to attend, along with Bible study and hymn singing, which Snake refers to as "a constant effort to brainwash us and to eliminate our native culture from our lives" (63). This much we learn about living at the Mission Home, but not a single word is said about his public school experience in Winnebago, Nebraska, during this time.

When he is thirteen, in 1950, Snake says, he "went to school at Haskell Institute, a federal boarding school in Lawrence, Kansas," entering "as a high-school freshman" (64). This is a much larger school than any he has attended thus far, "with approximately five hundred Indian students" (64) at the time, and it was "the first time in [his] life that [he] was exposed to many different tribal groups." He had earlier met only some Oneidas and Menominees at Neillsville. He finds this "a tremendous cultural change," and also "very stimulating to get to know many of these young people who came from distinct tribal backgrounds" (64). This had certainly been Esther Horne's experience at Haskell and the experience of other Haskell students as well. "The largest part of the student body," Snake observes, "were young people from the state of Oklahoma," and "probably eight or nine Winnebagos" (65).

Snake says that at Haskell he "began to get involved in athletic activities," playing some football and basketball but for the most part running cross-country. As "co-captain of the cross-country team, [he] used to run fifteen miles every evening to stay in shape" (64). He notes that life at Haskell is also regimented. Clock time involves a bell ringing to wake the students and then another bell "to go to the dining hall" (64) for breakfast. There are, in his recollection, a great many bells: one for class, one that "would ring when it was lunch time," another for "evening meal," and one marking "when it was time to go to bed" (65). As for religious observance, he says that in his time at Haskell, the students "were encouraged to attend church on Sunday" but that church attendance was not mandatory, and he "was one of those people that didn't go to church on Sunday at Haskell" (65).

This is because he "was still somewhat active in the Native American Church," having "attended prayer meetings from time to time, maybe once or twice a month" (65), something he had not earlier revealed. In spite of his mother's Reformed Church affiliation, and the fact that he had lived at the Reformed Church Mission Home, Snake says that he "never got involved in any non-Indian denomination" and considered the Native American Church to be his religion (65). "There wasn't any place in Lawrence, Kansas, to attend Native American Church meetings," but an uncle of his mother's "who had married into the Potawatomi tribe," would come and take Snake and his sister to a Native American Church meeting "about forty or fifty miles away from Lawrence" (65), on the Potawatomi reservation.

Of the few Winnebago students at Haskell, Snake writes that "they weren't any more attuned to the culture than [he] was," and he observes that the "circumstances at the school were kind of paradoxical. They didn't want us to practice our Indian ways but they didn't really deny them" (65). He shrewdly notes that the "Indian ways" the school encouraged were mostly "a propaganda tool to impress the non-Indian people in the surrounding community that we"—the Native student body—"were good people" (65). He makes clear that even in his day, despite the fact that "Haskell was an all-Indian institution, there was nothing Indian taught at the school." Although he had clearly seen it to be "a propaganda tool," he recognizes the Indian Club at Haskell as "the only organization which carried on any kind of cultural tradition" (66). Complicated as these matters are, he is nonetheless at an "all-Indian institution," and Reuben Snake continues to think of himself as all-Indian as well.

Snake speaks briefly of his teachers, noting that "they were predominantly non-Indian," and that some were "good teachers and there were some bad teachers." In that half the day is devoted to vocational training, Snake takes up radio and television repair under an instructor who "was a very good, caring person who had a genuine interest in teaching us" (66). He is especially impressed by Presley Wear, a Kiowa, who serves as freshman football coach. Snake's experience has been such that he "just couldn't believe that an Indian could be a teacher and a coach," and that this man "was the first role model [he] had." And the "head coach was a Potawatomi Indian, Doctor Tony Coffin. He was also a role model" (66).[16] This important matter is simply dropped, with Snake writing, "I was at Haskell about two and a half years. I went there in 1950 and I left in 1952" (66).

Then we once more encounter the kind of nonlinear chronology I had noted earlier. The sentence immediately following Snake's statement that he left Haskell in 1952 reads, "Like a lot of young people, I became involved in some things that I perhaps shouldn't have" (66). One might think he is going on to tell of "things" that happened just after his departure from school, as a youth of fifteen, still quite a young person. But this is not the case. Snake says, "Back in southern Minnesota, where I spent my summers with my family" (66), returning readers to the summers of 1943 and 1944, he "became involved in" hanging out "with non-Indian young people" in the southeastern Minnesota town of Albert Lea and drinking and fighting. It is also here—as we only now find out—that he would attend "prayer meetings of the Native American Church, and an occasional powwow." It is at the prayer meetings that "those old men would preach at us young guys to straighten up and act right, ... and leave the drinking alone." Snake elaborates on what he has said earlier in his discussion of religious worship at Haskell, stating, "When I was between ten and fifteen"—this would be 1947–52—"I attended prayer meetings once or twice a month," and it "used to give me real soul satisfaction to go to a Native American Church prayer meeting" (69). As for the advice offered by the older men, "It was good to hear but then it was hard to practice" (69).

In discussing his time at Haskell, Snake had not said anything about drinking between the ages of thirteen and fifteen. This information appears only in the following chapter, chapter 5, "From Student to Green Beret." There Snake says that he used to do "yard work perhaps two or three times during the week, in the evening after school and all day Saturday" (71). This is hard to reconcile with what he has said earlier, that he "used to run fifteen miles every evening to stay in shape" (64). How had he found the time? And how did he manage to run that distance regularly while drinking? However he did it, his work means that he has some money at the end of the week, and he and "some of his peers ... were always able to find somebody on the street to buy alcohol for them" (71). (Legal minimum drinking age in Minnesota in the early 1950s was twenty-one.) On one occasion Snake is drinking with a cousin and the two get into a fight, in which they "beat this one guy up pretty badly." Their "dorm supervisor" finds out, and the two are "put on restriction. For thirty days [they] couldn't go anywhere." This prompts his cousin to decide to leave the school and go home, and Snake decides to join him, returning to Minnesota—although "home" certainly might mean Black River Falls, Wisconsin, or even Winnebago, Nebraska—and enrolling "in school there" (72).

His mother was then working in a turkey-processing plant, rising at 4:30 in the morning to wake him and give him breakfast before walking some three miles in sub-zero weather to the job (72). He "was going to Albert Lea High School," but he wants to quit so that he can work and help his mother. She does not approve, but after his "sixteenth birthday" he does leave school, so that for a time he, his mother, and his stepfather "were all working at this produce house" (73). When he is seventeen, "in November of 1954" (73), he joins the army, although he is still under the legal age to enlist. Reuben Snake's schooling has come to an end.

Snake served as a soldier in Berlin and in Korea in the mid-1950s; became national chairman of the American Indian Movement in the 1970s; was elected to the Winnebago tribal council and became tribal chairman in 1977; going on to become president of the National Congress of American Indians in 1985. He traveled widely, addressing indigenous people's organizations in Canada, Mexico, South America, and Australia. Despite the poor health noted, and humble serpent though he claimed himself to be, he fought tirelessly, and ultimately successfully, for the right for Native American Church members to engage in the use of peyote for religious purposes.

19 Reuben Snake leading a Sunrise Ceremony in Central Park, New York City, 1992. Photograph by the Repatriation Foundation, reprinted courtesy of Jay C. Fikes.

A Letter from Thomas Wildcat Alford, a Returned Student Formerly at Hampton Institute

THE HAMPTON INSTITUTE WAS FAIRLY SYSTEMATIC IN COMPILING INFOR-
mation about its former students. In 1888, Helen Wilhelmina Ludlow
published *Ten Years' Work for Indians at the Hampton Normal and Agricultural
Institute* on behalf of the school. The book provides some information on
Hampton's experience educating freedmen and freedwomen since its opening
in 1868 but focuses on the program for Indian students that had begun in 1878.
Ludlow discusses such things as the Indians' diet, health and medical care, educational and vocational training, and also the relations at the school between
its black and Indian students. The book contains a "Report on Returned
Indian Students" compiled by Cora Folsom and addressed to Commissioner
of Indian Affairs John D. C. Atkins. This is made up of a number of "Letters
from Indian Graduates of Hampton" addressed to Hampton superintendent
General Samuel C. Armstrong. One of these is from Thomas Wildcat Alford,
whose autobiography opens part III of this volume.

Writing from Indian Territory, he offers some information—not a great
deal—as to his own situation and that of other returned students known
to him. I supplement that with information from Folsom's later account of
those students. I reproduce Alford's letter in full, without alteration. It may
have been edited by Helen Ludlow or Cora Folsom, but if so, I believe their
editing would have been light.

A LETTER FROM THOMAS WILDCAT ALFORD
OF THE ABSENTEE SHAWNEE TRIBE, GRADUATED 1882
Shawneetown, I[ndian]. T[erritory]. Feb. 6, 1888

GEN. S. C. ARMSTRONG

MY DEAR SIR: I have just received your letter asking me to make a statement of the course taken by Hampton and other Indian students since their leaving school, and other facts relating to them. I will cheerfully comply with the request, though unfortunately I feel unable to do justice to several who are not near me enough to learn how they are. Therefore my report will be confined only to those who are immediately in my vicinity.

Of students that have returned from Hampton I may say, all with one or two exceptions, are doing well, some very well, and there are others who are doing equally as well, perhaps, but of whom I cannot make statement accurately for reason above mentioned. The following are the names of the Indian students in this vicinity, not including myself.

John Downing, John King, Frank Chisholm, Antoine Gokey, Robbie Canalez, Mary King, Hattie Miles and Nellie Keokuk.

Of these who have done very well indeed are John Downing, John King, Mary King and Hattie Miles—4; fairly well, Antoine Gokey and Nellie Keokuk—2; indifferent, but seem coming up, Frank Chisholm—1; hopeless, Robbie Canalez—1. More than half of these I think did not receive the three years training allowed them, or if I remember aright, Antoine Gokey and Robbie Canalez were sent home for bad conduct.[1]

John Downing ever since he left school has been working faithfully, and is now married and happy living in Wichita agency, and is quite a successful cattle-raiser.[2]

John King has been faithful clerk here in an agency trader's store, getting from $35 to $40 per month, by which he is enabled to stock his farm of 80 acres—all under fence and cultivated—and sells a great deal of corn. He is the only one here who is quite successful in retaining his inheritance.[3]

Frank Chisholm is not so successful. He had too much of this world's goods awaiting him when he came from school, so that all he has done is to sell out his substance, until now he has but little. Frank is not particularly bad in any way, and for what indifference there is in him, his brothers, who are notorious rough characters, are responsible.

Robbie Canalez was quite young when he came home, and as his mother was a bad character, and his step-father a notorious horse-thief, it is not surprising that he became what he is—a thief. He is now hiding, a fugitive from justice.[4]

Mary King, soon after coming home, was employed as employes' cook in the Chilocco School near Kansas. She has since been married and is now doing very well.

Hattie Miles has married very well, and she and her husband kept a boarding house at this Agency for some time. Mr. King, her husband, is now Capt. of Agency Police, living in a good house and doing very well.[5]

Nellie Keokuk, I understand, has gone to some school in the States.[6]

Every one of these students wear [sic] citizen's dress.

There are about 12 students here from other schools who are doing fairly, considering their limited advantages of education they have had—6 girls and 6 boys. Of these who are doing very well indeed, 1; fairly well, 8; not ambitious and indifferent, 2.[7]

Now as request is also made for what I have done since leaving school, I will report briefly. As soon as I came home, I applied for work, but the agent told me there was no work. I then went over to the Missionary and applied for work. He hired me as interpreter for two or three months, when, through his influence, I obtained position as teacher in a day school among the Pottawatomies, where I taught one term of 8 months. In the summer of 1883 I was transferred to the Shawnees' boarding school of this place, where I taught from year to year until the time of my removal last fall. Since then I have been working about home first at one thing and then another. My savings have enabled me to own a little house of two rooms, beside out-buildings, a team of ponies, a wagon and a buggy, and about 45 head of cattle.

There are a great many obstacles in the way of returned Indian students which no one can enumerate. In the first place the returned student has still his natural propensities which were only made dormant, as it were, for the time being that he was surrounded by the comforts of civilization in a school. As soon as he is brought in contact with his people these forces are alive, being aroused by arguments of his people and other ways, and are at work in direct opposition to the principles he just learned in school, and, unless the student has something to do to direct his thoughts, or is uncommonly decided in his convictions (but 3 years are hardly long enough for that) or receives sympathy or encouragement, no one can fail to see which of these two forces will come out a conqueror. *Work* is the great remedy in this case, as I found out, and perhaps the only deliverance the students have, and as students in general, especially those of Hampton and Carlisle are willing to work. But here we come to the worst feature of the case. There is not enough work for them at the Agency or at home. It is true some have a chance to work at their parents' farm, but this is nothing like working one's own farm. They have been taught to realize that individual ownership of anything is the best. In their homes everything almost is in common. There is no incentive. Some one may ask, why don't they go to work then, open out their own farms, and build fences, &c.? Remember, they must have something to eat and to wear while they are splitting the rails and "turning the sod," and remember also their country and even the men surrounding them are called wild. In short they are surrounded with *nothing like anything in the States*. Even a white man who is bred in industry with all his ingenuity requires capital in one form or another to begin with and why not the Indian who is willing to work for that capital and only wants a chance. The white man alone can give that help.

No one can estimate the amount of difficulties these returned students meet with, until he has seen, felt, and knows it. The Congressional visitors and others have never visited places where the obstinate battles were fought, and consequently never saw the heroes of these battles. They never even come this far, I know. Its [sic] only a few places accessible by rail road they have visited, and then only stayed a few hours at one place; not long enough to get at the true state of things. Therefore their observations cannot be sustained by facts. They ought to visit every Agency, but they don't even do this.

There ought to be no report made upon the subject of what or no good the Eastern schools have done until every part of the Indian country is visited by an impartial committee, and every fact is weighed, and when this is done, in my opinion, there will be found an abundant testimony to the good work these schools are accomplishing. All agree that the Indian must be educated in order to become an intelligent citizen. If the Eastern schools are closed against him, what other schools can take their places? The Reservation schools have failed in part, if not wholly, to accomplish the same results, and the Gov't Industrial schools cannot do it. They are good as far as they go, but they cannot give the same thorough Christian learning that students receive in these Eastern schools, which is essential to good citizenship, and the only strong deliverance the Indian has from his present condition.

The Indian is to become citizen of the United States. He ought to have all the advantages to prepare himself, and there is no time when he needs more of such school [sic] as Hampton and Carlisle as now during his transition: and the returned student has better prospects of holding out in his new life since the tribal relation with all its evils are taken away, and he can secure his own individual farm, and everything that he raises is his.

With best wishes for Hampton's work, I am, respectfully,

T. W. ALFORD

Indian Boarding-School Students Mentioned in This Study, Vols. 1 and 2

THE FOLLOWING LISTING PROVIDES THE STUDENT'S FULL NAME, TRIBAL affiliation (if known), and the school or schools attended (in just a few cases, unknown). When the full name is unknown, I give the name as found in one of the autobiographical texts.

VOLUME I

Andrew	Hopi	Carlisle Indian School
Myrtle Begay	Navajo	Chinle Boarding School, Fort Apache Boarding School
Kay Bennett	Navajo	Toadlena Boarding School
Jason Betzinez	Apache	Carlisle Indian School
Big Helen	Hopi	Keam's Canyon School
Jeannette Blake	Navajo	Tuba City Boarding School
Paul Blatchford	Navajo	Rehoboth Christian School, Phoenix Indian School, Albuquerque Indian School
Howard Bogoutin	Navajo	Aneth Mission School, Shiprock Boarding School
William Cadman	Navajo	Albuquerque Indian School
Ramona Chihuahua Daklugie	Apache	Carlisle Indian School
Chris	Apache	Albuquerque Indian School, Santa Fe Indian School
Thomas Clani	Navajo	Shiprock Boarding School

Claude	Hopi/Tewa	Chilocco Indian School
Daklugie	Apache	Carlisle Indian School
Hoke Denetsosie	Navajo	Leupp Boarding School, Tuba City Boarding School, Phoenix Indian School
Amos Dugan	(?)	Chilocco Indian School
Glenbah	Navajo	Toadlena Boarding School
Tillman Hadley	Navajo	Blue Canyon/ Western Navajo Training School/ Tuba City Boarding School
Max Hanley	Navajo	Shiprock Boarding School, Sherman Institute, Ganado Boarding School, Albuquerque Boarding School
Esther Burnett Horne	Shoshone	Haskell Institute
Ira	Hopi	Keam's Canyon School
Irene	Hopi	Sherman Institute
Dezba Johnson	Navajo	Sherman Institute
Fred Kabotie	Hopi	Toreva Day School, Shungopavi Day School, Santa Fe Indian School
Edwin Kachina	Hopi	Keam's Canyon School, Phoenix Indian School
Lee Kansaswood	Navajo	Tuba City Boarding School, Sherman Institute
Jasper Kanseah	Apache	Carlisle Indian School
James Kaywaykla	Apache	Carlisle Indian School
Keedah	Navajo	Toadlena Boarding School
Samuel Kenoi	Apache	Carlisle Indian School, Chilocco Indian School
George P. Lee	Navajo	Shiprock Boarding School
Joe Lee	Navajo	Shiprock Boarding School
Lena	Navajo	Toadlena Boarding School
Louise	Hopi	Keam's Canyon School, Sherman Institute
Mrs. Bob Martin	Navajo	Fort Lewis Boarding School
Jack Mather	Apache	Carlisle Indian School
Mettie	Hopi	Sherman Institute
Frank Mitchell	Navajo	Fort Defiance Boarding School
Nah-deiz-az (Carlisle Kid)	Apache	Carlisle Indian School
Nancy	Navajo	Toadlena Boarding School

Nash	Hopi	Keam's Canyon School
Nellie/Gladys	Hopi	Keam's Canyon School
Edmund Nequatewa	Hopi	Keam's Canyon School, Phoenix Indian School
Dan Nicholas	Apache	Chilocco Indian School
Paul	Hopi	Phoenix Indian School
Irving Pawbinele	Hopi/Tewa	Phoenix Indian School
Polingaysi Qoyawayma	Hopi	Orayvi Day School, Sherman Institute
Tom Ration	Navajo	Albuquerque Indian School
Kesetta Roosevelt	Apache	Carlisle Indian School
Sam	Hopi	Phoenix Indian School
Emory Sekaquaptewa	Hopi	Orayvi Day School, Keam's Canyon School, Sherman Institute, Phoenix Indian School
Helen Sekaquaptewa	Hopi	Orayvi Day School, Keam's Canyon School, Phoenix Indian School
Robert Selena	Hopi	Keam's Canyon School
Anna Moore Shaw	Akimel O'odham	Mission Boarding School, Phoenix Indian School
Ross Shaw	Akimel O'odham	Phoenix Indian School
Irene Stewart	Navajo	Fort Defiance Boarding School, Haskell Institute
Don Talayesva	Hopi	Keam's Canyon School, Sherman Institute
Tawakwaptiwa	Hopi	Sherman Institute
Albert Yava	Hopi/Tewa	Polacca Day School, Keam's Canyon School, Chilocco Indian School

VOLUME 2

Alvina Alberts	Lakota	Grey Nun School (Fort Totten)
Paul Leon Alford	Absentee Shawnee	Hampton Institute
Pierrepont (Pierre) Alford	Absentee Shawnee	Hampton Institute
Reece Alford	Absentee Shawnee	Hampton Institute

Thomas Wildcat Alford	Absentee Shawnee	Hampton Institute
Thompson Alford	Absentee Shawnee	Hampton Institute
Webster Alford	Absentee Shawnee	Hampton Institute, Chilocco Indian School
Robert American Horse (Nakpa Kesela/Cut Ears)	Lakota	Carlisle Indian School
Charles Armstrong	Seneca	Hampton Institute
Joseph Armstrong	Seneca	Hampton Institute
Claude Arrow	Standing Rock Sioux	Hampton Institute
Lyman Bailey	Seneca	Hampton Institute
Audrey Banks	Leech Lake Ojibwe	Pipestone Indian School
Dennis Banks	Leech Lake Ojibwe	Pipestone Indian School, Wahpeton Indian School, Flandreau Indian School
Mark Banks	Leech Lake Ojibwe	Pipestone Indian School
Joe Bebeau	(?)	Pipestone Indian School
Wendell Big Crow	(?)	Saint Francis Mission School
Bishiu	White Earth Chippewa	Flandreau Indian School
Paul Black Bear	Dakota	Carlisle Indian School
Ben Benson	Mandan	Wahpeton Indian School
Tennyson Berry (Ah-ko-bah-setine)	Kiowa Apache	Carlisle Indian School, Chilocco Indian School
Joe Blackbear	Kiowa Apache	Kiowa Indian Boarding School
Aloysius Black Tail Deer (P-2)	Lakota	Holy Rosary Mission School
Baldwin Blue Horse	Dakota	Carlisle Indian School
Basil Brave Heart	Lakota	Holy Rosary Mission School (Red Cloud Indian School)
Gabby Brewer	(?)	Holy Rosary Mission School (Red Cloud Indian School)
Bernice Burnett	Shoshone	Haskell Institute
Gordon Burnett	Shoshone	Haskell Institute
Joe Bush	White Earth Chippewa	White Earth School, Beaulieu School
Claude	Comanche	Kiowa Indian Boarding School

Mary Crow Dog	Lakota	Saint Francis Mission School
Joe Crown	Leech Lake Ojibwe	St. Mary's Mission School, Pipestone Indian School
Cry Baby	(?)	Pipestone Indian School
Bill Day	(?)	Kiowa Indian Boarding School
John Downing	Absentee Shawnee	Hampton Institute
Ralph Eagleman	(?)	Saint Francis Mission School
Charles Alexander Eastman (Ohiyesa)	Santee Sioux	Flandreau Day School, Santee Normal School
John Sacred Cloud Eastman	Santee Sioux	Flandreau Day School Santee Normal School
Casper Edson	Arapaho	Carlisle Indian School
Adam Fortunate Eagle (Nordwall)	Red Lake Chippewa	Pipestone Indian School, Haskell Institute
Tom Gannon	(?)	Holy Rosary Mission School (Red Cloud Indian School)
Tim Giago	Lakota	Holy Rosary Mission School (Red Cloud Indian School)
Shirley Giago	Lakota	Holy Rosary Mission School (Red Cloud Indian School)
Albert Hensley	Winnebago	Carlisle Indian School
Tomson Highway	Canadian Cree	Guy Hill Indian Residential School
Esther Burnett Horne	Shoshone	Haskell Institute
Robert Horne	Hoopa	Haskell Institute
Frank Janis	Lakota	Carlisle Indian School
Buck Jones	(?)	Holy Rosary Mission School
Basil Johnston	Canadian Ojibwa	Saint Peter Claver's School
Bobbie Kills Among Many	Shoshone	Haskell Institute
John King	(?)	Hampton Institute
Knaska (Frog)	Dakota	Carlisle Indian School
Stiya Kowicura	Pueblo	Carlisle Indian School
Grant Lefthand	Southern Arapaho	Carlisle Indian School
Berenice Levchuk	Navajo	Fort Defiance Boarding School
George Levi	Arapaho	Haskell Institute
John Levi	Arapaho	Haskell Institute
Abraham Lincoln	Kiowa Apache	Kiowa Indian Boarding School

Ben Littlemoon	Lakota	Oglala Community High School
Pauline Littlemoon	Lakota	Oglala Community High School
Walter Littlemoon	Lakota	Oglala Community High School, Holy Rosary Mission School
Amos Lone Hill	Dakota	Carlisle Indian School
Alfred Mandan	Mandan	Santee Normal School
Edna Manitowabi	Canadian Ojibwa	Saint Joseph's School
Ida Marshall	(?)	Saint Francis Mission School
Andy Martinez	Paiute	Sherman Institute
Viola Martinez	Owens Valley Paiute	Sherman Institute
Mary	(?)	Pipestone Indian School
May	(?)	Holy Rosary Mission School (Red Cloud Indian School)
Nelson Metoxen	Oneida	Hampton Institute
Daniel Milk	Dakota	Carlisle Indian School
Mindi	White Earth Chippewa	Flandreau Indian School, Beaulieu Indian School
Barbara Moore-Richard (Mary Crow Dog)	Lakota	Saint Francis Mission School
Stephen Moran	Mixed-blood Dakota	Carlisle Indian School
George Morrison (Standing in the Northern, Lights Turning the Feather Around)	Grand Portage Lake Superior Chippewa	Hayward Indian School
Stanley Nordwall	Red Lake Ojibwe	Pipestone Indian School
Jim Northrup	Fond du Lac Anishinaabe	Pipestone Indian School, Brainerd Indian Training School
Judy Northrup	Fond du Lac Anishinaabe	Pipestone Indian School
Regina One Star	(?)	Saint Francis Mission School
Michael Oshkeneny	Menominee	Hampton Institute
Susan La Flesche Picotte	Omaha	Hampton Institute
Plenty Horses (Plenty Living Bear)	Lakota	Carlisle Indian School
Julia Powlas	Oneida	Carlisle Indian School
Purcell Powlas	Oneida	Pipestone Indian School
Louis Pretty Boy (Omaha)	(?)	Holy Rosary Mission School

Peter Razor	Fond du Lac Ojibwe	Owatonna School for Dependent and Neglected Children
Sarah Red Road/ Sarah Tackett/Sarah Mather	Lakota	Carlisle Indian School
Delphine Red Shirt	Lakota	Holy Rosary Mission School
Mattie Reid	Pueblo	Carlisle Indian School
Lawney Reyes	Sin-Aikst/ Lakes	Chemawa Indian School
Henry Roe Cloud	Winnebago	Genoa Day School, Santee Normal School
John Rogers (Wayquagishig)	White Earth Chippewa	Flandreau Indian School, White Earth School, Beaulieu School
Sague (Walking Stick)	Lakota	Holy Rosary Mission School
Howice Seonia	Pueblo	Carlisle Indian School
Bill Shakespeare	Arapaho	Carlisle Indian School
William Shakespeare (War Bonnet)	Arapaho	Carlisle Indian School
Reuben Snake	Winnebago	Neillsville Indian Mission School, Haskell Institute
Gertrude Spotted Tail	Lakota	Carlisle Indian School
Maud Spotted Tail	Lakota	Carlisle Indian School
Max Spotted Tail	Lakota	Carlisle Indian School
Pollock Spotted Tail	Lakota	Carlisle Indian School
William Spotted Tail (Stays at Home)	Lakota	Carlisle Indian School
Henry Standing Bear (Totola/Kills Little)	Lakota	Carlisle Indian School
Luther Standing Bear (Ota Kte/Kills Plenty)	Lakota	Carlisle Indian School
Victoria Standing Bear (Zintkaziwin/Yellow Bird)	Lakota	Carlisle Indian School
Willard Standing Bear (Wopotapi/Shot to Pieces)	Lakota	Carlisle Indian School
Maggie Stands Looking/ Maggie American Horse	Lakota	Carlisle Indian School
Robert Stuart	Mixed-blood Creek	Carlisle Indian School
Raymond Stewart	Brule Sioux	Carlisle Indian School
Madonna Swan	Lakota	Immaculate Conception School

Carl Sweezy (Black)	Southern Arapaho	Halstead School, Carlisle Indian School, Chilocco Indian School
Fieldie Sweezy	Southern Arapaho	Halstead School
Maud Swift Bear	Dakota	Carlisle Indian School
Charles Tackett	Mixed-blood Lakota	Carlisle Indian School
G. Wayne Tapio	Lakota	Holy Rosary Mission School
Jim Thorpe	Sac and Fox	Carlisle Indian School
Charles Trimble (Wobbie)	Lakota	Holy Rosary Mission School (Red Cloud Indian School)
Lucy Tsinah	San Carlos Apache	Carlisle Indian School
Clarence Three Stars (Packs the Dog)	Lakota	Carlisle Indian School
Glen Three Stars	Lakota	Oglala Community High School
Delores Two Stars	(?)	Pipestone Indian School
Frank Twist	Lakota	Carlisle Indian School
Lydia Whirlwind Soldier	Lakota	Saint Francis Mission School
Hugh Whirlwind Soldier/ Hugh Running Horse	Lakota	Carlisle Indian School
Whistler/Julian Whistler (Ya Slo)	Dakota	Carlisle Indian School
Julian Cook in Guts Whistler	Dakota	Carlisle Indian School
Melvin White Magpie	Lakota	Holy Rosary Mission School
Earnest White Thunder (Knocked-it-off/Wica-Karpa)	Dakota	Carlisle Indian School
Jane Willis (Geneish)	Canadian Cree	Fort George Anglican Residential School
Winter (Waniyetula)	Dakota	Carlisle Indian School
Arnold Woolworth (Big Tall Man)	Arapaho	Carlisle Indian School
Leo Wounded Foot (Tiny Tim)	Lakota	Holy Rosary Mission School
Chauncey Yellow Robe (Timber)	Brule Sioux	Carlisle Indian School
Richard Yellow Robe (Wounded)	Brule Sioux	Carlisle Indian School
Zitkala-Sa (Gertrude Simmons)	Yankton	Santee Normal School

NOTES

INTRODUCTION

1. Some of the material in this introduction appeared in the introduction to volume 1 of this study.

2. Thus, for example, we find Francis Leupp, commissioner of Indian Affairs from 1909 to 1913, writing, "I like the Indian for what is Indian in him. . . . Let us not make the mistake, in the process of absorbing them [sic], of washing out whatever is distinctly Indian" (quoted in Buchowska, *Negotiating* 71). This comes, of course, at a time when Bureau of Indian Affairs schools were working diligently to "wash out" the Indianness of their Indian students.

3. "Living in two worlds" was first used to describe the *problem* faced by Native people who, having grown up in largely traditional indigenous societies, had to adjust to the dominant settler society. In time, however, "teaching students to 'walk in two worlds'" became one of "the *goals* of education for indigenous groups in the United States," according to Rosemary Henze and Lauren Vanett (116, my emphasis), who offer a broad critique of this goal. "Ironically," they write, "the metaphor becomes a barrier [to] rather than a model of how to live in the world today" (123). Far more useful is W.E.B. Du Bois's concept of double consciousness, a condition in which, as Du Bois wrote, "One ever feels his twoness—an American, a Negro" (*Souls* 1)—or, in these instances, an American, an Indian. I take up this matter more fully in the discussion of Charles Eastman.

4. Genevieve Bell's dissertation is the fullest source for facts, figures, and statistics about Carlisle. See also Fear-Segal, Fear-Segal and Rose, Landis, and Witmer for further information about the school.

5. Goodale was married to the Santee Sioux medical doctor and activist Charles Alexander Eastman, and both knew and admired Pratt. Very late in his life Pratt dictated the memoir that would become *Battlefield and Classroom*. This was available to Goodale, although it was not published until 1964.

6. The slogan is regularly cited but the only place I have found it in print is in the text of a talk Pratt gave in 1892 called "The Advantages of Mingling Indians with Whites." He begins with the now-infamous remark of General Sheridan, "The only good Indian is a dead Indian" (in Prucha 1979 260), to which Pratt responds, "I agree with the sentiment, but only in this: that all the Indian there is in the race should be dead. Kill the Indian in him, and save the man!" (261). That man or woman would then enter mainstream society, "mingling" with whites. In that Pratt himself "always eschewed racial categorization for Indians" (Fear-Segal 2007 3), he radically underestimated the degree to which many whites did not wish to "mingle" with Indians, regardless of any "advantages" that might accrue to both.

7. The memorial wording is from www.arlingtoncemetery.net/rhpratt. htm. Joel Pfister writes that Pratt's own "formal schooling concluded when he was thirteen.... Thus he had approximately the level of education that Carlisle made available to students" (2009 37). Robert Trennert refers to the "new school discipline of 'domestic science'" as "a modern homemaking technique, developed as a means to bring stability and scientific management to the American family" in late nineteenth-century America and to "provide skills to the increasing number of women entering the work force" (1982 273). Hampton Institute opened its "domestic science" department in 1898 (Brudvig 2013).

8. "Once at St. Augustine, Pratt removed the prisoners' shackles and staked his military commission on permitting the Indians to police themselves" (Lindsey 1995 28). While it is possible to see this as a move toward producing the internalization of an oppressive order, it most certainly gave a degree of power, however circumscribed, to those who had been rendered powerless. See Brudvig (1996) for a fuller account of Pratt and Fort Marion.

9. Scott Riney notes that Pratt himself had been a tinsmith prior to joining the Union Army and showed no subsequent desire to practice the trade (1999 226 n.13).

10. Hampton had been established in 1868 by black and white members of the American Missionary Society to educate the freedmen, and the school began its Indian program ten years later, when Pratt joined Armstrong at the school. For more on Indian students at Hampton, see Hultgren, Molin, and Green (1989), Lindsey (1995), and in particular Brudvig (1996). See also the study of Thomas Wildcat Alford below. A detailed account of Carlisle's outing program is given in Bell, 165–97.

11. Lomawaima and McCarty quote this passage (65-6) which contains the phrase they use for the title of their study, *To Remain an Indian*.

12. Richard Drinnon titled his biography of Myer *Keeper of the Camps: Dillon S. Myer and American Racism*. On the last page of his essay, Cohen claimed that Myer was attempting to do to Native people what the U.S. had done to the Japanese Americans. He writes of Myer that "he knows best where other American citizens should live and what they should do, and has arranged that the entire force of government will operate to make people do what he deems to be in their best interests," for he is intent on "repeating, in peacetime, what has been aptly described as 'Our Worst Wartime Mistake'" (1953 390).

13. Although I refer occasionally to some Canadian boarding-school narratives—as here—all the texts considered in detail, with one exception, are from the United States.

14. The primary academic and, in general, the primary Western literate criterion for historical truth is factuality. For traditional oral societies—and for many in today's nascent post-literacy or secondary orality—the primary criterion for historical truth is publicly agreed-upon knowledge about the past, not factuality. For a further account of these differences, see my "America's Histories" (2002).

15. This is unhelpfully exaggerated. A more accurate historical example of "ethnic cleansing" is the "Sandy Lake Tragedy" referenced by Child (2014 278). A belated and little-known attempt at Indian removal, the "Sandy Lake Tragedy" came about when the government announced in 1850 that the site of annuity payments to the Lake Superior Chippewas would be moved from La Pointe, Wisconsin, to Sandy Lake, Minnesota. Contravening its own laws and treaties, the government did this in the hope that keeping the Chippewas away from home for the winter would break down their resistance to removal west of the Mississippi. But supplies were late in arriving, and what did come was completely inadequate to the people's needs. About 150 Native people died at Sandy Lake before it was decided to attempt the trip home, a trip on which some 230 more died, a Chippewa Trail of Tears.

16. The words I have omitted from my quotation of Warrior have him suggesting "that the boarding-school experience does not need the metaphor of some other group's experience to validate it" (2005 118). I understand him to mean that the experience of Native people in the boarding schools should be recognized as an instance of major historical trauma in its own right. This

is surely true. But such recognition is not undercut by comparison to other major historical traumas suffered by other communities.

17. See in particular Patricia Carter's "'Completely Discouraged': Women Teachers' Resistance in the Bureau of Indian Affairs Schools, 1900–1910." Several of these women wrote richly informative accounts of their time teaching in the boarding schools. Particularly valuable—and often quite lively—observations are offered by Estelle Aubrey Brown in *Stubborn Fool*.

18. Tom, Dick, Harry, Sally, or Mary were often given to precede a student's Indian name, which then became a surname assumed to derive from the student's father. On many occasions students' names were obliterated entirely and replaced by the attribution of names like William Shakespeare (for an Arapaho boy), or Abraham Lincoln (for a Kiowa Apache boy), schoolmates of a Pawnee Jane Eyre and a Yavapai Charles Dickens. Re-naming was a way to make things easier for teachers and administrators, to be sure, but it was also a way to de-Indianize the students. After the 1887 passage of the Dawes Act, allotting land to individual Indians, renaming took place beyond the boarding schools to make family relationships more apparent for the purpose of title to and inheritance of land. On this matter see Littlefield and Underhill (1971).

1. CHARLES EASTMAN'S
From the Deep Woods to Civilization

1. Although that may be excessive. Penelope Kelsey writes that "hake" means last, and Eastman's name, Hakadah, best translates "as 'little last', the 'dah' or 'dan' word ending commonly forming a diminutive of any noun" (56). The Buechel *Lakota Dictionary* gives *hakakta*, "last, the last, the youngest child, boy or girl" (2002 76), and the current standard, the *New Lakota Dictionary*, also has *hakakta*, defining it as "the youngest one, to be born last, be younger than" (145).

2. Both Carlos Montezuma (1866–1923), Yavapai, and Susan LaFlesche Picotte (1865–1915), a mixed-blood Omaha, received their medical degrees in 1889, just a year before Eastman. Dr. Montezuma received his degree from the Chicago Medical College of Northwestern University and then served as resident physician at the Carlisle School from 1893 to 1896, going on to operate a successful medical practice in Chicago. He and

Eastman corresponded frequently. Dr. LaFlesche Picotte graduated from the Hampton Institute in 1886 and received her degree from the Woman's Medical College of Pennsylvania at the top of her class. She served as agency physician for her Omaha people until poor health caused her to resign in 1894.

3. Eastman was an eastern or Santee Sioux, hence a Nakota, like Zitkala-Sa, a Yankton. She generally referred to herself as Dakota, however, and I use Dakota as a tribal identifier for Eastman as well. Luther Standing Bear was a western Sioux, Oglala (or Brulé), therefore Lakota. More is given on these distinctions in the discussions of Standing Bear and Zitkala-Sa to follow.

4. *From the Deep Woods to Civilization: Chapters in the Autobiography of an Indian*, was, as Eastman himself stated, his eighth book (1977 [1916] 185), and he published only one more, *Indian Heroes and Great Chieftains* (1920), for a total of nine books. Other numbers have been given, the confusion resulting from the fact that several of Eastman's books appeared in more than one edition, occasionally with a title different from the original. This would account for Raymond Wilson's attribution of two books to both Eastman and his wife, Elaine Goodale: *Wigwam Evenings* (1909) and *Smoky Day's Wigwam Evenings* (1910) (Wilson 1983 131). These are the same, however.

5. The death of their daughter, Irene, during the flu pandemic of 1918 is sometimes cited as contributing to the couple's difficulties, but these had existed for many years. Less frequently mentioned, as Sargent writes, is that Dr. Eastman "had an affair that produced an illegitimate child," causing "Elaine to demand that he leave the marriage" (2004 xii; 2005 xiii). The child, a girl born in 1919, used the name Bonno Hyessa, apparently a variant of Eastman's name, Ohiyesa (Sargent 2005 108–9). Goodale did not attend Charles Eastman's funeral in 1939, and in her papers, housed at Smith College, "there is no mention at all of Charles" (Miller 1978 70). She did, however, renew the copyright to *Deep Woods* in 1944, five years after Eastman's death.

6. But Miller also observes that Eastman got into difficulty as U.S. Indian inspector in 1925 because of his "tardiness" in finding someone who could type up his notes (69). That he could not type—along with other matters than his separation from Goodale—may have contributed to the fact that he published no books after they parted.

7. See Tatonetti (284) for a succinct but excellent summation of the debate concerning the division of labor in Eastman's books. For debates about Eastman's reputation, see Coskan-Johnson (in particular 112–15).

8. When referring to him as an author, I use Eastman; for references to earlier times, I mostly use Ohiyesa. Eastman also used Ohiyesa on many public occasions, and his only son, Charles Alexander Jr., was called Ohi by the family.

9. The Big Knives are the Americans, so-called because of the bayonets used by their troops and the swords worn by their officers. This uncle is his father's brother—although a father's brother, according to Lakota kinship terminology would be called "father."

10. Much of *Indian Boyhood* had first been serialized in *St. Nicholas: An Illustrated Magazine for Young Folks* in 1893 (Wilson 131). This material does not seem to have been revised for a more mature audience when published in book form.

11. Appearing with Eastman and John Oskison on the panel in Columbus, Ohio, for the first meeting of the Society of American Indians in 1911 was Joseph Griffis, who would publish his autobiography, *Tahan: Out of Savagery, into Civilization* in 1915, a year before Eastman's "from … to" book. Also in 1915, Henry Roe Cloud's autobiographical essay, "From Wigwam to Pulpit: A Red Man's Story of His Progress from Darkness to Light," appeared, and Roe Cloud was also a man Eastman knew. The "from … to" title was common to the period, frequently appearing in many of the immigrant autobiographies of the time, a subject I return to in discussing Thomas Wildcat Alford's *Civilization* in part III.

12. The first University of Nebraska Press edition of *From the Deep Woods* in 1977 reproduced the 1936 edition of the book and included that edition's brief foreword signed "E.G.E." Readers in 1936 would almost surely have known those were the initials of Elaine Goodale Eastman, although 1970s readers might not have recognized them. In her foreword Goodale observed that it was "by dint of much persuasion"—on her part, on the part of its readers, or both—that the story of *Indian Boyhood* would be "carried on" (xviii) in *Deep Woods*. Chapter 2, "My First School Days," had appeared earlier as "The School Days of an Indian" in two parts in the *Outlook*. Part I, called "My First Day in School," was published in the issue of April 13, 1907, and part II, "Discovering a New World," in the issue of April 20, 1907. Part I differs from what Eastman later put into his book in that it records

bits of dialogue between himself, his father, and his grandmother. I note a few other differences in passing.

13. The first paragraph may show signs of Elaine Goodale's editing. Eastman (apparently) describes the way in which this "pivotal day" of his life suddenly "turned" by means of the following extended simile: "as if a little mountain brook should pause and turn upon itself to gather strength for the long journey toward the unknown ocean" (1). Of course a Native author *might* write this way, but the anthropomorphizing of nature seems more typical of a late Victorian literariness like Goodale's. If this is indeed an example of her editing, it is not one that changes Eastman's meaning.

14. The Santee Sioux were pressured into signing two treaties in 1851 by which they ceded almost all their lands—large portions of southern and western Minnesota—in return for a modest annuity and a sum to be held in trust by the government for a period of fifty years. Very little of that money actually came to the Indians.

15. A total of 303 of the Indians were to be hanged, but President Lincoln reduced that number to 38, sparing Many Lightnings.

16. I do not know what he means by this. The proper way to ask a Dakota person's name is to ask, "How do they speak of you?" (see Ella Deloria 154)—a question that should present no difficulty to someone who might answer, "Ohiyesa," the winner.

17. Unlike most Indian boarding-school students, Eastman does not represent the *topos* of naming at the first schools he attended, and there have been several different accounts of how he got his English name. David Reed Miller writes, "Apparently while attending his first year at Santee Normal School, Santee Agency, Nebraska, Ohiyesa selected his new name" (70n1). Colin Calloway claims that his father "gave Ohiyesa his new name" (115), and Sargent writes: "Once back at Flandreau, Ohiyesa was baptized and given the English name Charles Alexander Eastman" (2005 44). None of these writers provides a source for their statements.

18. Zitkala-Sa would also attend the Santee School briefly in 1889, as would Henry Roe Cloud in 1897, going on to become the first Native American graduate of Yale University.

19. Reverend John Sacred Cloud Eastman was born in February 1849, the second child and the first son of Many Lightnings and Stands Sacred Woman. Imprisoned with his father in Davenport and also converted there, upon release he accompanied Many Lightnings to Flandreau, and in 1870

he made the 150-mile walk from Flandreau to Santee that Charles would undertake later. After further education he was ordained a minister and served as pastor of the First Presbyterian Church at Flandreau from 1876 to 1906. I have taken some of this information from a fascinating document, *"Eastman Cloud Man, Many Lightnings: An Anglo-Dakota Family," Compiled by William Bean (Great Grandson of John Eastman) for the Eastman Family Reunion, July 6, 1989, Flandreau, South Dakota*. It may be found at alejandrasbooks.org/www/Eastman-Cloud%20Man.pdf.

20. William Harney had fought in the war with Mexico and later led contingents of the army against the Sioux in the 1850s. Although born in Tennessee, he served as a Union general during the Civil War.

21. Beloit College was founded in 1846, before Wisconsin became a state, and Eastman's brother John was its first Indian student. Eastman entered Beloit College's preparatory program, not the college proper.

22. "Black Hawk's Rock River" does indeed flow through Beloit, although Black Hawk would only have known it much farther west, in what are now Iowa and Illinois.

23. These were the work of Late Woodlands people who had constructed them somewhere between 400 and 1200 CE. The mounds have since been designated as burial sites not to be disturbed.

24. Aaron Lucius Chapin was a graduate of Yale and the Union Theological Seminary. He was ordained a Presbyterian minister in 1844 and served as Beloit College's first president, from 1849 until his resignation in 1886.

25. One of these was Roger Leavitt, who reminisced: "We were told that a full blooded Sioux Indian … was across the hall from us. Thinking he might be homesick, and also somewhat curious, we rapped at his door and invited him to come into our room. We spent a most interesting hour. He was the first Indian I had ever seen dressed like a white man. He wore a white starched shirt and collar, and a necktie. His best suit which he had on, was as good as ours. He was quiet and reserved, but spoke well in reply to our many questions." From *the Beloit Alumnus*, December 1915, 5. I thank Frank Burwell, archivist of Beloit College, for this reference (personal communication April 26, 2017).

26. Ira Pettibone (1833–1917), a Civil War veteran, had come to Beloit as principal of the college's preparatory department—in which Eastman was enrolled—in 1871 and served in that capacity until 1881. I have this

information from his obituary in the *Citizen* (Winsted, CT), October 1, 1917, also sent me by Frank Burwell, archivist of Beloit College (personal communication April 26, 2017).

27. He had earlier noted his accomplishments in "elementary algebra and geometry" (50) at the Santee school, and he mentions here a "recent letter from a Beloit schoolmate," who wrote that Eastman was "the only boy who could beat him in algebra" (55). This may be Roger Leavitt, who commented in the piece earlier cited on Eastman's prowess at mathematics.

28. Eastman was probably aware of the fact that Abraham Lincoln had been a twenty-three-year-old volunteer in the Illinois militia in 1832 during the so-called Black Hawk War.

29. Eastman wrote that Riggs himself had graduated from Knox (58), which had been founded by anti-slavery reformers in 1837 and had strong connections to Presbyterianism and Congregationalism.

30. For example, David Murray: Eastman tells "of the eminent people he has met, and his successes in white society in a manner reminiscent of Booker T. Washington" (78). Washington's autobiography, *Up from Slavery* had appeared in 1901, just a year earlier than Eastman's first book.

31. In a lengthy letter to Wheelock in the summer of 1771 Occom had written, "I think your College has too much Worked by Grandeur for the Poor Indians, they'll never have much benefit of it" (in Peyer 78–79).

32. See Calloway for "Native Americans and Dartmouth." Eastman would portray Occom in several dramatic sketches performed at the college. His invocation of Occom is also coincidentally interesting because, as Joanna Brooks notes, Occom's is "the largest extant body of writing produced by an American Indian author before … Charles Eastman" (5).

33. See my study, *"That the People Might Live": Loss and Renewal in Native American Elegy.*

34. Kimball Union Academy, in Meriden, New Hampshire, about fourteen miles from Dartmouth in New Hanover, was founded in 1813 to prepare young men for the ministry. Its first graduating class in 1816 consisted of six male students; four young women who had also completed the school's program did not receive certificates of graduation. The school became co-ed in 1839.

35. If I have understood it correctly, the website African Americans @ Dartmouth College 1775–1950 (https://badahistory.net/) indicates that there were four or five black students at Dartmouth during the time Eastman

was there, so although he was the only Native American student, he was not the only student of color.

36. He "was a champion distance runner, played baseball and tennis, and boxed" (Calloway 117), holding Dartmouth's long-distance running record for three years. Eastman also joined a fraternity, and played whist (Wilson 32).

37. Kimball Union Academy, Dartmouth College, and Boston University Medical School were all private institutions at which tuition and fees amounted to a very substantial sum both then and now. Eastman says nothing in his autobiographical account about how he managed to pay for his education. As Colin Calloway explains, the Scottish Society for the Propagation of Christian Knowledge "financed Eastman's education at Kimball Union Academy and Dartmouth, paying for his tuition, board and rent, books, stationery, paper, stamps, clothing, shoes, rubber boots, oil, furniture, bedding, coal, firewood, washing and mending, and even fare to Nantucket and vacation expenses" (118).

The SSPCK had been established in 1709 to found Presbyterian schools in the Highlands of Scotland and also in the British colonies. It supported both Kimball Union and Dartmouth and continued to do so into the early twentieth century. According to Calloway, "Friends in Boston" supplied "the means for [Eastman] to pursue his medical studies" (118). These "friends" were probably Mr. and Mrs. Frank Woods, trustees of Amherst College, "with whom Eastman lived while attending medical school at Boston University" (Vigil 2015 67).

38. Eastman officially entered Dartmouth in 1883, and Emerson had died in 1882, so—not to put too fine a point on it—while he could indeed have met him *at* Dartmouth, that would have been before he was actually a Dartmouth student.

39. Malea Powell had suggested parallels between Eastman and Du Bois (214n), as had Robert Warrior (2005), who also references him in relation to Luther Standing Bear. More recently Kiara Vigil has noted that some of Eastman's texts were "in close dialogue with W. E. B. Du Bois" (Vigil 2015 50), a position also taken by Kyle Mays (discussed later).

40. I thank Professor Kiara Vigil (personal communication June 19, 2017) for informing me that Eastman's book had appeared in February of 1911. In a detailed account of Eastman, Du Bois, and the Universal Races Conference, Kyle Mays wrote that Eastman's title, *Soul of the Indian*, is "resonant with Du Bois's *Souls of Black Folks*" (Mays 2013 249). He notes that after the London Conference, Du Bois—who had become an "associate"

member of the Society of American Indians—published a photo of Eastman in the September 1911 issue of the NAACP's journal, the *Crisis*, which he edited (250).

41. Tova Cooper discusses more broadly what she calls Eastman's "attempts to rescue 'civilization' from its practitioners" (19). As for Christianity, I think Eastman is not at all sure that it can be "rescue[d] ... from its practitioners."

2. LUTHER STANDING BEAR'S
My People, the Sioux

1. Standing Bear sometimes gave his birth date as 1868, but Richard Ellis, in his introduction to the 1975 edition of *My People the Sioux*, noted that the "allotment schedule at Pine Ridge ... listed his date of birth as 1863, as did the census of 1932; so there is some question whether the government records are accurate or whether Standing Bear was correct" (xv). His Carlisle student information card listed him as 15 in 1879, and in response to a questionnaire from the School in 1890, Standing Bear wrote, "I am now twenty-six years old," making 1864 his birth date. (http://carlisleindian.dickinson.edu/documents/former-student-survey-responses-1890-part-5-5). In his 1931 "The Tragedy of the Sioux," reprinted at the end of the University of Nebraska Press edition of *Land of the Spotted Eagle*, he said, "I was born during the troublous days of the 60s, the exact year is not known" (260). In the discussion to follow I use the 1868 date, roughly.

2. *My People the Sioux* was originally published in 1928 with an introduction by the cowboy star of silent films, William S. Hart. It also contained photographs by E.A. Brininstool, a cowboy poet and an amateur historian of the Indian wars; by Clyde Champion, a photographer based in Alhambra, California, for whom Standing Bear had posed; and "drawings from the author" (title page). This has long been out of print. A second edition by the University of Nebraska Press appeared in 1975 with an introduction by Richard Ellis. Nebraska published a third edition in 2006 with a brief new introduction by Virginia Driving Hawk Sneve (it precedes Ellis's introduction, which is retained). Page numbers are the same in all three editions.

3. Standing Bear dedicated *My People the Sioux* "in loving memory" to his father, also named Standing Bear, whom he calls "a warrior of distinction [,] a great leader [,] and counselor among his people" (n.p.), stating

that his "father had previously held" the title of chief (274). The historian George Hyde, to the contrary, considered the elder Standing Bear one of the "unimportant men of various bands" (321). Richard Ellis had also noted the "possibility that Standing Bear overemphasized the importance of his father," observing that published histories do not mention the elder Standing Bear "as a significant Sioux leader" (1975 xv), although Ellis later amended this, acknowledging that the father "was undoubtedly a band leader" (1985 142). Further, although Luther Standing Bear pronounced both himself and his father Oglala chiefs, they were more likely Brulés. Ellis notes that "the record of agreement for land allotment in 1889 lists the elder Standing Bear as a member of the Brulés" (1975 xv), and Luther's Carlisle student file identifies him as a Brulé.

4. After the Dawes Allotment Act became law in 1887, Standing Bear accepted an allotment from the government, which held it in trust for him—as it did for all allottees—until he could obtain "fee patent," essentially individual title to the land. It was not until November, 1911 that he was able to do this.

5. Although some Native people had obtained citizenship, like Standing Bear, by accepting land allotments, and others by serving in the military, citizenship was not extended to all Indian people until President Coolidge signed the Indian Citizenship Act into law in June 1924. In *Land of the Spotted Eagle*, Standing Bear calls "the bill signed by President Coolidge … just another hoax" (245), although he had earlier believed—as Charles Eastman and many others had—that gaining citizenship would be important for Native people.

6. For Standing Bear's film roles see Vigil 298 n.118. Hazel Hertzberg places the AIPA "among local Pan-Indian clubs which sprang up in various cities. Many of them billed themselves as national organizations but in practice were confined to local areas" (233). Much later, in 1931, Standing Bear was involved with the National League for Justice to American Indians and, in 1936, with Jim Thorpe, in the Indian Actors Association. See Vigil's appendix (325–26) for a list of Indian reform associations of the period and their most prominent members.

7. Kiara Vigil reports an unfortunate and little-known event of Standing Bear's later life: "On May 6, 1935, the *Los Angeles Times* reported that Standing Bear had pleaded guilty to the charge of child molestation" (278), for which he received a one-year prison sentence. The victim appears to have

been an eight-year-old Paiute girl, although Vigil's research uncovered almost nothing about her. In his 1890 response to the Carlisle questionnaire, the youthful Standing Bear had written, "I have got along very well since I left school. The particular trouble I have had was about a girl." I have discovered nothing further about that earlier "particular trouble."

8. *Union Pacific* had an already well-known director in DeMille and an extraordinary cast, including Barbara Stanwyck, Joel McCrea, Anthony Quinn, Regis Toomey, Lon Chaney Jr., and Robert Preston, among others. Also in the full cast, but uncredited, was the pretend-Indian actor, Ironeyes Cody, born Espera de Corti. In 1939 the movie won the first Palme d'Or ever awarded by the Cannes Film Festival—which had to be canceled because of the outbreak of World War II. The award was finally presented to *Union Pacific* in 2002.

9. After his recruiting trip to the Rosebud Agency, Richard Pratt went on to Pine Ridge and, in September 1879, left with "sixty boys and twenty-four girls" (Ostler 149).

10. Pratt's "success teaching Indian prisoners at Fort Marion, in Florida," Jeffrey Ostler writes, "persuaded the army to let him take some of the prisoners to Hampton Institute" (150), his next posting. When he left Hampton he took several of them to Carlisle. Standing Bear refers to them as "prisoners," but that was not their status at the school.

11. In *Land of the Spotted Eagle* Standing Bear wrote of the time in 1879 when "there came to the Agency a party of white people from the East. Their presence aroused considerable excitement when it became known that these people were school teachers who wanted some Indian boys and girls to take away with them to train as were white boys and girls [trained]" (230). To encourage Lakota girls to come to Carlisle, Pratt brought with him Miss Sarah Mather, a direct descendant of Cotton Mather and a good friend of Harriet Beecher Stowe, who, with "her lifetime companion, Miss Rebecca Perritt" (Fear-Segal 2016b 211), had formerly taught some of the Indian prisoners in Pratt's charge at Fort Marion, Florida. Mather also taught at Carlisle for a time in its earliest days and, after leaving, visited the school often.

12. Standing Bear was given his father's name as a surname when he entered Carlisle, and in a scene I examine he "chose" the name Luther in the classroom. His student file lists him as "Luther Standing Bear (Kills Plenty)." Kills Plenty is a translation of Ota Kte, which would be his "honor" name.

As Ella Cara Deloria explained, "In Dakota, you do not say, if you are idiomatically correct, 'What is your name?' but, 'In what manner do they say of you?' That means, 'According to what deed are you known?' The deed of an ancestor was memorialized in a phrase applied to a descendant of his" (154). Standing Bear himself does not speak of having killed anyone, so the name Kills Plenty, as Ellis writes, would honor him by memorializing the fact that "his father had killed many Indian enemies" (1985 143).

13. *Land of the Spotted Eagle* is also available in three editions. The 1933 original edition had a very brief introduction by Professor Melvin R. Gilmore, whom Standing Bear describes in his preface as "Curator of Ethnology for the University of Michigan, Ann Arbor, Michigan" (2006 xxii). Then there is a 1978 edition by the University of Nebraska Press that retains the introductory material by Gilmore and Standing Bear and adds a foreword by Richard Ellis, followed by a 2006 edition that keeps Gilmore, Standing Bear, and Ellis, while preceding them with a new introduction by Joseph Marshall III. Here, too, pagination is the same in all three editions.

14. The elder Standing Bear went away for "about ten days, and then," his son writes, using money his son had been paid by the government for serving (unawares) as a scout, "returned all dressed up. He wore a collar, a necktie, a stiff shirt, and even carried a watch and chain," although he could not tell time. "Then he told his *wives* he … was going to open a store" (*My People* 98, my emphasis).

15. This is Zintkaziwin or Yellow Bird who would enter Carlisle three years later, in 1882.

16. The *New Lakota Dictionary* defines *wasicu* as a "white person, Caucasian, person of European or Euro-American ancestry or culture," adding that "the word does not imply skin color," and that the "origin of the word [is] unknown." The entry continues that "although several etymologies have been suggested, none of them seem conclusive" (625). For one set of suggested etymologies, see Eugene Buechel's *Lakota Dictionary* (352).

17. A somewhat different account is given in *Land*. Again no cleanup is described, but this time, Standing Bear writes, "the 'civilizing' process *began* … with clothes" (232, my emphasis).

18. On the next to last page of *My People* Standing Bear mentions encountering Mariana Burgess in California sometime during the First World War, noting that they "had not met since 1883" (287). "By the 1920s," Kiara Vigil writes, "Burgess was living 'all alone' in downtown Los Angeles

... and she aimed to use any free time or resources to help Native people in California" (194). Richard Ellis remarked: "Unfortunately, there are important gaps in this account [in *My People*], particularly relating to his marriages and to his activities in Los Angeles" (1985 151).

19. Robert American Horse, whose name Nakpa Kesela means Cut Ears, was the nephew of the Pine Ridge Agency chief American Horse. (The name means "He Has a White Man's Horse.")

20. Robert American Horse also showed himself quick to offer pithy commentary in an anecdote Richard Pratt included in his autobiography. Pratt writes of Clarence Three Stars, whom we will consider further, that he "had exceptional mental ability," although "he was at first disposed to bother his teacher," prompting the teacher to request that Pratt come to the classroom with the interpreter. Through the interpreter, Pratt ordered Three Stars to stand "at attention as a soldier," upon which Pratt asks, "What is the matter?" Three Stars then spoke rapidly in Lakota, "but his voice quavered." At this point American Horse "said something in Sioux at which all the others laughed." Pratt "asked the interpreter what Robert had said." The answer was: "Robert says to him, 'If you are so brave, what makes your voice shake so?'" (243).

21. In *Land of the Spotted Eagle* he gives a slightly different account: "Our first resentment was in having our hair cut," because it "has ever been the custom of Lakota men to wear long hair," so that "for days after being shorn we felt strange and uncomfortable" (189).

22. Describing the cleanup at the Pine Ridge boarding school, Thisba Morgan writes that the scrubbing the children endured during her time there "was nothing to the suffering their poor little feet were to endure when they were taken out of their soft flat-soled moccasins and put into the awful brogans furnished by the United States Government. They limped and shuffled about trying to learn to walk in the heavy things that were blistering their feet, some leaving bleeding sores which often became badly infected" (26). Brogans were heavy shoes or boots reaching to the ankle. One of the reasons they hurt the wearer's feet was that they were unpaired—they did not come in a "left" shoe and a "right," which made them cheaper to produce— so they would only take proper form after a good deal of painful wear. The Pine Ridge Boarding School would become the Oglala Community High School. Morgan, writing about 1958, called the school "a new fine institution of learning for the grandchildren of those pupils of the by-gone days"

(62). As we will see, however, Walter Littlemoon, who entered the school in 1947 at the age of five, describes unrelenting brutality on the part of the staff, not one of whom showed the concern of Thisba Morgan.

23. See Deloria's *Playing Indian*.

24. He is again much more critical in *Land*, where he observes that the "red flannel undergarments … given us for winter wear" caused him "discomfort [that] grew into actual torture" (234).

25. Beginning in 1872 Bishop William Hare "oversaw the establishment of Episcopal missions on all Sioux reservations in the Dakotas and Nebraska" (DeMallie and Parks 11–12). For an account of a prominent Dakota family's long relationship to the Episcopal Church see Vine Deloria Sr., in DeMallie and Parks.

26. The book champions Carlisle "civilization" against the savagery of—in this case—Pueblo Indian culture. Its narrative dramatizes the ostensibly fact-based difficulties of its protagonist to maintain Carlisle standards and, most particularly, to avoid participating in the "primitive" dances of her Pueblo. The author of the novel is "Embe," or "M. B.," Mariana Burgess. Its title borrows the name of Stiya Kowacura or Koykuri, a Laguna Pueblo student at Carlisle who entered in 1886 and was discharged because of ill health in 1892. The young woman in the photo used as a frontispiece (see figure 5), however, is Lucy Tsisnah, a San Carlos Apache woman. See Jacqueline Fear-Segal (2004), and Amelia Katanski for useful discussions of *Stiya*.

27. Clarence Three Stars (Packs the Dog) entered Carlisle with Standing Bear in October 1879 and left in the fall of 1884. Thisba Morgan wrote that when she came to teach at the Oglala Boarding School at Pine Ridge in 1890, she "succeeded Clarence Three-Stars, … who had attended the Indian School at Carlisle, Pa., and had returned to the reservation to work among his people" (23).

28. William Spotted Tail (Stays at Home), age eighteen; Oliver Spotted Tail (Pulls, or Bugler), age fifteen; Max Spotted Tail (Talks with Bears), age fourteen; Pollock Spotted Tail, age nine; Hugh Whirlwind Soldier (Hugh Running Horse), age eight; along with Sarah Spotted Tail Red Road, or Sarah Mather, age eighteen, all entered the school with Standing Bear on October 6, 1879. They are all the children of Chief Spotted Tail except for Whirlwind Soldier, who was his grandson. All of them left Carlisle with Spotted Tail on June 23, 1880. Oliver returned to Carlisle in 1882, when his sister Gertrude Spotted Tail first entered, and Max was re-admitted in 1883.

29. I have not found a record for a granddaughter of Chief Spotted Tail at Carlisle.

30. Tackett is listed as a mixed-blood in the Carlisle student records—this would explain his ability with English—and he, too, entered Carlisle in October 1879, the oldest of the Lakotas, at the age of twenty-seven. He was the husband of Sarah Tackett, who, as noted, is also listed as Red Road, Sarah Mather Red Road, and Sarah Spotted Tail Red Road. Tackett left with her and the other Spotted Tail children in June 1880.

31. Standing Bear's chronology is mistaken. Spotted Tail left Carlisle with the children on June 23, 1880. He was killed in August 1881, so news of his death could not have come "During the early part of 1881"—unless Standing Bear is thinking of the 1881 school year, the early part of which would indeed be September 1881.

32. See Sidney Harring's *Crow Dog's Case* for a full account of the dispute between Crow Dog and Spotted Tail. On August 5, 1881, Crow Dog shot and killed Spotted Tail. Crow Dog was captured, tried, convicted of murder, and sentenced to hang—despite the fact that the "families of both men had met, and, following tribal law, settled the matter for $600 in cash, eight horses, and one blanket" (Harring 1). Crow Dog's case was appealed all the way to the U.S. Supreme Court, which ruled, in *Ex Parte Crow Dog* (1883), that the U.S. "had no criminal jurisdiction over Indian tribes in 'Indian Country'" (Harring 1), a clear victory for Native sovereignty. This was overturned a year later when Congress passed the Major Crimes Act of 1884.

33. Fear-Segal writes that when a new cemetery was established in 1927, "Earnest was reinterred in plot C12, and ... on this site stands a stone that reads, 'Ernest, Son of Chief White Thunder, Sioux, December 14, 1880'" (2016a 168).

34. Allen Trachtenberg uses this incident to begin a chapter on Standing Bear that he calls "The Great Bridge," and in which he uses the idea of "bridging" to understand Standing Bear's life and writing. He notes that "there is no mention of the Carlisle School band in the *Opening Ceremonies of the New York and Brooklyn Bridge, May 24, 1883*," but he finds "no reason to doubt Standing Bear's account (332n2).

35. Standing Bear had entered Carlisle in October, 1879, so his third year had been up in May, 1882. In November 1883 a fourteen-year-old Brulé from Rosebud named Plenty Horses, or Plenty Living Bear, would enter Carlisle, departing in July 1889, as noted in the introduction. Standing Bear

may have recognized him from home and may have encountered him at school. Luther's brother, Henry Standing Bear, also entered in 1883, along with two Sicangu brothers from Rosebud. One, called Timber, was renamed Chauncey Yellow Robe; the other, Wounded, was given the name Richard Yellow Robe. The three are shown in the cover illustration, first upon their entrance to the school and then three years later, in one of John Choate's "before" and "after" photographs. Chauncey Yellow Robe graduated with honors in 1895, and he went on to a prominent career as an Indian activist, working with the Society of American Indians. He also had a major role in the film *The Silent Enemy* (1930). Standing Bear makes no mention of either of the Yellow Robe brothers or of Plenty Horses.

36. The Carlisle *School News*, for June, 1882 reports Teller's visit. It has him addressing "the scholars who are returning to their homes" (2), and assuring them that if they later wished to return to Carlisle, he would do his best to help them do so. It does not quote Teller as asking who would like to stay on, as Standing Bear describes, but of course it is possible that he did exactly that.

37. Standing Bear writes that Stuart "was one of the boys who had been brought up from the South before the Sioux boys and girls came to the school" (177). If that is correct, then Stuart, not Standing Bear, might have been "the first Indian boy to step inside the Carlisle Indian School grounds" (133). Stuart's Carlisle file, however, gives the date of his entrance to the school as January 1881, which would be later than the time Standing Bear entered. The file has him leaving the school in November 1883, so if it is accurate, he could not have been a candidate for the outing assignment to Wanamaker's Department Store, which, as I will describe further, began early in the spring 1884.

38. Lucy Maddox writes of Standing Bear that "the problem that worried him most" was "how to please, simultaneously, two men (who could hardly have been more different from one another) whom he admired and whose approval he very much desired: his father and Richard Pratt" (156). Contrary to Maddox, I find Pratt and the elder Standing Bear in important respects more nearly similar than different. Both had been warriors—Pratt fought in the Civil War—and both urged Standing Bear to be brave unto death. The two men also seemed to get along well when they met.

39. The John Wanamaker department store in Philadelphia had been established at the abandoned Pennsylvania Railroad Station in Philadelphia in 1876. It was the first retail establishment to use electric illumination

(1878) and the telephone (1879). It also had a tea room and restaurant to encourage women to visit and to shop. Consistent with practice at the time, Wanamaker hired only white Protestant males. Trachtenberg notes that Wanamaker sold boys' and girls' clothing to the Carlisle school and had a correspondence with Pratt (329 n.32).

40. His student file records that he officially left Carlisle in July, 1885.

41. Sitting Bull had an older sister, born about 1827, called Good Feather Woman in English; she appears with him and some of his children in a photo taken at Fort Randall in 1881 that is available on several websites. It is likely that he also had two younger sisters, Brown Shawl Woman and Twin Woman, who were twins, the Sitting Bull Family Tree website giving 1835 as the birth year for both. Whichever of Sitting Bull's sisters this was, she would probably not have been Standing Bear's aunt by blood relationship.

42. Charles Spencer Chaplin had not yet been born at the time of Standing Bear's homecoming in 1884, although he was a silent film star at the time Standing Bear wrote. The reference to "Jew comedians" reflects the casual anti-Semitism of the 1920s and Standing Bear's awareness that vaudeville performers like Jack Benny, the Marx Brothers, and George Burns were Jewish. Although often thought Jewish by Jews and gentiles alike, the likelihood is that Chaplin was not, in fact, Jewish. See Epstein.

43. This would be Nellie DeCory, whom he married in 1886 and then left to marry Laura Cloud Shield Levering (Sprague 40). Kiara Vigil quotes a letter from Levering in which she writes that Standing Bear left her as well (280). Later, in Los Angeles, Standing Bear lived with May Jones Montoya/ Sunflower until his death (Vigil 282).

44. This would put him at odds with Mariana Burgess, who abhorred traditional Native dances and made Stiya's refusal to take part in those performed at her Pueblo a critical point of her novel. In *Land*, Standing Bear would affirm: "Even when studying under the missionary, I went to the dances of my tribe" (237).

45. Richard Ellis mentions a letter dated May 2, 1933, from Standing Bear to President Franklin Roosevelt "proposing a bill that would require public schools to teach a course on Indian history, religion, philosophy, art and culture" (1975 xx n.3). I don't know whether Standing Bear had read DuBois, but he is echoed here. Du Bois had written that the Negro "would not Africanize America, for America has too much to teach the world and Africa. He would not bleach his Negro soul in a flood of white Americanism, for he knows that Negro blood has a message for the world" (45).

3. ZITKALA-SA'S "IMPRESSIONS OF AN INDIAN CHILDHOOD," "THE SCHOOL DAYS OF AN INDIAN GIRL," AND "AN INDIAN TEACHER AMONG INDIANS"

1. Philippe Lejeune long ago made the case for what he called "*le pacte autobiographique*" as an agreement between the author and the reader that an autobiographical text did indeed make truth-claims. Soon after Lejeune, Elizabeth Bruss wrote of "the autobiographical pact" (10), as affirming the "truth-value" of an autobiographical text, so that "the audience is expected to accept these reports as true" (11). Whatever the situation today, this "pact" would have been operative at the turn of the twentieth century. It is also the case that if one looks to Dakota coup stories as a type of indigenous auto-biography, exactly the same pact between teller and listener pertains. Agnes Picotte has noted that Zitkala-Sa sometimes presents as her own what was "told to her by people who had actually experienced the situations and circumstances ... described" (xv). For speculation on the generic status of Zitkala-Sa's autobiographical essays, see Katanski, and Spack.

2. See Roumiana Velikova's more recent account of the ways in which Zitkala-Sa's early texts are highly "tropic," rich in tropes and literary devices that aim for esthetic effect, regardless of historical accuracy.

3. The Sioux, as they have generically been called, can be separated into three large divisions based on differences in their spoken language, from east to west: the Nakota, Dakota, and Lakota. The more easterly Yankton, Zitkala-Sa's Nakota People (also Eastman's Santee People), pronounced certain words with an N, while, to the west, the Dakota used a D, and still farther west, the Lakota (like Luther Standing Bear) said L. Thus Zitkala-Sa might have named herself Zitkana-Sa, or more likely Zitkada-Sa, because she consistently referred to herself and her people as Dakotas. The Zitkala-Sa she chose probably should have been Zitkala-Sawin, -win being the marker of a feminine name, like the names of her friends Thowin and Judewin, or that of her mother, "Tate I yohin Win ("Reaches for the Wind, or Every Wind" (Lewandowski 2016 17)). Susan Dominguez writes that she did sometimes sign her name Zitkala-Sawin (11). She signed her let-ters to Carlos Montezuma (discussed later) "Zitkala"—and contemporary students, assuming that to be a first name, have occasionally referenced her—mistakenly—as "Ms. Sa."

4. Her mother almost surely spoke the Yankton dialect—Nakota—although she might well have been comfortable with other Siouan dialects. Ella Cara Deloria, for example, born at Yankton in 1889, wrote that although she grew up among the Tetons on the Standing Rock reservation, and "spoke Teton"—Dakota—there, she was "thoroughly at home in the Yankton dialect because [her] father and mother never abandoned it and [she] heard it daily" (1952 n.p.). Her nephew Vine Deloria Jr. wrote that she "spoke all three dialects of the Sioux language, although she was most familiar with the 'd' dialect" (1998 xiv), perhaps also true of Zitkala-Sa. All page references to Zitkala-Sa's three autobiographies in the 1900 *Atlantic Monthly* are from the 2003 reprint of her writings edited by Cathy Davidson and Ada Norris.

5. Dominguez writes that "'Gertie Felker' is the name listed on the Yankton Presbyterian Mission rolls" (97 n.113), Felker being her father's name. She was called Gertrude Simmons, the name of her mother's previous husband, John Haystings Simmons, at the schools she attended and also at Carlisle during the time she was employed there. Dominguez cites a *Washington Evening Post* interview with her conducted in 1936, in which "she revealed … that she was 'christened Zitkala-Sa.'" This, Dominguez says, "corrects the record regarding her birth name" (9). But Dominguez's source for this "correction," is what Zitkala-Sa told the *Post*, and just as what she told the *Post* for that story's headline was untrue—she was not a descendant of Sitting Bull—so, too, is this false. Zitkala-Sa was a name she chose for herself in 1898 (discussed later), and if she was given an Indian name at birth she never revealed it, nor has anyone found a record of it.

6. David Simmons was one of "eleven children from the Yankton Agency" (Spack 2002 57) brought to Hampton by Richard Pratt himself in November 1879 (Spack 2002 56), when David was twelve years old (Dominguez 129). If he had just returned from spending three years there, the time would be 1882, and Zitkala-Sa would be six years old, not eight, as her text has it.

7. Spoken Dakota—spoken Nakota as well—does not have a V sound, hence "Dawee" for Davey. My thanks to Dr. Julian Rice for this information (personal communication, October 3, 2017), and to Professor Scott Lyons for raising the question (personal communication, October 2, 2017). David Simmons would marry a woman named Victoria (discussed later) who, Tadeusz Lewandowski informs me, was called "Wickie" (personal communication, October 3, 2017).

8. Felker appears to have left little trace. There has been some speculation that he was French, although Felker does not seem to be a French name; that he may have had a problem with alcohol; and that he probably left his wife before their child was born. But the extensive research of, for example, Susan Dominguez, Ruth Spack, and Tadeusz Lewandowski has turned up no further information about him.

9. All references to Dakota people and "shingled hair" that I have been able to find allude only to Zitkala-Sa. If "shingled" hair did indeed identify "cowards," such a haircut would have been exclusive to men. John Miles, superintendent of the Cheyenne-Arapaho Agency in Indian Territory, in a letter of 1875, wrote that the son of one of the old war chiefs was attending the Arapaho Boarding School "with his hair 'shingled' close and neat, as is required of all" (home.epix.net/~landis/bullbear.html). I do not know whether Arapahoes considered such a haircut the mark of a coward.

10. Both Fisher's 1985 reprint and Davidson and Norris's 2003 reprint have "passwood." But this, as they all might have guessed, is a typo. Page 188 of the original in the *Atlantic Monthly* has "password."

11. Zitkala-Sa would later become a Catholic and send her son to Catholic boarding school; and she had a Mormon funeral service. While she may indeed at this time have yet been a "pagan," Christianity of some form did not remain merely a "superstitious idea" to her.

12. It was, as I have said, highly untraditional. Many years ago William Bevis wrote of "the insufferability of individuality" (592) in the six Native American novels he was studying, adding that "Emerson's 'Thou art unto thyself a law' is the exact opposite of Native American knowledge" (597). As for being marked out as an individual at school, Ella Deloria wrote, "I soon realized in... mission school that it was improper to be too smart. So even when I knew the answers ... I knew enough to keep still.... Once you learned to live under the spell of the average, you were all right. Everyone liked you then, and you had many friends" (1952 n.p.). I thank Bruce Kirby, reference librarian in the Manuscript Division of the Library of Congress, for a scan of Deloria's brief autobiography written for Margaret Mead about 1952 (personal communication September 7, 2017).

13. Zitkala-Sa would have been a candidate for the traditional girl's puberty ceremony at Yankton—if it was still practiced—almost surely before becoming a teen. The ceremony had been of great importance to the Oglala Lakota, and in *The Sacred Pipe*, Black Elk tells a story of its origin and first performance (J. Brown 116–26). Madonna Swan, a Lakota woman born in

1928 on the Cheyenne River reservation north and west of Yankton, titles a section of her autobiography *"Ishna Ti Cha Lowan*—Becoming a Woman" (40–43), and describes the ceremony for her first menstruation still being performed around 1940. A detailed ethnographic account of the Lakota ceremony appears in Marla Powers, 66–72.

14. In "Why I Am a Pagan," published two years later, she describes a visit from an Indian preacher to their home and says of her mother that "she, too, is now a follower of the new superstition" (803), using the same terminology she had earlier used (see note 11). I quote from the original in the *Atlantic Monthly* because Fisher, and also Davidson and Norris, print only the 1921 revised (it adds a short paragraph at the end) and retitled version called "The Great Spirit."

15. Rather than deriving from an anti-ethnographic stance, I think it may come from Zitkala-Sa's sense that her mostly white audience is not especially interested in cultural accuracy, nor was cultural accuracy a concern of hers. Susan Dominguez quotes a letter from Zitkala-Sa to the anthropologist Alice Fletcher, in which she asks to borrow an Indian dress to perform in—although she must know that Fletcher had not worked with Dakota people. The reason she asks is because the dress she had originally wanted to borrow from Angel DeCora, a Winnebago woman, was not available (Dominguez 157). James Mooney, Zitkala-Sa's opponent in the 1918 debate about Native use of peyote (discussed later), attacked her "tribal mélange" of dress in performance; his acerbic comments can be found in the Davidson and Norris compilation (xxiii) and in Lewandowski (2016 141).

16. Unlike Charles Eastman and Luther Standing Bear, Zitkala-Sa gives no dates and mentions no historical events of importance to Native American people. Of course, the two older men wrote much later than she did, at a time when dominant-culture reaction to some of these events had cooled. It is also the case that the Yanktons had not taken part in the Custer fight and, for the most part, did not participate in the Ghost Dance. (Joseph Iron Eye Dudley, however, records a detailed eyewitness account of a Yankton Ghost Dance narrated by his grandmother, in what was probably the fall of 1890 [74–82]). Nor does Zitkala-Sa name a single Native person of note—odd, in that her audience was surely interested in world-historical Indians.

17. Although many of the students at White's were apparently "at their own request received into membership with the South Wabash Monthly Meeting of Friends" (Green 14), Zitkala-Sa was not. Nearby Earlham College, which she attended on her graduation from White's, was founded

"as a Friends Boarding School in 1847," and "became in 1859 the second Quaker college in the world ... to provide a 'guarded religious education for the children of Friends'" (Hamm xi). But Zitkala-Sa does not seem ever to have joined the Friends Meeting.

18. By suggesting that her time at Earlham was not *exclusively* lonely and painful, I don't mean to imply that it wasn't at all lonely and painful. The tension the youthful Zitkala-Sa is feeling among the white people with whom she is supposed to be at ease was described poignantly by Vine Deloria Sr., writing late in his life. "There is constantly," Deloria says, " a slight strain in my associations with white people. From time to time, I have to go off by myself and relive that early culture ... recalling the ways of the Standing Rock people of sixty years ago.... The only way I can tell that I have never really crossed over is the strain I am bound to feel after being in the white world without any re-creation for some time" (194–95). I have no doubt Zitkala-Sa would have had much the same feeling.

19. Lewandowski cites a letter written by W. C. Dennis in 1938 in which Dennis recalls: "We naturally expected that as Seniors our class would sweep everything before it in the Oratorical Contest and to have this little Indian girl in the Freshman class beat our best was quite a surprise for us although I must say that I think we all took the defeat very nicely and supported her loyally when she went on to the State Contest" (Lewandowski 2016 207 n.45), which she soon would do.

20. Lewandowski suggests that Zitkala-Sa would likely have taken first place had not a southern judge objected to her brief critical remarks on slavery and given her a particularly low mark (2016 208 n.58; see also Dominguez 128). For the statewide contest Zitkala-Sa rewrote her winning speech at Earlham called "Side by Side" and printed in the *Earlhamite*. It is the revised version that appears in the volume edited by Davidson and Norris, and I have been unable to find the original.

21. Although it is within a single sentence that she gets from the contest to her room, it was in fact a lengthy and, indeed, triumphal passage. After taking the train from Indianapolis where the statewide contest had been held to Richmond, she was met at the station by Earlham's oratory coach, who escorted her to the college in "a specially prepared horse-drawn carriage 'brilliant with college colors' and escorted by 'mounted attendants.' At Earlham, the student body greeted Simmons with cheers at the campus gates, which had been decorated in her honor" (Lewandowski 2016 26–27).

She would also be "praised at a special reception" and receive "a congratulatory telegram" from the college president (2016 27).

22. Dr. Leon Speroff, author of a lengthy biography of Carlos Montezuma, may well have had an early statement like this in mind—doubtless along with things she wrote later—when he claims that Zitkala-sa "was one of the first influential people to insist on a modern sense of tribalism" (207). I think he means by this what is currently called tribal nationalism or sovereignty. Such a view needs to take into account, however, the fact that Zitkala-Sa does not usually refer to her people or other Native peoples by their tribal names, but, rather as her "race"—common enough in her day—and she does not express her aims in national terms. Hazel Hertzberg, referring to her first posting, along with her husband, among the Utes, writes that "Mrs. Bonnin was to play an important role in Pan-Indian affairs over the next two decades," although at the time, "she was only at the beginning of her career as a Pan-Indian leader" (138). I believe one can cite sufficient material from Zitkala-Sa's later writings to justify Lewandowski's observation—he is speaking of her work on *The Sun Dance Opera* (1913)—that they are marked by her "Sioux-centrism" (2016 80), although unlike Lewandowski, I do not see her as a forerunner of Red Power.

23. Barbara Landis, Carlisle Indian School biographer for the Cumberland County Historical Society, had put together a website called "Zitkala-Sa (aka Gertrude Simmons) at Carlisle," http://home.epix.net/~landis/zitkalasa.html. I have it from Lewandowski's biography (2016 210 n.8), and I first accessed it on August 25, 2017. The website gathers mentions of "Miss Simmons" in the school's newsletter, the *Indian Helper*, from her arrival in 1897 until 1900, after she had toured with the Carlisle Band (discussed later). The pages are not numbered, but each issue can be identified by the volume, number, and date. I provide only the date of each cited item.

24. David Simmons married a woman named Victoria in 1891 (Ludlow 1893 342), and in June 1901 Zitkala-Sa wrote to Carlos Montezuma to say that it was Victoria's behavior that moved her to take that name and no longer use Gertie Simmons. She wrote: "I have a half brother whose name is Simmons. Once my own father scolded my brother; and my mother took such offense from it that eventually it resulted in a parting—so as I grew I was called by my brother's name—Simmons. I bore it a long time till my brother's wife—angry with me because I insisted on getting an education said I had deserted home and I might give up my brother's name 'Simmons'

too" (in Lewandowski 2016 55; I have not found it in the 2018 collection). Because her father had left her mother either before or immediately after her birth, Zitkala-Sa can only have heard from her mother of him scolding David Simmons or learned of that scolding causing a "parting" between her parents. The account she gives here of her naming, although cited by a great many critics as factual, is simply not true. She left White's for Earlham in 1895 and continued to be known as Gertrude Simmons all through her education and early in her employment at Carlisle.

She took her new name while employed at Carlisle, "around 1898" (Lewandowski 2016 12), a decision that had nothing whatever to do with Victoria Simmons. Lewandowski cites Dominguez as the source of his observation that the "first recorded use of the name Zitkala-Sa appears written on the back" (2016 34) of a portrait photograph taken of her by Gertrude Kasebier in 1898 (Dominguez 147), when she was posing for Kasebier and her assistant, as we will see.

25. Whoever the alcoholic white doctor may have been, it was Dr. Carlos Montezuma who had previously been physician at Carlisle, from 1893 until 1896, just before Zitkala-Sa arrived. And it would be Dr. Montezuma, not the "inebriate paleface," who would accompany the Carlisle band on a tour of the east with Zitkala-Sa as featured soloist in the spring of 1900, apparently when the two first met. Estelle Brown, herself a teacher at several Indian boarding schools, did note, however, that sometime after 1902—after Zitkala-Sa's time at Carlisle—the Indian Bureau "found it necessary to lower the requirements for [Indian] Service physicians to get doctors to enter," thereby bringing "a safe salary within reach of the failures and incompetents found in all professions" (Brown 204–5).

26. Brown, who taught at the far less prestigious Crow Creek and Leupp boarding schools, wrote that Carlisle's "prestige and fame were generally known. For an Indian to say that he was a graduate of Carlisle"—as Luther Standing Bear had said—"was, in the Indian Service, equivalent to a degree from Harvard" (207).

27. Ah-nen-la-de-ni describes this practice at his Pennsylvania school, modeled after Carlisle. See his story in part III of this volume.

28. Something approaching a "rhetoric of pedagogical resistance" and "a scathing indictment" of the boarding school's ethnocidal ideology and practice by a Dakota woman would not come for another hundred years in the powerful account of Lydia Whirlwind Soldier (see chapter 4, this volume).

29. Susan Dominguez wrote that the death of Wheelock's young child was the crucial factor in the Carlisle Band not traveling to Paris (155). Whether the child's death would have led to the trip being cancelled if sufficient funds had been collected is impossible to know. Many of the students who had played in Carlisle's bands continued to play once they were home, forming reservation bands, some of which continue to perform today. For Indian band musicians then and now, see the DVD *Sousa on the Rez: Marching to the Beat of a Different Drum.*

30. Note that a considerable number of Native people who meant, like Zitkala-Sa, to "spend [their] energies in a work for the Indian race" (104), chose to work at Carlisle. The Omaha anthropologist and novelist Francis LaFlesche was associated with the school as early as 1886. In 1889 he married Rosa Bourassa, a Chippewa, who had been a student at Carlisle, and she returned to the school to serve as outing clerk in 1913. (Pratt left the school in 1904; it closed in 1918.) Charles Eastman had been outing agent in 1900. The Winnebago artist Angel DeCora, who had illustrated LaFlesche's novel *The Middle Five* (and also Mariana Burgess's *Stiya*) and who would illustrate Zitkala-Sa's *American Indian Stories*, taught art at the school from 1906 to 1915. For a biography of DeCora, see Waggoner. Albert Exendine, of Cherokee and Delaware background, and a teammate and friend of Jim Thorpe on Pop Warner's championship Carlisle football teams, would go on to coach at Carlisle in 1910, before moving to Georgetown and then Occidental College. Gabe Parker, who had been superintendent of Armstrong Academy for Choctaw Boys, and in 1914 the superintendent of the Five Civilized Tribes, was employed at Carlisle in 1916. The better-known Parkers, Ely and Arthur, were on the school staff in 1909 and 1916, respectively. The Cherokee writer and activist John Milton Oskison worked at Carlisle in 1916. The Reverend Sherman Coolidge, an Arapaho, served at the school about 1914, when he was active as well in the Society of American Indians. Charles Dagenett, a Peoria, was employed by the school in 1911 as an "Indian Craftsman." A founder and leader of the Society of American Indians, Dagenett would become the highest-ranking Indian in the Bureau of Indian Affairs. Most of these people worked at Carlisle after Pratt had left, but the school's reputation had been solidly established during the years of Pratt's superintendency. Most of this information comes from the index to Linda Witmer's *The Indian Industrial School*, and it was kindly sent to me by Jim Gerencser of the Carlisle Digital Resources Center. He

wrote: "The list is probably not complete or comprehensive" (personal communication August 2, 2017), and, I would add, the dates it gives—and thus some of the dates I have given—are sometimes approximate. Good biographies are needed for many of these interesting Native people.

31. In response to a student follow-up questionnaire from the school, Howice Seonia in 1910 wrote that she was a "housewife" living in New Mexico. She is identified in the Carlisle records as married to R. Marmon, and a 1910 letter to her from Superintendent Moses Friedman addresses her as Mrs. Robert G. Marmon. Robert Gunn Marmon (1848–1933) was the great-grandfather of author Leslie Marmon Silko. He had come to Laguna after the Civil War and married a Pueblo woman, whose name I have not discovered. Sometime after his wife died he married her sister, Maria Analla, also formerly a Carlisle student, whom Silko refers to as Grandma A'mooh. But Robert Gunn Marmon was almost forty years older than Howice Seonia and I suspect this Robert G. Marmon was not her husband. If that is the case, I cannot identify the man Howice Seonia married.

32. As recorded in the *Indian Helper* for Friday, April 28, 1899: "A large and beautiful wreath of white roses from Miss Gertrude Simmons [Zitkala Sa] of Boston, to whom Thomas Marshall was engaged to be married" was received "to be placed on his grave." This is the first use in the *Helper* of her recently chosen new name.

33. On March 5, 1901, Zitkala-Sa wrote to Montezuma, "I will say just what I think. I fear no man.... I do respect the conscious spirit within me for whose being or going I cannot account" (Lewandowski 2018 25). On March 17 she wrote to him, "I am bound to live my own life! I think it better to be alone in my work" (Lewandowski 2018 26, underlining in original). On April 19, 1901, she wrote to Montezuma: "I have to be content to do what I feel without explaining or justifying myself. I must live because I must" (Lewandowski 2018 34). In these letters she is championing the Emersonian dictum quoted by Bevis—and approved by Carlisle—"Thou art unto thyself a law." But however moving these sentiments may be—and I find her doing some of her best and most impassioned writing in her letters to Montezuma—they do not derive from Dakota culture. Rather, they are evidence of the way Zitkala-Sa has been *changed* by her education. In contrast to Emerson, Bevis quotes Janine Windy Boy-Pease, "To be alone, that would be abject poverty to a Crow" (in Bevis 580).

34. Civil service exams had been required for employment in the Indian schools since 1891, but Zitkala-Sa does not seem to have taken

one—although she was indeed a classroom teacher. The *Indian Helper* for Friday, February 4, 1898, notes someone at Door # 6 "just as Miss Simmons' pupils were passing out to Assembly Hall to take a lesson in singing. When asked to sum up the difficulties of her room in one word, she said, 'Language.'" It would have been fascinating had Miss Simmons chosen to elaborate on that one-word response for her readers. Anne Ruggles Gere writes that "the full extent of [Zitkala'Sa's] teaching remains undiscussed" (2005 62). This is hardly a surprise considering that she herself said absolutely nothing about her experience as an "Indian teacher."

35. Zitkala-Sa had met the prominent photographer Gertrude Kasebier probably in the spring of 1898, and stayed with her in New York during the summer of that year, posing for Kasebier and her assistant, Joseph Keiley, in some version of traditional costume and also as a proper Victorian lady with violin and book. See Kasebier for seven photographic portraits of Zitkala-Sa, some of which also appear in Lewandowski (2016 and 2018). They are very striking.

It was Kasebier, Lewandowski writes, who encouraged Zitkala-Sa "to explore the limits of her talent" (2016 34), by engaging in further study of the violin. She did study violin in Boston, as already noted, although Susan Dominguez found "no record of her ever having been enrolled in the New England Conservatory of music" (151–52), nor any record for her at the Boston Conservatory of Music (177 n.46). Barbara Michaels stated that Zitkala-Sa had "studied tuition-free with Eugene Gruenberg of the New England Conservatory," but also that "Conservatory records are very incomplete and contain no reference to Simmons" (169 n.42), apparently corroborating Dominguez. More recently, however, Kiara Vigil cites a "'Class Card' for Gertrude E. [?] Simmons, New England Conservatory Archives, Boston, MA" (215 n.5). I have scans of Pratt's letters from Lewandowski, to whom I am grateful.

36. Through Kasebier, Zitkala-Sa met Joseph Holland Day, a prominent photographer in Boston. Day introduced her to Bliss Perry, who had recently been made editor of the *Atlantic Monthly*, and he encouraged her to write for the periodical (Lewandowski 2016 37). The *Atlantic* published such notable writers as Henry James, Edith Wharton, William Dean Howells, and, among western writers, Mary Austin and Owen Wister; Jack London had a story in the January 1900 number in which Zitkala-Sa's "Impressions of an Indian Childhood" appeared. But that issue also contained chapter 31 of Mary Johnston's *To Have and to Hold: A Tale of Providence in Colonial*

Jamestown, a gory and grossly savagist novel. Lewandowski provides an excellent brief account of its racist sentiments (2016 213–14 n.66), and also observes that the novel was so popular that it "was credited with expanding the *Atlantic Monthly*'s readership almost twofold" (214 n.66). Another section of Johnston's novel appeared along with "The School Days of an Indian Girl" in the February 1900 *Atlantic Monthly.* That issue also contained poems by John Vance Cheney, who regularly appeared in other prestigious periodicals of the time, and whose collected works fill eight volumes. I have found him as unreadable today as Mary Johnston (but for different reasons). My point in remarking this is not to diminish the importance of Zitkala-Sa's appearance in the *Atlantic Monthly.* The editor believed her work would interest the journal's readership; it did, and it continues to interest readers today. But along with Henry James and Edith Wharton, the magazine also published Mary Johnston and John Vance Cheney, something I mention—once more—to contextualize Zitkala-Sa's work, not to denigrate it.

37. She also alerts white visitors to the fact that "They were paying a liberal fee to the government employees in whose able hands lay the small forest of Indian timber" (113). This is an insult to both her white and Native colleagues at Carlisle specifically and to the teaching corps in the Indian Service's schools generally. Whether "able" or not at all "able"—and at Carlisle, as I have said, Pratt had many applicants for positions to choose from—teachers and staff at the schools did not receive anything remotely like "a liberal fee" for their services, something Zitkala-Sa knew very well. Her own annual salary as assistant teacher is listed in the 1898 Report of the Commissioner of Indian Affairs as $540 per annum. This is equivalent to something like $5,144 in 2019 purchasing power. As superintendent, Pratt was paid $1,000 per year, which would be about $28,654 today, hardly a princely sum. Further, Marianna Burgess as teacher and in charge of printing, along with her companion Anne Ely, also a teacher and in charge of the outing program, each earned $1,000, the same salary as Pratt, and again very far from "a liberal fee." To get a better sense of the situation of these "government employees," see Carter. Once more I recommend Estelle Aubrey Brown's sharp, lively, and detailed account of being a teacher in the Indian boarding schools. Brown, only a year younger than Zitkala-Sa but with considerably more experience, taught at the poorly provisioned Crow Creek School in South Dakota for "six hundred dollars per annum" (Brown 20).

38. Katanski quotes the Santee School's paper, the *Red Man and Helper* for June 1900, which reported that Zitkala-Sa "is utterly unthankful for all

that has been done for her by the pale faces, which in her case is considerable" (124). She thinks this was probably not written by Pratt, but "perhaps encompass[ed] Pratt's feelings for [Zitkala-Sa]" (124). Fully aware of the pitfalls of appearing to sympathize with Pratt in this regard, I can nonetheless understand why he and the author of the piece might well have thought her "unthankful" to at least some "pale faces."

She could not be "unthankful" to the paleface Unthanks—pun unavoidable—who made it possible for her to learn to play the piano and violin and to attend Earlham. It was through her association with Carlisle that she met Gertrude Kasebier, and the school provided her with many opportunities to come to public attention. It is also the case that Zitkala-Sa "headed for Boston to study violin, supported by a grant *from the Commissioner of Indian Affairs*" (Lewandowski 2016 34–35, my emphasis), a surprising source of paleface support for this endeavor! A fuller account of the responses to Zitkala-Sa's essays and one more sympathetic to her than mine can be found in Katanski (123–29).

39. Pratt's letter to Chamberlin contains the nasty observation that if not for her schooling, Zitkala-Sa might have been a "poor squaw ... probably married to some young, no-account Indian" (in Lewandowski 2016 46). He also writes, however: "It has been on the mind of Dr. Chas. A. Eastman, who is an employe here, to write something to counteract it"—her account of the school, that is. Pratt makes clear to Chamberlin, "I am treating her with the utmost kindness," something his letters show to be true—although his "kindness" had a good deal of self-interest behind it.

40. Lewandowski writes that "despite their subversive content, the writings [the three *Atlantic Monthly* essays] won critical acclaim.... Zitkala-Sa became the toast of the Boston literati" (2016 43). As should be clear, I believe the essays won "critical acclaim" precisely because they weren't "subversive" at all. Zitkala-Sa asks her elite audience to feel for the sensitive Indian child at boarding school and not be fooled by some of the school's showcasing. These were not difficult tasks for turn-of-the-twentieth-century " "literati."

41. For any readers whose Longfellow may be rusty, "The Famine," section 20 of *Hiawatha*, runs to 180 lines and builds to the death of Minnehaha, the wife of Hiawatha, from starvation—Zitkala-Sa had led the Minnehaha Glee Club at Carlisle. Many lines are devoted to Hiawatha's unsuccessful hunt for game in a bitter winter, followed by his return to find his beloved dead. Although the historical and legendary Hiawatha was Iroquois,

Longfellow made him Ojibwe. He made Minnehaha "Dacotah" despite the fact that Dakotas and Ojibwes were traditional enemies.

In a letter to John Wanamaker on March 20, 1900—seeking financial support for the Carlisle band—Pratt wrote, "Saturday afternoon the President and Mrs. McKinley and ladies of the cabinet listened to them [the band] and Zitkala Sa in the White House for more than an hour and seemed to be highly entertained." The *Indian Helper* also recorded her triumphs.

42. Carlos Montezuma (1866–1923), a Yavapai from Arizona, was captured in a raid by Akimel O'odham (Pimas) about 1871. His captors sold him for thirty dollars to Carlo Gentile, an Italian photographer, artist, and gold prospector, and it was Gentile who gave the child the name Carlos Montezuma. After school in Illinois and, in the late 1870s, in Brooklyn and Yonkers, New York, Montezuma enrolled at the University of Illinois, and then at the Chicago Medical College, from which he received his MD in 1889. He was one of the founders of the Society of American Indians in 1911 and also published his own Indian rights paper called *Wassaja*, his Indian name as a child. He was for many years deeply involved in Yavapai struggles for land and water rights on the Fort McDowell Reservation, where he was buried. For fuller accounts see Iverson (1982) and Speroff (2004–5).

43. Ruth Spack has found a letter from him to Zitkala-Sa, "a copy of which he kept in his collection," dated July 29, 1902, after Montezuma had learned of her marriage to Raymond Bonnin in May of that year. Spack calls the letter "chillingly formal" (2001 183). Montezuma addresses Zitkala-Sa as "Madam" and asks her to pay for a sixty-year-old ring he had given her, which she had lost. I think its formality represents an effort to control an anguish sufficiently great to garble the doctor's syntax and diction.

44. The letters have been examined by many scholars, among them Susan Dominguez, Amelia Katanski, Kiara Vigil, and Tadeusz Lewandowski, who has recently published them with full annotation (2018). In them Ruth Spack finds that Zitkala-Sa "strengthens her philosophical and political stance" on such issues as "marriage, patriarchy, writing, culture, education, and the power structure of the United States" (2001 173). I don't see Zitkala-Sa *strengthening* her stances in the letters but, rather, attempting to articulate them for the very first time. There simply is no "stance" on these issues in Zitkala-Sa's early work.

In the first of her letters to Montezuma, dated February 9, 1901, just prior to their Chicago meeting, she writes that she is "expecting to teach next year in the government school in Yankton Agency S-D" (Lewandowski

2018 19). Lewandowski concludes from this that "Zitkala-Sa had already planned to return to Yankton to make her life" (2016 215 n.18), a plan that I believe was still tentative, in that she had been extremely agitated by her mother on her last visits to Yankton. I suggest that it was in countering Montezuma's fierce determination *not* to serve in the Indian Service on the reservations that she would work out her own equally fierce determination to try to do exactly that.

45. It is also while she is writing to Montezuma that she publishes what I consider her strongest literary work, "The Soft-Hearted Sioux," in *Harper's Monthly* for October 1901. Her "The Indian Dance: A Protest against Its Abolition" would appear only a few months later, in January 1902, in the *Boston Evening Transcript*, and in it Zitkala-Sa weighed in on what would continue to be an important issue for at least two decades more. She treats the question of Indian dance in a prose significantly stronger than that of the autobiographical essays of 1900.

46. Zitkala-Sa supported the war effort; Montezuma, however, raised some serious questions about it. Zitkala-Sa died in 1938 and Raymond Bonnin in 1942. I don't know when the gravestone at Arlington was set and inscribed. It reads:

Raymond T. Bonnin
United States Army

The dates of his birth and his death are not given. Below, in slightly larger letters:

HIS WIFE
Gertrude Simmons Bonnin
"Zitkala-Sa" of the Sioux Indians
1876–1938.

47. Mooney had had a good deal of experience with the peyote use of the Kiowas, Plains Apaches, and Southern Arapahos, and felt strongly—as did Carlos Montezuma——that Native people were entitled to determine their own religious practices. But Zitkala-Sa, Pratt, and the Eastmans worked successfully to oppose the legalization of peyote for religious purposes and also to discredit Mooney more broadly. Zitkala-Sa's opposition to peyote may have involved concerns that it might be abused in a manner similar to the increasing abuse of alcohol by some Native people. I thank Professor Scott Lyons for this latter observation (personal communication October 2, 2017).

4. WALTER LITTLEMOON'S *They Called Me Uncivilized*, TIM GIAGO'S *The Children Left Behind*, LYDIA WHIRLWIND SOLDIER'S "MEMORIES," AND MARY CROW DOG'S *Lakota Woman*

1. Erdoes had earlier collaborated with John Fire Lame Deer on his autobiography, *Lame Deer, Seeker of Visions* (1972), and he would again collaborate with Crow Dog—this time using the name Mary Brave Bird—on another autobiography, *Ohitika Woman* (1993). He was also involved in the production of Dennis Banks's autobiography published in 2004.

2. A copy of the "Contract for St. Francis Mission School, Rosebud Reservation, South Dakota," between the Bureau of Catholic Indian Missions and the commissioner of Indian Affairs for the 1906 school year is given in full as appendix B to Prucha, 209–13.

3. Carole Barrett and Marcia Wolter Britton quote Phyllis Young, one of the Lakota former boarding-school students they recorded, for the title of their essay, "'You didn't dare try to be Indian.'" But Barrett and Britton do not say when Young attended school.

4. Her 1999 volume of verse, *Memory Songs*, for the most part does not treat her school experiences, although the poem "Dreams from the Storage Closet" derives in part from punishments meted out at SFMS.

5. A film about him called *The Thick Dark Fog* (2011) was directed by Randy Vasquez and is available as a DVD.

6. Littlemoon and Jane Ridgway had come upon Dr. Judith Herman's book *Trauma and Recovery* first published in 1992. They contacted her, and were referred by her to Shorin. Herman had written, "Naming the syndrome of complex post-traumatic stress disorder"—a name she had introduced into the professional literature—"represents an essential step toward granting those who have endured prolonged exploitation a measure of the recognition they deserve" (22). She added, "The traumatized person is often relieved simply to learn the true [sic] name of her condition" (158). This was very much the case with Walter Littlemoon. Giago, Whirlwind Soldier, and Crow Dog, so far as their autobiographies reveal, did not seek professional treatment and, like a number of trauma survivors, achieved their healing by other means.

7. Walter Littlemoon was a member of the community occupied by the AIM activists, and his recollection of the events that transpired is bitterly critical of them. See his autobiography (69–79).

8. Section 2 of Article 1 of the SFMS contract for 1906 stipulated "that no pupil is to be enrolled under this contract who is under six" (in Prucha 210). But Lydia Whirlwind Soldier was not the only under-aged child at an Indian boarding school.

9. The brutal and abusive practices of the St. Francis and Holy Rosary Mission schools were replicated at other Catholic Indian boarding schools, but some Native students report much better treatment at the Catholic schools they attended. For example, Madonna Swan, a Lakota woman born in 1928, attended Immaculate Conception School in Stephan, South Dakota, from1935 until 1944, when she had to leave because of "chanhu sica [bad lungs]" (Swan 64), tuberculosis, fairly common at the schools. Her brief remarks about the sisters and the "priest who was superintendent" (51) record only their concern and kindness. Mark St. Pierre, with whom Swan worked to produce her autobiography, writes that "although loneliness was always a problem, Madonna liked the school and most of the Sisters who worked there" (187 n.37). Sister Carol Berg (1989) interviewed eight women who had attended Saint Benedict's Boarding School on the White Earth Chippewa reservation in Minnesota at various times between 1909 and 1945, and they all report positive memories of their time there. Their responses may or may not have been affected by the fact that the interviewer was a nun. Delphine Red Shirt, who attended Holy Rosary Mission School in the late 1960s, has only good things to say about it, as later noted.

10. Littlemoon, Giago, and Crow Dog did not have to undergo the *topos* of renaming that so many earlier Native students experienced. But Lydia Whirlwind Soldier writes that at school, she "had even lost [her] name. The Whirlwind was taken out of [her] name, so [she] became known as Lydia W. Soldier" (Whirlwind Soldier 207). As Ella Deloria has observed: "In Dakota, you do not say, if you are idiomatically correct, 'What is your name?' but, 'In what manner do they say of you?' That means, 'According to what deed are you known?' The deed of an ancestor was memorialized in a phrase applied to a descendant of his" (154). Whirlwind Soldier's grandfather had said to her, "'Remember who you are; remember where you got your name. Respect your name; be good and make us proud.... Whirlwind Soldier is your name'" (207). Lydia Whirlwind Soldier could not do that as Lydia W. Soldier.

11. DDT had come into use in 1942, having been developed to kill head and body lice that spread typhus among American troops during the Second World War. By 1947, when Littlemoon entered OCHS, it had made its way to most of the Indian boarding schools.

12. The next morning Littlemoon finds the "same two women ... still carrying their sticks, yelling out in harsh voices words [he] couldn't understand." They "grabbed different boys and beat them with their sticks. Those boys had wet their beds" (40). The boys "hadn't been shown the room to pee in, with the strange, shiny white things on the wall," but the "women didn't care. They beat and beat and beat" (40). Even when the children knew where the facilities were, however, bedwetting at the schools was not an unusual occurrence. Tim Giago devotes a poem in *Children Left Behind* to "The Bed Wetters" who sleep "In a far corner of the dorm/Segregated from the rest of us/In their own private hell" (28). Both Adam Fortunate Eagle and Dennis Banks write of "a place called the 'stink dorm'" at the Pipestone school: "Any boy who wet his bed was put in there for a week" (Banks 28).

13. At the Fort Defiance boarding school, Berenice Levchuk speaks of the students' hands bleeding from regular use of lye soap: "we washed dishes with powdered lye soap; we washed face and hands, showered, and shampooed with bar lye soap." She writes that "Furthermore, our unsympathetic matron ... refused to give us any Vaseline for our chapped hands and faces" (183).

14. James Carroll recorded that, "One of the more unusual chores performed by the Indian girls and the sisters at Saint Francis and Holy Rosary was the annual ritual of renewing the mattresses at the schools. Each year the girls and the sisters would use the husks from the corn crop to make new mattresses for the entire institution" (143). I suspect this practice was no longer in effect when Mary Crow Dog was at Saint Francis.

15. A word about traditional Lakota distinctions between excellence and competition may be in order here. Charles Eastman, for example, was proud of gaining Ohiyesa, the Winner, as his name, and traditional Lakota people certainly wished to excel. But it was not proper to put oneself forward at the expense of others. Gordon MacGregor writes: "The ideal of Dakota life in the old days was cooperation,"—as Lydia Whirlwind Soldier had learned from her grandmother—"and, although competition was permitted adults in limited fields of activity"—such as "winning war honors, giving away property, and adhering to womanly virtues" (138 n.1)—"it was not taught the young child.... Severe criticism was exerted on the child who sought to 'shine' in unapproved ways before he was old enough" (135).

16. Dr. Chu, with reference to Dr. Herman, refers to the situation of children "being held in a state of captivity, under the control of a perpetrator of abuse, and unable to escape," as similar to that of children in "concentration

camps, prisoner of war camps, and prisons," or wherever there is "severe and chronic childhood abuse" (35).

In the afterword to the 2015 edition of her book, Herman cites Jennifer Freyd's term "institutional betrayal" (254) to name an aspect of what boarding-school students experienced. This was doubly so for students at the Catholic schools, who found themselves betrayed not only by the institution of the school but the institution of the Church as well.

17. Saint Francis, in 1886, and Holy Rosary, in 1888, were both established by German Jesuits and staffed by Franciscan sisters, mostly German; the "1900 census reported most of the sisters at the Indian boarding schools to be foreign-born" (Carroll 63). A gradual conversion to American control, however, "had taken place by 1920" (Carroll 101). Tim Giago observed that "many of the nuns, priests and brothers came to America from Germany and other European countries and spoke very poor English themselves" (141), adding bitterly that these people would administer "a slap across the face or worse" to Indian children who "spoke in their own Lakota tongue" because they, like many of the teachers, "could not speak English" very well (141). By the 1960s, when Mary Crow Dog attended school, it is unlikely that "many of the nuns were German immigrants" (Crow Dog 35). She adds that "for the sake of objectivity [fairness?]," she should "mention that two of the German fathers were great linguists and the only Lakota-English dictionaries and grammars which are worth anything were put together by them" (35).

Her reference is to Father Eugen or Eugene Buechel (1874–1954) and the much younger Paul Manhart (1927–2008). Born in Omaha, Manhart was not a "German father," nor was he a "great linguist." Buechel, who was born in Germany and also was a "great linguist," published *A Grammar of Lakota* in 1939, when Manhart was twelve. He had been superintendent of both Saint Francis Mission School and Holy Rosary, and worked with Black Elk, who had been a Catholic catechist. In 1955, shortly after Buechel's death, Father John Bryde—(Tim Giago mentions him)—principal at HRMS, and himself a student of Lakota language, asked Manhart to work with materials Buechel had left, and the first edition of the Buechel-Manhart dictionary appeared in 1970.

18. Delphine Red Shirt, an Oglala-Brulé poet, autobiographer, and professor of Lakota language, born in 1957, first attended public school in Gordon, Nebraska, and found it pleasant enough except for the fact that she was the only Native student there. She then went to government boarding school from the fourth to sixth grade, and she experienced it as "massive,

sterile, and empty in an inexplicable way" (98), although she was relieved not to be "the only 'Indian' in the classroom" (99) . She then went to Holy Rosary Mission School, the name of which had changed to Red Cloud Indian School in 1969. She writes that the "nuns and teachers at the Catholic school" taught "with heart and feeling for the children in it" (98). If so, the school had changed very considerably from the time Tim Giago was there.

19. Andrea Smith, in a chapter called "Boarding School Abuses and the Case for Reparations," claims that the boarding schools went so far as to "violate … a number of human rights legal standards" (42), and she makes the case for government reparations to boarding-school students and their descendants.

20. MacGregor wrote of this practice at OCHS that "in some serious cases, the boys send the offender down the 'belt line,' which is unofficially sanctioned" (145). In Walter Littlemoon's time at OCHS, the "gauntlet" or "belt line" seems to have been officially sanctioned, initiated by the authorities not "the boys." Barrett and Britton quote Ben Benson, who says that at his North Dakota school about this time there were "really severe—beatings … they called it the 'belt line.' … You'd really get hit" (19). Dennis Banks attended the Pipestone Indian Industrial School in western Minnesota roughly in this period, and he describes the "school's punishment for running away" as "the 'hot line.'" The returned runaway "had to run between two rows of other kids, who held sticks and switches" (27).

21. Something similar is among the recollections of Alvina Alberts, who is quoted by Barrett and Britton as saying she "had broken bones in her hands. I didn't know until I went to the hospital after I was fifty some years old" (19). Perhaps she, too, had learned that this was "not something that one cried over" (Whirlwind Soldier 170) at school.

22. Whirlwind Soldier's experience is a painfully specific illustration of Dr. James Chu's observation that survivors of childhood trauma "developed fundamental assumptions about the world as malevolent and about themselves as defective and powerless" (xiii), assumptions that must be overcome for healing to take place.

23. In an obituary for Mary Crow Dog by David P. Ball that appeared in Tim Giago's newspaper, *Indian Country Today*, on March 14, 2013, Ball quotes a photographer named Owen Luck, who reported that Crow Dog had told him "what it was like to be raped in the mission school—the nuns had participated in this." This asserts that Crow Dog was raped at SFMS, either by one or more of the nuns or by someone else with the complicity of the

nuns, and it has been cited by others. But it is not what Crow Dog actually wrote about being raped. In *Lakota Woman* she said, "I was forcefully raped when I was fourteen or fifteen. A good-looking young man said, 'Come over here, kid, let me buy you a soda.'... He was about twice my weight and a foot taller than I am. He just threw me on the ground and pinned me down. I do not want to remember the details" (67). Terrible as this is, it has nothing to do with the mission school.

24. We know the name of at least one predatory priest at SFMS during the time Mary Crow Dog was a student there, a man who specialized in the abuse of younger girls. In a letter dated July 23, 1968, Fr. Richard T. Jones, S.J. wrote: "Chappy had his problems—drinking to excess, fooling around with little girls—he had them down the basement of our building in the dark where we found a pair of panties torn ... the girl situation is known in the sense that he is around little girls very much, but Larry Coons ... [he appears to be employed by the school] has asked that Brother Chappy not be around his two little ones. So ... another challenge for us." Treating this as though it were merely a case of someone leaving dirty socks around, Jones writes that he "had a nice talk with him on these points and he took it all nicely." Jones's letters indicate that by 1970 Brother Francis Chapman did, in fact, seem to be a changed man, although by 1973 he had resumed familiar patterns of drunkenness and abuse.

Jones's letters were entered into evidence in cases brought against St. Francis Mission by Ralph Eagleman, Ida Marshall, Wendell Big Crow, Regina One Star, and two others. After many trials and many appeals, charges against Chapman were dismissed in 2014 (he had died in 1990). In this case, as in others brought against sexual abusers at the Catholic boarding schools and against the Catholic dioceses themselves, charges were often dismissed because they were brought after the statute of limitations had expired. In that South Dakota only passed a statute of limitations for these particular crimes in 2010, right around the time that several of the cases were filed, counsel for the plaintiffs appealed numerous times with varying results. Charges against the dioceses were also sometimes dismissed because there was no law at the time the alleged acts took place requiring that they be reported to the relevant authorities. These dismissals were often appealed as well. The first Child Abuse Prevention and Treatment Act, making reporting of any abuse allegations mandatory, was passed only in 1974 (Chu 10). For Jones's letters see mediad.publicbroadcasting.net/p/sdpb/files/201304/EX%20A.pdf.

25. Tomson Highway's novel *The Kiss of the Fur Queen* (1998) provides the fullest, most graphically detailed account of sexual abuse at a Catholic residential school for Indians. This is a work of fiction, but it is substantially based upon the experiences of Highway and his brother at the Guy Hill Residential School in Manitoba.

26. Specific details of what was allegedly done to these children are given in the complaints brought against the staff of each of the Catholic boarding schools and the various Catholic dioceses. In the case of multiple Native plaintiffs identified only by their initials brought against the Catholic Diocese of Sioux Falls, Tekakwitha Indian Mission of Sisseton, South Dakota, and a great many named individuals (e.g., Brother Henry Susman, Sister Theresa, Father John Pohlen, and Sister Gabrini, among others), the alleged abuses are described in page after page of the complaint. Although these things did not take place at SFMS, HRMS (or, for that matter, at OCHS), it is extremely likely that similar things happened at those institutions as well. The complaint against Tekakwitha Mission is fifty-eight pages long, comprising 267 sections. I will cite only a few of the allegations.

Plaintiff F.W. alleges that when he was between the ages of four and eight, about 1946–50, he was sexually abused by Father Edward Hess and Sister Gabrini. Hess "sexually abused Plaintiff by coming to Plaintiff's bed in the dormitory at night, sitting on Plaintiff's bed and groping and fondling Plaintiff's penis. FATHER HESS would also give Plaintiff wine at the church after service and would grope and fondle Plaintiff's penis in the church" (section 184, p. 31). During the same time period, Sister Gabrini "who was in charge of bathing Plaintiff, would caress, touch and fondle Plaintiff's penis, masturbating Plaintiff until Plaintiff got an erection" (section 184, p. 31).

Plaintiff A.H., who was between the ages of seven and nine in the years 1957–59, alleges that Father John Pohlen "would take Plaintiff to a private office and he would remove Plaintiff's underwear and touch and fondle Plaintiff's vagina. FATHER POHLEN also penetrated Plaintiff's vagina with his fingers on multiple occasions. Plaintiff was also sexually abused by other priests whose name she does not recall. These priests fondled Plaintiff and touched and groped Plaintiff between her legs" (section 191, pp. 32–33). The case was brought in July 2010 and dismissed in November 2017 on the grounds of having been brought too late, as specified by the belatedly passed statute of limitations. I thank Karl Thoennes III, administrator, Second Judicial Circuit, State of South Dakota, for several personal communications (November 20, 2017) informing me of this case's resolution. It is possible that further litigation has ensued. The case can be found at www.bishop-accountability.org/news2010/07_08/100814abbott.pdf.

27. Like Whirlwind Soldier and Tim Giago, I had also thought that there was indeed something like a cycle of abuse. Dr. Herman states, however, that "the great majority of survivors neither abuse nor neglect their children" (114), although Dr. Chu's observation soon to follow about the learning of parental skills tends more nearly to corroborate what Whirlwind Soldier, Giago, and I had surmised.

28. Glen Three Stars was almost surely related to Clarence Three Stars, the Carlisle student who worked with Luther Standing Bear at the John Wanamaker store in Philadelphia in the summer of 1884. He was a star athlete at OCHS when Walter Littlemoon was in his first years at the school, so Littlemoon may or may not have been aware of him.

29. Gordon MacGregor's study of conditions at schools in the region in 1943 found that unlike Lydia Whirlwind Soldier's father, many Lakota families thought that it was "quite acceptable to escape personal conflict by running away, and no stigma is attached to such action. Hence it is to be expected that children who do not adjust easily to school will run away. Moreover, the child is not punished when he runs home" (137).

30. Recalling the names as necessary for healing appears in the work of many Native writers. There is, to be sure, N. Scott Momaday's autobiography called *The Names*, but nearest to what Giago and Littlemoon have done, I think, is the end of the fourth and the fifth and last stanza of Kimberly Blaeser's poem "Recite the Names of All the Suicided Indians":

> Go deaf if you must he said
> but keep singing your name
> your life
> keep singing
> your name
> your life.
> *Nagamon.*
> Sing.
> v
> So let me
> chant
> you

each one
the names
of all
the suicided
Indians

5. JOHN ROGERS'S *Red World and White*

1. Rogers writes the name Way Quah Gishig, but it is the more usual practice today to connect the syllables, Wayquahgishig, as I do when referring to him as the protagonist of the narrative. Linguists, however, write the name, Wekwaa-gizhig, the last part, *-gizhig*, meaning day or sky, a common ending for Anishinaabe men's names. The first part, *wekwaa*, means "end of a place, horizon," and "dawn of day" is a likely enough translation. It is important to note, however, that the true "meaning of a name comes in the vision of the namegiver and does not come from the linguistic elements in its expression." For all of this information I am grateful to Professor John D. Nichols (personal communication May 22, 2018).

2. Rogers spoke of himself as Chippewa. Some contemporary Chippewa people prefer Ojibwe, while others use their own Algonquian name, Anishinaabe, as I have just done. For the most part, however, I use Chippewa, as Rogers did.

3. Melissa Meyer writes that his widow "described Rogers as a self-employed interior decorator who enjoyed painting and playing golf" (iv).

4. The White Earth reservation, in northwestern Minnesota, the largest in the state, is named for the white clay in the soil. It was established in 1868, following the signing of a treaty by ten Anishinaabe chiefs and President Andrew Johnson a year earlier. In 1934 White Earth ratified the Indian Reorganization Act, joining with five other Ojibwe bands to become the "Minnesota Chippewa Tribe." Gerald Vizenor's chapter "History of White Earth," reprints important documents relevant to the early days of the reservation.

5. Wade Popp of the National Archives and Records Administration's Kansas City office found in volume 1 of the school's Enrollment Register a John Rogers, Chippewa, listed as having been enrolled at the school from 1899 to 1905, for six years, although not the same six years that Rogers specifies (personal communication April 24, 2018).

6. Meyer notes that at about this time Anishinaabe families began to gather ginseng and snakeroot not only for their own use but to sell to whites for pharmacological purposes (xii).

7. Forests around Cass Lake, Minnesota, had been logged commercially as early as 1898, and as Melissa Meyer writes, Rogers's "story barely alludes to the deforestation of northern Minnesota's red and white pine forests" in these years. The concern for the trees expressed here by the young man is indeed his only allusion to what Meyer calls the "environmental devastation" (xiv) of the forests, leading finally to the end of the timber industry in the region by the mid-1920s (Tanner 97).

8. Nanabush or Nanabozho (there are other spellings as well) is the trickster figure and culture hero of the Anishinaabe, with great powers, mischievous and otherwise (e.g., he is said to be the founder of the important Midewiwin or Medicine Lodge ceremony, discussed later). He can appear in many forms but is often represented as a rabbit.

9. All three printings of Rogers's book spell his name on the first page as Way quah gishig and here, late in the book, as Way quah gisgig. In that his father's name is given as Pin de gay gisgig, this later spelling of Rogers's name might suggest to readers that he bears his father's surname. But Anishinaabe naming practices, similar to the naming practices of other Native peoples, do not assign any part of the father's name to his children. After a child is born Anishinaabe parents call upon a medicine person, who chooses the appropriate name. As noted, *gishig, gisgig* (this may be a typo, although either *h* or *g* might be used), or *giizhig*, meaning "day" or "sky," is a common element of men's names; that father and son both have it in their names is probably a coincidence. The first part of Biindige-gizhig's name, *biindige*, I have learned from Professor Nichols, is a verb form, "he/she enters," used as a prefix (personal communication May 22, 2018). Rogers gives no translation for his father's name.

10. Rogers's father says of the lake they cross to get to his home "This is Loss Lake" (137). I have been unable to find a Loss Lake in Minnesota, and I suspect that Rogers has either misremembered the name of the lake or else this should read Lost Lake, which does exist. Dick Lyons, who grew up in the Cass Lake area in the 1940s and 1950s, remembers *two* Lost Lakes but no Loss Lake, and his son, Professor Scott Lyons, knows of a third Lost Lake (personal communication from Scott Lyons, April 10, 2018). There are perhaps others.

11. "It's a Long Way Back to Mother's Knee," was composed by Halsey Mohr in 1907, the earliest Rogers could have heard it. This would make him about seventeen when he joins his father.

12. This is a Mide scroll, and there is a substantial literature on Mide scrolls, with several of the studies providing illustrations of them. General accounts are given by the Ojibwe writers William Warren (1885) and Basil Johnston (2014 and 1982), and there are careful accounts as well as in the work of Walter Hoffman (1891) and Michael Angel (2002) referenced below. See also the studies by Fred Blessing (1963 and 1977), Selwyn Dewdney (1975) and Richard Nelson (1983). Following passage of the Native American Graves Protection and Repatriation Act (NAGPRA) in 1990, the Smithsonian Institution along with some other institutions holding Mide scrolls returned them to petitioning Native communities.

13. The Battle of Bear Island took place between Ojibwes and the American Army on the Leech Lake reservation in the fall of 1898. A fine poetic account of the "war" at Bear Island is Gerald Vizenor's *Bear Island: The War at Sugar Point*.

14. The Midewiwin is an important ceremonial, performance of which long preceded the arrival of the Europeans who produced the earliest written accounts of it. These date from a letter by the Frenchman Antoine Denis Raudot in 1710 and later a description by the French geographer Joseph Nicollet from the 1830s. Henry Schoolcraft (1992[1839]) wrote of it using Nicollet's work (unattributed; it was not published until the 1970s), and also information provided by his mixed-blood Chippewa brother-in-law, George Johnston. As noted, the Ojibwe historian William Warren published on the Midewiwin in 1885; and Walter Hoffman gave a detailed account in his 1885–86 Annual Report to the Smithsonian Institution (1891). More recent accounts are those of Harold Hickerson (1974) and Ruth Landes (1968, from work done in the 1930s). The Canadian Ojibwa author Basil Johnston has also published on the Midewiwin, as noted earlier. The latest and best account I know is that of Michael Angel (2002) who wrote, "There can be little doubt that the Midewiwin is deeply rooted in Ojibwa culture," and "forms an integral part of their world view.... It did not arise as some form of crisis or revitalization cult in response to Euro-American contact" (183). As for Christian elements in the ceremony, Angel writes, "any incorporation that may have occurred was carried out in terms of the Ojibwa world view, not the Christian Euro-American one" (184).

6. GEORGE MORRISON'S *Turning the Feather Around*

1. His editor, Margot Galt, writes that she began "audio taping for this book" (10) in 1994, and "halfway through the taping, George and Hazel"—Morrison's former wife, the artist, Hazel Belvo, who remained a close friend—"decided that her voice should enter in dialogue with his to cover the years they lived together" (11); thus the second section of the book ascribes passages either to Morrison or to Belvo. Galt states that in the book, "George's first telling stands, unless we corrected it together" (11).

2. Valuable, however, is "George Morrison," a detailed account of Morrison and his work by Gerald Vizenor, who was for many years a friend.

3. Chippewa City is now abandoned. Already in decline when Morrison was born, it was largely obliterated by the construction of U.S. Highway 61, which began in 1926. Robert Zimmerman, *aka* Bob Dylan, born in Duluth and raised in Hibbing, Minnesota, referenced it in his sixth album, *Highway 61 Revisited* (1965).

4. This was the Civilian Conservation Corps for unmarried, unemployed young men under Roosevelt's New Deal.

7. PETER RAZOR'S *While the Locust Slept*

1. The Fond du Lac Band of Lake Superior Chippewa is one of the six nations that make up the Minnesota Chippewa Tribe.

2. A condensed version of Razor's life story appears in the song "Where the North Wind Blows," track number 6 of Curtis and Loretta's CD, "When There's Good to Be Done."

3. A number of praising quotations and several blurbs appear before the front matter, and the book was recognized in brief notices by *Publishers Weekly* and *Kirkus Reviews*. But although it won the Minnesota Book Award for 2002, I have not found any reviews.

4. His reference is actually to the cicada, although cicadas are often called locusts.

5. Harvey Ronglien, only a year older than Peter Razor, came to the Owatonna school in 1932 at the age of five and remained there until the school closed in 1945. A condensed version of Ronglien's story appears on

Curtis and Loretta's CD, "When There's Good to be Done," in the song "Case 9164." Ronglien has also written a "Memoir" of his time at Owatonna, called *A Boy from C-11: Case #9164*, published in 2006, five years after Razor's book. He mentions *While the Locust Slept*, although he does not seem to have known Razor himself—despite the fact that both of them were at the school together for more than a decade. I'll reference Ronglien's account on occasion to contextualize some of what Razor reports.

6. Ronglien notes that "adoption rates were extremely low (5%)," especially in the immediate post-Depression years, so that "many older children were placed out on indenture contracts until age 18" (25), as would be the case with Razor. Adoption rates for Native or African American children were even lower than 5%.

7. Ronglien says he ran away four times but doesn't "remember a severe punishment" for those attempts. He does note that he's "heard stories from others who were severely punished for running away" (58) and also that "boys who repeatedly ran away" from Owatonna "were reassigned to Red Wing Reform School" (55). Bob Dylan recorded the song "The Walls of Red Wing" in 1963 (released only in 1991).

8. Tanya Cooper writes that "*the latest Congressional study* [2012] *has found that African American and Native American children are at greater risk for child maltreatment than children of other races*" (215, italics in original), both institutionally and in foster care, the main focus of her study.

9. Some of the attacks reported by Peter Razor are hard to believe, but I do not think they are instances of falsely recovered memories because of the names and dates he provides, the records he occasionally cites, and the abundant details he gives. Ronglien makes clear that the "severity of punishment … depended on the cottage the child lived in. It was all up to the matron who made [the] rules" (63). He recalls that besides "getting slapped," he received "two beatings from Miss Morgan that crossed the line." She beat him with a "radiator brush" so badly that he "was bruised for weeks on [his] back and arms." On another occasion, she "beat [his] head against a wall so viciously that"—like Razor—he "thought she was going to kill [him]" (65).

10. Razor does not report having observed or experienced sexual abuse of any kind at the school. But the extremity of the violence perpetrated by staff at Owatonna and, in particular, what appears to be an almost complete lack of accountability, makes me certain that it occurred. Ronglien explicitly describes two instances of sexual abuse he endured at Owatonna (59–60).

11. Mary Razer was an important consultant for Densmore, who wrote of her beadwork that "Mrs. Frank Razer is ... serious, steady and always industrious. Her original patterns are ... constrained, a larger portion are strictly conventional, and there is evidence of painstaking care throughout her work" (80). Photographs by Densmore of Razer pulling in and mending gill nets are reproduced in Bruce White's book (114, 139), as is a studio portrait of her and her family taken between 1915 and 1920 (142).

8. ADAM FORTUNATE EAGLE'S *Pipestone: My Life in an Indian Boarding School,* DENNIS BANKS'S "YELLOW BUS," AND JIM NORTHRUP'S "FAMILIES—*Nindanawemanaaganag*"

1. The Pipestone school is in Pipestone, Minnesota, so named for a quarry of smooth, red, easily worked sandstone used by Native people for centuries to make ceremonial pipes. As a result of a visit made to the quarry by the painter George Catlin in 1835, it is sometimes called catlinite. The Pipestone National Monument was established in 1937, and presently only enrolled Native Americans may quarry the pipestone.

2. A Canadian text well worth mention in this regard is Jane Willis's *Geneish: An Indian Girlhood* (1973). Willis, born in 1940, is mixed-blood Canadian Cree, from St. George's Island, Québec. She describes her time at the Anglican residential school on the island, up through her eighth grade graduation, "ten and a half ... years in Indian boarding schools—ten and a half years of boot camp" (195). Basil Johnston's *Indian School Days* (1988) is also an extended account of a Canadian Ojibwa's experiences in a Catholic boarding school in northern Ontario.

3. Fortunate Eagle's endnotes to his introduction give the source for this quotation as p. 128 of a book called *John Collier's Crusade for Indian Reform, 1920–1954*, by Kenneth Phelps (187). The author of that book, however, is Kenneth Philp, and the quotation from Collier does not appear on p. 128. Fortunate Eagle, to be sure, is not an academic scholar, and I suspect he found the quotation elsewhere and mistakenly attributed it to a page in Philp's book. I have not been able to source it, but it strikes me as accurately expressing things Collier said and wrote on many occasions.

4. This was the case, as noted, for many of the Indian boarding schools. Lawney Reyes, who attended the Chemawa School in Oregon from 1940

to 1942, wrote that he "became aware that most of the students came to Chemawa because of problems at home.... All of us were poor, and our families were unable to support us" (97). This had been true of Walter Littlemoon's mother and of Tim Giago's parents and would also be the case with Dennis Banks's mother and Jim Northrup's.

5. Fortunate Eagle reprints twelve of the twenty-one short biographies given in Reynolds's dissertation. Reynolds compiled these biographies from "Case histories of students by county welfare boards" (48 n.2), which were the authorities in charge of certifying need on the part of the students for them to qualify for Pipestone—see later discussion for Banks and Northrup. All of the twelve files he selected describe what he calls "sordid background experiences" (165). Nineteen of the twenty-one children described by Reynolds clearly came from difficult family situations.

6. Student files for former Pipestone students are available for those who are deceased, or for those still living who attended more than seventy-five years ago, so that Adam Nordwall's records were not available from the Pipestone School at the time of writing (2019). Nonetheless, I have no doubt that he and his siblings were taken to Pipestone because their mother applied to have them enrolled.

7. I again refer to the boy represented in the book as Nordwall and to the author of the book as Fortunate Eagle, for the most part.

8. In a brief reminiscence called "My School Days," Purcell Powless, a Wisconsin Oneida who came to the Pipestone school in 1937, his time there overlapping Fortunate Eagle's, recalled that the school had "nice warm beds" and "pretty good food" (85).

9. As previously noted, in 1929 Commissioner of Indian Affairs Charles Burke had issued Circular 2526 "forbidding corporal punishment altogether at Indian schools" (Trennert 1989 603). Nonetheless, as we have seen, staff at the Catholic mission schools and the secular Oglala Community High School in South Dakota continued to beat children mercilessly, as did the staff at many of the schools. This does not seem to have been the case at Pipestone, although contrary to official policy, school staff certainly did administer corporal punishment.

10. The boys' "parching place" is next to their vegetable garden, "across the north side of the [school] grounds." Nordwall has learned "that Mr. Burns, a Southern Cheyenne from Oklahoma, told the other employees to stay away from the parching place because it's the boys' sacred area."

Nordwall says, "I'm really proud that grownups respect our traditional ways" (123). After parching some corn and handing it out to other students and to staff as well, "One of the older boys says, 'We have to carry on our old ways'," to which Nordwall responds, "I'm beginning to understand" (124). Lawney Reyes had said of Saturday afternoon semi-clandestine gatherings of boys from many tribes at Chemawa to make and drink coffee that "these experiences helped me develop for the first time the feeling of being an Indian" (112).

11. Nordwall and some of the other boys "play the game we call Name the Indians," and they make a list of the Indian staff at the school, noting which of them had graduated from Haskell or Carlisle. The game on this occasion is prompted by a letter from his mother—who had gone "to the Flandreau Indian School" (95) nearby—in which she asks whether there are "any Indians working … at Pipestone" (95).

12. In his introduction Fortunate Eagle noted that although he "never attended the mission school, the older members of his family did." But "some of the more horrific stories" they recounted, he says, he "chose not to write because he could not get independent confirmation" (xiv). This suggests that he was able to "get independent confirmation" for the "horrific stories" he did write.

13. Further confirmation of this comes from Powless, who wrote, "I hear they forbade our language at these schools." This would not have affected him, he says, "since I didn't know my language." But, he recalls, the "Winnebago … and Sioux spoke their language in small groups at the school and yet no one bothered them at the time" (85).

14. He tells many stories from his life in *Contrary Warrior: The Life and Times of Adam Fortunate Eagle*, a film by John Ferry (2010).

15. The files are in Record Group 75 of the Records of the Bureau of Indian Affairs, National Archives Identifier 599708, located at the National Archives in Kansas City, Missouri. I have Banks's records from Wade Popp, archives specialist, sent on April 23, 2018. I thank him for his help.

16. As noted earlier, DDT had been developed in 1942 to kill head and body lice that spread typhus among the American troops. It may well have been approved for use in the Indian boarding schools only a year later. Lydia Whirlwind Soldier, as we have seen, had it applied to her head in 1946.

17. This would be 1948. Esther Burnett Horne, a Shoshone woman whose story we will consider later, had come to the Wahpeton Indian School

in 1930—the only Indian teacher there at the time—and the eleven-year old Dennis Banks was indeed her student. Horne writes that at a meeting of the Minnesota Education Association in 1969, Banks came up to her, put his arms around her, and said, "Mrs. Horne, you know, you might well have been called the mother of AIM." As Banks recalled, this was because she told her Indian students, "Keep your heads up.... And don't be a puppet on somebody else's string" (Horne and McBeth 129).

18. Reyes, whose years at Chemawa, like those of Nordwall at Pipestone, were during the period when corporal punishment was officially prohibited, also describes the belt line for serious infractions: "About twenty-four or thirty students would remove their belts and form two lines. The offender had to run between the lines, and the members of the belt line struck his back and legs as he ran through" (116).

19. The reference is to Gerald Vizenor's sharply critical portrait of Banks, "Dennis of Wounded Knee," in his *The People Named the Chippewa* which I found as incisive in a recent re-reading as I had when I first read it more than thirty years ago.

20. I have these once more from Wade Popp of the National Archives and Records Administration, sent on July 31, 2018.

21. My information comes from a copy of a letter sent to the U.S. Department of the Interior on August 22, 1949, by Ernest Rylander on behalf of the Saint Louis County Welfare Board requesting that James Northrup Jr. and Judith Northrup be admitted to the Pipestone School. There is also a letter addressed to Jim Northrup. Both letters are included in Northrup's student file from Pipestone.

22. Ronglien had noted that at Owatonna, "the night watchman would come through twice each night to wake the bed wetters" (31) in the hope that if they then used the facilities they might not wet their beds.

23. Tim Giago, at the Holy Rosary Mission School only a few years earlier, had addressed this matter, as we have seen, and Harvey Ronglien, at Owatonna, described quite explicitly what happened when "one of the older boys crawled in bed with [him]." Ronglien writes that although this was "repeated ... a couple of times, ... [he] never said a word to anyone" (60).

24. As noted, absences in the Pipestone student records were marked by an "A." Running away was marked by a "D" for "deserted." There is no "D" and no absences at all are recorded for Northrup's first year at the school. I suspect this is lax reporting on the part of his teacher.

25. Northrup's poem "Ditched" treats his first year at Pipestone. It begins:

A first grader
A federal boarding school
Pipestone
Said anin to the
first grown up
Got an icy blue-eyed stare
in return
Got a beating
from a
second grader for crying
about the stare

Anin is the casual or informal Ojibwe term for "hello." Unlike what he tells his mother in the poem, in his prose recollections Northrup got slapped by the blue-eyed grown-up (and also got beat up by a second grader).

26. Although found only in a very few places in the United States other than at Pipestone, Minnesota, pipestone also occurs on the Lac Courte Oreilles Ojibwe reservation in Sawyer County, Wisconsin, about 125 miles southeast of Fond du Lac.

27. I had thought the nickname was one Northrup had mockingly bestowed on the man to indicate an unappealing self-love or self-satisfaction on his part. But an obituary for Gale, who died on February 11, 2013 (legacy.com), states that he was widely known among the students at the Brainerd School as "Chief Hugs Himself," and that it was "a title he loved."

9. EDNA MANITOWABI'S
"AN OJIBWA GIRL IN THE CITY"

1. The author's name is also altered from Manitowabi to Manitobawabi, although this is probably an awkward typographical error.

2. Interviewing her in the *Toronto Star*, Deborah Dundas noted that she went to school in Spanish, Ontario, which is indeed about seventy miles from her home on Manitoulin Island. The Spanish Ontario Catholic residential schools were Saint Peter Claver for boys (which Basil Johnston attended

about a decade earlier, and where he was sexually abused) and Saint Joseph for girls. I believe Saint Joseph's is probably the school Manitowabi attended.

3. David Brumble's 1981 *Annotated Bibliography* lists it and provides a fine summary (88–89). Gretchen Battaile and Kathleen Mullen Sands also list it and accurately summarize it in their bibliography of Native women's autobiographies. Their summary concludes with the observation that "the style is terse and self-analytical, more sociological than literary" (164). My sense is that the terseness and self-analysis are powerfully expressive from a literary perspective.

4. Both the original journal publication and the small press book are available, although neither is easily found. Several booksellers list the reprint but have no copies for sale. Page references differ, so with quoted material, I give pages first for the journal and then for the book.

5. In keeping with the de-Canadianizing and generalizing of the reprint, page 5 has her "go to the city," not to "Toronto." I'll note some other changes of this nature in the text.

6. They are called Bob and Marsha in the original publication and renamed Fred and Gerta in the reprint, although all the names are surely fictional.

7. Abortion had been illegal in Canada until Prime Minister Pierre Elliott Trudeau's Liberal Party obtained passage of the Criminal Law Amendment Act of 1969. This amended a provision of the Canadian constitution criminalizing abortion so as to allow it if a committee of doctors agreed that it was necessary for the physical or mental well-being of the mother. In 1988 the provision that had only been amended in 1969 was ruled unconstitutional, the result being to make abortion more generally legal and available—although different Canadian provinces have different provisions for administering the law. It is my sense that Manitowabi is speaking of a time just a bit earlier than 1969.

10. THOMAS WILDCAT ALFORD'S *Civilization*

1. The 1936 edition—also published by Oklahoma—had a title page that read, "*Civilization*, as told to Florence Drake by Thomas Wildcat Alford." On the new title page the book is called "*Civilization and the Story of the Absentee Shawnees*, as told to Florence Drake by Thomas Wildcat

Alford, with a Foreword by Angie Debo." The 1979 edition is a facsimile of the 1936 edition, so pagination is the same in both.

2. Alford quotes a Shawnee chief in favor of schooling as saying, "It would enable us to use the club of white man's wisdom against him in defense of our customs" (73).

3. There are today three federally recognized Shawnee nations in Oklahoma: the Absentee Shawnee, the Eastern Shawnee of Oklahoma, and the Shawnee Tribe, formerly part of the Cherokee Nation. The 2015 census recorded the number of Shawnee speakers as 255, mostly in Oklahoma and elderly, thus making Shawnee an endangered language.

4. There is also the matter of his arranging allotments for Shawnee families without their consent, as I note later. Other impediments to such recuperation are found in his 1888 letter to Samuel Armstrong, which is reprinted in full in Appendix A.

5. See James Axtell's classic essay "The White Indians of Colonial America," and also Levernier and Cohen's *Indians and Their Captives* and Strong's *Captive Selves*.

6. His account is consistent with the description of Shawnee naming practices given by Erminie and Carl Voegelin just a year earlier. Although Alford had served as a consultant to the Voegelins, Erminie Voegelin, in her review of *Civilization*, was dismissive of its ethnographic usefulness, writing, "As his knowledge of Shawnee ethnography is limited, Alford can rarely give a well rounded description of Shawnee culture" (536). She did note some exceptions.

7. A valuable account of how Hampton Indian students used periodicals like the *Southern Workman* can be found in Emery (2012).

8. While still in service, his father had sent home a "big blue overcoat," the sleeves of which his mother turned into leggings for the boy (12), after which he became "known among [his] companions as 'soldier'" (13).

9. This is Tecumseh's grandson, Wapameeto, "Gives light as he walks," about whom Alford will have more to say (171–76). He was born in Texas about 1834 and in 1872 became chief of the non-progressive Shawnees, who were called Big Jim's Band. He was consistent in opposing the allotment of Shawnee land, and after they were allotted, he took his people to Mexico in 1900, where he contracted smallpox and "succumbed September 30, 1900" (175).

10. Alice Longfellow provided eight scholarships for Indian students to Hampton (Ludlow 1893 515). The government also subsidized Hampton's

Indian students for a period of three years. Robert Engs writes that its super-intendent, Samuel Chapman Armstrong, agreed to accept Native students at a school established for the freedmen of the south in part because "a gov-ernment stipend was assured for each" (xiv).

11. Fortress Monroe was located at the southern tip of the Virginia pen-insula, in Hampton, Virginia. Although Virginia had joined the Confederacy, Fortress Monroe remained in Union control throughout the Civil War, and represented a site of freedom for runaway slaves. General Samuel Armstrong (1839–93), the son of American missionaries in Hawai'i, after serving in the Union army, was appointed Superintendent of the Freedmen's Bureau of the 9th District, Virginia, in 1866. With support from the American Missionary Association, he established the Hampton Normal and Agricultural Institute in 1868, to educate black men and women to become teachers of their people. He and Richard Pratt, another Union officer, established the Indian Program at Hampton in 1878, and Hampton—it is, today, Hampton University—continued to educate Indians along with blacks until 1923, when the Indian Program closed. Booker T. Washington, who had come to Hampton in 1872 as both a student and a janitor served as "house father" to the Indians.

12. Common practice was for each Indian upon arrival to be "given a black roommate in order to aid in the acquisition of civilized manners" (Engs 118). In that Alford and his friend had already acquired a fair degree of "civilized manners," they may not have roomed with a black student. But Alford would have known that many of the Indians did.

13. And very much the case with Hampton's Native students, who, as Robert Engs notes, did not take well to the school's southern diet (122).

14. In chapter 3 of his autobiography, *Up from Slavery*, Washington also comments on the newness of "the use of the bath tub and the tooth brush" (44).

15. Jon L. Brudvig's compilation of the names and brief histories of the Native students at Hampton does not list many runaways, although it is clear that some Native students adjusted to the school less well than Alford. A Seneca named Charles Armstrong—it is likely that he was named at the school for Hampton's founder—was deemed "unsatisfactory and troublesome," while Joseph Armstrong—also likely named for General Armstrong—left "due to failing health," as did another Seneca, Lyman Bailey. Claude Arrow, a Standing Rock Sioux, was noted for "Dancing and loafing." Frank Gauthier, a Menominee, was expelled for unspecified bad conduct. These students were not at Hampton during Alford's time, but surely he would have encountered others who also had difficulties, became ill, or ran

away. Robert Engs observes that Hampton, like Carlisle and other schools, had a jail on campus (107). And, as I will note later, Alford's brother and one of his sons had difficulties at Hampton.

16. Alford did not become hereditary chief, although he did become a chief by government appointment. In 1893 he served as one of seven Shawnees on a Business Committee "to represent the Absentee Shawnees as a tribe in all dealings with the United States." The committee members' names were forwarded to Washington, ostensibly in alphabetical order, and, Alford writes, "As my name was first on the list, I was made chairman automatically and was in reality at last in the position of chief or principal adviser of my people, recognized as such by the government at Washington" (161); recognized by the government in Washington but not necessarily by his own people.

17. General Armstrong's parents were Presbyterian missionaries in Hawaii, and he was true to their faith. Florence Drake's account of Tecumseh, Oklahoma, at the turn of the twentieth century lists the names of many members of various local churches, but Alford's does not appear among them. At some point he became a freemason, and a masonic graveside service was held at his burial in 1938.

18. The first Native students to graduate from Hampton in 1882 were Thomas Wildcat Alford, John Downing (Eastern Cherokee), and Michael Oshkenenny (Menominee) (Lindsey 119). The government supported Indian students for only three years at Hampton, although the curriculum was a five-year program, equivalent to the completion of high school. Graduates might then enter the Normal School for two years if they wished to continue.

19. Helen Ludlow noted that Alford also taught briefly at the Chilocco Indian School (1893 345), where records list him as also "disciplinarian" and "farmer" for the school.

20. We are not told the denomination of the unnamed Sioux woman, nor did Alford reveal his sectarian choice, although I am guessing it was Presbyterian.

21. Brudvig's notes on former Hampton male Indian students indicate that Paul Leon Alford was "Expelled for drinking." Thomas Wildcat Alford's younger brother, Thompson, spent four years at Hampton, during which time Brudvig notes that he was "wild and hard to control" (www.twofrog.com/hamptonmale1.txt). This had likewise been Cora Folsom's sense of the young man, although she also observed that he had a "happy good nature" (443). He left the school in 1889, going home to live with his brother, and a

year later went to the Chilocco Indian School. Obviously not all the Alfords were model students.

22. Although Alford himself and also the WorldCat library catalogue list his translation as a translation of the *four* gospels into Shawnee, the two separate copies of that book I have been able to see translate the Gospel of Matthew only.

23. Paul Alford was at Hampton from 1902 to 1907 (just when he was expelled for drinking I can't say). Pierre attended from 1900 to 1903, when he graduated. Charles Reece was there from 1902 to 1906, when he too graduated. There were Alford daughters as well, but their names do not appear on Brudvig's list of female Hampton students (www.twofrog.com/hamptonfem1.txt). Although no one of these many children would have been allowed to speak Shawnee, Charles Reece and Pierrepont did have Indian names: "Palagonesemo=Single Voice" for the former and "Welamiamo" for the latter (Brudvig 1996 348).

24. She appears to give two dates for the letter in question, March 11, 1889, and January 10, 1887. It is my guess that Alford admitted his subterfuge in the later communication. In 1890 Indian Territory became Oklahoma Territory, which it remained until statehood in 1907.

25. In his 1882 "Graduating Address" Alford announced his desire to lead his people "out of the darkness of barbarism and ignorance into the path of peace and prosperity," and he concluded with the hope that "we shall come together with a Bible in one hand and a hoe in the other ... to fit ourselves for that great brotherhood of mankind" (78). There are echoes here of Booker T. Washington, whom Alford does not mention in his autobiography, as I have said. A major concern of the address is to make the case that the government will do better to "civilize" the Indians by means of education rather than by force of arms, because, among other things, the latter is very expensive.

II. JOE BLACKBEAR'S *Jim Whitewolf: The Life of a Kiowa Apache Indian*, AND CARL SWEEZY'S *The Arapaho Way: Memoir of an Indian Boyhood*

1. Federally recognized as the Apache Tribe of Oklahoma, the Nadiishadena, "our people," were referred to in the literature as the Kiowa Apache or Plains Apache. Schweinfurth (2002) and Jordan (1965) make clear that

the people today disapprove of the closeness to the Kiowa implied by the first appellation and prefer to be called Plains Apache (to distinguish them from the Fort Sill Apache) or, as in the constitution they adopted in 1972, simply Apache. Brant quotes James Mooney's observation that they were Kiowa in everything but language (Brant 1969 11; Mooney 1979 169), but this is true only in the most general sense. Plains Apache people spoke a Na-Dene or southern Athabascan language (Navajo "din'e," Apache "nde" or "indeh," the People), while the Kiowas spoke a Tanoan language. The last fluent speaker of Plains Apache, Alfred Chalepah Sr., died in 2008. In her dissertation on Chalepah, which I will cite further, Michelle Stokely noted that it was only in 1999 that "an Apachean alphabet system" of writing the language was "adopted by tribal resolution" (19). Stokely, Schweinfurth, and Jordan (1965) all make clear that "Jim Whitewolf" was Joe Blackbear.

2. Webster observes that "*Jim Whitewolf* is clearly modeled after Opler's *Apache Odyssey: A Journey Between Two Worlds*" (Webster 2007 302), published the same year as Brant's book, 1969. I have not been able to discover why a period of twenty years separated Brant's research from the publication of the book on which it is based.

3. Webster's 2009 essay examines Brant's introduction to *Jim Whitewolf* in comparison to William Bittle's essay (1962) on the Apache revival of the *Manatidie* or Blackfeet Society Dance. He finds that Brant "paints the Plains Apache as victims and pawns in a world largely outside tribal members' understanding" (302), while in Bittle's work they appear as "intentional agents that have desires and motivations" (302). Webster writes that whereas Brant's "sympathy for the Plains Apache lies in their victimhood," Bittle's lies in their "creativity" (310). Although Webster does not consider the autobiography itself, his account of the introduction is consistent with what I am calling Brant's ironic presentation of Joe Blackbear's life.

4. I have not sought to specify the type of master plot structuring the boarding-school narratives considered thus far, nor will I do so for those next considered. All the boarding-school narratives discussed in this book, because they bear witness to the author's survival as an individual, as an Indian, and as a speaking subject, may generally be considered comic in their plot structure.

5. See my "Figures and the Law" for an account of how the Cherokees, in the late 1820s, sent memorials to Congress seeking to defeat the Indian Removal Act by showing that the tragic narrative on which the act was based—a story in which it was sad but inevitable and just that the Natives go—was false, and attempting to install in its place an ironic narrative—strictly

a case of might making right, an injustice. N. Scott Momaday represents Kiowa history as a tragic narrative of decline in *The Way to Rainy Mountain*. I read Momaday's book that way in "*That the People Might Live*," 134–44.

6. William Bittle's generous review of the book nonetheless observed that Brant's "remarks on such conveniences... are now [in 1969–70, not 1949] meaningless" (1970 884).

7. An approximate version of what it was like appeared in Brant's 1963 publication of an "origin of peyote" story Blackbear had narrated in Apache. That story had been translated by Wallace Redbone, also the translator for the autobiography, whom Brant "fictionalized" (1969 viii) as Wallace Whitebone. Here is a sample of how Brant presented Blackbear's English in 1963: "They were Lipan Apaches. It was very hot and dry there. All the water had dried up. They had no food or water and there was none around them.... It was early in the morning. The boy went out in the mountains" (180). As noted later, he reproduced this story word for word in *Jim Whitewolf.*

8. Joe Blackbear's father appears a few times in the narrative but he is never named. He was known as Old Man Blackbear, and he had served with the U.S. Army during the Red River War of 1874. He told stories about his experiences during that war to his son, Joe, who includes some of them in *Jim Whitewolf.* In her study of Alfred Chalepah Sr., Michelle Stokely writes that Chalepah—who was born in 1910—said that when he was a child, his "favorite storyteller was Old Man Blackbear, a respected elder" (105). Chalepah heard a version of a story called "How We/They Got Peyote" (Stokely 110) from Old Man Blackbear—a strong adherent of the Native American Church—who told it to his son, Joe, and to his grandson, Ray, Joe's son and Willy's father.

9. Plains Apaches, like southwestern Apaches, strongly exhibited what Michael Hittman has called "ghost fright" (1997 180), or ritual avoidance of the dead. See Opler, and Schweinfurth, 123–27. Curiously, this was true as well of the Paiutes among whom the Ghost Dance religion began. For discussion, see Hittman, 1973 and 1997. Although Blackbear's people also avoided the dead, did not speak their names, and did not welcome their possible return, they nonetheless mostly shared their Kiowa neighbors' enthusiasm for the Ghost Dance. An interesting early account of the Kiowa Sun Dance or Kado is that of Hugh Lenox Scott. See also Kracht.

10. The Reverend John Jasper Methvin (1846–1941), a veteran of the Confederate Army and a Methodist missionary, came to Anadarko in

1887, "appointed," as he wrote, "to missionary work among the wild tribes" (166). He opened the Methvin Methodist Institute in 1890. See Clyde Ellis (1996a) for the recollections of several students who had attended the Methvin school. Sally McBeth wrote that "Saint Patrick's Catholic Mission and School in Anadarko and the Methvin Methodist Mission Institute were the two most important mission schools located within the research area" (1983 75); that is, in west-central Oklahoma.

11. Kay Schweinfurth had access to a great many unpublished interviews Brant had conducted with Blackbear in 1949. As cited by Schweinfurth, these present information and stories about many aspects of traditional Plains Apache culture, which, had Brant included some of them, would once more have complicated his presentation of Blackbear as representative of a "disintegrating" culture.

12. N. Scott Momaday's play "The Indolent Boys" takes place at the Kiowa boarding school in Anadarko. It concerns an incident that occurred during the winter of 1891, before Joe Blackbear enrolled at the school. Barton Wherritt, the school disciplinarian, had whipped a Kiowa boy named Sethaide (Momaday calls him Seta), prompting the boy to run away with two other Kiowa students. They were overtaken by a blizzard and froze to death, which, when they heard, led Kiowa people to descend on the school. They were met there by G. P. Gregory, the superintendent, but did not find Wherritt, who hid from them. Joe Blackbear was not a Kiowa, but he came to the school in the fall of the year this happened, and it seems inconceivable that he had not heard about it. Nonetheless, nothing of this is mentioned, either because he did not speak of it or because Charles Brant did not see fit to include whatever he might have said.

13. Almost all Native nations had a version of the hand game, also called the stick game or bone game, which involves betting on who will guess correctly the number of bones or sticks hidden in a player's hands. That Brant has not provided an ethnographic note here is curious—ironic—because as Schweinfurth makes clear, the hand game is not merely an amusement for the Plains Apache but also appears in a creation story, in which "the prize in the hand game, survival and governance of the universe, went to the humans and the animals who defeated the monsters" (26). She cites at some length one of "the most enduring of the creation stories," a hand game tale in which "Coyote had the starring role" (31). The version she gives is by Ray Blackbear—who would have heard it from his father, his grandfather, or both (32).

14. Ray Blackbear told Julia Jordan that his father "speaks about three different languages. He can talk Comanche like you're talking English" (1968 12).

15. This is the Rev. J. J. Methvin, whom Blackbear had named earlier in his narration.

16. In the book's fifth and final chapter Blackbear says, "When I was in school I had a good friend named Claude. He was a Comanche boy. I played marbles with him and he always gave me fruit and things his father brought him" (117). Claude got sick at school, was sent home, and died. His father then gave Blackbear "a good horse, a saddle, and bridle that he had intended for his own boy. I was just like his own son" (117). He also taught Blackbear to prepare a medicine made from "a certain root." Blackbear says he used this medicine when his son, "Ben" (Ray Blackbear), had a stomach ache that no one could cure. He gathered the root and made the medicine for his son, who got well.

17. Peyote buttons are to be found in northern Mexico, and the peoples of the former Indian Territory obtained them first from Lipan Apaches, the peyote religion coming to the southern Plains about 1880, or possibly introduced to the Plains Apaches earlier, about 1875, by a man named Nayokogal (Jordan 1968 35). Although the religious services came to include a great many Christian elements, the use of peyote in them met with widespread opposition. James Mooney worked with Kiowas, Arapahos (as we will see further), and others to help them get the Native American Church incorporated in Oklahoma in 1918—the year Charles Eastman, Zitkala-Sa, and Richard Pratt beat him in the fight before Congress to legalize peyote for religious use nationally. Peyote use in Native American Church services did not become legal until 1993–94. For Plains Apache peyotism, see Brant (1963) and Bittle (1960).

18. Ray Blackbear had gone to live with his grandfather, Old Man Blackbear, in 1911, when he was eight (Jordan 1968 9) and learned from him about early Plains Apache peyotists, among them Tennyson Berry, "the only early Kiowa-Apache peyotist to have been a student at Carlisle" (Stewart 85). He also was well aware of his father's relation to peyotism. In 1968, just a year before his death, responding to Julia Jordan's question, "Did your father ever go down to Laredo to get peyote?" Ray Blackbear said, "Oh yeah. He been down there several times. And he's always been a great help to these leaders. He carry drum for them and build fire for them.... He knows the songs, and he knows the prayers" (in Jordan 1968 12).

19. He writes of tribal names: "In the beginning, we Arapaho called ourselves by a different name that meant 'Our Own Kind of People,'" before being called Arapaho, which "means trader" (2), probably a Pawnee word for his people.

20. It was only ten years later, in 1905, as Bass writes, "on a cross-country tour with an Indian baseball team"—more on that later—that Sweezy "went to the Lewis and Clark Exposition in Portland, Oregon," and came "upon some of his work in an Indian exhibit from the Smithsonian Institution" (ix), something of which the young man might well have been proud.

21. Bass included twenty-two color reproductions of Sweezy's paintings in the book, and says of them that they are "without any of the embellishments or fusion that might have made his art a hybrid form" (viii). She is writing, to be sure, before "hybridity" became a positive term. I have found very little commentary on Sweezy's art, but further exploration of Bass's estimate would be useful.

22. A Northern Arapaho who had preceded Sweezy at Carlisle was War Bonnet, renamed William Shakespeare by the school. He had arrived in 1881, perhaps the year of Sweezy's birth, and left after three years. It is interesting to note that rather than finding the school-given name grotesque or insulting, War Bonnet must have been pleased by it, in that he named his son Bill Shakespeare. For Bill Shakespeare, see Fowler.

23. It is, of course, Bass who gives it only two paragraphs. But I suspect that here and elsewhere, it is not that she chose to cut material but, rather, that Sweezy just did not say much about these things. The chapters containing ethnographic material are more fully detailed—either because he spoke more about these things or because she questioned him about them.

24. Sweezy's Carlisle student record has him arriving at the school in August 1896 and leaving in July 1897. If, as he says, he worked on a farm for *two* summers, that would mean he received an outing assignment immediately upon arriving and another very shortly before he left—although he left because of ill health. Coincidentally, Hattie Powless, a Wisconsin Oneida woman who would become Sweezy's wife, arrived at Carlisle in the same month that he left. One of thirty-one Powless (or Powlas) Oneidas to attend Carlisle (Hauptman and McLester 288), she arrived at the age of twelve and graduated ten years later. Sweezy says that it was when he came "to Rainy Mountain to take charge of the Government school ... that [he] met Hattie Powless, an Oneida who was a matron there" (40). He does not mention that she was a Carlisle graduate.

25. The Chilocco Indian Agricultural School in Indian Territory opened in 1884 with 150 students, all from Plains nations. Like the other federal boarding schools, it operated according to a strict military regimen and offered half a day of academic classes and half a day of vocational training to its male and female students. It closed in 1980.

26. Sweezy does not say whether he played baseball at Chilocco, although at the time, as Jeffrey Powers-Beck noted, so far as Indian baseball was concerned, "the major baseball power was Chilocco" (518).

12. AH-NEN-LA-DE-NI'S "AN INDIAN BOY'S STORY"

1. I have used the pagination of the original text from the *Independent*, July 1903, which can be found online at archive.org/details/p2independen-55newy?q=ah-nen-la-de-ni. After its periodical publication, "An Indian Boy's Story" was reprinted in a volume edited by then editor of the *Independent*, Hamilton Holt, called *The Life Stories of Undistinguished Americans* (1906). It has been reprinted in several recent anthologies.

2. The *Independent* was founded in 1848 by Congregationalists, one of whom, Henry C. Bowen, made it an important voice in the anti-slavery movement. Bowen was the grandfather of Hamilton Holt, who took over the editorship, serving from 1897 to 1921 and completely secularizing the magazine. (Holt would continue his grandfather's legacy, playing a role in the founding of the National Association for the Advancement of Colored People in 1909.) Like the *Atlantic Monthly*, the *Independent* published literary and political writing. Between 1896 and 1921, for example, every president of the United States had written for the magazine—which also was very much open to "undistinguished Americans."

3. He writes that his mother "would have nothing to do with the medicines" (1780) his father made and sold. Her mother, "a pure-blooded Indian," was "a doctor of a different sort than [his] father," and he realizes he would have learned much if he had paid attention to his grandmother when she "took [him] about in the woods ... to gather herbs, and ... roots and leaves ... how to dry and prepare them ... and what sicknesses they were good for" (1780).

4. Although Daniel La France does not seem ever to have become a Mohawk chief, Brenda La France and Ron La France have been Mohawk

tribal chiefs recently. I do not know whether they are related to Daniel La France. See also note 12.

5. It is not clear why he would need permission either to go to Carlisle or to serve in the war. He is nineteen years old, and his eight years at the institute exceed what had been agreed upon, that the "boys and girls were supposed to remain at the school for five years," after which," as he understood it, they "were free from any obligation" (1784).

6. Of the two poems he includes, here in its entirety is the shorter one, called "The Indian's Conception:

When first the white man's ships appeared
To Redmen of this wooded strand,
The Redmen gazed, and vastly feared,
That they could not those "birds" withstand;
As they mistook the ships for birds.
And this ill omen came quite true—
For later came more; hungrier birds.

7. During the Civil War women had served as nurses in the hospitals behind the lines, while each fighting unit had a contingent of male nurses to provide immediate aid and care for those wounded in battle. As is well known, Walt Whitman served—in an amateur and volunteer capacity—as a Civil War nurse, and some of his experiences are conveyed in the poem, "The Wound Dresser," with further accounts in the prose of *Specimen Days*. When the Army Nurse Corps was established in 1901 it was for women only, and although men continued to be "wound dressers" in battle during World Wars I and II, it was not until 1955 that President Eisenhower signed the Bolton Act into law, providing commissions for qualified male nurses in the reserve corps.

8. See "What to the Slave Is the Fourth of July?," an address delivered in Rochester, New York, in 1852. My reference is to Douglass's observation: "This Fourth of July is *yours* not *mine*. You may rejoice, I must mourn" (116, emphasis in original).

9. The Indian Rights Association was an all-white organization founded in Philadelphia in 1882. Like the Lake Mohonk Friends of the Indian, it was committed to the assimilation of American Indians, advocating for their citizenship and full civil rights, but with no understanding of the special treaty

relation between Indian nations and the U.S. government. Lawrence Lindley was the extremely active secretary of the main branch in Philadelphia, at this time. Ah-nen-la-de-ni does not say with whom he and his fellow students were in contact.

10. This was Estelle Reel, superintendent of Indian Schools from 1898 to 1910. "The *Uniform Course of Study* she developed for the schools ... influenced generations of students" (Lomawaima 1996 5).

11. There were actually two Vreeland Bills, sponsored by Republican Senator Edward Vreeland, from Cataraugus County in New York. Both dealt with the allotment of Seneca lands. In 1902 they each passed the House but both were defeated in the Senate. Although the Bills did not immediately affect the Mohawk reservation, Ah-nen-la-de-ni believed that had they passed, his St. Regis reservation might have been next to be threatened with allotment.

12. See note 4 for the two recent chiefs. Ms. Amberdawn La France of the St. Regis Mohawk Environment Division wrote to me in 2018 that she had heard of "An Indian Boy's Story" but did not know of a Daniel La France (personal communication January 22, 2018).

13. ESTHER BURNETT HORNE'S *Essie's Story*

1. McBeth consistently refers to her as Essie, and I have earlier found the use of first names in this manner on the part of many editors, amanuenses, and scholars to be patronizing —as it would be were I to call Horne "Essie." But that is not the case here: considering the length and closeness of the two women's relationship, for McBeth to refer to her as "Horne" would instantiate a false objectifying distance, one that simply was not present in their work together.

2. McBeth provides a detailed account of the historical case for Sacajawea's death in 1812—even the spelling of her name is a matter of some dispute, most contemporary sources using Sacagawea—while noting a number of uncertainties in the written record. She also provides the background for the oral tradition's adoption of the 1884 date for her passing—which was supported by a study done by Charles Eastman for the commissioner of Indian Affairs in 1925 and is also accepted by some ethnographers and ethnohistorians today. Briefly, the oral tradition has it that a woman named Porivo, buried on the Wind River reservation in 1884, was

actually Sacajawea, who had come back to her people sometime before 1868. Here, too, the oral tradition provides an account many Shoshones accept as *true* although it may not be *factual*. Thomas Johnson's review of *Essie's Story* treats this matter in detail and supports the 1812 date for Sacajawea's death.

3. Irene Stewart (1907–98), a Navajo woman, had arrived at Haskell in 1922, just two years before Esther Horne, and graduated from ninth grade in 1926. Although invited to re-enroll for high school, she did not return. "The one thing [she] never stopped regretting," Stewart wrote, "was not having gone back to Haskell to finish" (34). Her time at the school and Horne's overlapped, but neither mentions the other. For Stewart, see volume 1.

4. An "overseas cap" was the soft cloth cap that had been introduced among American soldiers during World War I, replacing the "Montana" campaign hats—stiff, broad brim, felt hats with high crowns—that had earlier been worn.

5. McBeth's introduction references "Horne's pro-boarding school testimony as recorded in a hearing before a U.S. Senate Select Committee on Indian Affairs (1982)" (xiii), and in her review of *Essie's Story*, Elizabeth Bugaighis remarked Horne's determination to "contest the one-dimensional image that the boarding schools produced nothing but lonely and confused children" (356). As we have seen in considerable detail, the boarding schools did indeed produce a great number of "lonely and confused children," although most former Haskell students continue to express a positive view of their experience. Suzanna Buchowska's study (2016), based on interviews with recent Haskell graduates, affirms that to this day "students have become a close-knit community creating friendships ... that have reached outside the school's premises and beyond the point of graduation," and that "community at Haskell became a new tribe and home for many" (55).

6. She does not, however, mention a single case in which a student ran off—as she does not mention a single act of student resistance. In that a punishment has been established for "going AWOL," there must surely have been runaways.

7. McBeth does, however, contribute an endnote quoting Horne as saying she "wouldn't want any of [her] children to have to go through a belt line!" and stating the degree to which other boarding-school students "objected to being held responsible for punishing their classmates" (187 n.8).

8. The dominance of the Haskell Fighting Indians of 1926 is indicated by the scores of their first three games, which they won 65-0, 57-0, and 55-0,

later beating Bucknell 36-0 and Michigan State 40-7. The elaborate Haskell Homecoming event that took place in October 1926 also included the dedication of a new Haskell Stadium, and was attended by hundreds of Indians from near and far, who filled the local hotels and also pitched camps on the Kansas (or Kaw) River. The festivities went on for several days, and were widely reported in the press, so it is not possible that Horne was unaware of them, although she makes no mention of them. For a detailed account of the 1926 Haskell Homecoming see Rader.

9. John Levi was known as "the Jim Thorpe of Haskell" (Buchowska 248), and Thorpe himself is said to have called Levi the greatest athlete he'd ever seen. See McDonald; Bloom; and Oxendine.

10. Irene Stewart had noted that Oklahoma Osage students at Haskell in these years had oil money, but like Horne, she and other Navajo young women, did not (29). The Osages made large contributions toward the construction of the new Haskell Stadium dedicated in 1926, as did the Quapaws (whose wealth came not from oil but from lead and zinc).

11. This was somewhat more daring than Horne indicates because Prohibition was then in effect. The nineteenth amendment to the Constitution, prohibiting the manufacture, sale, or transportation of alcohol, had been passed in 1919, followed by the 1920 Volstead Act providing Congress means for enforcing Prohibition. Beer was thus illegal at the time. (Prohibition was not repealed until 1933.)

12. In her very first teaching position at the Eufaula Boarding School, in Eufaula, Oklahoma, Horne found that some of her students "appeared to be of black ancestry," although they were listed as Creeks. She learns that they were "Creek Freedmen ... the offspring of former black slaves of the Creek Indians" who "had become enrolled members of the Creek tribe" after Emancipation (56). Although she doesn't "remember that there was any fighting among the students who were all Indian, mixed-blood, or black" (56), she does report that "after a particularly delicious meal," she "walked into the kitchen to compliment the cook." For doing so, she is called into the office of the school superintendent, where she is reprimanded because "'we do not associate with or talk to the colored cooks,'" and she is ordered "'to refrain from this practice in the future.'" Horne writes that she "chalked up [the superintendent's] remarks to ignorance and the part of the country that we were in" (57), and, one might add, to the year, 1929.

14. VIOLA MARTINEZ, *California Paiute: Living in Two Worlds*

1. Diana Meyers Bahr writes that "Viola has no written record of her birth. Oral tradition places her birth in 1917" (174 n.1). "Oral tradition" does not place events in numbered years. Bahr means that people in the community generally believe she was born in 1917. The obituary for Martinez in the *Los Angeles Times* gives her birthdate as July 26, 1914, a date that presumes a "written record"—although I cannot say whether one actually exists.

2. Bahr is a bit confusing here as well. Martinez was a student at Sherman from 1927 to 1932 and then boarded at Sherman while taking her senior year of high school at the nearby Riverside Polytechnical School (68), a public school. She next attended Riverside Junior College and "worked assisting the dormitory matrons at Sherman Institute" (70). She then enrolled in Santa Barbara State College (now the University of California–Santa Barbara), and graduated in 1939, "with a bachelor of science degree in home economics and a secondary teaching credential" (76). All told, this would be roughly "twelve years" away at school.

3. My quotations of Martinez's words are, strictly speaking, quotations of Bahr quoting Martinez, but double quotation marks are too awkward in appearance to use.

4. The conventional spelling is Minnehaha, from the name Longfellow gave to Hiawatha's beloved, and the girls who lived in the dorm were known as the Minnehaha Girls. The name was widely used, and as noted, Zitkala-Sa was in charge of the Minnehaha Glee Club at Carlisle.

5. Bahr quotes Martinez as saying, "the one time I did go home, I escorted my *cousin* in a casket to the reservation" (53, my emphasis). A few pages later Bahr writes: "Viola returned home to Owens Valley only once in twelve years, the trip to accompany the body of her *niece*, the daughter of one of her much older brothers" (59, my emphasis). The difference may involve Paiute reckoning of kinship relations, or it may be an error. Bahr assures readers that she and Martinez reviewed both the transcript of the interviews and the "first draft of the manuscript" (170) together, but apparently neither of them caught the discrepancy between "cousin" and "niece."

6. It is worth mentioning in this regard that a boyfriend of hers, a football player and "a very handsome man," asked Viola Meroney (as she

was then) to marry him, "but I wouldn't marry him because he was not Indian" (74). The man she did marry, Andy Martinez, was Paiute, and she had met him at Sherman.

15. REUBEN SNAKE'S *Your Humble Serpent*

1. There are two federally recognized Winnebago or Ho-Chunk peoples, the Winnebago Tribe of Nebraska and the Ho-Chunk Nation of Wisconsin. The latter changed their name from Winnebago to Ho-Chunk in their 1994 Constitution. Ho-Chunk comes from their own Siouan language, and it means "people of the great or sacred voice or speech," or perhaps "big fish people": there is disagreement as to the exact meaning. The copious notes on these matters by Snake's editor, Jay Fikes (251–53) are very useful. Snake was an enrolled member of the Nebraska Winnebago tribe, although he spent much time among the Ho-Chunk of Wisconsin.

2. Omer Stewart writes that "by 1889, peyotism had diffused beyond Indian Territory to the Winnebago of northeastern Nebraska" (148) and to Wisconsin as well. Paul Radin's *The Winnebago Tribe*, originally published in 1923, has the fullest account of the people's early encounters with peyote, including "Albert Hensley's Account of the Peyote" (349–52). Hensley, who had attended Carlisle, was credited with introducing elements of the New Testament into the peyote ceremonies.

3. According to Stewart: "The 'roadman' is the leader of the all-night peyote ceremony, the 'peyote meeting.' The name refers to the 'peyote road,' a line incised along the crescent of the half-moon altar on which participants are asked to concentrate in the belief that 'the road' will lead their thoughts and prayers to the supernatural—in modern times often designated as 'God the Father'" (60).

4. See his "Huichol Indian Identity and Adaptation."

5. Fikes notes that the name "indicates the manner in which a snake elevates its head in self-defense" (25–26).

6. The Winnebago Medicine Lodge Society has some parallels with the Anishinaabe Midewiwin. Fikes provides useful commentary (257).

7. Neillsville was neither a government-run boarding school nor, like some of the Catholic schools, a contract school. The school was "supported by the subcommittee of the Board of National Missions … within the Reformed Church of Wisconsin" (R. Johnson 12–13), a private church school.

8. This is Reverend Benjamin Stucki, who had been superintendent since 1921, when the school opened in Neillsville. The "founder" was his father, Reverend Jacob Stucki.

9. Wisconsin did not prohibit corporal punishment in its public schools until 1988. The Wisconsin law does not apply to private schools, like Neillsville, which are still free to adopt their own policies.

10. Hideki Tojo, general of the Japanese Imperial Army and prime minister of Japan from 1941 to 1944, was closely allied with Nazi Germany and Fascist Italy during the Second World War.

11. The film, *Your Humble Serpent: The Wisdom of Reuben Snake* (1996), includes an interview with Snake in which he says it was in boarding school that he first had the sense that he would one day be a leader of his people. That early intuition is not represented in the autobiography.

12. Another Nebraska Winnebago man to attain great prominence was Henry Roe Cloud (1884–1950), the first full-blood Indian to graduate from Yale University. At seven years old Roe Cloud attended the Genoa Day School on the reservation in Nebraska, and then spent some time at a residential government boarding school, also on the reservation. He attended the Santee Normal School, which Charles Eastman and Zitkala-Sa had attended and, after graduating in 1902, was admitted to the Mount Hermon School (as Eastman had been). He entered Yale in 1906 and graduated in 1910, going on to be prominent in Indian education and Indian affairs more broadly. For his own very sketchy account of his education, see Roe Cloud, "From Wigwam to Pulpit," a brief autobiography published in 1915, just one year before Eastman's "from—to" autobiography. For a full account of Roe Cloud's life and achievements see Pfister (2009).

13. Little Abner, usually written Li'l Abner, a caricature country bumpkin, was the protagonist of a hugely popular cartoon series drawn by Al Capp that ran in many newspapers from 1934 to 1977. The shoes he wore "in the comics"—when he wore shoes—were produced and sold as Li'l Abners: rough, heavy, cheaply made brogans, also called stogies. They were made through the 1970s, and both originals and copies are available online today.

14. They are contained in several boxes of "Series 3: Biographical (1971–96)" of the Reuben Snake Papers.

15. There was, however, a Reformed Winnebago Indian Mission School in Winnebago, Nebraska, that was open from 1912 to 1953, and it is unclear why Snake's mother did not enroll her children there.

16. I have found no information about Presley Wear. Dr. Tony Coffin, Prairie Band Potawatomi, was head coach and athletic director at Haskell. The Coffin Sports Complex at the school, completed in 1981, was named for him.

APPENDIX A

1. Placing students in these categories seems to have been a Hampton practice. In 1893, for example, Folsom concluded that of the 460 students of whom she was aware, the condition of 98 was "excellent," 219 "good," 91 "fair," 35 "poor," and 17 "bad" (487). Folsom later wrote of "ANTOINE GOKEY or Gautier, *Kit-ti-kul-la-ho* (Spotted Tail), three-fourths Sac and Fox, about 25 years of age," that he came to Hampton in June 1882, and left in October 1883. "His record for industry was not good, but a generous heart prompted him to do acts of kindness that endeared him to many friends. A reckless life brought on disease and in March, '90, he died" (386). For Canalez, see later detail.

2. Folsom wrote that Downing's first position on his return was that of agency policeman, after which he was able to build a house and start a cattle ranch and farm. He had large herds, and "hogs and chickens enough to delight the heart of any farmer." She visited the Downings in 1889 and found everywhere "reminders of Hampton; even the children knew the names of their father's old teachers and friends" (329).

3. Folsom recorded that John King had been made the local postmaster in 1891, despite what she noted as his poor English (396).

4. Folsom describes Canalez as the son of a "Mexican outlaw and desperado." He had returned from Hampton "on expiration of time, Oct., '83, fell into the gang from which he had come, and lived a wild, reckless life until caught and imprisoned" (359).

5. Hattie Miles, Folsom wrote, after leaving Hampton went to Haskell Institute for about a year with her classmate, Nellie Keokuk. On her return home, as Alford notes, she married Michael King. But King would die in 1890, and since her husband's death, Folsom judges, Miles's "record of character has been very unsatisfactory" (386).

6. The States as distinct from Indian Territory and other United States territories. But Alford has obviously lost touch with her, for as Folsom later wrote, she had died in 1884 (385).

7. That reckoning leaves one student unaccounted for.

Adams, David Wallace. "Beyond Bleakness: The Brighter Side of
    Boarding Schools, 1870–1940." In *Boarding School Blues:
    Revisiting American Indian Educational Experiences*, ed. Clifford
    Trafzer, Jean Keller, and Lorene Sisquoc, 35–64. Lincoln:
    University of Nebraska Press, 2006.

———. *Education for Extinction: American Indians and the Boarding School
    Experience, 1875–1928*. Lawrence: University of Kansas Press,
    1995.

Ahern, Wilbert. "Review of David Wallace Adams' *Education for
    Extinction*." *Minnesota History* 55 (1996): 88–89.

———. "Review of Frederick Hoxie's *A Final Promise*." *Minnesota History*
    49 (1985): 254.

African Americans @ Dartmouth College 1775–1950. https://badahis-
    tory.net/.

Ah-nen-la-de-ni. "An Indian Boy's Story." *Independent,* vol. 60,
    no. 1848, July 2, 1903, 1780–87. archive.org/details/
    p2independen55newy?q=ah-nen-la-de-ni.

Alcoff, Linda, and Laura Gray. "Survivor Discourse: Transgression or
    Recuperation?" *Signs* 18 (1993): 260–90.

Alford, Thomas Wildcat. *Civilization.* Norman: University of Oklahoma
    Press, 1979 [1936].

———. *The Gospel of Our Lord and Saviour Jesus Christ according to
    Matthew, Translated into the Shawnee Language.* Xenia, OH: Dr.
    W. A. Galloway, Nay-Nah-Ko-Nah-Kah, 1929.

———. "Graduating Address of Thomas Wildcat Alford." *Southern
    Workman* 11 (July 1882): 78.

———. "Letters from Indian Graduates of Hampton." In Helen
    Wilhelmina Ludlow, *Ten Years Work for Indians at the Hampton
    Normal and Agricultural Institute,* 47–51. Hampton, VA: Hampton
    Normal and Agricultural Institute, 1888.

Angel, Michael. *Preserving the Sacred: Historical Perspectives on the Ojibwa Midewiwin*. Winnipeg, Manitoba, Canada: University of Manitoba Press, 2002.

Andrews, Thomas. "Turning the Tables on Assimilation …" *Western Historical Quarterly* 33 (2002): 407–30.

Antin, Mary. *From Plotzk to Boston*. Miami, FL: Hardpress Publishing, 2012 [1889].

———. *Promised Land*. Miami, FL: Hardpress Publishing, 2012 [1912].

Anzaldúa, Gloria. *Borderlands: The New Mestiza*. San Francisco, CA: Spinsters/Aunt Lute, 1987.

Axtell, James. "The White Indians of Colonial America." *William and Mary Quarterly* 32 (1975): 55–88.

Bahr, Diana Meyers, ed. *Viola Martinez, California Paiute: Living in Two Worlds*. Norman: University of Oklahoma Press, 2003.

Banks, Dennis, with Richard Erdoes. *Ojibwa Warrior: Dennis Banks and the Rise of the American Indian Movement*. Norman: University of Oklahoma Press, 2004.

Barrett, Carole, and Marcia Wolter Britton. "'You didn't dare try to be Indian': Oral Histories of Former Indian Boarding School Students." *North Dakota History* 64 (1997): 4–25.

Bass, Althea. "Foreword." In Carl Sweezy, *The Arapaho Way: A Memoir of an Indian Boyhood*, ed. Althea Bass, vii–x. New York: Clarkson Potter, 1966.

Bataille, Gretchen, and Kathleen Mullen Sands. *American Indian Women Telling Their Lives*. Lincoln: University of Nebraska Press, 1984.

Bean, William. *Eastman, Cloud Man, Many Lightnings: An Anglo-Dakota Family. Compiled by William Bean (Great Grandson of John Eastman) for the Eastman Family Reunion, July 6, 1989, Flandreau, South Dakota*. Alejandrasbooks.org/www/Eastman-Cloud%20Man.pdf.

Beckett, Samuel. *Waiting for Godot*. New York: Grove Press, 1954.

Bell, Genevieve. "Telling Stories out of School: Remembering the Carlisle Indian Industrial School, 1879–1918." PhD diss., Department of Anthropology, Stanford University, 1998.

Beloit Alumnus, December 1915.

Berg, Carol. "'Climbing Learners' Hill': Benedictines at White Earth, 1878–1945." PhD diss., University of Minnesota, 1981.

———. "Memories of an Indian Boarding School: White Earth, Minnesota, 1909–1945." *Midwest Review* 11 (1989): 27–36.

Berry, Brewton. *The Education of the American Indian: A Survey of the Literature.* Washington, DC: U.S. Department of Health, Education, and Welfare Bureau of Research, 1968.

Bevis, William. "Native American Novels: Homing In." In *Recovering the Word: Essays on Native American Literature,* ed. Brian Swann and Arnold Krupat, 580–620. Berkeley: University of California Press, 1987.

Bittle, William. "The Curative Aspects of Peyote." *Bios* 31 (1960): 140–48.

———. "Ethnography and Ethnology: Jim Whitewolf." *American Anthropologist* 72 (1970): 883–84.

———. "The Manatidie: A Focus for Kiowa Apache Tribal Identity." *Plains Anthropologist* 7 (1962): 152–63.

Blaeser, Kimberly. *Gerald Vizenor: Writing in the Oral Tradition.* Norman: University of Oklahoma Press, 1996.

———. "Recite the Names of All the Suicided Indians." In *Absentee Indians & Other Poems,* 7–9. East Lansing: Michigan State University Press, 2002.

Blessing, Fred. "Birchbark Mide Scrolls from Minnesota." *Minnesota Archeologist* 25 (1963): 89–142.

———. *The Ojibway Indians Observed: Papers of Fred K. Blessing, Jr. on the Ojibway Indians from the Minnesota Archeologist.* Saint Paul: Minnesota Archeological Society, 1977.

Bloom, John. *To Show What an Indian Can Do: Sports at Native American Boarding Schools.* Minneapolis: University of Minnesota Press, 2005.

Bok, Edward. *The Americanization of Edward Bok: The Autobiography of a Dutch Boy Fifty Years After.* New York: Scribner's, 1920.

Bowker, Kathie Marie. "The Boarding School Legacy: Ten Contemporary Lakota Women Tell Their Stories." EdD diss., Montana State University, 2007.

Braatz, Timothy. "Foreword." In *All of My People Were Killed: The Memoir of Mike Burns (Hoomothya), a Captive Indian,* iii–xii. Prescott, AZ: Sharlot Hall Museum, 2010.

Brant, Charles. *Jim Whitewolf: The Life of a Kiowa Apache Indian.* New York: Dover, 1969.

——."Joe Blackbear's Story of the Origin of the Peyote Religion." *Plains Anthropologist* 8 (1963): 180–81.

——. "Kiowa Apache Culture History: Some Further Observations." *Southwestern Journal of Anthropology* 9 (1953): 195–202.

Brave Bird, Mary, with Richard Erdoes. *Ohitika Woman*. New York: Grove, 1993.

Bremner, Robert, ed. *Children and Youth in America: A Documentary History*, vol. 2: *1866–1932*. Cambridge: Harvard University Press, 1971.

Britten, Thomas. *American Indians in World War I: At War and At Home*. Albuquerque: University of New Mexico Press, 1997.

Brooks, Joanna. *American Lazarus: Religion and the Rise of African-American and Native American Literatures*. New York: Oxford University Press, 2003.

Brown, Estelle. *Stubborn Fool: A Narrative*. Caldwell, ID: Caxton, 1952.

Brown, Joseph Epes, ed. *The Sacred Pipe: Black Elk's Account of the Seven Rites of the Oglala Sioux*. Norman: University of Oklahoma Press, 1953.

Brudvig, Jon. "Bridging the Cultural Divide: American Indians at Hampton Institute, 1878–1923." PhD diss., College of William and Mary, 1996.

——. "Hampton Normal and Agricultural Institute: American Indian Female Students (1878–1923)." www.twofrog.com/hamptonfem1.txt.

——. "Hampton Normal and Agricultural Institute: American Indian Male Students (1878–1923)." www.twofrog.com/hamptonmale1.txt.

——. "'Make Haste Slowly': The Experiences of American Indian Women at Hampton, 1978–1923." 2013. www.sc.edu/nas/files/2013/03/Proceedings-2005.Brudvig.pdf.

Bruguier, Leonard Rufus. "The Yankton Sioux Tribe: People of the Pipestone, 1634–1888." PhD diss., Oklahoma State University, 1993.

Brumble, H. David. *American Indian Autobiography*. Berkeley: University of California Press, 1988.

——. *An Annotated Bibliography of American Indian and Eskimo Autobiographies*. Lincoln: University of Nebraska Press, 1981.

Brumley, Kim. *Chilocco: Memories of a Native American Boarding School.* Fairfax, OK: Guardian Publishing, 2010.

Bruss, Elizabeth. *Autobiographical Acts: The Changing Situation of a Literary Genre.* Baltimore, MD: Johns Hopkins University Press, 1976.

Brunhouse, Robert. "The Founding of the Carlisle Indian School." *Pennsylvania History* 6 (1939): 72–85.

Buchowska, Suzanna. *Negotiating Native American Identities: The Role of Tradition, Narrative, and Language at Haskell Indian Nations University.* Poznan, Poland: UAM, 2016.

Buechel, Eugene. *A Grammar of Lakota, the Language of the Teton Sioux.* Rosebud, SD: Rosebud Educational Society, 1939.

Buechel, Eugene, and Paul Manhart. *Lakota Dictionary: Lakota-English/ English-Lakota.* Lincoln: University of Nebraska Press, 2002 [1970].

Bugaighis, Elizabeth. "Review of *Essie's Story.*" *History of Education Quarterly* 40 (2000): 355–57.

Burwell, Frank. Personal communication, April 26, 2017.

Calloway, Colin. *The Indian History of an American Institution: Native Americans and Dartmouth.* Lebanon, NH: Dartmouth College Press, 2010.

Cantiello, Jessica Wells. "School Pictures: Photographs in the Memoirs of White Teachers of Native American Children." *a/b: Autobiography Studies* 29 (2014): 79–106.

Carlisle Indian School Digital Resource Center, http://carlisleindian.dickinson.edu/documents/former-student-survey-responses-1890-5-5.

Carroll, James. *Seeds of Faith: Catholic Indian Boarding Schools.* New York: Garland, 2000.

Carter, Patricia. "'Completely Discouraged': Women Teachers' Resistance in the Bureau of Indian Affairs Schools, 1900–1910." *Frontiers* 15 (1995): 53–86.

Cary, Elizabeth Luther. "Recent Writings by American Indians." *The Book Buyer: A Monthly Review of American Literature*, February 1902, 23–25.

Child, Brenda. "The Boarding School as Metaphor." In *Hemispheric Perspectives on the History of Indigenous Education*, ed. Brenda Child and Brian Klopotek, 267–84. Santa Fe, NM: School for Advanced Research Press, 2014.

——. *Boarding School Seasons: American Indian Families, 1900–1940.*
    Lincoln: University of Nebraska Press, 1998.

——. "Runaway Boys, Resistant Girls: Rebellion at Flandreau and
    Haskell, 1900–1940. *Journal of American Indian Education* 35
    (1996): 49–57.

Chu, James. *Rebuilding Shattered Lives: Treating Complex PTSD and
    Dissociative Disorders,* 2nd edition. Hoboken, NJ: Wiley, 2011.

Churchill, Ward. *Kill the Indian, Save the Man: The Genocidal Impact of
    American Indian Residential Schools.* San Francisco: City Lights,
    2004.

Citizen (Winsted, Connecticut), October 1, 1917.

Clark, Carol Lea. "Charles Alexander Eastman (Ohiyesa) and Elaine
    Goodale Eastman: A Cross-Cultural Collaboration." *Tulsa Studies
    in Women's Literature* 13 (1994): 271–80.

Clifton, James, ed. *Being and Becoming Indian: Biographical Studies of North
    American Frontiers.* Chicago, IL: Dorsey Press, 1989.

Cohen, Felix. "Erosion of Indian Rights, 1950–3: A Case Study in
    Bureaucracy." *Yale Law School Journal* 62 (1953): 348–90.

Coleman, Michael. *American Indian Children at School, 1850–1930.*
    Jackson: University Press of Mississippi, 1993.

Contrary Warrior: The Life and Times of Adam Fortunate Eagle, film by John
    Ferry, 2010.

Cooper, Tanya. "Racial Bias in American Foster Care: The National
    Debate." *Marquette Law Review* 97 (2013): 215–77.

Cooper, Tova. "On Autobiography, Boy Scouts, and Citizenship:
    Revisiting Charles Alexander Eastman's *Deep Woods.*" *Arizona
    Quarterly* 65 (2009): 1–35.

Copeland, Marion. *Charles Alexander Eastman (Ohiyesa).* Boise, ID: Boise
    State University Press, 1978.

Coskan-Johnson, Gale. "'What Writer Would Not Be an Indian for
    a While?' Charles Alexander Eastman, Critical Memory, and
    Audience." *Studies in American Indian Literatures* 18 (2006):
    105–31.

Crow Dog, Mary, with Richard Erdoes. *Lakota Woman.* New York:
    Harper, 1990.

Deloria, Ella Cara. "Ella Deloria's Life." Margaret Mead Papers.
    Manuscript Division, Library of Congress, box 58, "Publications
    and Other Writings, 1952."

———. *Speaking of Indians*. Lincoln: University of Nebraska Press, 1998 [1944].

Deloria, Philip. *Indians in Unexpected Places*. Lawrence: University Press of Kansas, 2004.

———. *Playing Indian*. New Haven: Yale University Press, 1998.

Deloria, Vine Sr. "The Establishment of Christianity Among the Sioux." In *Sioux Indian Religion: Tradition and Innovation*, ed. Raymond DeMallie and Douglas Parks, 91–112. Norman: University of Oklahoma Press, 1987.

———. "The Standing Rock Reservation: A Personal Reminiscence." *South Dakota Review* 9 (1971): 167–95.

Deloria, Vine Jr. "Introduction." In Ella Cara Deloria, *Speaking of Indians*, i–xxii. Lincoln: University of Nebraska Press, 1998.

DeMallie, Raymond, and Douglas Parks, eds. *Sioux Indian Religion: Tradition and Innovation*. Norman: University of Oklahoma Press, 1987.

Densmore, Frances. *Chippewa Customs*. St. Paul: Minnesota Historical Society, 1979 [1929].

Dewdney, Selwyn. *Sacred Scrolls of the Southern Ojibway*. Toronto: University of Toronto Press, 1975.

Dominguez, Susan Rose. "The Gertrude Bonnin Story: From Yankton Destiny to American History, 1904–1938." PhD diss., Michigan State University, 2005.

Douglass, Frederick. "What to the Slave Is the Fourth of July?" In *The Oxford Frederick Douglass Reader*, ed. William Andrews, 108–30. New York: Oxford, 1996.

Drake, Florence. "Tecumseh at the Turn of the Century." *Chronicles of Oklahoma* 38 (1960): 397–408.

Drinnon, Richard. *Keeper of the Concentration Camps: Dillon S. Myer and American Racism*. Berkeley: University of California Press, 1987.

Du Bois, W. E. B. *The Souls of Black Folk*. New York: Bantam, 1989 [1903].

———. "The Negro Race in the United States of America." In *Inter-Racial Problems: Papers from the First Universal Races Congress Held in London in 1911*, ed. Gustav Spiller, 348–63 (New York: Citadel Press, 1970).

Dudley, Joseph Iron Eye. *Choteau Creek: A Sioux Reminiscence*. Lincoln: University of Nebraska Press, 1992.

Dundas, Deborah. "Interview with Edna Manitowabi." *Toronto Star*, April 6, 2018, n.p.

Eastman, Charles Alexander. *From the Deep Woods to Civilization: Chapters in the Autobiography of an Indian*. Lincoln: University of Nebraska Press, 1977 [1916].

———. *Indian Boyhood*. New York: Dover, 1971 [1902].

———. "The North American Indian." In *Inter-Racial Problems: Papers from the First Universal Races Congress Held in London in 1911*, ed. Gustav Spiller, 367–76. New York: Citadel Press, 1970 [1911].

———. *Report to the Commissioner of Indian affairs (Investigation of Sacajawea's Final Burial Place)*. Letter dated March 2, 1925. United States Department of the Interior, Office of Indian Affairs, Washington, DC.

———. "Response" to "Indians in the Professions." In *Report of the Executive Council of the Proceedings of the First Annual Conference of the Society of American Indians*. 108–9. Washington, DC, 1912.

———. *The Soul of the Indian*. Lincoln: University of Nebraska Press, 1980 [1911].

Eastman, Elaine Goodale. *Pratt: The Red Man's Moses*. Norman: University of Oklahoma Press, 1935.

———. *Sister to the Sioux: The Memoirs of Elaine Goodale Eastman, 1885–1891*. Ed. Kay Graber. Lincoln: University of Nebraska Press, 2004 [1978].

Ellinghaus, Katherine. *Taking Assimilation to Heart: Marriages of White Women and Indigenous Men in the United States and Australia, 1887–1937*. Lincoln: University of Nebraska Press, 2006.

Ellis, Clyde. "Boarding School Life at the Kiowa-Comanche Agency, 1893–1920." *Historian* 58 (1996a): 777–93.

———. *To Change Them Forever: Indian Education at the Rainy Mountain Boarding School, 1893–1926*. Norman: University of Oklahoma Press, 1996b.

Ellis, Richard N. "Foreword." In Luther Standing Bear, *Land of the Spotted Eagle*, xiii–xx. Lincoln: University of Nebraska Press, 1978.

———. "Introduction." In Luther Standing Bear, *My People the Sioux*, ix–xx. Lincoln: University of Nebraska Press, 1975.

———. "'I would raise him to be Indian'." In *Essays on Nineteenth and Twentieth Century Native American Lives*, ed. L. G. Moses and Raymond Wilson, 139–58. Albuquerque: University of New Mexico Press, 1985.

Embe (Mariana Burgess). *Stiya, a Carlisle Indian Girl at Home.*
    Cambridge, MA: Riverside Press, 1891.

Emery, Jacqueline. "Writing Against Erasure: Native American Students
    at Hampton Institute and the Periodical Press." *American
    Periodicals* 22 (2012): 178–98.

Emery, Jacqueline, ed. *Recovering Native American Writings in the Boarding
    School Press.* Lincoln: University of Nebraska Press, 2017.

Engs, Robert. *Educating the Disfranchised and Disinherited: Samuel
    Chapman Armstrong and Hampton Institute, 1839–1893,* Knoxville:
    University of Tennessee Press, 1999.

Enoch, Jessica. "Resisting the Script of Indian Education: Zitkala-Sa and
    the Carlisle Indian School." *College English.* 65 (2002):117–41.

Epstein, Lawrence. *The Haunted Smile: The Story of Jewish Comedians in
    America.* New York: Public Affairs, 2002.

Fear, Jacqueline. "The 'Civilization' of Thomas Wildcat Alford." *Revue
    francaise d'études américaines* 17 (1983): 295–310.

Fear-Segal, Jacqueline. "Eyes in the Text: Mariana Burgess and *The
    Indian Helper.*" In *Blue Pencils and Hidden Hands: Women Editing
    Periodicals, 1830–1910,* ed. Sharon Harris with Ellen Garvey, 123–
    43. Boston: Northwestern University Press, 2004.

———. "The History and Reclamation of a Sacred Space: The Indian
    School Cemetery." In *Carlisle Indian Industrial School: Indigenous
    Histories, Memories, and Reclamations,* ed. Fear-Segal and Barbara
    Rose, 152–84. Lincoln: University of Nebraska Press, 2016a.

———. "The Lost Ones: Piecing together the Story." In *Carlisle Indian
    Industrial School: Indigenous Histories, Memories, and Reclamations,*
    ed. Fear-Segal and Barbara Rose, 201–32. Lincoln: University of
    Nebraska Press, 2016b.

———. *White Man's Club: Schools, Race, and the Struggle of Indian
    Acculturation.* Lincoln: University of Nebraska Press, 2007.

Fear-Segal, Jacqueline, and Barbara Rose. "Introduction." In *Carlisle
    Indian Industrial School,* ed. Jacqueline Fear-Segal and Barbara
    Rose, 1–34. Lincoln: University of Nebraska Press, 2016.

Fikes, Jay. "Huichol Indian Identity and Adaptation." PhD diss.,
    University of Michigan, 1985.

Fisher, Dexter. "Foreword." In Zitkala-Sa, *American Indian Stories,* v–xx.
    Lincoln: University of Nebraska Press, 1985.

Folsom, Cora. "Record of Returned Indian Students." In Helen Wilhelmina Ludlow, *Twenty-Two Years Work of Hampton Normal and Industrial Institute at Hampton, Virginia*, 317–486. Hampton, VA: Hampton Normal School Press, 1893.

Fortunate Eagle, Adam, with Tim Findley. *Heart of the Rock: The Indian Invasion of Alcatraz*. Norman: University of Oklahoma Press, 2002.

———. *Pipestone: My Life in an Indian Boarding School*. Norman: University of Oklahoma Press, 2010.

Fowler, Loretta. "Oral Historian or Ethnologist? The Career of Bill Shakespeare, Northern Arapahoe, 1901–1975." In *American Indian Intellectuals*, ed. Margot Liberty, 227–40. St. Paul, MN: West Publishing Company, 1978.

Foucault, Michel. *Discipline and Punish: The Birth of the Prison*. New York: Pantheon, 1977 [1975].

Frye, Northrop. *Anatomy of Criticism: Four Essays*. Princeton, NJ: Princeton University Press, 1957.

Gagnon, Gregory. *Culture and Customs of the Sioux Indians*. Lincoln: University of Nebraska Press, 2012.

Gannon, Tom. "Immigration as Cultural Imperialism: An Indian Boarding School Experience or the Peer Gynt Suite and the Seventh Cavalry Café." *Great Plains Quarterly* 34 (2014): 111–22.

Gere, Anne Ruggles. "Indian Heart/White Man's Head: Native-American Teachers in Indian Schools, 1890–1930." *History of Education Quarterly* 45 (2005): 38–65.

Gerencser, Jim. Personal communication, August 20, 2018.

Giago, Tim. *The Aboriginal Sin: Reflections on the Holy Rosary Mission School (Red Cloud Indian School)*. San Francisco, CA: Indian Historian Press, 1978.

———. *Children Left Behind: The Dark Legacy of Indian Mission Boarding Schools*. Santa Fe, NM: Clear Light Publishing, 2006.

Gram, John. *Education at the Edge of Empire: Negotiating Pueblo Identity in New Mexico's Indian Boarding Schools*. Seattle: University of Washington Press, 2015.

Green, Alice. *White's Institute: A Glimpse into Its Past and Present*. Muncie, IN: Scott Printing Company, 1929.

Guenther, Richard. "The Santee Normal Training School." *Nebraska History* 51 (1970): 359–78.

Hafen, P. Jane, ed. *Dreams and Thunder: Stories, Poems, and* The Sun Dance Opera. Lincoln: University of Nebraska Press, 2001.

Hamm, Thomas. *Earlham College: A History, 1847–1997.* Bloomington: Indiana University Press, 1997.

Harring, Sidney. *Crow Dog's Case: American Indian Sovereignty, Tribal Law, and United States Law in the Nineteenth Century.* Cambridge: Cambridge University Press, 1994.

Hauptman, Laurence. "From Carlisle to Carnegie Hall: The Musical Career of Dennison Wheelock." In *The Oneida Indians in the Age of Allotment, 1860–1920,* ed. Laurence Hauptman and L. Gordon McLester III, 112–38. Norman: University of Oklahoma Press, 2006.

Hauptman, Laurence M., and L. Gordon McLester III, eds. *The Oneida Indians in the Age of Allotment, 1860–1920.* Norman: University of Oklahoma Press, 2006.

Henze, Rosemary, and Lauren Vanett. "To Walk in Two Worlds: Or More? Challenging a Common Metaphor of Native Education." *Anthropology and Education Quarterly* 24 (1993): 116–34.

Herman, Judith. *Trauma and Recovery: The Aftermath of Violence—From Domestic Abuse to Political Terror,* with a new epilogue by the author. New York: Basic Books, 2015 [1992].

Hertzberg, Hazel. *The Search for an American Indian Identity: Modern Pan-Indian Movements.* Syracuse, NY: Syracuse University Press, 1971.

Hickerson, Harold. *Ethnohistory of the Chippewa in Central Minnesota.* New York: Garland, 1974.

Highway, Thomson. *The Kiss of the Fur Queen.* Norman: University of Oklahoma Press, 1998.

Hittman, Michael. "The 1870 Ghost Dance at the Walker River Reservation: A Reconstruction." *Ethnohistory* 20 (1973): 247–78.

———. *Wovoka and the Ghost Dance,* ed. Don Lynch. Expanded ed. Lincoln: University of Nebraska Press, 1997.

Hoffman, Walter. *The Mide'wiwin or, "Grand Medicine Society" of the Ojibwa.* Annual Report of the Bureau of Ethnology (1885–86). Washington, DC: Government Printing Office, 1891.

Holt, Aaron. Personal communication, April 2, 2018.

Horne, Esther Burnett, and Sally McBeth. *Essie's Story: The Life and Legacy of a Shoshone Teacher.* Lincoln: University of Nebraska Press, 1998.

Hyde, George. *Spotted Tail's Folk: A History of the Brulé Sioux.* Norman: University of Oklahoma Press, 1974 [1961].

Iverson, Peter. *Carlos Montezuma and the Changing World of American Indians.* Albuquerque: University of New Mexico Press, 1982.

Jacobs, Margaret. "The Eastmans and the Luhans: Interracial Marriage between White Women and Native American Men, 1875–1935." *Frontiers* 23 (2002): 29–54.

Johnson, Thomas. "Review of *Essie's Story.*" *Ethnohistory* 51 (2004): 454–57.

Johnston, Basil. "Foreword." In Sam McKegney, *Magic Weapons: Aboriginal Writers Remaking Community After Residential School*, 3–9. Winnipeg: University of Manitoba Press, 2007.

———. *Indian School Days.* Norman: University of Oklahoma Press, 1988.

———. *Ojibway Ceremonies.* Toronto: McClelland and Stewart, 1982.

———. *Ojibway Heritage.* Lincoln: University of Nebraska Press, 2014 [1976].

Jordan, Julia. "Ethnobotany of the Kiowa Apache." PhD diss., University of Oklahoma, 1965.

———. "Interview with Ray Blackbear, 2/8/1968." Doris Duke Oral History Project, University of Oklahoma, T-222-1, 1–17.

Kafka, Franz. *The Trial,* trans. David Wylie. New York: Dover, 2003 [1925].

Kasebier, Gertrude. *Buffalo Bill's Wild West Warriors: A Photographic History*, with introduction and text by Michelle Delaney. Washington, DC: Smithsonian National Museum of American History–Collins Publishers, 2002.

Katanski, Amelia. *Learning to Write "Indian": The Boarding School Experience and American Indian Literature.* Norman: University of Oklahoma Press, 2006.

Kelsey, Penelope. *Tribal Theory in Native American Literature: Dakota and Hodenosaunee Writing and Indigenous Worldviews.* Lincoln: University of Nebraska Press, 2008.

Kenny, Michael. "A Place for Memory: The Interface between Individual and Collective History." *Comparative Studies in Society and History* 41 (1999): 420–37.

———. "The Recovered Memory Controversy: An Anthropologist's View." *Journal of Psychiatry and the Law* 23 (1995): 437–60.

Kirby, Bruce. Personal communication, September 17, 2017.

Kracht, Benjamin. "The Kiowa Ghost Dance, 1894–1916: An Unheralded Revitalization Movement." *Ethnohistory* 39 (1992): 452–77.

Krupat, Arnold. *All that Remains: Varieties of Indigenous Expression.* Lincoln: University of Nebraska Press, 2009.

———. "America's Histories." In *Red Matters: Native American Studies,* 48–75. Philadelphia: University of Pennsylvania Press, 2002.

———. *Boarding-School Voices: Carlisle Indian Students Speak.* Lincoln: University of Nebraska Press, forthcoming.

———. *Changed Forever: American Indian Boarding-School Literature,* vol. 1. Albany: State University of New York Press, 2018.

———. "Figures and the Law." In *Ethnocriticism: Ethnography, History, Literature,* 129–72. Berkeley: University of California Press, 1992.

———. *For Those Who Come After: A Study of Native American Autobiography.* Berkeley: University of California Press, 1985.

———. *Red Matters: Native American Studies.* Philadelphia: University of Pennsylvania Press, 2002.

———. *"That the People Might Live": Loss and Renewal in Native American Elegy.* Ithaca, NY: Cornell University Press, 2012.

———. "Trickster Tales Revisited." In *All That Remains,* 1–26. Lincoln: University of Nebraska Press, 2009.

———. *The Voice in the Margin: Native American Literature and the Canon.* Berkeley: University of California Press, 1989.

LaFlesche, Francis. *The Middle Five: Indian Schoolboys of the Omaha Tribe.* Lincoln: University of Nebraska Press, 1963 [1900].

Lame Deer/John Fire, and Richard Erdoes. *Lame Deer, Seeker of Visions: The Life of a Sioux Medicine Man.* New York: Simon and Schuster, 1972.

Landes, Ruth. *Ojibwa Religion and the Midewiwin.* Madison: University of Wisconsin Press, 1968.

Landis, Barbara. "Carlisle Indian Industrial School History." http://home. epix.net/~/landis/history.html.

Landrum, Cynthia. "Acculturation of the Dakota Sioux: The Boarding School Experience for Students at Flandreau and Pipestone Schools." PhD diss., Oklahoma State University, 2002.

Lejeune, Philippe. *Le pacte autobiographique.* Paris: Editions du Seuil, 1975.

Levchuk, Berenice. "Leaving Home for Carlisle Indian School." In *Reinventing the Enemy's Language: Contemporary Native Women's*

Writings of North America, ed. Joy Harjo and Gloria Bird, 175–86. New York: Norton, 1997.

Lewandowski, Tadeusz. Personal communication, October 3, 2017.

———. *Red Bird, Red Power: The Life and Legacy of Zitkala-Sa*. Norman: University of Oklahoma Press, 2016.

Lewandowski, Tadeusz, ed. *Zitkala-Sa: Letters, Speeches, and Unpublished Writings, 1898–1929*. Leiden, Netherlands: Brill, 2018.

Leyburn, James. "Review of *Civilization* by Thomas Wildcat Alford." *American Sociological Review* 1 (1936): 1038–39.

Lindsey, Donal. *Indians at Hampton Institute, 1877–1923*. Urbana: University of Illinois Press, 1995.

Littlemoon, Walter, with Jane Ridgway. *They Called Me Uncivilized: The Memoir of an Everyday Lakota Man from Wounded Knee*. Bloomington, IN: iUniverse, 2009.

Lomawaima, K. Tsianina. "Estelle Reel, Superintendent of Indian Schools, 1898–1910: Politics, Curriculum, and Land." *Journal of Indian Education* 35 (1996): 5–31.

———. *They Called It Prairie Light: The Story of Chilocco Indian School*. Lincoln: University of Nebraska Press, 1994.

Lomawaima, K. Tsianina, and Teresa McCarty. *"To Remain an Indian: Lessons in Democracy from a Century of Native American Education*. New York: Teachers College–Columbia University. 2006.

Ludlow, Helen Wilhelmina. *Ten Years' Work for Indians at the Hampton Normal and Agricultural Institute*. Hampton, VA: Hampton Institute, 1888.

———. *Twenty-Two Years Work of Hampton Normal and Industrial Institute at Hampton, Virginia*. Hampton, VA: Hampton Normal School Press, 1893.

Lyons, Scott. Personal communications, October 2, 2017, April 10, 2018.

———. *X-Marks: Native Signatures of Assent*. Minneapolis: University of Minnesota Press, 2010.

MacGregor, Gordon, with the collaboration of Royal Hassrick and William Henry. *Warriors without Weapons: A Study of the Society and Personality Development of the Pine Ridge Sioux*. Chicago: University of Chicago Press, 1946.

Maddox, Lucy. *Citizen Indians: Native American Intellectuals, Race, and Reform*. Ithaca, NY: Cornell University Press, 2001.

Manitobawabi, Edna. *An Indian Girl in the City.* Buffalo, NY: Friends of Malatesta, n.d. [1971?].

Manitowabi, Edna. "An Ojibwa Girl in the City." *This Magazine Is about Schools* 4 (1970): 8–24.

Mays, Kyle. "Transnational Progressivism: African Americans, Native Americans, and the Universal Races Congress of 1911." *American Indian Quarterly* 25 (2013): 243–61.

McBeth, Sally. *Ethnic Identity and the Boarding School Experience of West-Central Oklahoma American Indians.* Lanham, MD: University Press of America, 1983.

———. "Introduction: Methodological and Cultural Concerns of Collecting and Coauthoring a Life History." In Esther Burnett Horne and Sally McBeth, *Essie's Story*, xi–xli. Lincoln: University of Nebraska Press, 1998.

McFee, Malcolm "The 150% Man, a Product of Blackfeet Acculturation." *American Anthropologist* 70 (1968): 1096–1108.

McGillycuddy, Julia. *McGillycuddy, Agent: A Biography of Dr. Valentine T. McGillycuddy.* Palo Alto, CA: Stanford University Press, 1941.

Meriam, Lewis, comp. *The Problem of Indian Administration: Report of a Survey made at the Request of the Honorable Hubert Work, Secretary of the Interior, and submitted to him, February 21, 1928.* Baltimore: Johns Hopkins University Press, 1928.

Methvin, J. J. "Reminiscences of Life Among the Indians." *Chronicles of Oklahoma* 5 (1927): 166–79.

Meyer, Melissa. "Foreword." In John Rogers, *Red World and White: Memories of a Chippewa Boyhood*, iii–xxi. Norman: University of Oklahoma Press, 1996.

Michaels, Barbara. *Gertrude Kasebier: The Photographer and Her Photographs.* New York: Harry N. Abrams, 1992.

Miller, David Reed. "Charles Alexander Eastman, Santee Sioux, 1858–1939." In *American Indian Intellectuals*, ed. Margot Liberty, 61–73. St. Paul, MN: West Publishing Company, 1978.

Momaday, N. Scott. "The Indolent Boys." *Three Plays.* Norman: University of Oklahoma Press, 2007, 1–71.

———. " The Moon in Two Windows." *Three Plays.* Norman: University of Oklahoma Press, 2007, 105–77.

———. *The Way to Rainy Mountain.* Albuquerque: University of New Mexico Press, 1969.

Montezuma, Carlos. "Changing Is Not Vanishing." In *Changing Is Not Vanishing: A Collection of American Indian Poetry to 1930,* ed. Robert Dale Parker, 287–88. Philadelphia: University of Pennsylvania Press, 2011.

Mooney, James. *Calendar History of the Kiowa Indians.* Washington, DC: Smithsonian Institution Press, 1979 [1898].

———. *The Ghost-Dance Religion and Wounded Knee.* New York: Dover, 1973 [1896].

Morgan, Thisba Hutson. "Reminiscences of My Days in the Land of the Oglalla Sioux." *South Dakota Historical Collections* 29 (1958): 21–46.

Morrison, George, with Margot Fortunato Galt. *Turning the Feather Around: My Life in Art.* St. Paul: Minnesota Historical Society Press, 1998.

Nelson, Richard. "Inscribed Birchbark Scrolls and Other Objects of the Midwiwin." *Papers of the Fourteenth Algonquian Conference* 14 (1983): 397–408.

New Lakota Dictionary: Lakhótiyapi: English, English: Lakhótiyapi. Bloomington, IN, Pierre, SD: Lakota Language Consortium, 2011.

Nichols, John D. Personal communication, May 22, 2018.

Nichols, John D., and Earl Nyholm, eds. *A Concise Dictionary of Minnesota Ojibwe.* Minneapolis: University of Minnesota Press, 1995.

Nicollet, Joseph. *The Journals of Joseph N. Nicollet: A Scientist on the Mississippi Headwater with Notes on Indian Life, 1836–37,* trans. André Fertey, ed. Martha Coleman Bray. St. Paul: Minnesota Historical Society, 1970.

Northrup, Jim. "Ditched." In *Walking the Rez Road,* 72. Stillwater, MN: Voyageur Press, 1993.

———. "FAMILIES—*Nindanawemaaganag.*" In *The Rez Road Follies: Canoes, Casinos, Computers, and Birch Bark Baskets,* 1–36. Minneapolis: University of Minnesota Press, 1997.

———. "Thou shalt not use a siphon hose as a credit card." *Indian Country Today,* April 6, 2007.

Opler, Morris. *An Apache Life-Way: The Economic, Social, and Religious Institutions of the Chiricahua Indians.* Chicago: University of Chicago Press, 1941.

Ostler, Jeffrey. *The Plains Sioux and U.S. Colonialism from Lewis and Clark to Wounded Knee*. New York: Cambridge University Press, 2004.

Oxendine, Joseph. *American Indian Sports Heritage*. Champaign, IL: Human Kinetics Books, 1988.

Parker, Robert Dale, ed. *Changing Is Not Vanishing: A collection of American Indian Poetry to 1930*. Philadelphia: University of Pennsylvania Press, 2011.

Peterson, Erik. "'An Indian … An American': Ethnicity, Assimilation, and Balance in Charles Eastman's *From the Deep Woods to Civilization.*" In *Early Native American Writing: New Critical Essays*, ed. Helen Jaskoski, 173–89. New York: Cambridge University Press, 1996.

Peyer, Bernd. *The Tutor'd Mind: Indian Missionary-Writers in Antebellum America*. Amherst: University of Massachusetts Press, 1997.

Pfister, Joel. *The Yale Indian: The Education of Henry Roe Cloud*. Durham, NC: Duke University Press, 2009.

Picotte, Agnes. "Foreword." In *Old Indian Legends*, retold by Zitkala-Sa, xi–xviii. Lincoln: University of Nebraska Press, 1985.

Popp, Wade. Personal communications, January 5, 2018, April 18, 2018.

Powell, Malea. "Imagining the New Indian: Listening to the Rhetoric of Survivance in Charles Eastman's *From the Deep Woods to Civilization.*" *Paradoxa* 15 (2001): 211–26.

Powers, Marla. *Oglala Women: Myth, Ritual, and Reality*. Chicago: University of Chicago Press, 1986.

Powers-Beck, Jeffrey. "'Chief': The American Indian Integration of Baseball, 1897–1945." *American Indian Quarterly* 25 (2001): 508–38.

Powless, Purcell. "My School Days." In *The Oneida Indians in the Age of Allotment*, ed. Laurence Hauptman and L. Gordon McLester III, 84–88. Norman: University of Oklahoma Press, 2006.

Pratt, Richard. "The Advantages of Mingling Indians with Whites." In *Americanizing the American Indians: Writings by the "Friends of the Indian," 1880–1900*, ed. Francis Paul Prucha, 260–71. Cambridge, MA: Harvard University Press, 1973.

———. *Battlefield and Classroom: Four Decades with the American Indian, 1867–1904*, edited and with an Introduction by Robert Utley. New Haven, CT: Yale University Press, 1964.

————. Richard Henry Pratt (biographical sketch), Arlington National Cemetery website, www.arlingtoncemetery.net/rhpratt.htm.

————. Richard Henry Pratt Papers, Yale Collection of Western Americana, Beinecke Rare Book and Manuscript Library, WA MSS S-1174, Yale University.

Prucha, Francis Paul. *The Churches and the Indian Schools: 1888–1912.* Lincoln: University of Nebraska Press, 1979.

Rader, Benjamin. "'The Greatest Drama in Indian Life': Experiments in Native American Identity and Resistance at the Haskell Institute Homecoming of 1926." *Western Historical Quarterly* 35 (2004): 429–50.

Radin, Paul. *The Winnebago Tribe.* Lincoln: University of Nebraska Press, 2010 [1923].

Raudot, Antoine Denis. *Letters from North America,* Belleville, Ontario: 1980 [1710].

Razor, Peter. *While the Locust Slept.* Saint Paul: Minnesota Historical Society, 2001.

Red Shirt, Delphine. *Bead on an Anthill: A Lakota Childhood.* Lincoln: University of Nebraska Press, 1999.

Reyes, Lawney. *White Grizzly Bear's Legacy: Learning to Be Indian.* Seattle: University of Washington Press, 2002.

Reyhner, Jon, and Jeanne Elder. *American Indian Education: A History.* Norman: University of Oklahoma Press, 2004.

Reynolds, Gaylord. "The History of Pipestone Indian School." Master's thesis in the Graduate School, University of South Dakota, 1952.

Rice, Julian. Personal communication, October 3, 2017.

Ridgway, Jane, and Walter Littlemoon. "Response." *Applied Anthropologist* 30 (2010): 52–53.

Riney, Scott. *The Rapid City Indian School: 1898–1933.* Norman: University of Oklahoma Press, 1999.

Roe Cloud, Henry. "From Wigwam to Pulpit: A Red Man's Story of His Progress from Darkness to Light." *Missionary Review of the World* 38 (1915): 329–39.

Rogers, John (Chief Snow Cloud). *A Chippewa Speaks.* Hollywood, CA: Snow Cloud Publishers, 1957.

————. *Red World and White: Memories of a Chippewa Boyhood.* Norman: University of Oklahoma Press, 1996.

Ronglien, Harvey. *A Boy from C-11: Case # 9164.* N.p.: Graham Megyeri Books, 2006.

Sargent, Theodore. "Introduction." In *Sister to the Sioux: The Memoirs of Elaine Goodale Eastman, 1885–1891*, ed. Kay Graber, i–xiii. Lincoln: University of Nebraska Press, 2004.

———. *Life of Elaine Goodale Eastman.* Lincoln: University of Nebraska Press, 2005.

Sargent, Theodore, and Raymond Wilson. "Elaine Goodale Eastman: Author and Indian Reformer." In *The Human Tradition in America between the Wars, 1920–1945*, ed. Donald Whisenhunt, 89–104. Lanham, MD: Rowman and Littlefield, 2002.

Schoolcraft, Henry Rowe. *Algic Researches: Indian Tales and Legends*, ed. W. K. McNeil. Baltimore, MD: Genealogical Publishing Company, 1992 [1839].

Schweinfurth, Kay Parker. *Prayer on Top of the Earth: The Spiritual Universe of the Plains Apaches.* Boulder: University of Colorado Press, 2002.

Scott, Hugh Lenox. "Notes on the Sun Dance or Kado." *American Anthropologist* 13 (1911): 345–79.

Shillinger, Sarah. *A Case Study of the American Indian Boarding School Movement: An Oral History of St. Joseph's Indian Industrial School.* Lewiston, NY: Edwin Mellen Press, 2008.

Smith, Andrea. *Conquest: Sexual Violence and American Indian Genocide.* Cambridge: South End Press, 2005.

Snake, Reuben, as told to Jay Fikes. *Reuben Snake: Your Humble Serpent, Indian Visionary and Activist.* Sante Fe, NM: Clear Light Publishers, 1996.

Snake, Reuben, Gary Rhine, Hayna Brown, et al. *Your Humble Serpent: The Wisdom of Reuben Snake.* DVD. Peacedream Productions, 1996.

Sousa on the Rez: Marching to the Beat of a Different Drum. Kanopy Streaming, 2012.

Southwick, Sally. *Building on a Borrowed Past: Place and Identity in Pipestone, Minnesota.* Athens: Ohio University Press, 2005.

Southern Workman 9, no. 7 (July 1882): 78.

——— 32, no. 7 (July 1903): 290.

Spack, Ruth. *America's Second Tongue: American Indian Education and the Ownership of English,1860–1900.* Lincoln: University of Nebraska Press, 2002.

———. "Dis/engagement: Zitkala-Sa's Letters to Carlos Montezuma, 1901–1902." *MELUS* 26 (2001): 173–204.

———. "Re-visioning Sioux Women: Zitkala-Sa's Revolutionary *American Indian Stories.*" *Legacy: A Journal of American Women Writers* 14 (1997): 25–42.

Speck, Frank. "Review of *Civilization* by Thomas Wildcat Alford." *Journal of American Folklore* 50 (1937): 299–300.

Speroff, Leon. *Carlos Montezuma, M.D.: A Yavapai American Hero.* Portland, OR: Arnica Publishing, 2004–5.

Spiller, Gustav, ed. *Inter-Racial Problems: Papers from the First Universal Races Congress Held in London in 1911.* New York: Citadel Press, 1970.

Sprague, Donovin Arleigh. *Rosebud Sioux.* Charleston, SC: Arcadia, 2005.

Standing Bear, Luther. *Indian Boyhood.* New York: Dover, 1971 [1931].

———. *Land of the Spotted Eagle.* Lincoln: University of Nebraska Press, 1978 [1933].

———. *My People, the Sioux.* Lincoln: University of Nebraska Press, 1975 [1928].

Stewart, Omer. *Peyote Religion: A History.* Norman: University of Oklahoma Press, 1987.

Stokely, Michelle. "My Father's Name was Zahtah: Constructing the Life History of Alfred Chalepah, Sr." PhD diss., University of Oklahoma, 2003.

Strong, Pauline Turner. *Captive Selves, Captivating Others: The Politics and Poetics of Colonial American Captivity Narratives.* Boulder, CO: Westview Press, 1999.

Student Case File of Dennis J. Banks. Record Group 75, Records of the Bureau of Indian Affairs. Pipestone Indian School, National Archives Identifier 599708.

Swan, Madonna, as told through Mark St. Pierre. *Madonna Swan: A Lakota Woman's Story.* Norman: University of Oklahoma Press, 1991.

Sweezy, Carl. *The Arapaho Way: A Memoir of an Indian Boyhood*, ed. Althea Bass. New York: Clarkson Potter, 1966.

Szasz, Margaret. *Education and the American Indian: The Road to Self-Determination since 1928.* 3rd ed. Albuquerque: University of New Mexico Press, 1999 [1974].

Tahan (Joseph Griffis). *Tahan: Out of Savagery, into Civilization.* New York: George H. Doran, 1915.

Tanner, Helen Hornbeck. *The Ojibwa*. New York: Chelsea House, 1992.

Tatonetti, Lisa. "Disrupting a Story of Loss: Charles Eastman and Nicholas Black Elk Narrate Survivance." *Western American Literature* 39 (2004): 279–311.

The Thick, Dark Fog. Randy Vasquez, director. High Valley Films, 2012.

Thoennes, Karl. Personal communication, November 20, 2017.

Trachtenberg, Alan. *Shades of Hiawatha: Staging Indians, Making Americans, 1880–1930*. New York: Hill and Wang, 2004.

Trafzer, Clifford, Jean Keller, and Lorene Sisquoc, eds. *Boarding School Blues: Revisiting American Indian Educational Experiences*. Lincoln: University of Nebraska Press, 2006.

Trennert, Robert. *Alternative to Extinction: Federal Indian Policy and the Beginnings of the Reservation System, 1846–51*. Philadelphia: Temple University Press, 1975.

———. "Corporal Punishment and the Politics of Indian Reform." *History of Education Quarterly* 29 (1989): 595–617.

———. "Educating Indian Girls at Non-Reservation Boarding Schools, 1878–1920." *Western Historical Quarterly* 13 (1982): 271–90.

———. *The Phoenix Indian School: Forced Assimilation in Arizona, 1891–1935*. Norman: University of Oklahoma Press, 1988.

Utley, Robert. *The Last Days of the Sioux Nation*. New Haven: Yale University Press, 1963.

———. "The Ordeal of Plenty Horses." *American Heritage* 26 (1974): 15–19, 82–86.

Velikova, Roumiana. "Troping in Zitkala-Sa's Autobiographical Writings, 1900–1921." *Arizona Quarterly* 51 (2000): 49–64.

Vigil, Kiara. *Indigenous Intellectuals: Sovereignty, Citizenship, and the American Imagination, 1880–1930*. New York: Cambridge University Press, 2015.

———. Personal communication, June 19, 2017.

Vizenor, Gerald. *Bear Island: The War at Sugar Point*. Minneapolis: University of Minnesota Press, 2006.

———. *The Everlasting Sky: Voices of the Anishinaabe People*. St. Paul: Minnesota Historical Society Press, 2000.

———. "George Morrison." In *Native Liberty: Natural Reason and Cultural Survivance*, 207–26. Lincoln: University of Nebraska Press, 2009.

———. "History of White Earth." In *Escorts to White Earth: 1868 to 1968, 100 Year Reservation*, 133–67. Minneapolis, MN: Four Winds, 1968.

———. *The People Named the Chippewa: Narrative Histories*. Minneapolis: University of Minnesota Press, 1984.

———. *Touchwood: A Collection of Ojibway Prose*. St. Paul, MN: New Rivers Press, 1987.

Voegelin, Carl, and Erminie Voegelin. "Shawnee Name Groups." *American Anthropologist* 37 (1935): 617–35.

Voegelin, Erminie. "Review of *Civilization* by Thomas Wildcat Alford." *American Anthropologist* 39 (1937): 536–37.

Vonnegut, Kurt. *Slaughterhouse Five*. New York: Delacorte Press, 1969.

Waggoner, Linda. *Fire Light: The Life of Angel De Cora, Winnebago Artist*. Norman: University of Oklahoma Press, 2008.

Warren, William. *History of the Ojibway People*. St. Paul: Minnesota Historical Society Press, 1984 [1885].

Warrior, Robert. "Deloria and Mathews in the Context of American Indian Intellectual Traditions from 1890 to 1990." In *Tribal Secrets: Recovering American Indian Intellectual Traditions*, 1–44. Minneapolis: University of Minnesota Press, 1999.

———. "The Work of Indian Pupils: Narratives of Learning in Native American Literature." *The People and the Word: Reading Native Nonfiction*. Minneapolis: University of Minnesota Press, 2005, 95–142.

Washington, Booker T. *Up from Slavery*. New York: Doubleday, 1998 [1901].

Watras, Joseph. "Progressive Education and Native American Schools, 1929–1950. *Educational Foundations* 18 (2004): 81–105.

Webster, Anthony. "Reading William Bittle and Charles Brant: On Ethnographic Representations of 'Contemporary' Plains Apache." *Plains Anthropologist* 52 (2007): 301–15.

Whirlwind Soldier, Lydia. "Memories." In *Shaping Survival: Essays by Four American Indian Tribal Women*, ed. Jack Marken and Charles Woodard, 159–214. Lanham, MD: Scarecrow Press, 2001.

———. *Memory Songs*. Sioux Falls, SD: Center for Western Studies, 1999.

White, Bruce. *We Are at Home: Pictures of the Ojibwe People*. St. Paul: Minnesota Historical Society, 2008.

White, Hayden. *Metahistory: The Historical Imagination in Nineteenth-Century Europe*. Baltimore, MD: Johns Hopkins University Press, 1973.

Whitman, Walt. *Specimen Days and Collect*. New York: Dover, 2012 [1882].

———."The Wound Dresser." In *Complete Poetry and Collected Prose*. New York: Library of America, 2008.

Whitewolf, Jim [Joe Blackbear]. *Jim Whitewolf: The Life of a Kiowa Apache Indian*, ed. Charles Brant. New York: Dover, 1969.

Wightman, Abigail. "Disappointing Indigeneity: Powwow and Participation Among the Plains Apache." *Ethnology* 51 (2012): 55–74.

Willis, Jane. *Geneish: An Indian Girlhood*. Toronto: New Press, 1973.

Wilson, Raymond. *Ohiyesa: Charles Eastman, Santee Sioux*. Champagne: University of Illinois Press, 1983.

Witmer, Linda. *The Indian Industrial School, Carlisle, Pennsylvania, 1879–1918*. Carlisle, PA: Cumberland County Historical Society, 2000.

Wong, Hertha. *Sending My Heart Back Across the Years: Tradition and Innovation in Native American Autobiography*. New York: Oxford, 1992.

Ziibiwing Center of Anishinaabe Culture and Lifeways. *American Indian Boarding Schools: An Exploration of Global Ethnic and Cultural Cleansing* ("Supplementary Curriculum Guide"). Michigan: Ziibiwing Center, Saginaw Chippewa Indian Tribe, 2004.

Zitkala-Sa. *American Indian Stories, Legends, and Other Writings*, ed. Cathy Davidson and Ada Norris. New York: Penguin, 2003.

———. "The School Days of an Indian Girl." *Atlantic Monthly* 85 (February 1900): 185–94.

———. "Why I Am a Pagan." *Atlantic Monthly* 90 (December 1902), 801–3.

INDEX

Note: Page numbers in italics indicate illustrations.

CPSIA information can be obtained
at www.ICGtesting.com
Printed in the USA
BVHW030914010721
610973BV00007B/102

9 781438 480060